LB1507.R6 1982   **62913**

ROBISON
DESIGNING CURRICULUM FOR
EARLY CHILDHOOD

DATE DUE			
DEC 6 '89	MAY 1 3 '98		
MAR 7 '90	NOV 2 4 '99		
MAY 2 '90	APR 2 1 '04		
OCT 17 '90	DEC 1 5 '05		
MAR 6 '91			
DEC 11 '91			
APR 1 '92			
5/27/92			
FEB 1 8 '98			

DATE DUE

WITHDRAWN FROM THE EVAN'S LIBRARY AT FMCC

FULTON-MONTGOMERY COMMUNITY
COLLEGE LIBRARY

Designing Curriculum for Early Childhood

Designing Curriculum for Early Childhood

HELEN F. ROBISON
Baruch College, CUNY

SYDNEY L. SCHWARTZ
Queens College, CUNY

ALLYN AND BACON, INC.
Boston   London   Sydney   Toronto

*In memory of
Kenneth D. Wann,
our doctoral advisor and beloved colleague*

Copyright © 1982 by Allyn and Bacon, Inc., 470 Atlantic Avenue, Boston, Massachusetts 02210. All rights reserved. No part of the material protected by this copyright notice may be reproduced or utilized in any form or by any means, electronic or mechanical, including photocopying, recording, or by any information storage and retrieval system, without written permission from the copyright owner.

Printed in the United States of America.
10 9 8 7 6 5

Library of Congress Cataloging in Publication Data

Schwartz, Sydney L. (Sydney Lisbeth)
   Designing curriculum for early childhood.

   Includes bibliographies and index.
   1. Education, Primary—Curricula—Planning.
I. Robison, Helen F. II. Title.
LB1507.S28   372.19   81-12754
ISBN 0-205-07725-0   AACR2

Contents

Preface   ix

I FRAMEWORK FOR CURRICULUM   1

1 Curriculum Framework   2
Perplexing Curriculum Problems   4
Need for Curriculum Framework   7
Curriculum Components   8
Summary   8
Exercises   8
Bibliography   8

2 Curriculum Form   9
Curriculum as a Happening   10
Curriculum as All the Child's Experiences in School   12
Curriculum as Plans for Teaching   12
Curiculum as a Syllabus   14
Curriculum as a Program   15
Curriculum Definitions Compared   15
Summary   16
Exercises   16
Bibliography   16

3 Values and Objectives   17
Objectives   19
Long-Range and Short-Range Objectives   21
Changing Curriculum Goals   24
Summary   26
Exercises   26
Bibliography   26

4 Views of Knowledge   28
Classes of Content   29
Summary   42
Exercises   42
Bibliography   42

5 Views of Child Development   43
Maturationist View   45
Cultural Training Views   47
Cognitive-Developmental View   51
Curriculum Implications of Kohlberg's Categories   56
Child Development Views and the Curriculum   56
Other Views of Development   58
Summary   60
Exercises   62
Bibliography   62

6 Sequencing Curriculum   63
Content Order versus Developmental Order   66
Common Guidelines for Sequencing   68

Sequencing Fact Accumulation   75
Sequencing Skill Accumulation   76
Sequencing in Subject Areas and Academic Disciplines   81
Key Concepts as a Basis for Sequencing   83
Themes as a Basis for Curriculum Sequencing   85
Task Analyis as a Tool of Sequencing   88
Developmental Theory and Sequencing   90
Summary   94
Exercises   94
Bibliography   94

7 Designing Curriculum: Putting Components Together   96
Analysis of Selection   99
Problems in Curriculum Design for the Young   100
Summary   104
Exercises   104
Bibliography   104

II TEACHERS AND TEACHING   105

8 Meeting Children's Social-Emotional Needs   106
The Development of the Self-Concept   108
Teaching Strategies to Meet Children's Social-Emotional Needs   111
Learning from Children with Handicaps   114
The Teaching Team   117
Summary   118
Exercises   119
Bibliography   119

9 Design of Space and Activities   120
Use of Space   121
Rules and Routines   124
Instructional Activities   126
Summary   129
Exercises   130
Bibliography   130

10 Teaching Roles and Strategies   131
The Teacher as a Person   132
Teaching Roles   133
Child Development Views and Teacher Roles   134
Teacher Strategies   135
The Strategy of Asking Questions   137
Summary   143
Exercises   143
Bibliography   143

11 Diagnostic Teaching: Determining Children's Needs   144
Informal Diagnostic Procedures   145
Diagnostic Teaching in Piagetian-based Programs   152
Formal Diagnostic Procedures   153
Summary   156
Exercises   156
Bibliography   156

III A PROTOTYPE CURRICULUM   159

12 Framework for a Prototype Curriculum   160
Curriculum Form   162
Goals and Values   162
Knowledge Selection   167
Views of Development and Learning   168
Sequencing the Curriculum   169
Children's Social-Emotional Needs   170
The Environment and Learning Activities   170
Views of Teaching   171
Prototype Form   172
Summary   174
Exercises   175
Bibliography   175

13 **Prototype Curriculum: Science and Mathematics** 176
    Instructional Approach: Beginning Sorting and Classification 178
    Charting the Mathematics and Science Areas 181
    Mathematics 185
    Science 205
    Summary 208
    Exercises 210
    Bibliography 210

14 **Prototype Curriculum: Music and the Arts** 212
    Music 214
    Art 223
    Summary 233
    Exercises 234
    Bibliography 234

15 **Prototype Curriculum: Language Development and Beginning Reading** 235
    Language Development 236
    Goals and Teaching Approach 238
    Literature 242
    Beginning Reading and Writing 249
    Approaches to Beginning Reading 252
    A Comprehensive Approach 254
    Summary 260
    Exercises 260
    Bibliography 260

IV CURRICULUM RESOURCES 263

16 **Resources for a Vital Curriculum** 264
    The Natural Environment 266
    Human Geography 276
    Human Resources 280
    Summary 292
    Exercises 292
    Bibliography 293

17 **Social and Political Forces and the Curriculum** 294
    Changing Family Composition 296
    Mobility 298
    Sexism 299
    Racism and Poverty 300
    Poverty and Schooling 301
    National Dispersion of Immigrants 304
    Value Changes 305
    Community Involvement 307
    Summary 308
    Exercises 308
    Bibliography 308

Appendix A Tests 311
Appendix B Teacher-made Diagnostic Recording Forms 319
Index 334
About the Authors 342

Preface

Early childhood education has traditionally focused on the needs of children during the early years and on the affective and physical environment required to meet these needs. In terms of curriculum, this emphasis meant making decisions on materials and activities, room arrangement, daily schedules, and occasional trips. Curriculum became the sum of intuitive decisions made by the sensitive, skillful teacher who knew how to provide for the needs of young children.

In the contemporary world, in which accountability is stressed in both the public and private sectors, early childhood educators are challenged to be articulate about what children are gaining from early childhood programs. Articulation requires a definition of what curriculum means in the classroom. If programs for young children are to continue to be designed by early childhood educators, it is imperative that standards for accountability grow out of clear program goals and accomplishments.

We find that our preservice and inservice students have great need for a conceptual framework within which to make curriculum decisions. They urgently need to understand how the components of a curriculum interrelate and what is the range of options actually available.

The major purpose of this book is to feature the bases for curriculum decisions in early childhood education and discuss the range of available options. A second purpose is to highlight the rich resources that may be tapped to fit any curriculum design. While we have a commitment to the curriculum design detailed in Section Three of this text, we hope our decisions will illustrate and facilitate the process of design and development for others. We seek to pursue the curriculum questions teachers ask by mapping the range of procedures and belief systems from which choices may be made.

Section One of this text discusses the curriculum components and their interrelatedness. This section deals with the framework of the curriculum, emphasizing child development, knowledge, and sequencing principles in relation to curriculum purposes, values, and form.

The second section reviews the professional knowledge base for making teaching decisions, including learning activities and teaching behaviors.

The third section illustrates the first two sections, combining these to show one specific curriculum design.

The fourth section focuses on the extensive curriculum resources for young children that help give programs vitality and individuality.

No program can utilize the fullness of available resources. This book offers a wealth of possibilities for curriculum design. Teachers are challenged to make appropriate selections that provide for the uniqueness of their class group, meeting the needs and interests of both children and teachers.

ACKNOWLEDGMENTS

To the following day care centers, nursery schools, and public elementary schools for cooperation in providing classrooms for photographing children: International Nursery School and Kindergarten, Merrick "Y" Day Care Center, Joseph DiMarco Day Care Center, Southeast Queens Self-Help, and Public School 397 in Brooklyn.

To Richard Gordon for his invaluable assistance in photographing children.

To Johanna K. Mott for her continuing help in clarifying presentation of ideas and testing them with teachers.

To our families for their support and patience during our preoccupation with this book.

We also wish to acknowledge the major contribution Maureen Herman made to the mathematics curriculum in an earlier text of ours, *Learning at an Early Age*, vol. 2, on which the prototype described in the present text is based.

I Framework for Curriculum

As professors of early childhood education who are teaching undergraduate or graduate students, we have found a need for a text that could help our students analyze curriculum development in logical and coherent ways. We especially wanted to enable students to construct a conceptual framework that would support functional bases for making daily and long-term decisions.

Section One, therefore, analyzes the components of a curriculum framework. It also offers a range of theories and beliefs about each component in a curriculum design. Illustrations are used to show how ideas might be translated into practice.

Chapter 1 deals with the need for a curriculum framework, illustrating the kinds of problems encountered when teachers are unaware of the options and range of possibilities. In Chapter 2, the varieties, strengths, and limits of curriculum form are described. Values and objectives are analyzed in Chapter 3. While generally taken for granted, views of knowledge and ideas of what should be taught are given a fresh look in Chapter 4. A more familiar component—views of child development—is reviewed in Chapter 5 for its implications for curriculum design. Chapter 6 challenges teachers to make decisions about what to teach next and how to order instruction. Suggestions for coordinating all curriculum components are included in Chapter 7.

1 Curriculum Framework

Creative curriculum designing can be within every teacher's competence. Inspiration is personal and unique, but the curriculum designing process requires an objective series of decisions united by logical consistency. We turn to art for definitions of creative design. For the artist, design "is the organization of parts into a coherent whole."[1] This organizing process is purposeful and requires a series of decisions. Each decision narrows remaining choices, so that the one "best solution" emerges. Marjorie Bevlin identifies steps in the process of design, which applies to curriculum as well as to art.[2] The steps focus on:

1. defining the purpose,
2. analyzing the options,
3. selecting the design features,
4. producing the design,
5. evaluating the design—does it measure up to your intentions?

Teachers start with many more givens than the artist. But creative design in both cases is a matter of asking questions and making decisions that build a unified pattern or product. This book seeks to help teachers identify the decisions they have to make to conceive and produce an interesting design.

1. Marjorie Elliott Bevlin, *Design through Discovery* (New York: Holt, Rinehart and Winston, 1980), p. 2.
2. Ibid., pp. 32–34.

When a three-year-old silently climbs on the teacher's lap and hands him a book expecting to be read to, one can easily forget that teaching is a complex act involving many decisions. For most of us, it would seem natural to open the book and begin reading. Ideas about curriculum, child development and learning, and teaching skills seem far removed from such a warm, intimate interaction with a young child. However, when five more children try to crowd on the same lap, at the same time, the need for teaching decisions becomes evident. In reality, the first lap-sitter posed decisions as comprehensive as did the additional five children, such as:

1. whether to use the book to initiate a conversation about classroom activities or to use the book in other ways;
2. whether to restrict the interaction to a hug or some form of emotional support, without reading the book;
3. whether to read the book's pictures or its narrative, or to ask the child questions about her or his experiences, or to ask the child to "read" the book;
4. whether to wait for the child's initiative before deciding how to respond.

Any one of these decisions, or many others, might be right in this situation, depending on the teacher's views about goals, curriculum, and children, and on the teacher's knowledge about a particular child. Similar views about goals for children could lead to different decisons, if the curriculum approaches are different. For example, of two teachers valuing independence, one might hug the child and ignore the book, while the other might invite the child to read the story. In the former case, the primary concern might be to foster children's ability to pursue tasks of their own choosing. In the latter case, the teacher might be featuring vocabulary development and reading skills.

Teachers in early childhood settings face an unending challenge to decide *what to teach*, *when to teach*, and *how to teach*. On what basis does a teacher decide to introduce a new musical game, plan an art activity, place new science materials on a table, or begin a rhyming activity with a small group? Under what conditions does a teacher enter into the children's activities, initiating conversations and asking questions? When does the teacher increase children's responsibilities to solve their own social conflicts or to monitor the routines of the program?

As difficult as these decisions are, it is even more difficult to provide a cogent explanation of the reasons for the decisions to others. Imagine having to explain why the teacher chose to ignore the three-year-old's book selection and redirected the child into activities? Such an analysis would require some statement about goals for the program, curriculum values, and a developmental view, not only of three-year-olds but of this particular child. It certainly would not do to justify basing such an action on feelings such as, "It seemed right at the time," or "I felt that was what the child really needed." Nor would it be sufficient to rely on rules such as, "During playtime, children are expected to play with each other and with the materials. We don't spend time with them alone during playtime." Neither of these approaches deals with the most important question of the goals for children and the program or the reasons for rules.

PERPLEXING CURRICULUM PROBLEMS

The difficulty of defining curriculum and the basis for teaching decisions often leads to frustration for teachers of young children. The struggle to identify program goals is a major problem. Once identified, goals need some preference order—which are more important? Which are less important? Another need teachers have is to judge their own effectiveness in teaching. But teaching effectiveness cannot be judged in a vacuum; it must be related to goals. Effectiveness in teaching reading cannot be evaluated if this is not a program goal. Yet, for teachers to experience personal and professional satisfactions and confidence in their teaching decisions, they must have a sense of effectiveness and autonomy. Accountability to parents and the community can only rest on teacher judgments that what was intended was well done.

The following experiences typify the kinds of perplexing questions that provoke frustration for thoughtful and conscientious teachers.

A Question of Instructional Effectiveness

The teacher in a classroom of four-year-olds was working to expand her program by changing materials provided during the free-choice period and by introducing new activities during group periods. The teacher reported the following problem to a graduate class, requesting help in deciding what to do next.

Using a suggestion in a section of an early childhood textbook, *What They Can Learn*, the teacher arranged some materials to stimulate exploration of the properties of light.[3] In accordance with the description in the book, the teacher placed a pencil in a glass of water on the science table.

3. Catherine Landreth, *Preschool Learning and Teaching* (New York: Harper & Row, 1972), pp. 73–83.

One child soon became fascinated with the apparent bend in the pencil, the distortion caused by the light passing through the water. As predicted by the textbook author, the child spent a great deal of time putting the pencil in and out of the water, making comments that reflected his perceptions. Each time the child placed the pencil in the water, he inquired, "Who bent my pencil?" When removing the pencil from the water, he commented, "Now it's straight."

Up to this point, the teacher expressed satisfaction with her instructional effectiveness. In keeping wth her view of how curriculum ought to develop, through children's interests, the plan was going well. However, her conviction that children learn through their own actions and experiments was beginning to threaten her sense of instructional effectiveness. The teacher was puzzled about how to help this child understand that the pencil does not change shape in water but only appears to do so. For this teacher, instructional effectiveness essentially required that children acquire accurate information but not through teacher "telling."

The teacher reported a number of attempts to help the child discover that the pencil did not really bend in the water. These included expanding the exploration to more materials, such as the child's own fingers, sticks, pipe cleaners, wire strips, and solid metal rods. But to no avail. The child always returned to the pencil and his concern with its shape when the pencil was placed in the water.

As this situation was discussed in the graduate class over a period of weeks, it became clearer that the teacher had conflicting views of knowledge, learning, and teaching. On the one hand, she was deeply committed to supporting the child's discovery and encouraging his "figuring out." On the other hand, she was unable to accept the understanding the child was working out because it was not "right." Teachers who value discovery-type learning have to come to terms with the probability that knowledge is made up of ideas constructed by the learner. If it is understood that children are going to build understandings their own way, the teacher must expect temporary "wrong" answers on the way to better ones.

In this situation, there was no resolution to the teacher's feeling of *instructional ineffectiveness*. Her views on how children learn prohibited her from trying to explain the phenomenon of light refraction, but she could not feel comfortable with the child's inaccurate perceptions. However, from this experience, the teacher was able to identify in what ways her views of knowledge required more careful review of the kinds of materials she offers the children. She decided that, in the future, she would select materials and activities from which children would be likely to develop reasonably accurate understandings rather quickly. In this way, she could preserve her discovery approach while also meeting her standards for children to acquire accurate knowledge.

A Question of Professional Autonomy

A new teacher in a classroom of three-year-olds decided to change the lunch routine to conform with one she had used during student teaching. Instead of having all children wait at the bathroom doorway together for toileting and hand washing and then wait at the tables for a few children to complete table setting and lunch serving, she gathered the children on the floor for finger plays and action songs. From this grouping, the table setters of the day went to complete their tasks with the help of the assistant teacher, and the handwashing routine was accomplished by sending two children at a time to the bathroom.

When the director viewed this redesigned lunch routine, she expressed disapproval. She expected all children to be seated at the tables during the table-setting process. In the director's view, as she explained it to the teacher, the new procedure required most of the children to be waited on by a few. In her idea of curriculum, routines constituted such an important part of the program that all children had to be included, either as watchers or doers. No competing activity could go on at the same time.

The teacher was unable to explain her new procedure in curricular terms. She found herself making such justifications as, "It's really nice," "It's not so hectic," and "The children really enjoy it." Since the director was not convinced by such explanations, the routine was returned to the standard format for that center.

Frustrated, this teacher sought the advice of her college professor. Was she wrong? What was the matter with the plan? How could she explain it to her director? As the teacher explored why the plan was desirable, she discovered that her values included increased instructional time and reduced waiting time. Her new procedure, as she saw it, involved all children in actual activity, that is, she viewed learning as an active process. The table setters had continuing guidance as they worked through the task of providing a complete set of utensils at each setting, and the hand washers were actively involved in their independent task. At the same time, most of the group were expanding their learnings through finger plays and action songs.

In this instance, the two views of curriculum as encompassing all aspects of the program were similar. However, the teacher's idea that active involvement meant doing rather than waiting and watching did not conform with the director's requirement of total grouping for all routines. Since the teacher was unable to articulate her views, the differences could not be analyzed, and she lost her chance for autonomy in making this teaching decision.

A Question of Accountability

It was open school night, and parents were visiting in their children's classroom. They took this opportunity to find out more about the program from the teacher of the five-year-olds. Some of their questions were:

- "What do the children do all day?"
- "What else do they do besides play?"
- "What do you teach them?"
- "Why don't the children have homework?"

The teacher briefly explained the great importance of play in children's learning. The group times were described as periods when the children heard stories and talked about experiences as a way to improve language skills. The teacher covered a range of program activities, such as motor skills in arts, crafts, and physical games, prereading skills through listening games, instruction in name writing, symbol reading in card games, mathematical skills in woodworking, musical activities, and the routines of the program. Most important, the teacher explained, was that the children were learning how to get along with each other and that they enjoyed school activities.

The parents responded to this explanation with approving nods and smiles. However, they restated the original question about what is being taught. They understood that children learn from each other and through using the materials, but they also believed that the teacher's job was more than watching over learning—it was teaching. They expressed their conviction, in a variety of ways, that there should be more instruction and homework.

This teacher was unable to meet the standards of accountability for this group of parents. Her description of *instructional effectiveness* was too general for them to understand. Ultimately, she lost her *autonomy*, since the the parents, who paid the tuition, would not be satisfied until duplicated sheets were used for instruction and homework.

The teachers in this school then began the difficult process of defining curriculum in clear enough terms so that parents not only could understand it, but also could see how the program activities achieved the curriculum goals. The project of curriculum construction thus became a guideline for accountability.

A Question of Personal and Professional Satisfaction

Any one of the experiences just described could seriously limit a teacher's sense of personal and professional satisfaction. Increasingly, the early childhood teacher is required to master curriculum content, ideas, knowledge of child development, and communication skills with both children and adults. Weakness in any one of these areas can lead to loss of a sense of instructional effectiveness, autonomy, or accountability.

Personal and professional satisfaction grows out of a continuing sense of control of teaching decisions and feedback that reflects effectiveness. That is, the results, of one's teaching decisions are essentially as expected. This means selecting activities and teaching methods that support program goals and values. Selection implies knowing and considering the scope of options.

NEED FOR CURRICULUM FRAMEWORK

How does a teacher develop the skills of decision making that reflect a reliable basis for performance? We believe such skills grow out of familiarity with the variety of approaches to knowledge, program, child development and learning, and teaching. Each of these views defines a range of decisions that have clear limits.

Beyond these limits, different views emerge. As teachers identify the point of view and the range of teaching decisions contained in each approach, how to coordinate planning with on-the-spot decisions becomes clearer. This means that, if as a kindergarten teacher I really like the informal, open-education type of program, I can describe the features that appeal to me, and I can confidently implement these features in my classroom. If, instead, I want permission to substitute a different program, such as a Piagetian-based curriculum, I can clearly state my reasons for preferring one to the other and can defend my choices.

By exploring views of knowledge, child development and learning, and teaching and sequencing curriculum, this book will help the classroom teacher understand the different curriculum approaches for young children. Although it is true that the major task of the early childhood teacher is to provide an environment in which children flourish, it is equally true that there is no single model for such an environment. There are differing ideas about what "flourish" means, and it is the major task of this book to highlight its many possibilities.

Children can respond to a teacher's expectations more readily if there is continuity in teaching designs and expectations for children. These expectations often grow out of unspecified assumptions of what is valuable for children to know and do, and how they learn best. Teachers need to specify their ideas about curriculum and to make teaching decisions that are likely to lead to intended successful experiences for children. Readers are encouraged to identify those ideas that reflect their views in each major component of curriculum and to test the meaning of these ideas in interactions with children. Contradictions, discontinuities, and unrelated program activities show up readily as ideas are translated into teaching plans and activities. If teachers of young children construct a framework to guide program design and teaching decisions, these can serve as a basis for personal and professional review of instructional effectiveness.

CURRICULUM COMPONENTS

Visit a variety of educational settings for children two and one-half to six years of age and note the similarities and differences in the children's experiences. Some programs differ from others in the way the rooms are arranged and the way teaching occurs. That is, to the observer, a classroom where children are seated in a group for long periods, for activities directed by the teacher, looks different from one in which the children move freely, engaging in activities of their own choosing. But the teachers in both of these classrooms may offer the same views about what children need, how they learn, and what kind of curriculum is desirable. It is just as likely that the views of the teachers will differ as much about the way they teach as they will about the content they are using. Observers are often surprised and confused when what they see and hear are not the same.

SUMMARY

Two continuous concerns of teachers are *how* to relate to children individually and in groups, and *what* to teach. While in reality these concerns tend to be interdependent, curriculum planning for what to teach is distinct from the teaching methods and the management of the setting. The curriculum is the educational reason for young children to be in kindergarten, day care, Head Start, or primary-grade classes. In this first section, we will examine the range of ideas that can serve as a framework for making curricular and programmatic decisions. The major components considered are:

1. curriculum form,
2. values and objectives,
3. views of knowledge,
4. views of child development,
5. sequencing curriculum.

A conceptual framework should make it easier for the teacher to make such decisions; to feel more secure that the decisions are well based; and to communicate the logic of her decisions to others, including children, parents, assistants, supervisors, and administrators.

EXERCISES

1. Write a brief observation of an instructional activity observed in an early childhood classroom.
    a. Determine the goals and values.
    b. Identify the content, or summarize what children seemed to be learning.
    c. List problems in answering (a) and (b) above.
2. Analyze an instructional plan you prepared and/or implemented in teaching for:
    a. goals and values;
    b. curriculum content and how it relates to goals and values. Is there a clear relationship? If not, how could the plan be changed to make goals and values specifically relate to content?

BIBLIOGRAPHY

Bevlin, Marjorie Elliott. *Design through Discovery.* New York: Holt, Rinehart and Winston, 1980.

Landreth, Catherine. *Preschool Learning and Teaching.* New York: Harper & Row, 1972.

2 Curriculum Form

If you ask a director of an early childhood center, "May I see your curriculum?" the director might hand you a brochure to read or explain that no written form of the curriculum exists but that it can be described orally. The form of the curriculum can vary from a written, detailed program to a set of ideas and beliefs that can only be grasped by observing the program. The curriculum of the early childhood program may take many different forms—from a happening to a syllabus to a program. The form usually derives from how curriculum is defined. Major definitions of curriculum discussed in this chapter include:

1. a *happening*, in which children's choices dominate and teachers support children's activities;
2. *all the child's experiences in school*, from both the child's perspective and the teacher's;
3. *plans for teaching*, in which teachers plan activities for the day, week, or longer periods;
4. a *syllabus*, which details a series of instructional goals to be achieved in designated subject or content areas;
5. a *program* based on one approach or theory.

As these definitions of curriculum are discussed, you are encouraged to identify similarities and differences in the approaches.

CURRICULUM AS A HAPPENING

Curriculum is "what happens" when most of the choices are left to the child. The teacher trusts the child to decide how to spend time in school and expects that any choices the child makes will be constructive and appropriate for that child at that time. Since it is unpredictable how the program will go on any one day, until children make their choices and become involved in their selected activities, the teacher does not plan for content selection in advance. However, the teacher stands ready to respond to the ebb and flow of children's activities, sensitive to individual children, their needs and interests. Such a curriculum approach requires a teacher with rich resources, one who can comfortably make on-the-spot decisions.

The following statement from a book on children's play is representative of this broad view of early childhood curriculum, which has a long-standing tradition:

> The early years are filled with rapid growth in all aspects of children's development. A desire to enhance development contributes to an interest in providing a rich variety of learning opportunities for children to promote physical, social, emotional and intellectual growth. For young children, play is the most appropriate medium to present such learning opportunities.[1]

1. Gail Bjorklund, *Planning for Play: A Developmental Approach* (Columbus, Ohio: Charles E. Merrill, 1978), p. 59.

Within this view of content, much of what happens depends on advance arrangement of an environment in which children's choices can be made. This includes organization of materials and management procedures to assure orderliness and to avoid chaos. It is probable that, without dictating content, the teacher influences it by the attractiveness and interest surrounding selected experiences. This view of curriculum regards all learning as equally valuable. Children's choices are vital, since where children find interest and value, they invest themselves without needing external motivation.

However, most teachers who leave choices to the child concerning what to deal with in school are not content to face each day with so many unknowns. Consequently, they plan such things as (1) a time schedule for length and sequence of periods in the program, activity period, cleanup, snack, group time and/or music period, and (2) specific activities or materials that stimulate involvement. With time schedules and specific activities planned, the unknowns are considerably reduced.

When curriculum is viewed as *what happens*, there is a clear valuing of process over any specific content, since what is valued is the child's interest and way of being involved in learning activities or experiences. Human relationships are also high on the values list, as the child experiences respect, trustfulness, support, and autonomy in activities. The process goals of this curriculum may be selected from such outcomes as problem solving, task construction, task design, or discovery of physical properties of the environment. Such psychosocial skills as leading, following, cooperating, expressing oneself, valuing oneself, or having self-confidence may be important values. Other process goals might be to enjoy school, use time effectively, or think and act independently.

Teaching flows from children's choices and behaviors and cannot be plotted in advance. Teaching roles are specified to include observing, reflecting, elaborating, modeling, evaluating, and planning.[2] The planning role is defined as "gathering information through observation and interaction with children and using this information to select appropriate play experiences which will extend and support play."[3] It should be noted that this planning function does not suggest the use of sources external to the children.

The important sources for curriculum in this definition are the children themselves. It should not be inferred that this curriculum approach lacks content. On the contrary, there is likely to be a great deal of content in such a curriculum, selected on the basis of the teacher's analysis of children's needs and interests.

This mode of curriculum development rests on intuitive, on-the-spot decisions. The repertoire from which teaching decisions are made grows out of prior experience with children's activities and knowledge of child development. Sources that are helpful for the teacher are tradition, or what has been useful in the past, as well as information and advice from other teachers and educators about what else is new and useful.

Advocates of this approach cite its strengths as being personalistic, humanistic, and unbounded. Assumptions are not made as to what "should" be happening, nor are children viewed as alike and interchangeable. Ideally, the child is central to all possible choices, and the teacher supports these choices to the extent that the teacher perceives them as conducive to furthering development.

Critics note that teachers do, in fact, make many choices in arranging the environment and the schedule and in selecting which of the many expressed interests and needs of children to emphasize. Additionally, critics cite the need for experienced, insightful, and resourceful teachers to be able to make such on-the-spot decisions continually. Especially difficult, critics say, is coordinating with team members to initiate or respond to children's actions.

2. Ibid., p. 71.
3. Ibid., p. 78.

CURRICULUM AS ALL THE CHILD'S EXPERIENCES IN SCHOOL

The concept of curriculum as being everything the child experiences in school is an attempt to acknowledge the often dominant influence of the hidden curriculum, or of incidental and unplanned events that may overshadow teaching plans in personal significance to the child. It allows that not everything that is planned to be taught is learned. It also suggests that much school experience, of which teachers may be unaware, has unintended effects.

This view of curriculum is reflected in today's movement toward meeting the ethnic needs of children. It alerts teachers and schools to the meaning of *ambience*, the atmosphere of the classroom; *group dynamics*, the way members of the group react to each other; and the importance of *affect*, the emotional communications between people. It is a useful tool in many situations where social change is rapidly creating new and unfamiliar social groupings. For example, when one day care center began absorbing many non-English speaking children, multiple challenges arose in dealing with the language barrier and a different set of social behaviors and cultural values. The teachers' lack of skills with the language of the newly enrolled group created unintended experiences for children. Teachers continued to have conversations only with parents of the English-speaking children, at arrival and dismissal, limiting interchanges with non-English speaking parents to smiles and nods. The hidden curriculum, in this case, involved an apparent valuing of one set of parents over another.

This view of curriculum features the impact of external social forces that subtly influence the in-class experiences. The young child is especially vulnerable to a breach in the need for security, trust, and respect for his or her values and traditions. Advocates of this approach to curriculum emphasize the need to examine all aspects of interpersonal relationships to assure continuity of learning for the children. This approach is limited by the enormity of the task of examining all aspects of interactions. Since so many interactions that occur are actually beyond the control or knowledge of the teacher, planning and reviewing a curriculum of this type assumes enormous proportions.

An important advantage of this definition of curriculum is the possibility of increasing teacher sensitivity to the effects on children of unplanned as well as of intended experiences. Advocates are especially alert to social change and to the need to review traditional practices that may lose purpose in new contexts. Clearly, teachers are required to take more account of the context in which learning takes place, to be more sophisticated about the many unpredictable ways that cultural practices affect learning outcomes.

Teachers, however, may throw up their hands when given so much responsibility. They may need far more supervisory support. A team backup is especially needed here, reinforced by volunteers or recruits from new groups to be accommodated by the schools. Most challenging to the teacher who prefers advanced planning is the unexpected nature of outcomes or the consciousness of lack of control.

CURRICULUM AS PLANS FOR TEACHING

Plans for teaching are increasingly required by day care directors, supervisors, and elementary school principals. General curriculum theory has for a long time defined curriculum as plans for teaching. A sampling of representative definitions follows:

1. Johnson defines curriculum as "a structured series of learning outcomes."[4]
2. Zais defines curriculum as "a plan for the education of the learners."[5]

---

4. Mauritz N. Johnson, "Definitions and Models in Curriculum Theory," in Edmund C. Short and George D. Marconnit, eds., *Contemporary Thought on Public School Curriculum* (Dubuque, Iowa: Wm. C. Brown, 1968), p. 44.

5. Robert S. Zais, *Curriculum Principles and Foundations* (New York: Thomas Y. Crowell, 1976), p. 10.

3. Taba views all curricula as containing certain elements; that is, a statement of specific objectives, some choices, and structuring content.[6]

Plans for teaching young children seem to have cycles of popularity. In the recent past, when child-centeredness predominated, plans were regarded as barriers to flexibility. This is currently changing to renewed emphasis on planning for selected outcomes.

Curriculum viewed as intentional planning may be very specific or broad, and it may feature short-range or long-range planning. Many examples of curriculum plans for early childhood programs are found in current curriculum texts. They vary in the degree of detail used to guide daily curriculum decisions: some plans are limited to a set of unrelated activities, while others may describe a series of activities in one topical or content area. The plans, whether written or oral, can relate to activities, content, processes, or some combination of the three. *Activities* describe what teachers and children do, while *content* describes facts, skills, and ideas selected for learning. On the other hand, *process* stresses long-term developmental patterns, such as classification. In general, these three features contrast action, ideas, and ways of thinking.

Plans that relate to activities often detail the teaching procedures. For example:

Planting Seeds — Activity Procedures
- For this activity, collect 10 lbs. of soil, enough milk cartons for each child, and marigold or other rapidly sprouting seeds. Examine materials with children; then place first soil and then seeds into planter and water. Place planters on window sill and examine daily.

Note that goals and children's learning processes are omitted from this activity plan.

6. Hilda Taba, *Curriculum Development: Theory and Practice* (New York: Harcourt, Brace & World, 1962), p. 10.

Focusing on content, plans may cite goals for children's learning. For example:

Planting Seeds — Content Focus
- *Goals:* Children learn that seeds are the source of new plants, and that seeds will sprout under special conditions. Also, they learn that different seeds produce different plants.
- While setting up planters with children, discuss prior experiences with plants at home, out-of-doors, focusing on differences between plants. Anticipate the growth of the newly planted seeds, using a sample plant to illustrate the type of plant that will grow.

Here the focus is on how to teach and what content to teach.

Plans which feature process goals may stress learning procedures. For example:

Planting Seeds — Process Goals
- In a seed-planting activity with children, focus children's attention on the properties of the materials, encouraging comparison and contrast of form, texture, color, and size. Encourage prediction of what will happen to soil when water is added and to seed when it is planted. Encourage children to formulate experiments to test their predictions. Encourage children to discuss their experiments and to formulate their understandings. Stimulate arguments and challenges.

Advocates of curriculum plans view planning as the professional basis for teaching. It serves beginners and experienced teachers alike by helping them to anticipate children's needs, interests, and activities and to organize the materials and environment to meet them. Supporters of this approach claim that by anticipating alternatives such planning increases teaching options, in contrast to the limited options that might be considered at the moment.

They claim that any plans worth using with young children usually require considerable flexibility.

For those who seek to avoid rigidity by avoiding planfulness, R. F. Dearden cautions that

> In the fashion to throw out frameworks as rigid barriers, or as artificial or watertight compartments, it has gone unnoticed that frameworks can protect as well as restrict. They can save the individual from his own biases and from losing his direction in largely immediate practical preoccupations.[7]

Dearden reminds us of how useful a framework can be in practice.

Critics of written plans for teaching highlight the possibility that teachers will cease to observe children closely and instead follow written or formulated plans inflexibly. Many experienced early childhood teachers refuse to write plans for teaching lest these reduce spontaneity and flexibility in responding daily to children's perceived needs. These teachers, however, often indicate that they act on implicit plans—some made in advance and requiring preparation, others developed as the situation requires.

CURRICULUM AS A SYLLABUS

A comprehensive set of written plans constitutes a syllabus, which serves as a long-range guide for curriculum. It identifies what is to be taught, and usually in what sequence, and for what objectives. Many local and state education authorities in the United States require such a syllabus to be published for prekindergarten and kindergarten levels, as well as for the grades. Many education departments issue syllabi to guide local school districts. Such syllabi formalize early childhood programs, establishing them as educational entities related to the educational enterprise. Advocates and critics of the view of curriculum as a syllabus cite the same arguments as those cited for curriculum as plans for teaching. The security of having a written guide offers the primary value, while the confining aspects of a plan written in advance is seen as a severe limit. The written form establishes expectations of what the program will accomplish with the children, and it may facilitate assessment and evaluation processes and induction of new teachers.

To the parents in a community whose taxes support public schools, or whose fees are paid to day care, nursery school, or profit-making early childhood centers, the idea of a published syllabus detailing the curriculum is very appealing. It looks substantial, authoritative, and official. It seems to promise that much thought has gone into planning for early learning, that the planning is well based on experience and research, and that it is reliable. Indeed, most such publications reflect great care and selectivity.

A curriculum embodied in a syllabus seems to assure that there will be some unity and predictability in the young child's school experiences and even in outcomes. Teachers and their assistants are often just as pleased as parents, supervisors, and administrators to have such written curriculum plans to follow. They provide a document for those who ask about the curriculum, since such questions are often difficult to answer.

Needless to say, a written curriculum is no better than one that exists only in practice. It may or may not offer the flexibility needed to adapt, revise, and keep it up to date. The nature of teaching in our culture usually gives early childhood teachers many possibilities for ignoring a syllabus they do not find useful, or for varying and adapting it in countless ways.

To the extent that teachers themselves participate in the writing of the syllabus, with regular revisions it may be a helpful tool for reviewing ideas about young children's learning needs for and evaluating theory and research that may have implications for classroom practice. The process of writing or rewriting a sylla-

---

7. R. F. Dearden, *Problems in Primary Education* (London: Routledge & Kegan Paul, 1976), p. 96.

bus helps teachers to clarify and update their ideas. Once these ideas take written form, communication with parents and others is greatly facilitated.

The published syllabi vary in the same way that written plans vary. Some are not really prescriptive of content or methodology. Until recently, they tended to offer a good paraphrase of child development philosophy and suggestions for useful topics, themes, units, trips, and holiday events. Others that are very prescriptive include behavioral objectives, such as tying shoelaces, writing one's name, and counting to ten. Minimum competencies may be listed, for example, the ability to sit quietly for fifteen minutes listening to a story, or the ability to listen to others and wait one's turn in a group discussion with ten other children.

CURRICULUM AS A PROGRAM

The term *curriculum* is often used to describe a particular program, such as a Montessori program or an academically oriented program. Programs have also been titled "compensatory," "Head Start," "Follow Through," and "developmental," among others. The name of the program may or may not identify the particular curriculum being followed or constructed. Montessori schools are associated with the theories and materials developed by Maria Montessori. Head Start programs have no similar unifying theory or unique approach.

Within the past ten years a number of textbooks for early childhood have been published that describe programs with distinctive curriculum patterns. It is important to note that curriculum as a program is best reflected by those that feature a coordinated set of plans related to underlying theory and program goals.

CURRICULUM DEFINITIONS COMPARED

The foregoing discussion indicates the many different ways curriculum is used or defined. There is no overriding right way to define this basic educational term. Definitions are value-laden. We select the meanings that give value to our own priorities.

From the process-oriented perspective, two distinctive views emerge. One view defines curriculum as "what happens." Learning is a seamless whole, and whatever interests the child is useful for constructive development. Continuity is in the child, not in ideas or bodies of knowledge, nor in activities or experiences. Just as it has been shown that when infants select their own food they tend to eat a balanced, nutritious diet, so it is thought that children select for their school learning the kinds of activities and materials especially right for fulfilling their needs and for optimal development. This view assumes the preschool child is as free of exterior influences on choices as is the infant.[8]

The other view of process-oriented curriculum shows less willingness to give young children much choice, and guidance is planned in advance. Agreeing that the child's own activity and reflections are the basic ways children construct a system of reasoning and ideas about the world, teachers and curriculum planners are more willing to observe carefully what the child chooses to deal with and how reasoning develops. The teacher may choose to challenge, probe, stimulate, interest, or redirect the child in explorations that might suggest more complex questions or ideas. The curriculum in this case is likely to be somewhat more selective. However, selections tend to be based on the kind of tasks that interest children and that may open new challenges for them.

In contrast to a process orientation, curriculum plans may be more comprehensive, including identified content, possible sequencing and pacing, as well as evaluation of outcomes compared with plans. The published syllabus, if specific about scope and sequence, offers an even more detailed base for evaluation and a

---

8. C. M. Davis, "Self Selection of Diet by Newly Weaned Infants," *American Journal of Diseases of Children*, 36 (1928): 651–679.

unified, public statement of objectives and goals to assess. The uniformity is often more apparent than real, but it may exert considerable pressure—especially on novice teachers—to adapt children's learning experiences to those specified in written documents.

Using the definitions discussed, you are encouraged to identify the form that seems most in accord with your professional views. The curriculum form that seems most desirable is likely to be the one that is most familiar. It will be helpful to review these preferences while reading the following chapters on related components.

SUMMARY

Curriculum form, which is based on the curriculum definition used, may take such forms as (1) a happening, (2) the totality of all the child's experiences in school, (3) plans for teaching, (4) a syllabus, or (5) a program.

Happenings are features where children's choices predominate. *The totality of school experiences* recognize the influences of the hidden curriculum or the reality of daily life in school. *Plans for teaching* recognize teacher centrality in curriculum and the advantages of thoughtful teacher decision making. The *syllabus* is usually a written document, issued by local or state education authorities, that attempts to unify teaching purposes and communicate these to parents. And last, when curriculum is viewed as *a program*, it represents an attempt to distinguish a coherent set of unique characteristics as a design for learning, such as the Montessori program.

EXERCISES

1. Prepare an instructional activity plan for a specific classroom, choosing your preferred form.
    a. Find a colleague or fellow student who has chosen a different form and compare your preferred form with his or hers.
    b. Discuss reasons for your preference and advantages and disadvantages of possible forms.
2. Interview at least two teachers about their preferences for instructional forms.
3. Review two early childhood textbooks and identify author preferences for curriculum form.

BIBLIOGRAPHY

Bjorklund, Gail. *Planning for Play: A Developmental Approach.* Columbus, Ohio: Charles E. Merrill, 1978.

Davis, C. M. "Self Selection of Diet by Newly Weaned Infants." *American Journal of Diseases of Children,* 36 (1928): 651–679.

Dearden, R. F. *Problems in Primary Education.* London: Routledge & Kegan Paul, 1976.

Johnson, Mauritz N. "Definitions and Models in Curriculum Theory." In Edmund Short and George Marconnit, eds. *Contemporary Thought on Public School Curriculum.* Dubuque, Iowa: Wm. C. Brown, 1968.

Taba, Hilda. *Curriculum Development: Theory and Practice.* New York: Harcourt, Brace & World, 1962.

Zais, Robert S. *Curriculum Principles and Foundations.* New York: Thomas Y. Crowell, 1976.

3 Values and Objectives

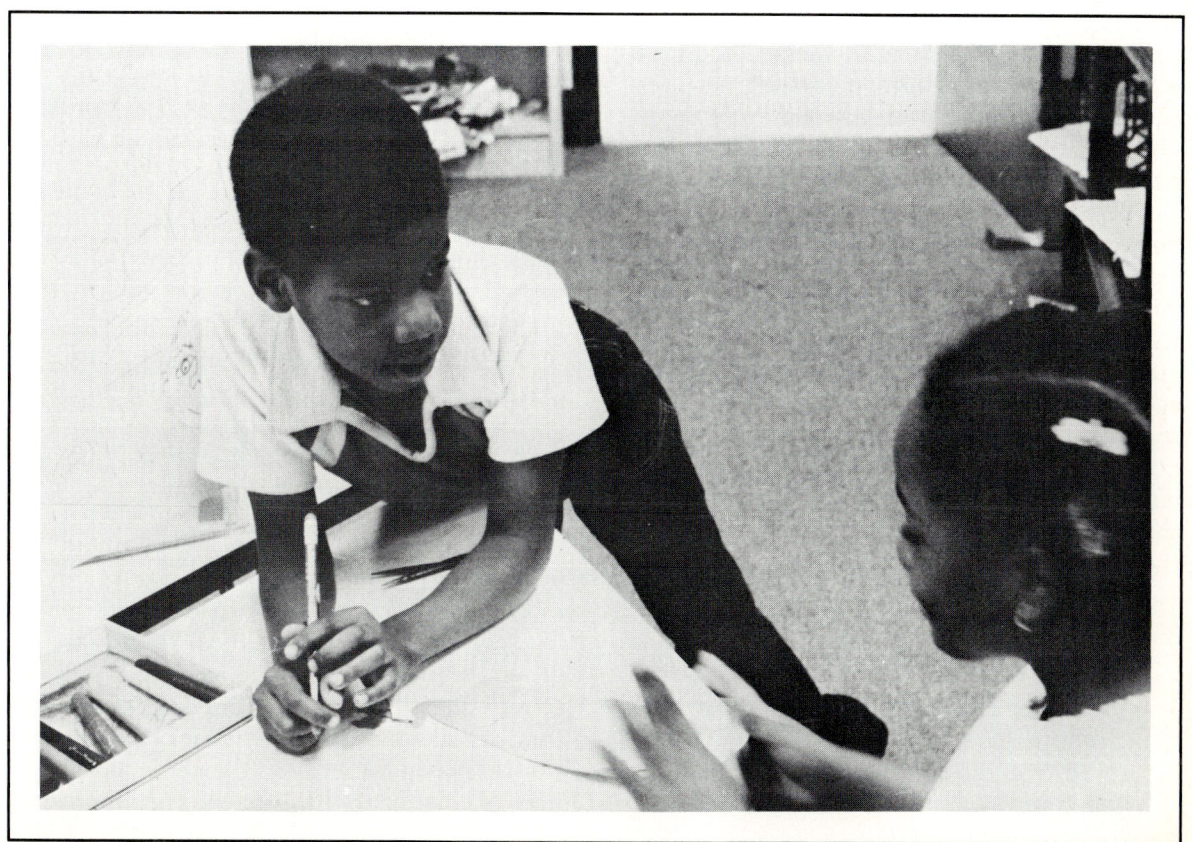

One of the primary components of curriculum development is the collection of ideas about purposes and objectives, values and goals. These four terms tend to be used interchangeably, and there will be no attempt here to make fine distinctions among them. However, you might notice in the literature generally that purposes and values are linked with long-term concerns while goals usually designate an instructional or short-term objective. The reasons for curriculum decisions can only be explained in relation to one's purposes and values.

The educational values are challenged in all forms of early childhood education. What objectives are being followed, and what choices have been made among the various possibilities for curriculum construction? When evaluating prospective centers, parents and funding agencies alike frequently hear the same objectives claimed by vastly different schools.

Some educators in early childhood prefer to build curriculum directly on values rather than translate values into objectives. For example, the general value of independence may be elaborated into a series of specific objectives such as:

1. to develop the skills of personal care with clothing, food, and grooming;
2. to develop the social skills of cooperation and group awareness;
3. to develop curiosity, inquiry skills, and problem solving skills;
4. to develop choice-making behavior.

These values define hoped-for outcomes without breaking down into specific goals of learning activities.

A major function of objectives is to distinguish one program from another. For example, a program with academic skill goals can be easily distinguished from a program with social-emotional development goals. Another function of goals is to serve as a basis for examination of consistency and continuity of program. A program with the stated goal of fostering independence would be inconsistent with a program design that fails to provide the children with choices. Ultimately, the objectives serve as an ever-present basis for making planning and teaching decisions.

Whether values are detailed into objectives specifically or generally is a challenging question for teachers. If the teacher chooses to make specific lists of aims, the parents and others may view the program too narrowly, looking only for evidence that specific objectives have been accomplished. In contrast, if general values are the guide, it is often difficult to recognize the variety of children's activities that can accomplish these values. The distinction between general and specific objectives may be equated to the difference between long-range and short-range objectives. The nature or content of objectives is discussed in the next section, followed by an examination of the differences between long-term and short-term objectives.

OBJECTIVES

The content of curriculum goals may be organized in a variety of ways. Sources for goal selection include areas of human growth and development, curriculum content, cultural values, and community needs. Irrespective of the areas used, objectives will overlap. For example, general goals in growth and development may focus on:

1. affective or personality development;
2. cognitive development;
3. skill development, including physical, social, or academic skills.

Affective and personality development goals feature enhancing the way the children feel about themselves, the way they deal with their emotions, and their sense of confidence, competence, independence, and importance or worthwhileness. To achieve a sense of competence or independence, some skills are required. These may include the physical skills needed for dressing and eating, climbing and running, and cutting with scissors and pouring paint. They may also include the social skills needed for the give-and-take in play situations. Consequently, a focus on affective and personality development goals is likely to lead to the selection of skill development goals.

Cognitive development goals feature children's ways of acquiring knowledge-building concepts, testing ideas, and solving problems. This kind of learning is dependent on young children's active manipulation of materials in the environment, requiring *skills* of coordination.

Using a similar kind of category system, a study of twenty-two Follow-Through programs originally funded in 1968 broadly divided the programs, primarily according to their purposes, into four categories as follows:[1]

1. *Behaviorist types*, with precise requirements for instruction and reinforcement: Their purposes are to reinforce children for desired behavior for success in school.
2. *Cognitive growth programs:* these seek to facilitate the normal "stage-wise growth of these processes."
3. *Self-actualization programs:* these help the child learn to become competent in his or her own physical and social environment.
4. *Programs responsive to the needs and wishes of the community:* unlike the previous three, this fourth category, it should be noted, gives no clue to the type of curriculum likely to be considered responsive to any specific community. These programs, tend to be oriented to a racial or ethnic group—such as an American Indian tribe or a black group with separatist orientation—wishing to maintain a culturally distinct group within the larger community.

While Follow-Through programs represented a wide range of curricular types among those available in early childhood education, federal funding was limited to selected schools serving disadvantaged young children who had already experienced Project Head Start. There was no consideration for the many children who came from homes not economically disadvantaged.

Another way of categorizing objectives might be in terms of the following kinds of outcomes:

1. social utility,
2. social responsibility,
3. skills,
4. knowledge of common culture,
5. knowledge of special culture,
6. personal development.

1. Eleanor E. Maccoby and Miriam Zeller, *Experiments in Primary Education: Aspects of Project Follow Through* (New York: Harcourt, Brace, Jovanovich, 1970), pp. 25–26.

As shown in Table 3–1, some of these are by no means mutually exclusive. For example, in category one, *social utility*, there are skills that are desired by a community because practical skills decrease dependency needs, but these skills would also contribute to personal development in many ways (category six), as well as to other areas. It is equally true that items

TABLE 3.1. Curriculum goals

A. SOCIAL GOALS
1. *Social Utility*
   a. practical living skills
   b. vocational preparation
   c. personal survival
   d. obedience
   e. conformity
   f. coping skills
   g. self-management
   h. self-discipline
   i. health
   j. safety

2. *Social Responsibility*
   a. democratic values
   b. social justice
   c. ethical behavior
   d. reconstruction of society
   e. earth survival
   f. international harmony
   g. preparation of citizenship
   h. honesty
   i. sharing
   j. mainstreaming
   k. nonsexist behavior
   l. nonstereotyping thought

B. KNOWLEDGE GOALS AND SKILL GOALS
3. *Knowledge of Common Culture*
   a. transmission of culture
   b. liberal arts
   c. master standard English
   d. literacy
4. *Knowledge of Special Culture*
   a. ethnic/racial pride
   b. being bicultural
   c. being bilingual
   d. cultural separation
   e. parental preferences

5. *Skills*
   a. motor skills
   b. readiness for primary grades
   c. mastery of basic skills
   d. woodworking skills
   e. block-building skills
   f. skills in the arts and music
   g. athletic skills
   h. health skills and habits

C. INDIVIDUAL DEVELOPMENT GOALS
6. *Personal Development*
   a. personal satisfaction
   b. cognitive development
   c. mental powers
   d. creativity
   e. recreational interests
   f. aesthetic pursuits
   g. learning how to learn
   h. love of books and reading
   i. mental health
   j. autonomy
   k. understanding one's world
   l. social relationships
   m. broadening interests
   n. psychosocial security
   o. health and safety
   p. emotional therapy
   q. sense of identity
   r. self-concept
   s. self-valuing
   t. self-actualization

listed under "Social Responsibility" (category two) could also be listed under one or more of the other categories. Yet there are distinctions of emphasis. Where personal development is one of the highest values, there is less interest in the way children educated in these values will respond to social needs or subordinate individual interests to group requirements. The opposite extreme is also well illustrated in those programs emphasizing group interests or needs over individual development.

As noted above, no matter which system is used to categorize goals, the categories will inevitably overlap. However, the use of some kind of system for selecting goals facilitates a clarification of values—what is most important. This clarification serves as a check on overemphasizing secondary goals at the expense of primary goals. If, for example, a primary goal was to stimulate creativity, instruction in the use of art tools would be a secondary goal, requiring less emphasis than would encouraging children to experiment with the tools. Goal selection provides the framework for making long-term decisions and choosing short-term goals to achieve the primary objectives.

LONG-RANGE AND SHORT-RANGE OBJECTIVES

Long-term objectives tend to provide a frame for thinking, and short-term objectives tend to reflect plans for teaching. The long-term objectives often describe the goals of an early childhood center, an entire school, or some part of it. Short-term objectives tend to be specific for a day, week, or month and are more closely tied to day-to-day curriculum activities.

In a sense, the long-term goals are reflective of the philosophical or theoretical commitment of the curriculum designers, while the short-term goals reflect teaching style or practice.

As has been pointed out by Hilda Taba, large, complex, long-range objectives do not really guide curriculum design.[2] If the objectives are too general, no particular design can flow from it. Several reasons account for this:

1. No one grade or school level has any specific responsibility for broad outcomes, therefore, no one design is forthcoming.
2. No one grade or school level *could* achieve those objectives, which take years to accomplish.
3. Large objectives can be achieved by a variety of designs. If the kindergarten's objective is stated as being "the child's maximum development socially, emotionally, physically, and intellectually," it does not require any one curriculum over others.

Broad objectives tend to provide a frame for thinking about more specific objectives of curriculum, how they should be designed. Table 3-2 lists a sample of program goals that provides the framework for thinking about more specific objectives. For example, a general goal of acquiring language-processing skills leads to such specific goals as auditory sequential memory—"remembering in proper sequence what has been heard"—and grammatical closure—"the ability to use and interpret syntax and grammatical constructs."[3]

Long-term objectives serve as guidelines for program development and review and generate shorter-range objectives. Many long-range objectives are resistant to measurement or evaluation. Short-term goals, which give direction to daily teaching decisions, are often mea-

---

2. Hilda Taba, *Curriculum Development: Theory and Practice.* (New York: Harcourt, Brace & World, 1962), p. 196.
3. Merle Karnes, R. Reid Zehrbach, and James Teska, "Conceptualization of the Goal Curriculum," in Mary Carol Day and Ronald Parker, eds., *The Preschool in Action*, 2nd ed. (Boston: Allyn and Bacon, 1977), p. 264.

TABLE 3.2. Sample program goals

Goal statements	Program
". . . supporting, stimulating and guiding . . . developmental processes of competence, individuality, socialization and integration."[a]	Bank Street developmental-interaction approach (Long-range goals)
Preparing child to succeed in elementary school. 1. "development of communication skills and language processes that are correlates of academic success"; 2. "to become motivated" by experiencing success; 3. "acquire effective information-processing skills."[b]	Karnes, GOAL curriculum game-oriented activities for learning (Long-range goals, detailed)
". . . to provide an environment in which children will have ample opportunity to experience changes (discontinuity) in all four areas of knowledge and freedom to construct an understanding that bridges the differences."[c]	Forman and Kuschner, Piaget-based curriculum (Long-range goals)

"The development of the entire personality, with particular emphasis on intellectual and moral autonomy."[d]
• *Social-emotional objectives*
  1. to feel secure with adults
  2. to respect the feelings and rights of others and to begin to coordinate different points of view (decentering and cooperating)
  3. to be independent and alert and curious[e]
• *Cognitive objectives*
  1. to come up with interesting ideas, problems, and questions
  2. to put things into relationships and notice similarities and differences[f]
	Kamii, Piaget-derived curriculum (Long-range and some specific shorter-range goals)

[a]Barbara Biber, "A Developmental-Interaction Approach," in Mary Carol Day and Ronald Parker, eds., *The Preschool in Action*, 2nd ed. (Boston: Allyn and Bacon, 1977), pp. 264–267.

[b]Merle Karnes, R. Reid Zehrbach, and James Teska, "Conceptualization of the Goal Curriculum," in Mary Carol Day and Ronald Parker, eds., *The Preschool in Action*, 2nd ed. (Boston: Allyn and Bacon, 1977), pp. 264–267.

[c]George E. Forman and David S. Kuschner, *The Child's Construction of Knowledge: Piaget for Teaching Children* (Monterey, Calif.: Brooks/Cole, 1977), p. 46.

[d]Constance Kamii and Rheta DeVries, "Piaget for Early Education," in Mary Carol Day and Ronald Parker, eds., *The Preschool in Action*, 2nd ed. (Boston: Allyn and Bacon, 1977), p. 392.

[e]Ibid., p. 393.

[f]Ibid., p. 394.

sureable but are subject to isolation, one from the other, unless drawn from a larger framework that serves to integrate the parts.

A long-term goal, "to feel secure with adults" from Table 3-2, can generate such short-term goals as:

1. separate comfortably from parents at school entrance;
2. ask for help when needed for personal and learning needs;
3. express feelings, negative or positive, to school staff;
4. give affection to teaching staff;
5. maintain one's point of view even when challenged by adults.

Implications

A review of curriculum form described in Chapter 1 indicates that some forms are more likely to depend primarily on long-term goals without detailing how these goals are achieved in smaller steps. Yet teachers following such forms are required to make decisions toward short-term goals that are assumed to fit the broad objectives. For example, teachers using the form of "curriculum is what happens," often choose to enrich the children's environment and encourage more "happenings" by introducing new materials, activities, and experiences. The teacher's decision to change the environment reflects a short-term goal of sparking new interest in a preselected area. At this point, a long-range objective of enhancing children's learning is translated into a specific activity.

A serious consideration of the function of long-term goals and short-term objectives related to curriculum form allows teachers to avoid the fruitless argument of which kinds of goals are preferred and leads to a continuous clarification of the relationship between broad and specific goals.

Goals and Values

It is often difficult to distinguish goals from values, since values are an integral part of goal development. Values held in common by early childhood educators account for the fact that different programs agree on several points. In his study of twenty-two Follow-Through programs designed to continue Head-Start benefits, Ellis Evans found six points of agreement on values and goals:[4]

1. Every curriculum must start where the child is. There is an assumption here that some kind of effort will be made to assess this for each child.[5]
2. Within the limitations of resources available, the instruction should be individualized for each child.
3. If the child is not learning, it is not the fault of the child but of the program, materials, or methods. Evans points out that, while each curriculum requires the right conditions for learning, each curriculum assumes different ideas as to what these conditions are.
4. Clear goals are necessary for educational planning and curriculum delivery, though here again, goals vary widely with each program.
5. There are specific school-appropriate behaviors required for learning, such as task orientation, rather than distractibility, and motivation to learn academic content.
6. The child should feel good about experiences in school.

Note that of the six points of agreement, the first four refer to values. Common values do not necessarily lead to similar curriculum deci-

---

4. Ellis Evans, *Contemporary Influences in Early Childhood Education*, 2nd ed. (New York: Holt, Rinehart & Winston, 1975), pp. 15-16.
5. See Chapter 11 for an extensive review of procedures available to determine where a child is in relationship to preexisting curriculum goals.

sions. Value statements are too abstract and far-removed from program implementation to find ready translation into method, content, or context. For example, the first point cited above, starting where the child is, could be consistent with many different procedures. It does not address itself to the content or the goals. Similarly, point 2 features individualizing but does not indicate toward what goal or in what way. Points 5 and 6 more closely reflect goals and are primarily personal development goals.

CHANGING CURRICULUM GOALS

The three sources of influence on curriculum goals are the nature of knowledge, the expectations of society, and the current state of theory and research about how children develop and learn. Although there may be periods of dramatic change in educators' views of knowledge, as noted in Chapter 4, or in our research about learning, tradition acts as a brake on sudden change from any of the three sources. Expectations of society about curriculum goals can be seriously disrupted by strong social movements, which shake tradition and set the condition for changing curriculum goals.

History and Tradition

The force of tradition resisting change and being self-perpetuating is a useful metaphor, but it should be noted that there is never one clear tradition. Historically, more than one idea about objectives has always been around in early childhood education. Which is the "true" tradition is frequently a matter of choice and selection.

The kindergarten was originated by Friedrich Froebel in Germany before 1850. His curriculum was based on the idea that children learn through directed play, and he designed materials to achieve his stated values and objectives. His curriculum featured finger plays, which are still used; "gifts," or objects to be manipulated in specific ways; and various ways to emphasize unity of person and God, including the still-popular circle time.

Very specific records, made by participants in the kindergarten movement in the United States in the early 1900s, document a severe split between those who were more literal, or traditional, in their interpretation of Froebel's writings, and those who were breaking away from such literalism, introducing "new" ideas, materials, and activities into the kindergarten curriculum.[6] For example, dolls, doll play, and large construction blocks, which were not part of Froebel's curriculum, became popular in American kindergardens, creating great tension among the very literate kindergarten theorists and practitioners. As a result of this split, the newer ideas and materials won out, and a tradition was born before World War I. Several new traditions came into being after that, one which sprang from ideas of Sigmund Freud as these became known to American educators, another from John Dewey's ideas about progressive education.

Freudian theory emphasized unconscious motivation, the beginnings of sexual development, the inevitable conflicts between social expectations and spontaneous behavior, as in toilet training or eating habits, and above all, the impact of emotions on behavior. Dewey stressed freedom of choice; he believed the child's activity was essential to purposeful learning and that the child's interest motivated and gave meaningfulness to learning; and he emphasized the social group as a vehicle of teaching children democratic processes. All these ideas were new, but as they spread, another tradition came into being.[7]

6. Evelyn Weber, *The Kindergarten: Its Encounter with Educational Thought in America* (New York: Teachers College Press, 1969), pp. 126–129.
7. Harry Good and James Teller, *A History of American Education*, 3rd ed. (New York: Macmillan, 1973), pp. 379–380.

Kindergartens were incorporated into public schools beginning in 1870 and by World War I were part of the public schools in all big cities, except in the South and the Southwest. By 1947-48, almost 60 percent of large-city school systems in the United States had kindergartens.[8] As of October 1976, over 81 percent of five-year-olds in the United States were enrolled in schools, mostly kindergartens, and another 10.69 percent of five-year-olds were in primary grades.[9] Kindergarten education is now very close to being as universal as elementary school education.

Soon after World War II, there were attempts to describe the "best" in early childhood schooling and to look on early childhood education as a single developmental stage from age two or three to age seven or eight without drastic interruption.[10] This approach bridges conventional divisions in school organization by including preschool through second grade in one school design. It is interesting to note thirty years later that this view is still an idea that has not yet become reality.

What is considered traditional is usually what becomes well known, is easily communicated, and is expected. In times of social turbulence, such as the sixties, so much criticism surges forward and with such force that, while some of the criticism vanishes when the social pressures ease, some of it surely has enduring effects. Really radical change rarely occurs on any large scale, simply because schools and staffs usually continue to do what they know best how to do. The pressures of the sixties for openness, humanistic forms of schooling, acceptance of much variety, and individualistic learning styles and procedures quietly changed in the seventies to pressures for literacy, conformity, discipline, learning in more standard ways, and for achievement in the "basics." The pendulum continues to swing back and forth in predictable patterns. In summary, tradition as a source of goals exerts both a positive and negative force on goal selection. From a positive view, tradition protects against widespread radical changes without the test of time. Simultaneously, tradition often inhibits a valid testing of new ideas.

Social Movements

Broad social movements inevitably affect the objectives and the content of early childhood education. Whether it is the ecology movement, women's liberation, or universal use of television, what affects the lives of children and their families inevitably affects goals for young children. A brief sampling of forces and related effects is listed in Table 3–3 to illustrate the impact of social movements and forces. Children who watch a great deal of television have a different set of life experiences than those who once listened to radio or spent their days outdoors. School goals reflect these changes. For example, movement education received a major boost when it was discovered how much time young children spend in the sedentary activity of television watching.

It often seems that trends change with alarming rapidity. Taxpayer revolts tend to reduce public financial support for education among other services. "Accountability" movements ebb and flow, with demands for evidence that the public is getting its money's worth from schools. Both of these trends are partly due to the pattern of declining birth rates, with an increasingly larger portion of the American population in the older age brackets. Older citizens generally constitute a group more concerned with their current income needs than with the future social needs of the society.

---

8. R. Freeman Butts and Lawrence A. Cremin, *A History of Education in American Culture* (New York: Holt, Rinehart & Winston, 1953), p. 586.

9. U.S. Department of Health, Education and Welfare, National Center for Educational Statistics, *Digest of Educational Statistics*, 1977–1978.

10. See the summary of Piaget's cognitive stages in Chapter 5.

TABLE 3.3. Social movements and forces

	Movement/forces	Sample effects
1.	Increasing technical nature of modern industry	Technological assets: high energy use. Technological problems: environmental pollution, which affects child health.
2.	Rising rates of divorce and nonmarriage	One-parent families, mostly headed by working mothers with need for increased infant and child care services.
3.	Women's liberation and equal-rights movement	Demands for nonsexist education to eliminate stereotypes in education and job aspirations.
4.	Universal ownership of television sets	Extensive viewing of daytime and evening television by young children: the phenomenon of television-as-babysitter.
5.	Urban decay	Housing problems; overcrowding; and inadequate recreational, medical, vocational, and other facilities. School dropouts, juvenile delinquency, and school children as victims of drug and alcohol abuse. Crime poverty, malnutrition, and alarming birth rates for very young girls.

SUMMARY

Terms used interchangeably by authorities in the field include *goals*, *objectives*, *values*, and *purposes*. Despite differences in the use of terms, all programs have long-term goals and short-term objectives.

Values are often general terms such as autonomy or literacy. Therefore, while they do not mandate any specific kind of program, values set the boundaries for inclusion or exclusion of objectives. Long-term goals serve as the basis on which teachers derive specific short-term objectives to guide program planning.

The content of goals may include affective, cognitive, or skill development statements. Skills may be physical, social, or academic. Curriculum goals do not usually change rapidly. While society during periods of social, political, or economic upheaval may make dramatic changes in demands on schools, in reality, tradition and teacher skills serve to resist drastic change.

EXERCISES

1. List the five long-term goals for early childhood curriculum you consider most important. Indicate which are process and which are product goals. Indicate which are affective and which are not affective goals.
2. For each goal listed, identify at least three subgoals, or short-term objectives.
3. Compare your lists with your colleagues or fellow students.

BIBLIOGRAPHY

Biber, Barbara. "A Developmental-Interaction Approach." In Mary Carol Day and Ronald Parker, eds., *The Preschool in Action*, 2nd ed. Boston: Allyn and Bacon, 1977.

Butts, R. Freeman, and Cremin, Lawrence A. *A History of Education in American Culture* New York: Holt, Rinehart & Winston, 1953.

Evans, Ellis. *Contemporary Influences in Early Childhood Education*, 2nd ed. New York: Holt, Rinehart & Winston, 1975

Forman, George E., and Kuschner, David S. *The Child's Construction of Knowledge: Piaget for Teaching Children.* Monterey, Calif.: Brooks/Cole, 1977.

Good, Harry, and Teller, James. *A History of American Education*, 3rd ed. New York: Macmillan, 1973.

Kamii, Constance, and DeVries, Rheta. "Piaget for Early Education." In Mary Carol Day and Ronald Parker, eds., *The Preschool in Action*, 2nd ed. Boston: Allyn and Bacon, 1977.

Karnes, Merle; Zehrbach, R. Reid; and Teska, James. "Conceptualization of the Goal Curriculum." In Mary Carol Day and Ronald Parker, eds., *The Preschool in Action*, 2nd ed. Boston: Allyn and Bacon, 1977.

Maccoby, Eleanor E., and Zeller, Miriam. *Experiments in Primary Education: Aspects of Project Follow Through.* New York: Harcourt, Brace, Jovanovich, 1970.

Taba, Hilda. *Curriculum Development: Theory and Practice.* New York: Harcourt, Brace & World, 1962.

U.S. Department of Health, Education and Welfare, National Center for Educational Statistics. *Digest of Educational Statistics, 1977–1978.*

Weber, Evelyn. *The Kindergarten: Its Encounter with Educational Thought in America.* New York: Teachers College Press, 1969.

4 Views of Knowledge

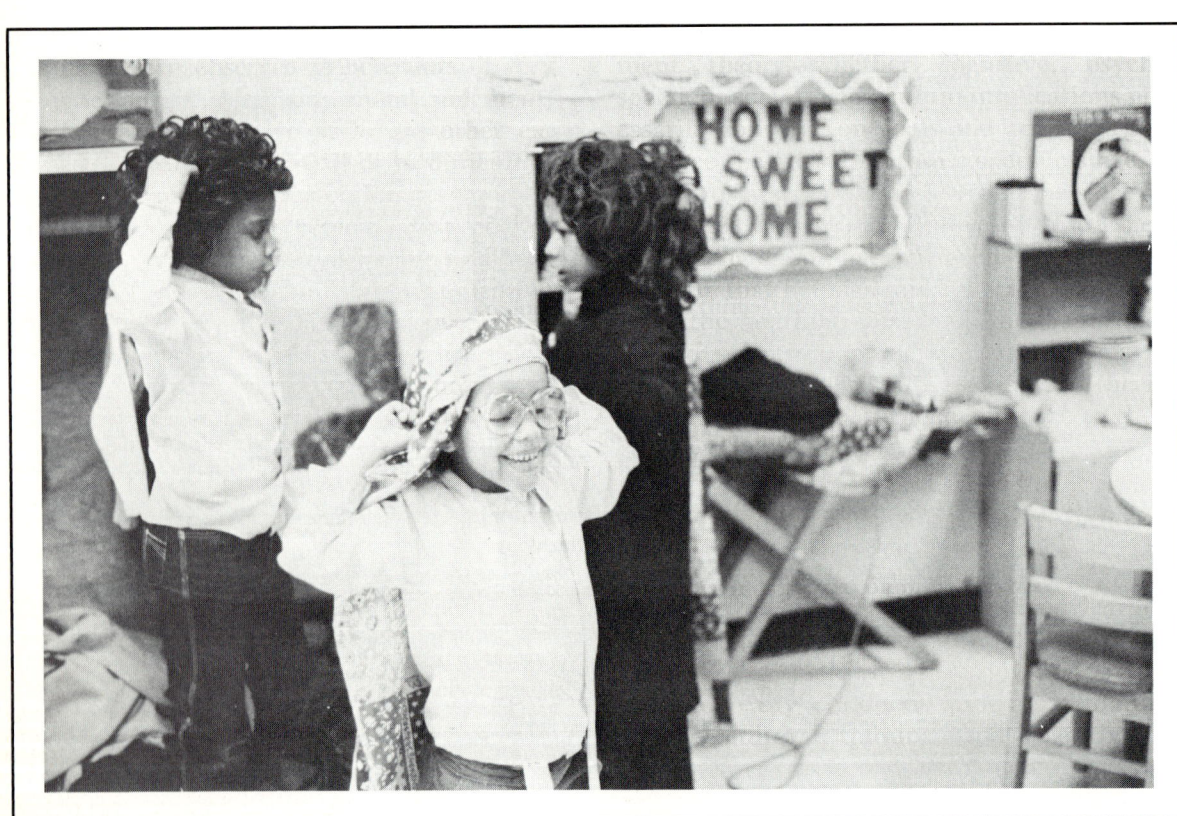

What should young children be taught? Content questions are raised in every quarter by teachers and other school personnel, parents, community leaders, governmental organizations, and the general public. It has been pointed out that data is lacking about what is best for children, and thus early childhood content tends to be the result of individual judgments about what children should learn.[1]

Since educators make judgments from different perspectives and values, content selections vary widely, ranging from daily-living survival skills, to Montessori, Piagetian-based, academic, British Infant School, behaviorist, humanist, and other designs. To develop a satisfactory curriculum that accomplishes what you intend requires not only clarification of your views of how children grow and learn (to be discussed in Chapter 5), but also consideration of your views of knowledge, or what is to be learned. Positions vary as to what kinds of learning are worth curriculum emphasis. In this chapter, we will discuss *classes* of knowledge, or the clustering of different kinds of content on which curriculum designs are built.

---

1. Ellis D. Evans, *Contemporary Influences in Early Childhood Education*, 2nd ed. (New York: Holt, Rinehart & Winston, 1975), p. 377 and passim.

CLASSES OF CONTENT

At least six classes of content are among the different answers available to the knowledge question for early childhood teachers. You are likely to find these classes of content familiar, for they identify curriculum patterns found everywhere. These classes include primary focus on (1) accumulation of facts, (2) skill development, (3) subject areas, (4) academic disciplines, (5) themes, and (6) holistic approaches. As each class of content is discussed, it is important to remember that in practice there is rarely a pure illustration of any one class. Nevertheless, the discussion of each class may alert you to the real differences in content likely to be encountered in early childhood classrooms.

Fact Accumulation

Fact accumulation exists in practically every kind of curriculum, but it can be either the major component or a very minor part of a design built on one or more of the other classes. Young children tend to be "fact collectors," while they continually explore the world of materials and find new ways to use them. Consequently, this approach to curriculum content is often viewed as fitting in closely with the developmental pattern of young children.

A *fact-accumulation approach* to curriculum leads to high valuing of the details of children's experiences and observations. Whether the teacher selects a set of facts or identifies facts as the daily program develops, the most important content of teaching is made up of the items that children are expected to acquire. For young children, who are in the process of learning almost everything, facts range from the descriptive labels of size, color, shape, texture, density, temperature, weight, and other physical attributes, to events, both current and historical.

In a program that holds accumulation of facts as a primary value, the teacher is likely to schedule daily lessons featuring a set of facts. In early childhood classrooms, familiar fact-accumulation lessons stress such content as:

1. names of colors;
2. names of animals and of animal sounds, habitats, and characteristics;
3. names of musical instruments;
4. differentiating objects of different densities into hard and soft;
5. calendar reading, including names of the days of week, date, month, year, season, usually stressing the sequence of numbers;
6. daily weather observations and descriptions;
7. summarizing observations after a group trip, stressing "We saw—" and "We did—";
8. history lessons stressing the facts of a given holiday, for example, a lesson on Thanksgiving entitled "Thanksgiving Long Ago and Today";
9. show-and-tell sessions, emphasizing each child's factual summary;
10. evaluating comprehension after story reading, emphasizing the facts of the story, especially the "who," "what," "when," and sometimes "why."

Programs that value fact accumulation may use planned lessons or other formats. Some teachers feature facts throughout the program as they initiate conversations with children and respond to children's questions and discussions. For example, a conversation about a child's painting may focus on color or shape labels. A discussion of block constructions is likely to feature the identification of functional parts, such as the door, window, and roof of the garage. As children collect leaves in the fall, teachers may name the trees, the color or shape of the leaves, or the number of points on a leaf.

This continuing focus on the facts of experience reflects a valuing of fact accumulation as the dominant class of content if other kinds of content are excluded or little used. One way to identify this focus is to analyze the content of formal or informal tests used in the classroom. Teachers often say they are stimulating vocabulary development, and, of course, naming and verbalizing the facts of observations, experiences, and events is a well-tested method of expanding children's language skills.

Strengths and limitations The strength of this approach in early childhood is that young children are natural fact accumulators, and these facts are often the substance of their communication. Proponents of this approach hold that children need to learn many facts. Teachers cannot develop other classes of content without a basic collection of facts on which to build. It does not require more of children than they can accomplish, while at the same time it furnishes a base for other content.

One limitation of the fact-accumulation approach is that children tend to accumulate those facts that they perceive as important, and these are not necessarily the same facts the teacher's intends them to learn. Consequently, curriculum planning based primarily on fact accumulation is unreliable in terms of outcomes. A further limitation of this approach is that it tends to encourage lecturing as an efficient way to deliver facts. Lecturing, or telling, is generally unproductive with very young children. Additionally, a teacher's valuing of facts tends to limit children's discussions and testing of ideas. Unnecessary restrictions may be placed on children's curiosity, creative efforts, experimentation, or personal ways to collect, organize, and use the facts of experience. Memory may be prized, in this emphasis, over the numerous ways people think and learn about the world.

Skill Accumulation

Skill accumulation, long a popular basis for curriculum in the elementary grades, has extended to early childhood classrooms also. The demand for academic skills is most notable in urban centers, where strong pressures come from the community for improved reading scores and school success. Under this recent pressure, skill-drill programs in phonics, word recognition, counting, and writing alphabet letters have developed in early childhood programs that leave little time for other content.

However, skill accumulation is not necessarily confined to the academic side. Montessori programs for young children have as a major focus *coping skills*, such as dressing, tying shoelaces, buttoning clothing, and robing and disrobing outerwear, *cleaning skills*, such as washing tables and utensils and replacing materials in containers on shelves after use, and *pouring skills*, practicing first with solids like rice, and later with liquids.[2]

The activities included in a skill-accumulation program are usually scheduled for frequent repetition over a period of time. Repetitive practice may vary from formal skill drill led by the teacher, to voluntary playful practice or games. As indicated above, the valued content may be standard academic skills, physical skills, or both. They often include social skills, such as waiting one's turn or using conventional rules of politeness to show consideration of others.

Skill-practice activities in early childhood classrooms include the following:

1. Academic skills: the three Rs
   a. name recognition: using name cards or name lists to practice recognizing written names, one's own and others;
   b. counting skills: practicing counting a set of objects, a set of sounds such as claps or drumbeats, or a pictured set of things;
   c. handwriting skills: tracing and copying one's name, geometric forms, letters, numerals, or other forms;
   d. reading alphabet letters, numerals, and sight words.
2. Personal management skills
   a. practice tying shoelaces; buttoning and closing zippers; and managing rubbers, boots, and outer clothing;
   b. practice pouring liquids, using a fork at meals, or shelving play materials according to a stated pattern;
   c. practice hand-washing and bathroom routines.
3. Physical/motor skills
   a. practice using scissors: cutting on a line and cutting out predrawn forms;
   b. practice using a pencil: tracing objects, stencils, and straight-edge objects for drawing lines;
   c. learn to hop and skip by practicing to music;
   d. learn to coordinate arm and leg movements using jump ropes or hoops;
   e. practice ball catching and throwing;
   f. calisthenic exercises;
   g. practice dance steps or rhythms.

Strengths and limitations Skills encompass many possibilities. They emphasize practice activities, drilling for mastery, that is, learning

---

2. Maria Montessori, *The Montessori Method* (New York: Bentley, 1964).

something so well that it can be done automatically. A major strength of the skill approach to curriculum is the visibility of what is learned. In this era of accountability, skills can be demonstrated to a demanding public as proof that schools are teaching. Another asset is the ease with which skill-learning needs can be identified for young children, individually and in groups. Young children have many useful skills they need to learn. Most skills are functional and contribute to children's needs for independence and autonomy.

A major limitation of this approach is the amount of time needed for practice and the difficulties involved in sustaining young children's attention on teacher-selected practice activities. While parents value skills, they also value their children's enthusiasm for school. The value questions often narrow down to how soon children are expected to master the selected skills—as soon as possible, or through practice toward mastery, or in a more relaxed timetable without required schedules of mastery.

The primary grades have traditionally carried the brunt of basic academic skill practice, and six- and seven-year-olds expect to learn to read and write. Developmental readiness and society's expectations coincide for most of this age group. However, critical problems can develop for younger children if expectations exceed comfortable achievement levels.

All programs value skills, just as all programs value facts. But there is a large gap between skill accumulation as a basis for curriculum and including skills along with other valued content. Few people would argue against skills in the curriculum. Few would advocate a curriculum that includes only skills.

Subjects

Schools in the United States have a long-standing tradition of making subjects the mainstay of the elementary school curriculum. This tradition is now visible in early childhood programs as well. A *subject* may be thought of as a content area that has been a standard part of the school curriculum, including not only the three Rs but also social studies, health and safety, and language arts. Subjects such as language arts and social studies are a mixture of content areas arranged for the convenience of teaching. The mixed areas are like a stew for which everyone has a preferred recipe drawn from the disciplines that make up the area. For example, social studies draws from the disciplines of history, sociology, anthropology, political science, economics, and geography.

Until recently, kindergartens, day care, and other preschool settings were able to keep their distance from the subject curricula of the early grades. Today, however, early childhood curriculum books increasingly categorize program activities into subject groupings. A typical example of recommended lessons in social studies found in one text includes:[3]

1. Citizenship education: to develop the understanding that each person has worth and dignity, plan an activity in which each child is introduced and then initiate a discussion about the ways children are alike and yet different. Use books, songs, pictures, and discussion.
2. Anthropology: to develop the understanding that people live according to certain values, skills, and traditions, talk about the ways each family celebrates birthdays, or consider what each child values most.

In this text, a teaching unit is recommended for further development of each topic. Social studies topics recommended for units include "Our Homes," "Money Is Used for Many Things," and "Many People Help Us."[4]

---

3. Sarah Leeper, Ruth Dales, Doris Skipper, and Ralph Witherspoon, *Good Schools for Young Children*, 3rd ed. (New York: Macmillan, 1974), pp. 258–281.
4. Ibid., pp. 268–269.

The subject-matter approach is reflected not only in planned lessons but also in room arrangement patterns and in time scheduling. Teachers often set up a writing corner, a math corner, a reading area, and an art area. Classrooms that combine subjects might have a math-science interest center, a language arts center, and a creative arts center (or the language arts and creative arts might be combined). Scheduled program activities are clearly designated as one subject or another. The teacher may announce the science lesson for the day, before or after other subjects, in specific slots in the day's schedule.

Projects and units are developed by many teachers in order to integrate the two or more subjects. A class project of making a bird feeder integrates math (measurement and shape), science (classification of birds and types of bird food), reading (using written sources of information on all parts of the project), writing (narratives of experience, or labels of items in the project, or both). Many early childhood teachers justify their preference for projects by listing the content by subjects and by demonstrating the stimulating aspects of such forms of learning.

Projects can, of course, be thought of either as curriculum or methodology. The project can be the selected content, or it can be the way the teacher helps children learn the subject content. In a highly acclaimed 1938 French film, *Passion for Life*, a rural schoolmaster chooses a curriculum project (printing a school newspaper) to overcome the children's failure to learn the subject curriculum (reading, writing, history, math, and other subjects). The children's personal interest, activity, and motivation, as the film shows, accomplished what the more traditional curriculum was unable to—competency in passing the French national academic exams.

Strengths and limitations The strengths of this approach stem from its familiarity to parents and teachers. Textbooks, workbooks, and practice exercises are available in abundance for children in kindergarten and the primary grades. Similarly, tests conform to subject boundaries through many years of accommodation. For all classes, communication about school curricula with parents and others is easy and unambiguous when subjects are discussed. However, this simplicity is a weakness as well as a strength. Where subjects are taught separately, it limits variety, enrichment, and integrating projects, which give vigor to the curriculum. Those who oppose a subject approach to content claim that children are more holistic, or that their interests and skills are not ready for narrow concentration on single subjects. They feel this approach restricts the personal interests of teachers and children and the excitement for new social movements, such as ecology, which do not readily conform to subject niches.

Those who criticize integrating subjects through projects or units focus on the subordination of the content to the activity. Genuine supporters of the subject approach reject projects as unnecessary doctoring of subjects, with a loss of efficiency in achieving content goals.

Thematic Selection

Themes, topics, and units of work together represent another class of content frequently used in early childhood programs. *Thematic selection* breaks the boundaries of subjects to help create order and unity in children's school experiences. The logic of content and the psychological patterns of development are thought to be more easily interrelated in thematic than in subject approaches. Themes represent an effort to integrate curriculum and to retain the design of interest center activity, which has been the traditional format for programs for young children for a long time. The thematic approach to curriculum features children's interest in activities on broad topics or themes related to important community events, holidays, or interesting occurrences.

An example of this curriculum in many early childhood programs is the succession of a common set of themes in a fixed order, beginning in autumn with the changing seasons, followed by such holiday emphases as Columbus Day, Halloween, Thanksgiving, Chanukah, and Christmas. The activities developed around these themes are intended to integrate academic learning from a number of subject areas and contribute to the development of concepts. In addition, this curriculum provides flexibility in activities to meet children's individual interests. Thus the flexibility of the thematic approach to curriculum makes it universally adaptable.

Implementation of a theme may permeate the classroom for a number of weeks. Through the selected theme, activities feature exploring understanding and building skills in language, mathematics, science, social studies, social skills, and expressive or creative abilities.

The theme of transportation illustrates the pervasive quality of this approach to an early childhood curriculum. The theme of transportation suggests making trips that allow firsthand experiences; having discussions; using books as resources; narrating experiences for written booklets and for illustrations and photographs; reconstructing vehicles, roadways, and other related structures; and dramatizing the roles of people involved. The classroom activities that can initiate a transportation theme accompanied by one or more trips to transportation centers include:

1. dramatic play,
2. block constructions,
3. model building with craft materials,
4. storytelling of individual experiences,
5. pictorial representations with various media,
6. reading books on the theme.

Thematic selections of curriculum may be weekly topics or units or extended clusters of topical units. Brief units, such as focus on pets, the circus, or nutrition, are most often planned for one week, perhaps two. These limited units are completed and succeeded by other topics, with no intent to relate one to another. The objective is a broad, surface acquaintance with many topics, rather than in-depth study of a few.

Units draw their focus from current events of topical interest taken from the lives of the children in the class, the local environment, or the national scene. A circus in town, a child's new baby brother or sister, a new pet, National Health Week, spring, and a national holiday represent a small sample of units and unit clusters. Typically, most unit topics reflect the here-and-now criterion advocated in the 1920s by Lucy Sprague Mitchell. She cautioned teachers to concentrate on the visible and available content that was familiar to the child and that could be encountered with some frequency.[5]

The racial and ethnic awareness sparked by the civil rights movement of the sixties led to the addition of themes related to cultural traditions and cultural pluralism. Black History Week and Puerto Rican Discovery Week are units that have taken root in early childhood classrooms in geographic areas where there are large concentrations of blacks and Puerto Ricans. In different communities, the cultural patterns, holidays, and special interests of other ethnic groups are often featured, including Mexican and South American Hispanic groups, American Indians, Chinese and other Oriental groups, Norwegian, Hungarian, Polish, Greek, Italian, and Armenian groups. The national movement against sexism requires awareness of sexist themes, materials, and activities and use of nonstereotyped formats.

Table 4-1 reviews the kinds of content likely to appear in the curriculum related to the four classes of content already discussed and the two to be discussed next. The question

---

5. Lucy Sprague Mitchell, *Young Geographers*. (New York: John Day, 1934).

TABLE 4.1. Examples of classes of content

Knowledge sources	Content examples	
1. Facts	Colors and shapes Number names in order Names of months and days of week	Weather observations Stories of Columbus, Pilgrims, George Washington, and Abraham Lincoln
2. Skills	*Academic* Counting in sequence Letter recognition Phonics Number writing *Social* Making friends Sharing Taking turns Using conventional rules of politeness	*Coping* Personal cleanliness Clothing management Eating Classroom cleanup *Process* Information seeking Problem setting Pursuing personal areas of curiosity Learning how to learn
3. Subjects Formal integration of subjects is referred to as an *integrated curriculum*	Reading Social studies Math and Science Language arts	Music Arithmetic Health Education Physical Education
4. Themes A combination of subjects and skills is also referred to as an *integrated curriculum*	*Historical and Current Events* Columbus day Washington's birthday Halloween Spring Circus	*Topics* Transportation Community services Communication Families Nutrition
5. Structure of disciplines, key concepts	*Math:* scts, subsets, geometric shape, equivalent sets, greater than–less than, congruent length, longer, shorter *Physical Science:* force, energy, motion *Life Science:* adaptation is a factor in all plant and animal life *Economics:* Key prices are determined in the market place largely by supply and demand	
6. Holistic	Need for friendship Need for belonging and acceptance, approval, and respect Need for sense of competence, independence, and autonomy Social responsibilities in class, at home, and in the community Need for a healthful, nonpolluted environment Maintenance of personal well-being Need for survival skills	

of the source of integrated curriculum is answered in two ways. One form is simply combining subject areas, essentially the subject approach. The thematic approach represents the second type of integrated curriculum, which really subordinates subjects to ideas and activities.

Strengths and limitations The strength of the thematic approach is that it offers strong integrative elements with a clear focus. Flexibility and adaptability to different teachers and children is another strength. Children's understandings of their experiences can be worked out in playful classroom and playground activities and in individual and small-group discussions that feature children's ideas. Art often turns out to be the most integrative of the many classroom activities. Motivation, interest, and activity may be very strong in this category.

Among the limitations of the thematic approach is the questionable assumption that it assures predictable learning outcomes. But varied and personal learnings may result. Despite extensive experiences with a theme, such as the network of community services, a child may conclude that the uniform makes the mail person. Furthermore, since young children lack historical time concepts, they may view historical themes as contemporary incidents. Productive themes may be limited by lack of materials or previous experience in their development by teaching staff. This tends to limit selection to the well-tried topics, which may be less stimulating to children and teachers.

Structured Disciplines

Disciplines are rather well-defined bodies of knowledge. In disciplines such as mathematics, physics, and psychology, scholars and researchers fashion new knowledge, pattern their own fields in fairly well-accepted ways, and use distinctive forms of inquiry, or ways of knowing. It is as though the human knowledge pie were to be divided up by the experts in each area. Expertise tends to be narrow and deep, and to work at the edges of what is known, to capture more knowledge, and to push the edges further out.

The disciplines, as defined by scholars and researchers, offer the most highly structured forms of our accumulated knowledge. However, disciplines are not usually structured for teaching but for research and new knowledge construction. In the fifties and sixties, suggestions about how to use the structured disciplines for curriculum purposes led to the identification of key concepts as a basis for redesigning early childhood programs.[6]

Key concepts are big ideas that serve to organize what is known in a discipline of knowledge. For example, seven key concepts in science, identified by Gerald Craig, are listed in Table 4–2, along with subordinate concepts that might relate to an early childhood curriculum.[7] Note that the big ideas can be related to almost any learning activity in the classroom, whether initiated by children or teacher. For example, the concept of change can be featured as children play with paints, play-dough, or crayons or as they engage in cooking experiences or cleanup. Similarly, the concept of balance can be featured under the same conditions, when teachers and children note that as more crayon appears on the paper, the stick of crayon gets shorter, or as the paint brushes get cleaner, the water becomes more discolored.

Table 4–3 gives a summary of distinctive statements about using structured disciplines as the basis for curriculum. The theorists listed stress the advantages of the disciplines ap-

---

6. Jerome Bruner, "Process of Education Revisited," in Glen Haas, ed., *Curriculum Planning: A New Approach*. (Boston: Allyn and Bacon, 1977), p. 197.

7. Gerald Craig, *Science for the Elementary School Teacher*, 5th ed. (Waltham, Mass.: Blaisdell Publishing, 1966), pp. 92–100.

proach in helping teachers organize content more clearly and authentically. They stress that organizing content for teaching means coordinating child development ideas with content selection. They do not require that these disciplines be treated as separate subjects. Consequently, content from the disciplines as recommended by these theorists always includes some recommendation about how to teach content organized from the disciplines. It should be noted that there is considerable emphasis on methodology by those who advocate a structured disciplines approach to content. Phenix features the "lure to discovery," Hirst features "modes of thinking." Jerome Bruner, who popularized this approach, personally participated in testing the methodology.

TABLE 4.2.   Illustration of key concepts in science

	Craig's concepts[a]	Area[a]	Related concepts for young children
1.	The universe is very large.	Space	Some things take up more space than others.
			Space can be measured and compared with other spaces, smaller, larger, or same size.
2.	The earth is very old.	Time	Some people are older than others.
			Birthdays are ways to measure age.
			Age refers to life on earth.
3.	The universe is constantly changing.	Change	Growing means change in size.
			Children grow taller and heavier.
			The seasons keep on changing *forever*.
4.	Life is adapted to the environment.	Adaptation	When it's cold, we wear more clothes and heat the buildings.
			Animals and plants adapt to the environment in many ways.
5.	There are great variations in the universe.	Variety	Different types of animals and plants exist.
			People have skins of different colors.
6.	The interdependence of living things	Interrelationships	People need plants for food.
			Plants need sun, water, and nourishment to grow.
			Pets are loving and loyal, but they have special needs.
7.	The interaction of forces	Equilibrium and balance	When a moving ball bumps into a still ball, one begins to move while the other slows down.

[a]After Gerald Craig, *Science for the Elementary School Teacher*, 5th ed. (Waltham, Mass.: Blaisdell Publishing, 1966), pp. 92–100.

Lists of selected disciplines to be structured for children's learning experiences will necessarily differ, depending on who is making the list. The old liberal-arts group of disciplines, like Hirst's list in Table 4-3, tends to be included on most lists, though morals and religion may or may not be there. Despite long-held convictions that moral instruction does not belong in school, concerns for the school's role in moral development is clearly evident in today's literature in early childhood education and it has become an increasingly popular area for teaching and learning.

Strengths and limitations The major advantage offered for the key concepts approach proposed in the early sixties was that it was a way to overcome the limits of the fact-accumulation approach to the various subjects. Essentially, the argument is that fact accumulation is inefficient in the long run, while concept learning is economical, practical, and increasingly more

TABLE 4.3. Views of knowledge as structured disciplines

Theorist	Views of knowledge	Implications for curriculum
Phillip Phenix	A good discipline is knowledge that is organized for instruction, that simplifies understanding, that reveals significant patterns and relationships organized for thinking, and that has "dynamism," which is a "lure to discovery."	Only knowledge from the disciplines belongs in curriculum.[a]
Paul Hirst	While agreeing with Phenix's idea, Hirst proceeds to identify eight disciplines as fundamental for children's school learning: mathematics, physical science (botany, biology, physics, and chemistry), knowledge of persons (economics, psychology, political science, sociology, anthropology, and history), fine arts, literature, morals, religion, and philosophy. New knowledge is interdisciplinary.[c]	Curriculum need not parallel the structure of any discipline but must be well organized for teaching the age-stage of children.[b]
Richard Pring	Disciplines embody public traditions of thought and inquiry.	Seven principles of selection are: 1. social utility, 2. social responsibility 3. common culture, 4. cognitive concern, 5. personal satisfaction, 6. parental and social preference, 7. mental powers.[d]

[a]Phillip H. Phenix, *The Realms of Meaning* (New York: McGraw-Hill, 1964).
[b]Paul H. Hirst, *Knowledge and the Curriculum: A Collection of Philosophical Papers* (London: Routledge & Kegan Paul, 1974), p. 25.
[c]Ibid., p. 39.
[d]Richard Pring, "Curriculum Content: Principles of Selection," in Denis Lawton et al., eds., *Theory and Practice in Curriculum Studies* (London: Routledge & Kegan Paul, 1978), pp. 140-142.

significant as the child matures. Economy in learning is stressed because it is well established that strings of facts are hard to learn and remember, while well-organized classes of information having clear relationships to one another are much easier. It is practical to spend time teaching children material that they will not immediately forget, and that can be used with greater sophistication as they advance in school. The greater significance of this content is expected to derive from the increased depth of learning at more advanced age levels.

The key concepts approach projected a dazzling vision of schools making great leaps in the excellence and authenticity of the knowledge base. The strengths of the approach, as listed in Table 4-4, include the emphasis on updating the curriculum by moving its conceptual base closer to the high levels of contemporary scholarship. Instead of outmoded subject matter, it was expected that organizing concepts would help children understand and collect information with more comprehension and retention. The limits of this approach, as seen by those who do not favor it, are that

TABLE 4.4. Using structured disciplines for the curriculum base: contrasting points of view

Pro	*Con*
Ideas and discoveries are up-to-date, in contrast to outdated facts.	Outside sciences, structure of disciplines material is unavailable or sketchy, and principles for structuring knowledge are lacking.
Use of key concepts as the organizing pattern and the unique inquiry methods of the disciplines reduce the need to memorize lengthy lists of facts.	Key concepts are difficult to find or construct in usable form.
Concept learning facilitates the sorting of facts for use and serves as a way of retaining facts.	Splintering of total curriculum into narrowly defined disciplines limits the ordering of facts across disciplines and bars more holistic forms of learning.
Spiraling curriculum, offering the same conceptual material at increasingly higher levels, provides unity of curriculum from youngest to oldest students and facilitates more advanced reasoning capability.	Complex concepts cannot be "discovered" by young children, who are unsophisticated in reasoning and conceptualizing.
	Spiraling curriculum requires retraining teachers of young children, without allocating resources for this retraining.
	New instructional materials, outside the budgets of most programs for young children, are required.
Concept learning reduces need for time-consuming fact teaching, which is also inefficient due to the high rate of forgetting.	Concept learning does not fit the child-development approach to curriculum, which follows children's interests and personally felt needs.
	The results of research on *modes* of inquiry used by scholars in disciplines are not learnable or useful to young children; therefore, complex ideas would be substituted for facts to be memorized.

scholarly concepts would be too complex and too advanced for young children, that children would be expected to memorize concepts, and that the curriculum would be splintered into narrow fields, defined by the advanced scholars in those areas.

Interestingly, over half of these objections center on the methods rather than on the content. Despite a strong thrust toward discovery learning made by those who advocate such curriculum, critics see the same old method of memorization being applied to complex bundles of ideas that are no more meaningful to children than were the previous bundles of facts. Jerome Bruner, one of the initiators of the key concepts idea, noted later that he had no idea of the problems teacher education would encounter using this approach.[8] Problems of retraining teachers in a conceptual approach to content reflect the enormous difference between this approach and the long-established fact- or skill-accumulation bases for curriculum.

Holistic Curriculum

An undifferentiated curriculum can result from several of the approaches described above. *Undifferentiated* is used here to mean a lack of segmentation of the content into subjects or disciplines. The broad-themes approach is most likely to ignore traditional curriculum divisions and to select content without regard to subjects, integrated subjects, or disciplines. Many early childhood classrooms pursue an undifferentiated curriculum of various kinds. For example:

1. Piagetian-based curricula focus on modes of reasoning and acting on the environment.
2. Child development–based curricula focus on the child, offering activities and projects that seem to be within the child's capability and interest.
3. Behaviorist-based curricula seek to train the child to develop specific behaviors and skills that will accord with primary teachers' ideas of readiness for learning. Some behaviorist programs, however, may be attached to various types of differentiated content or to more familiar subjects.

The primary feature of an undifferentiated curriculum is that it does not emphasize bodies of knowledge but stresses some value other than content. Behaviorists might stress persistence in task completion, or "on-task" behaviors, while Piagetians stimulate cognitive reasoning, and child development teachers cultivate social-emotional development. This is merely to suggest how these approaches basically differ.

A popular form of holistic curriculum, for younger as well as older elementary school grades, is the *humanistic curriculum*. It is concerned with one's feelings about oneself and others. Content is selected to help children study such concerns and to develop more mature self-perceptions and social relationships. Nonsexist curricula are another holistic pattern because they help children to think about roles, vocations, and responsibilities without assuming that one's sex determines all limits and expectations.

In practice, the holistic curriculum appears to "happen." It can be viewed as a series of happenings flowing from children's interests and problems as they occur and from the use of unplanned events, such as a visit by a plumber to repair a pipe. Such a curriculum is described as informal since it grows out of the daily actions of children, rather than from a syllabus or plan. In fact, the actions and events the teacher emphasizes and the way they are developed depend on the teacher's views of child development, as noted above.

Strengths and limitations Teachers who follow an undifferentiated curriculum indicate that its advantages stem from the freedom and flexibility to follow children's interests and to

---

8. Bruner, "Process of Education Revisited," p. 179.

respond to their needs. Since young learners are active and spontaneous, teachers see such flexibility as responsive to the natural learning needs of children. In contrast, critics view this lack of planning as narrow and confining, for it is solely dependent on the teacher's existing knowledge of content and activities, and it is limited by the teacher's bias in judging children's needs. Without planning, critics say, teachers do not sense a need to expand their knowledge, to check their judgments against the research and experience of others, or to identify alternative activities for greater variety and range of learning. The pairing of strengths and criticisms relates primarily to values, as both views may acknowledge the freedom of choice and flexibility. In Table 4–5, these advantages and criticisms are paired, reflecting two sides of one coin.

Another advantage for young children's learning is the inclusion of children's feelings, attitudes, and concerns, which many teachers think determine children's potential for school success far more than what they learn. If children like school and feel competent to learn, advocates of this curriculum say, they will be able to master whatever they encounter in the primary grades.

TABLE 4.5. Holistic curriculum critiqued

Strengths	Weaknesses
Teachers can be more spontaneous without worrying about what subject is being taught.	Teachers use implicit criteria for knowledge selection without making these explicit.
	Teachers may fail to teach information required for later development or for continuing school success.
Holistic curriculum helps teachers focus more on children's learning than on instruction or teaching.	It emphasizes teacher bias in identifying children's needs, and teachers tend to make different decisions about the same child.
Teachers can use whatever they know and like—from what they have done or have seen or heard about—that seems to be enjoyable and worthwhile for children.	Holistic curriculum begs the question of what curriculum is, masking a refusal to deal with just what knowledge base is being used.
	It validates what is really a random, nonreflective approach to selecting content.
Since young children's learning is active, it is easier to improvise on the spot than to try to preplan.	The program is mindless, without identifying alternatives that are often needed to give direction and guidance to untutored and repetitive activities.
Cognitive concerns can deal with how children reason, rather than what they reason about.	Selected learning, based on teacher's own knowledge without reviewing the wealth of ideas in the literature and the research, is narrow.
Holistic curriculum can feature other criteria more important than what children learn, such as children's feelings, attitudes, and concerns.	Objective basis is lacking for self-evaluation in teaching or assessing children's progress, since all decisions are subjective.

SUMMARY

Six different classes of content were discussed, including (1) accumulation of facts, (2) accumulation of skills, (3) subjects, (4) disciplines, (5) themes, and (6) holistic curriculum. These classes represent differing emphases on the "what" of teaching, or the curriculum.

However, a class of content is rarely encountered in its pure form, as indicated above. Informal or open classrooms may have a truly undifferentiated or holistic curriculum, but more often there is an attachment of this approach to the "basics," to the "three Rs," or to some other content class, such as subjects or themes.

The discussion of views of knowledge in this chapter described classes of content, not methods of teaching. Criticisms of some classes of content, such as content organized into key concepts or structured according to disciplines, tend to stress problems of method more than selection of content. Since it is important to select content that is teachable, method problems are considered in Section Two, Chapters 8-11.

EXERCISES

1. Compare your views of knowledge for the preschool and for the primary grades. In what ways are they the same? How are they different? Why?

2. Select two different curriculum areas, such as mathematics and language arts. Review two early childhood texts to compare views of knowledge in each area.

BIBLIOGRAPHY

Bruner, Jerome. "Process of Education Revisited." In Glen Haas, ed., *Curriculum Planning: A New Approach*. Boston: Allyn and Bacon, 1977.

Craig, Gerald. *Science for the Elementary School Teacher*, 5th ed. Waltham, Mass.: Blaisdell Publishing, 1966.

Evans, Ellis D. *Contemporary Influences in Early Childhood Education*, 2nd ed. New York: Holt, Rinehart & Winston, 1975.

Hirst, Paul H. *Knowledge and the Curriculum: A Collection of Philosophical Papers*. London: Routledge & Kegan Paul, 1974.

Leeper, Sarah; Dales, Ruth; Skipper, Doris; and Witherspoon, Ralph. *Good Schools for Young Children*, 3rd ed. New York: Macmillan, 1974.

Mitchell, Lucy Sprague. *Young Geographers*. New York: John Day, 1934.

Montessori, Maria. *The Montessori Method*. New York: Bentley, 1964.

Phenix, Phillip H. *The Realms of Meaning*. New York: McGraw-Hill, 1964.

Pring, Richard, "Curriculum Content: Principles of Selection," In Denis Lawton et al., eds., *Theory and Practice in Curriculum Studies*. London: Routledge & Kegan Paul, 1978.

5 Views of Child Development

Curriculum decisions are strongly influenced by teachers' ideas about growth and development and how children learn. We will review three major approaches to development and learning in this chapter and discuss briefly some implications each approach has for curriculum. A first step to making curriculum decisions in early childhood education requires clarifying the major positions that exist to find the one that seems most persuasive. Of the three approaches described in this chapter—the maturationist, cultural-training, and cognitive-developmental—you are encouraged to identify which one most closely defines your view.

Each teacher brings strong convictions to the classroom about how children develop and learn. Theories of development and learning provide a basis for answering such questions as:

- Is the child a blank page on which home and school, parents and teacher write enduring messages?
- Is the child an empty pitcher to be filled with knowledge through schooling?
- Is the child a tender plant in the garden, waiting for good weather and feeding before unfolding?
- Is the child a young, immature person qualitatively different from adults, yet needing the same sense of respect?

Clearly, different teaching approaches are required for different answers to these questions. While development and learning are closely related, they are not the same. There are differences in meaning to be found in both theory and practice. *Development* is usually defined as genetically determined behavior, and *learning* as the change of behavior that occurs due to experience. We assume that you have already had a basic course in child development and educational psychology. The following sections include a capsule review of major approaches to development and learning that are in no way intended to substitute for such courses. Those of you who do not have this background are encouraged to use more extensive textbooks in child development and learning and to use the summaries in this text as a review of such studies.

Among theorists who have emphasized the early years, Lawrence Kohlberg's criteria for distinguishing one program from another contribute to clarification of the relationship between child development and learning theories, and early childhood programs.[1] He distinguishes between the maturationist, cultural training, and cognitive-developmental theories, which govern the wide range of early childhood programs currently in use. In the following discussion of views of child development and learning, we will use Kohlberg's three classes to correlate developmental and

---

1. Lawrence Kohlberg, "Early Education: A Cognitive-Developmental View," *Child Development*, 39 (1968): 1013–1062.

learning theories with curriculum practices. Then we will discuss other theories helpful in developing curriculum for young children.

MATURATIONIST VIEW

The maturationists, according to Kohlberg, regard biological, genetic, or internal factors as primarily responsible for the child's development.[2] The idea of a good seed that is well planted, reared in a benign environment, that unfolds and grows to its best potential, without unnecessary adult pressure, goes back at least to Rousseau in middle eighteenth-century France. It is also the central idea of the kindergarten movement initiated by Froebel in Germany early in the nineteenth century. Since, in this view, the child is born with the abilities and capacities that will mature with growth, the theory essentially requires a supportive and healthful environment. A frequently heard statement teachers make reflecting this view is:

> These children are their own best teachers, and they are going to learn and grow by themselves if we let them. In fact, the best thing we can do is to stay in the background unless we are needed.

Arnold Gesell's studies of children, which led to descriptions of normal stages of development, stressed maturation as the mechanism by which children reach each successive stage of development. Having examined and tested many young children, Gesell based his averages and stage ranges on his careful recordings of children's behaviors and task completions. If your child is four, he said, this is the stage the child is likely to be going through, and these are the things the child is likely to be able to do.[3] While Gesell's averages were well based, dealing with averages may make one forget the large variation that actually occurs at any one age or stage. However, he defined the sequence of stages clearly.

2. Ibid.
3. Arnold Gesell and Frances Ilg, *Infant and Child in the Culture of Today* (New York: Harper and Brothers, 1943).

Faced with examples of immature child behavior, the maturationist will say, "The child will outgrow it." Many types of behavior are in fact outgrown by most children, but the difficult question for both teachers and parents is, "How do you handle the child until she or he outgrows whatever needs outgrowing?" The maturationists offer two somewhat opposing answers. For children who are immature compared with their agemates, one answer points to the need for earlier schooling to support growth through a difficult period. The opposite answer is to delay school entrance, for example, until age seven. This solution—to give the grossly immature child a chance to outgrow infantile behavior at home without trying to cope with group social situations at school—is not popular with parents. The swelling ranks of working mothers, who need custodial as well as educational opportunities for their children, is a social change schools have to reckon with realistically.

While maturational patterns are thought of as something the child is born with, there are increasing observations that point to powerful environmental influences on such apparently genetic patterns as pace of development and of height growth. For example, studies at Harvard of severely retarded infants indicated the positive impact of environmental stimulation in advancing the pace of development. Changes in height patterns have been observed in California, where climate, diet, and living patterns, or some mixture of these, seem to be associated with taller children. Japanese children are also surpassing their parents' height patterns since World War II, possibly because of increased protein in the diet.

Gesell's work in establishing averages, or norms, for developmental changes, is often referred to as the *normative* approach. One unfortunate consequence of the normative approach is the tendency to label children "slow," "fast," or "average." Labeling a child becomes an unnecessary limitation when it affects how teachers work with children, what they expect of them, and how teachers value each child's potential as a student. There is some evidence that when children perceive teacher expectations, children try to live up to them, or they develop a style of learning that corresponds to teacher judgments. Pacing a child too rapidly may be as counterproductive as pacing too slowly.

Curriculum Implications of the Maturationist View

If development is maturational and internal and is little affected by environmental influences, the important message for the teacher is to wait until maturation occurs. The burden is on the child to develop the necessary readiness. This view also relieves the teacher of the need to find ways to move toward readiness, since it is unlikely to be hastened by teaching decisions.

This approach carries some problems. Waiting for readiness to happen may be the same as assuming that a child is unable to learn something he or she has had no opportunity to accomplish. Withholding learning opportunities for the optimum moment of readiness may instead contribute to the child's declining interest in learning, lack of security in feeling able to learn, and acceptance of adult suggestion that she or he is not learning well.

Ideally, the maturationist should offer a well-prepared environment for the children who are ready to use it appropriately. This would permit children to find their own levels of learning as they encounter interesting materials in an attractive setting. In such an environment, the teacher might deal with each child at the child's own level or group children together who appear to be similar in their readiness for the learnings to be developed.

But some maturationists do not trust a design that depends on having children find their own levels of learning. Instead, children are tested and then grouped on common levels. Many teachers are attracted to this approach because they think it makes planning and teaching easier if the group is more homogeneous. The same series of lessons, or learning experiences, are expected to be useful for the whole group, without the need to individualize methods or content, for a wide range of "readiness." There is, however, a difficult problem with this seemingly efficient approach: that is, that children are rarely homogeneous in all abilities and achievements. Grouping children on the basis of their verbal skills may not help them when learning mathematics, physical, or social skills. Other problems concern the many difficulties of testing young children adequately. Errors in judgment are inevitable.

Assuming that teachers can determine by testing or other evaluation methods exactly what children are ready for, teachers usually have access to packaged materials that purport to match various levels of readiness. For example, if the Metropolitan Achievement Test is used to determine readiness for reading instruction, as it often is in kindergarten or at the beginning of the first grade, those children above the desired cutoff score would be placed at the beginning of the reading sequence in whatever system is in use. Children scoring below the desired cutoff score might be retained in kindergarten for another year or placed in a "transitional" classroom where the teacher's approach may or may not be maturationist.

Summary of the Maturationist View

The maturationist view holds that the child is born with the abilities and capacities that essentially determine developmental potential. The learning environment or arrangement this view generates can be either a well-ordered environment with supportive, helpful teachers who guide the child through free choice of learning activities, or it can be the creation of homogeneous groups based on assessment of achievement.

CULTURAL TRAINING VIEWS

Opposite from maturationism is Kohlberg's category of cultural training, a behaviorist view that places the forces for development and learning largely outside the child in the environment. For behaviorists, generally, learning and development are not separate. Nor is learning thought to be different for younger than for older children. Older children, who have had time to learn more, are ready for higher steps on the learning ladder, and they have chained together more prior learning into concepts. In this view, it is not a different stage of development that enables older children to learn more complex material, but only more opportunity for prior learning. The more time provided for learning, according to behaviorists, the more the child is likely to have learned.

The behaviorist approach includes clearly defined views of how learning takes place. Learning occurs in small steps, in sequence, and in hierarchies. Bundles of learning accumulate and become the bases for more complex ideas or concepts. Behaviorist ideas and theories have become very complex, but the two major forms are the theories of *stimulus and response* (S-R) and of *conditioned response*. Neobehaviorist theories have generally tried to include what is missing from these two major types, that is, the internal or cognitive processes of the child.

Reinforcement

Reinforcement occurs when the teacher gives candies or hugs to the children who have produced the correct answer when a color name was requested. The hugs or the candies are *reinforcers*. So is praise for using a tool correctly or a treat for finishing first. Reinforcers take many forms, such as prizes, food, special privileges, stars, and choices of free-time activity. While most teachers do not think of themselves as behaviorists, they use reinforcers to insure that desired behaviors will recur or to make the child feel good about himself or herself. Most teachers find through experience that reinforcers are powerful tools to teach desired classroom behaviors, social skills, motor skills of many kinds, and numerous types of initial learning in many content areas, including beginning reading and mathematics.

In the classroom, when some children receive reinforcers or rewards that others want, the latter are seen as being deprived of something they want. Positive reinforcers, however, are regarded as being far more powerful in learning situations than any kind of negative reinforcement, such as deprivation or punishment. Punishment is not regarded as particularly useful except for its ability to stop undesirable behavior. Once the child is helped to cease whatever is unbearable or undesirable, positive reinforcers can be used to emphasize learning new behavior and to stimulate its recurrence. Punishment has the additional disadvantage that it must be quite severe to achieve the intended result, which is likely to make the child fearful of the teacher who uses punishment.

Another branch of behaviorism, called social learning theory, or learning by imitation, shows the way reinforced children become models for other children in the group. The teacher's reinforcement of one or two children shows other children what they have to do to get the same rewards. Providing that the nonreinforced children *like* the teacher, *do not dislike* the reinforced models, and *want* the reinforcement they see other children getting, social learning theory indicates that more children will voluntarily produce the desired behavior. Examples of this approach are frequently seen in classes for young children at story-reading time, when the teacher beams at the children who are sitting quietly, and says, "I like the way Mary, Joe, and Anita are sitting." Ideally, however, reinforcers are not selected for groups but for individual children, since all children do not respond to the same reinforcers.

Behavior Analysis

Learning through reinforcement of desired responses has been hailed as especially useful to eliminate errors in learning. Errorless learning is thought be easily designed, using small steps with feedback such as "That's right!" or "Good!" so children would not have to unlearn wrong answers. For teaching purposes, Ellis Evans offers a summary of the five principles of what has come to be called *behavior analysis:*[4]

1. *Specify expected outcomes.* This is the objective, or what you want the child to learn. The objective might be to discriminate a circle from a square on a set of cards or to produce the color labels of red or blue when shown samples of yarn or paper.
2. *Determine where to start.* Can the child do it now? Can the child understand the task? If the child has already learned the final, desired behavior, continue on to the next step or learning task. If not, decide where to start in the instructional sequence. If the child recognizes a circle but not a rectangle, the starting point may be different than if both shapes are equally unfamiliar.
3. *Design a teaching sequence.* Plan small steps in learning so that reinforcers can be given for each visible change in behavior.
4. *Identify reinforcers.* If the usual reinforcers do not work—if the correct answers do not recur—observe the child's self-selected activities, note what the child likes, and choose one of these as a possible reinforcer.
5. *Implement teaching plans to change behavior.* Often reinforcing step by step is necessary along the way to the desired goal. Initially, the child may be reinforced for any behavior that is somewhat similar to the desired behavior. Once desired behaviors have been acquired, reinforcers are gradually limited to reduce dependency. Finally, when the learned behavior is well established, the reinforcers are eliminated altogether.

Many teachers who deplore behaviorism as described above, because they see it as manipulating another person, would be amazed to discover that they often use it, but without its precision and sequence requirements. When teachers use behaviorist techniques loosely and without careful plans, they find it no more successful than other methods. Some teachers accept the behavior-analysis method as a useful alternative when other methods do not work, and they expect to discard it when the child makes enough progress to respond to more independent requirements. Other teachers regard behaviorist methods as wrong and immoral and strive to avoid them in teaching.

Unlike most other methods of teaching, behaviorist methods are based on substantial scholarly research. Behaviorism requires an active child, because reinforcement must be given for actions that are desirable. A truly passive child would pose numerous problems for behaviorists. However, the behaviorist teacher or the teacher using behaviorist methods *chooses* (1) which acts to elicit, reinforce, or both, (2) which acts to eliminate (extinguish) through nonreinforcement, (3) which reinforcers to apply, (4) on what schedule (the contingency schedule), and when to discontinue reinforcement. There are behaviorist procedures, however, that put almost all these decisions in the hands of the child, for control and independence.

The Curriculum from the Cultural Training View

Behaviorists hold a narrow and specific view of curriculum with clearly specified objectives. They assume that learning or knowledge can

---

4. Ellis D. Evans, *Contemporary Influences in Early Childhood Education* (New York: Holt, Rinehart & Winston, 1975), pp. 105–106.

be broken into bits and acquired, step by step, as the teacher reinforces in turn each item in the series. Learning is cumulative in this view, and each step leads to the next step.

Learning theorists have been inventive in devising ideas of cues, prompts, branching, and the like to guide teaching of units of knowledge. *Cues* are signals that call for attention and provide information a child may need. An example of a cue is a teacher's flicking the lights to signal the end of the work period while putting finger to lips to inform the group that talking should cease. *Prompts* are reminders of information the child may have forgotten, furnished in much the same way a stage prompter reminds an actor of forgotten lines. A teacher is using prompts when holding up word cards for a child to read, along with pictures that remind the child of what the words represent. *Branching* is a way to break down complex information into simpler parts, helping the child to master these first. For example, if a child is unable to join two subsets and find the number or sum of the two sets, *branching* content might include simpler counting activities that, when well learned, make possible the more complex operation of addition. A review of these helpful ways to structure content for teaching indicates the great extent to which most teachers already practice learning theory.

This approach does not define appropriate content. It deals with how learning occurs. However, it requires the kind of content that has specifically identified desired outcomes and that can be broken into small sequential steps. Unpredictable outcomes, intuitive leaps in thinking, and nonsegmented forms of learning cannot be handled well by this approach.

An example of a structured curriculum designed through behaviorist methods is the Primary Education Project, a Pittsburgh University design developed by Lauren Resnick during the late sixties, which sought to teach children the skills and concepts needed for success in school. Using cumulative learning theory as a guideline for organizing the curriculum, a hierarchy of learning goals was developed. These target tasks, or desired outcomes, were analyzed for the prior skills needed. For example, the classification tasks move through five units, each unit building on the preceding one, beginning with a unit on basic matching skills and ending with advanced matching skills.[5] Like most programs, this one is not purely behaviorist but a mixture of behaviorist and cognitive-developmental approaches. Its derivation of a curriculum and its view of learning, however, illustrate behaviorist patterns of curriculum design.

Different Opinions of the Cultural Training Approach

The essential arguments that arise between critics and supporters of the behaviorist view are listed in Table 5-1. Critics find the approach of controlling by manipulating external conditions undesirable and unacceptable, while supporters point out that teachers continuously choose which child behaviors to stimulate and which to discourage. In many cases there are only differences in degree of control, not in kind, between behaviorist and nonbehaviorist teachers. The real distinctions lie not so much in what teachers say or do, but in the central idea of how learning takes place and in values of learning outcomes.

Nonbehaviorists do not accept the notion that little bits of knowledge can be taught so that they add up to major conceptions and systems of thinking. They are not even interested in teaching little bits of knowledge, except for utilitarian purposes. Instead, they agree with Piaget that the child must construct his or her own ideas and cannot receive them from others. Further, nonbehaviorists reject the ethical implications of creating dependency on

---

5. Lauren B. Resnick, Margaret C. Wang, and Jerome Rosner, "Adaptive Education for Young Children: The Primary Education Project," in Mary Carol Day and Ronald K. Parker, eds., *The Preschool in Action*, 2nd ed. (Boston: Allyn and Bacon, 1977), pp. 220–251.

TABLE 5.1. The behaviorist view

Critics say	Supporters say
1. Behaviorism has a limited range that cannot apply to all types of learning.	Behaviorism works when other approaches fail and may be discontinued when the child responds to preferred methods.
2. Behaviorism fosters dependency by featuring extrinsic rewards rather than personal motives.	Behaviorism doesn't create dependency if self-control is featured with the child's choice of goals and reinforcers.
3. Behaviorism relies on bribery, *concrete rewards* such as cookies or stars, and *social approval*, such as special jobs and public praise.	Most teachers already use *concrete rewards* and *social approval* to encourage repetition of desired behavior.
4. Behaviorism does not deal with complex causes of behavior; it oversimplifies.	Causes of behavior are very complex and are beyond the scope of teaching, belonging to the field of therapy.
5. Behaviorism ignores children's thoughts and feelings, dealing only with their behavior.	Even if teachers could determine causes of behavior, teachers are not trained therapists.
6. Behaviorism is a mechanistic process, treating people as passive objects; thus it is dehumanizing and depersonalizing.	Using reinforcers specially selected for the individual is personalistic because it requires *detailed observation* of the behavior of each individual and *helps* the teacher drop punitive methods often used when "all else fails."

others for approval of one's thinking; this, they say, is morally wrong. Piagetian theorists, discussed in the next section, stress the great need of the child to reach "wrong" conclusions, as long as they are the child's own. Piagetians believe that the child will develop ever more complex thinking, independently, which should ultimately lead to more "correct" conclusions. The nonbehaviorist is not convinced that just because the child says the right word the meaning of that word is understood.

Another reason why "errorless" learning, which many behaviorists strive for, is regarded as destructive by nonbehaviorists is the assumption behaviorists make that children think like adults, needing only correction or reinforcement to achieve adult-like thinking. Since developmental views stress the qualitative difference between children's and adults' thinking (as we will discuss further in the next section, "Cognitive Developmental View"), there is controversy over whether the child can be taught by correction or reinforcement to think like an adult. Such attempts mask the qualitative differences in *how* children think and conceptualize knowledge, according to nonbehaviorists. However, there is increasing interest in applying behaviorist theories to learning at early stages, when goals are specific and often involve psychomotor skills and when reinforcement is likely to be most effective.

Implications of Behaviorism for Teaching

Behaviorist stress on external influences on learning requires many specific steps, with reinforcement at each step. This approach has limitless implications for teaching and curriculum. That is, if the child's development seems slow, it is likely that one or more of the following is true:

1. Instruction was not begun at the right step.
2. Steps were not small enough.
3. Feedback to the child was not well communicated.
4. Cues, prompts, branching, or other devices were not used when needed.
5. Reinforcers were not adequate.
6. The schedule of reinforcement was not appropriate.
7. The instructional design was not a successful construction.
8. The stimuli selected were inappropriate, and so on.

Since development is not really different from learning, causes for learning failures must always be sought externally, not in the child's neurological stage of development. This approach places great responsibility on teachers to design better learning plans, to identify curriculum units appropriate for individual children, to monitor children's progress diagnostically, to change plans that are not effective, and to know when successful learning has occurred. While this approach cannot prescribe curriculum, it requires the teacher to do so, selecting the kind of content that can be taught in small steps with predetermined outcomes.

COGNITIVE-DEVELOPMENTAL VIEW

Cognitive-developmental theorists, Kohlberg's third category, differ from maturationists, for whom internal growth factors are dominant, and from behaviorists, for whom external factors determine learning. Developmentalists are often called *interactionists*, because they view the child's development as the result of the interaction between genetic and environmental factors.

The developmental view has also come to be called *constructivism* because of the Piagetian theory of how children learn, or "construct," knowledge. According to this theory, the child initiates much exploratory activity, manipulating objects, acting on them in many ways, and organizing a system for thinking about the world. Through *assimilation* the child plays, pretending and imagining the way she or he wants the world to be. In the opposite process of *accommodation*, reality intrudes, requiring the child to be more objective or conventional in behaving and thinking. According to Piaget, there is a continuous balancing within the child between the extremes of assimilation (pretending and imagining) and accommodation (dealing with reality). As the child balances these two processes, thinking becomes increasingly adaptive, mature, and complex.

Piaget also found four different stages in the child's intellectual development, each qualitatively different from the others (as described in the following subsection). The child is not a miniature adult but a different sort of person whose development will depend not only on maturation, but also on experiences with people and objects, on logical-mathematical reasoning about those experiences, and on an internal force called *equilibration*. Social transmission, an important influence on development, includes the forces a culture brings to bear on the socialization of the young. Piaget offers a sophisticated view of the heredity-versus-environment controversy, giving great weight to both sides, because he believes it is through the interaction between them that intelligence is determined, or rather constructed.

Piaget's research is primarily focused on the intellectual aspect of development. Others, notably David Elkind, have generalized this view to all aspects of development.[6] This view conceives of the child as capable of making choices, initiating activities, applying abundant energies and thoughts constructively, and building ways of learning and thinking. The concepts that the child constructs are the child's own. They are fashioned by an individual out of experience of various kinds, in accordance with the reasoning capability available at any particular stage. In the young child, this reasoning capability is regarded as very different from mature thinking. Gradually, concepts and the child's way of reasoning and constructing ideas become more complex, advanced, objective, and mature. As the child completes one stage and enters the next, a different way of thinking develops, not more of the same. Autonomy, independence, internal motivation, and qualitatively different kinds of reasoning at each stage are required by this approach.

Summary of Piaget

According to Piaget, the four factors that influence cognitive development are:[7]

1. physical experiences with objects;
2. social experiences with people;
3. maturation, or neurological development;
4. equilibration, an internal mechanism in which there is continual balancing of the previous three factors, continued reorganization within the child, and constant tilting back and forth between the extremes of reality and personalistic thought.

Social experiences can be very important in creating doubts in the child's mind, when, for example, she finds out that an idea she has, which she thought everyone had, is quite different from that of her peers. Physical experiences in massive quantities are needed for the child to construct such concepts about the world as size, weight, length, time, mass, order, and relationships among them. Maturation is a limiting factor in that greater complexity of thinking requires greater complexity of neurological development. Maturation also makes possible the transitions from one stage to the next, to a different capability of understanding, always more complex and more mature.

The four major developmental stages Piaget has found are as follows.

1. *Sensorimotor stage.* This stage occurs from birth to about age two. In this stage, action *is* thought, and the many experiences the baby has with objects in the environment, with manipulations and actions, and with people build the basis for much future conceptualization. Major accomplishments of this stage, which precedes language development for the most part, are:
   a. *Object performance.* The baby comes to understand that the rattle that fell underneath the crib is still there, although it cannot be seen. It is no longer, "out of sight, out of mind."
   b. *Environmental permanence.* The car bed is the same car bed, whether it sits in the living room waiting for a ride, or is safely stowed in the car. Thus objects, people, and environmental features retain their essential identity, even when some changes are made, such as where they are, how many pieces they break down to, or how they are dressed, decorated, or covered.
   c. *Simple cause-and-effect.* The baby soon comes to understand that getting dressed in outdoor clothes means going outdoors, and these simple, repeated forms of cause-and-effect become understandable.

---

6. David Elkind, *Children and Adolescents* (New York: Oxford University Press, 1970).
7. Jean Piaget, *The Psychology of Intelligence* (New York: Harcourt, Brace & World, 1962).

d. *Self-identity*. The idea of being different from mother or others is a very important distinction between self and nonself.
   e. *Intentionality*. The baby comes to make decisions, decides what to do, with what, and where and resists strongly when others try to redirect the baby's actions. The baby is not just a reactor to external stimuli but an actor-initiator.
   f. *Deferred imitation*. This is the evidence of memory, when the child imitates something that happened or was present before and does not exist in the present.

For all stages, Piaget stresses both *continuity* and *discontinuity*, that is, the intellectual development of one stage is carried over to the next, but now more complex capability is built. Another important concept in stage development is *invariance* in the sequence of stages: the same sequence is always followed, although there is a great deal of individual variability in the pace at which children develop and in ages when stages are completed and entered.

2. *Intuitive intelligence*, or preoperational intelligence. This stage lasts from about age two to about six or seven. Important features of this stage of development are that:
   a. *Language develops*, advances, and becomes an important vehicle of communication, gradually substituting in many ways for action. Language development of a high order is achieved by the end of this stage. However, it must be stressed that Piaget does not equate speech and language with thinking. Thinking may be physical or mental but it is not the same as speech, or having vocabulary. He says thought structures speech, rather than the other way around.
   b. *Symbolic thinking*, using images, actions, and language, is an increasingly important way of thinking and reasoning.
   c. Children develop many ways of *conceptualizing* about their world, although reasoning is not reliably logical, but more intuitive.
   d. *Perceptual-boundedness*, however, continues to limit reasoning ability. Sensory information is dominant over reasoning when the two contradict each other.
   e. *Egocentricity* begins to diminish, but continues to prevent the child from differentiating her or his perspective from anyone else's.
   f. *Simple classification*, based on one variable at a time, dominates sorting and classifying activities. The child is unable to do multiple classification, or use more than one variable at the same time.
   g. *Transductive reasoning*, or reasoning from the specific to the specific, interferes with logical deduction and induction, relating specifics to generalities.
   h. *Animism*, or thinking that all objects are alive, or that those that move —such as water, wind, or kites—are alive, is a common characteristic of intuitive intelligence.
   i. *Realism*, or thinking that dreams or fantasies really exist outside of the human imagination, predispose young children to accept magic, or the idea that anything can happen or can cause anything else to happen. Reality and logical limits do not intrude on magical ideas.
   j. *Numerical concepts* develop and grow, first in relation to objects and later as symbols of numerosity, for example, that four is more than three.

The stage of intuitive intelligence is often a deceptive one, because at the end of this stage, there already is evidence of transition to the next, and samples of what seem like pure logic may be identified. However, what characterizes a stage for Piaget is not some examples but a whole system of thinking, integrated in its parts and representative of the system as a whole. One expects *some* logic from five- and six-year-olds, and one is not disappointed if it is understood that the logic is not stable and totally available for all purposes.

3. *Concrete Operations.* Thinking in concrete operations, from about age six or seven to about eleven or twelve, is the beginning of logical thinking, but not in the abstract; it is based on the real and concrete. No longer perception-bound, egocentric, or transductive in thinking, the child gradually learns as the stage advances to reason objectively, inductively, and deductively. The child learns to question or overcome sensory information when reason tells the child it cannot be so. For example, a group of seven- and eight-year-olds was invited to help harvest nuts from some nut trees. But the nuts were blown off by a great storm several days before. Many were on the ground and the host bought packages at the store and sprinkled more on the ground so that the children would not be disappointed in their harvesting party. The children were busily filling their sacks from pickings on the ground when one child looked perplexed and demanded to know how come all the nuts were on the ground, with none left on the trees. Here is an example of good reasoning, based on experience, which called into question the perceptual information available.

When water is poured from one container into a larger, narrower one, a child up to six or seven years old will think, "It looks like more," observing the most salient variable of height and ignoring the less salient one of width. Now in the stage of concrete operations, the child can look at both variables and understand how they coordinate to create a perceptually misleading appearance of more. The child can think, "It's taller, but it's narrower, so it's really the same," or, "It has to be the same, because nothing was added or taken away, therefore there is no change in the amount of water."

At the stage of concrete operations, the features of such thinking are *multiple classification* (coordinating more than one variable at a time), *transitivity* (things equal to other things are equal to each other; or if A = B, and B = C, then A = C), *class inclusion* (whole-part relations), *reversibility* (returning to the starting point, or reversing by canceling a line of thought), and *conservation* (recognition that objects remain unchanged despite various operations, such as different placement, order, arrangement, and the like), and *associativity* (finding different routes to the same conclusion).

Logical thinking is thus clearly established by the end of this stage, but it is built on concrete objects, with mastery of classification, relationships, and quantitative meanings. Where the younger child in the stage of intuitive intelligence focused on a limited part of a field, in this stage of concrete operations the child develops the ability to explore a field systematically and to integrate and arrange his or her thinking more easily and cogently.

4. *Formal Operations.* Formal operations are thought to begin to occur at about ages twelve to thirteen. This is the mature form of logical thinking, capable of abstract logic and mental manipulations. At this final, complex stage of thinking—which is thought to peak at about age sixteen and continue thereafter—maturity includes not only the abstract capability, but

the introspective ability to understand how one thinks and why.

It is not known what proportion of adolescents, or of adults for that matter, actually achieve this stage of formal operations, or use it systematically. Since experience is one of the contributing components leading to this stage, it is clear that not everyone becomes involved in such thinking, either for lack of necessity, or opportunity, or capability.

Curriculum Implications from the Cognitive-Developmental View

There are many contemporary cognitive-developmental programs. Each has its distinctive characteristics, but all share an open-ended view of children's growth and development. Process goals—that is, ways of learning and thinking—are valued more than the content acquired. There is also respect for each child's unique pace and mode of learning.

All programs of the cognitive-developmental type include such familiar early childhood learning activities as block building, dramatic play, puzzles, artwork, many kinds of materials to manipulate, music, and dance. These activities can be expected to appeal to young children almost anywhere and usually result in constructive and involving forms of individual and group play and work. In some programs, these standard activities constitute most of the curriculum offered to children, with small to large amounts of teacher intervention. In other programs, this base is attached to various forms of tutoring, direct teaching, or assigned cognitive tasks that are expected to encourage children to reason, classify, seriate, or otherwise demonstrate forms of what Piaget calls logico-mathematical reasoning.

Programs claiming a Piagetian base vary greatly in curriculum design. They are relatively new, so it is understandable that curriculum questions receive varied answers, until further experience or theorizing helps to identify major organizing principles and structure. Two such curricula that clearly derive from Piaget are those of Kamii and DeVries,[8] and of Forman and Kuschner.[9] These programs, which depend on the child's active self-involvement in learning, require an environment rich in resources and opportunities for experimental learning as well as teachers who can understand and diagnose the nature of the child's learning. It is essential that a teacher know how to challenge and support children's activity without taking over the children's function of constructing their own knowledge. By design or task invitation, teachers stimulate learning by extending challenges and setting up conditions for children to make discoveries. Making mistakes is an essential part of finding out and is valued as the child's own cognitive activity. Children are expected to correct their own mistakes in reasoning as they mature and think in more complex ways.

In a cognitive-developmental program, teachers cannot transmit ideas, concepts, or principles, as teachers are expected to do in a maturationist program; that is, teachers cannot lecture or explain. In both types of programs, however, teachers are expected to transmit to children arbitrary social knowledge, such as the names of things. However, even here there is a great difference in curriculum emphasis. Where maturationist teachers are expected to give great weight to vebal learning, cognitive-developmental teachers transmit such knowledge chiefly when it is useful and needed, not as a high priority of the program.

8. Constance Kamii and Rheta DeVries, *Physical Knowledge in Preschool Education: Implications of Piaget's Theory* (Englewood Cliffs, N.J.: Prentice-Hall, 1978).

9. George E. Forman and David S. Kuschner, *The Child's Construction of Knowledge: Piaget for Teaching Children.* Monterey, Calif.: Brooks/Cole, 1977.

Summary of the Cognitive-Developmental View

The cognitive-developmental view grows out of Piaget's conception that development and learning are transactional with mutual interaction between child and environment. This occurs in clearly differentiated stages, each of which has specific characteristics. Programs reflecting this view include the Piagetian-based programs of Kamii and DeVries, Forman and Kuschner, and others. Many programs representing the traditional child development approach currently include elements of the cognitive-developmental view. While this approach does not require a specific kind of curriculum, it defines curriculum chiefly in terms of developmental capabilities and learning needs and is more process oriented than the maturationist type. It shares with behaviorism the emphasis on process rather than on content.

CURRICULUM IMPLICATIONS OF KOHLBERG'S CATEGORIES

Comparing the three program categories in Kohlberg's scheme, it is interesting to note that curriculum design can be very *prescriptive* or it can be very *permissive*, in both maturationist and cognitive-developmental types.

Cultural training programs are highly prescriptive because the training is geared closely to specific cutural objectives, such as readiness for success in first-grade reading instruction. It is true in a broad sense that many different forms of curriculum might be selected, each one having as much likelihood as any other to produce readiness for success in first-grade reading instruction. In practice, sponsors of cultural-training programs tend to offer a specific curriculum, one that can be perceived as being relevant to its objectives and in which teachers and supervisors can be "trained."

A nonprescriptive approach to curriculum design is the essentially maturationist Bank Street College model of Head Start, whose developmental goals are mainly process-oriented including "thinking, expressing, probing, and coping behavior."[10] This model relies heavily on, but does not restrict itself to, well-tested nursery school activities, which are known to engage young children's interests in many ways and for many purposes. Unlike DISTAR, the Bereiter cultural training program, in which teachers are specifically trained in verbal behaviors for teaching, the Bank Street model requires teachers who can use great sensitivity in offering psychosocial guidance, as well as direct teaching.

Play is included in cognitive-developmental programs, since it is one of the major ways children learn. Most maturationist programs also feature play, since children are likely to generate many forms of play when they are given choices. Games, trips, and classroom visitations are also arranged by teachers in maturationist programs. In a cultural-training program, play, if included in the curriculum, is likely to be planned as a way to break tension, to relieve pressure, or to provide a break in the tightly planned teaching-learning schedule; but play is not part of the instructional curriculum.

CHILD DEVELOPMENT VIEWS AND THE CURRICULUM

None of the three approaches described above, as we have aready noted, require teachers to use certain content only. Content is not prescribed by the theories. But the theories define the *kinds* of content in harmony with the approach. Only the behaviorist view clearly requires a preselected, segmented, and carefully sequenced curriculum.

10. Barbara Biber, "A Developmental-Interaction Approach," in Mary Carol Day and Ronald K. Parker, eds., *The Preschool in Action*, 2nd ed. (Boston: Allyn and Bacon, 1977), p. 458.

Most programs seem to combine behaviorist and cognitive-developmental features with little sense of contradiction. You may well ask, if this is so, what difference does it make? Why not select the best features of different philosophies or programs and their curricula, without worrying about having a consistent approach?

In fact, analyses and selections of program objectives and of curricula serve basically to accentuate one's true expectation of outcomes. If selections from several different approaches are made and contradictory outcomes result, the educator should be aware of the breaks of logic in any rationale based on such choices. Since not everyone interprets programs and curricula in the same way, selections from different approaches require further analysis to identify relationships that are neither apparent nor well known. For example, some behaviorists say their approach is really very humanistic, and they offer substantial reasons and data to support this claim. Since universal acceptance of definitions for terms such as *humanistic* is lacking, controversies can seldom be settled by resort to sheer logic.

In one program design, which brings together Piagetian and cumulative learning (behaviorist) theory, the educators accept the Piagetian stress on natural development and general experience as the basis for cognitive development. But they add that it is possible to identify critical events for which instructional experiences can be provided to influence the child's cognitive development.[11] The major objective of this program is to assure the child of success in primary-grade learning—essentially a cultural training objective—but in this case the primary grades are seen as being continuous with the preschool program, for maximum effects to occur. Here it is expected that if children are successful in such a continuous program, they will also "become capable of controlling their own learning and social activities to a significant degree."[12] Quite a few early childhood programs for "disadvantaged" children, using a behaviorist mode, have theorized that successful learning experiences free children to become autonomous learners, free to make "mistakes" and to pursue ideas that the Piagetian mode stresses.

If you want certainty that children will learn a specific body of content correctly, you clearly hold a behaviorist view of child development. The content selected may be facts, skills, activities, values, attitudes, and even ideas or concepts. A mastery of specific content will not usually be accomplished in cognitive-developmental approaches to learning, which view children as being in a continuous state of developing and growing. Maturationists, as suggested earlier, often aim for such mastery by grouping children together who are regarded as ready to learn the desired content. Behaviorists may seek to accomplish the same mastery, not by grouping children by ability, but by sequencing learning tasks in the content in a systematic way to build the desired "ladders" of success.

Accepting "incorrect" reasoning as evidence of a child's current capacity also differentiates cognitive-developmentalists from behaviorists and maturationists. The Piagetian approach requires arranging experiences for the child so that *self-correction* eventually occurs as thinking skills also mature. Behaviorists aim chiefly for correcting errors immediately or structuring learning so that errors cannot occur. Maturationists may accept errors as inevitable in the growth process or seek to prevent them by matching learning to the capability the child is presumed to have. Developmental theorists not considered to be cognitive-developmentalist have analyzed child development in ways that suggest curriculum needs different from those of cognitive-developmentalists, as described in the following section.

---

11. Resnick, Wang, and Rosner, "Adaptive Education for Young Children," pp. 220–251.

12. Ibid., p. 221.

OTHER VIEWS OF DEVELOPMENT

Psychosocial-Developmental View

Erik Erikson is the leading theorist who has adapted Freudian psychoanalytical, stage-specific theories to human development.[13] Following Shakespeare, he divides the life span into eight stages representing critical periods of development. Each stage has a major task with specific success-failure outcomes. Each stage, like Piaget's, is more complex and mature than the preceding one, but problems not resolved at one stage keep returning until they are resolved.

Critical periods each pose a crisis of some kind. The first period is similar to Piaget's sensorimotor period of the first two years of life. Erikson, however, poses the first crisis as trust versus mistrust. In the next two years, it is autonomy or doubt that must be resolved. The fifth and sixth years are concerned with initiative or guilt. Next come the years of elementary school, ages six to eleven, during which the crisis to be resolved is industry versus inferiority feelings. The adolescent stage, ages twelve to eighteen, requires a resolution of identity or role confusion. The sixth stage of early adulthood concerns intimacy or isolation. The seventh, or middle age, deals with self-absorption. And for the eighth stage, in old age, the crisis is integrity or despair. These developmental emphases are of the social-emotional rather than cognitive sphere.

Curriculum implications of the psychosocial-developmental view Erikson's system of classifying stages and identifying the central crisis of each stage has been a valuable theoretical support for early childhood curricula that stress emotional development and psychosocial needs. His system offers more implications for the process than for the content of early childhood curriculum programs, but it emphasizes the importance of emotional and social growth.

The early childhood years of three to six span the two stages that feature achieving a sense of autonomy and of initiative. *Autonomy* means knowing the difference between one's self and others, primarily the nurturant adult of the infancy-toddler period. *Independence* is established as the child acquires the ability to function as a separate individual in a setting away from the mothering adult. *Initiative* means exploring or testing relationships and experiences without feeling guilty about pursuing one's own ideas. The sense of initiative is acquired as the child becomes comfortable making independent choices representing the child's own view rather than the views of adults important to the child. *Industry*, for the primary grades, means systematic work and visible achievements, such as learning to read.

Any curriculum design based on this theory of stages features supporting children as they deal with their own emotions and work through their relationships with peers and adults. Children's feelings, attitudes, and purposes are respected and valued. Primarily, children create their own activities while the teachers use appropriate opportunities to help children complete the task of the stage.

Social Learning Theory

The development of a body of theory and research on social learning, initiated chiefly by Albert Bandura but including other researchers, presents early childhood teachers with effective strategies for a wide range of possible learning. Social learning theory is an offshoot of behaviorism that offers theoretical support for much intuitive teaching while supplying specific criteria for its success. Used both for improvement of young children's behavior and for learning of various kinds, social learning theory, or learning by imitation, appears to be less manipulative of the child than general behaviorism.

---

13. Erik Erikson, *Childhood and Society*, 2nd ed. (New York: Norton, 1963).

According to Bandura, social learning occurs when a child *observes* another, or *model*, and then *imitates* the model's actions. Whereas Piagetian theory says concepts are internally constructed by the child, social learning theory says they can also be learned by watching others. This is achieved apparently unconsciously, although there must be a base for such learning in prior experience; that is, the child must understand the modeled behavior. Four basic processes involved in social learning as cited by Bandura are:[14]

1. *Attention.* To learn, the child must observe the model closely.
2. *Retention.* The child must transform the observed behavior into mental images and store them in memory.
3. *Motoric enactments.* The child must be physically capable of imitating the model.
4. *Motivation.* The child must be interested in imitating the model.

According to Bandura, three types of modeling effects can be achieved:

1. *Inhibition-disinhibition.* The model decreases or increases responses already known to the child.
2. *Facilitation.* The child is encouraged to use skills he or she already has, on observing that others, especially the model, are using them.
3. *Learning new responses.* In learning new responses, the child is highly selective of what parts of the observed behavior to imitate. This is dependent on the child's prior cognitive experience (what the child understands of what he or she sees), physical skills actually available, and degree of attention and interest.

The major encouragement of social learning in this approach comes from what the child sees happening to the model. If the model is reinforced for the performance, the reinforced behavior is more likely to be imitated. Effectiveness of the model may depend on what personal characteristics the model has, what the character of the observing child is like, and on how well-organized the modeled behavior appears. Children who are less competent, younger, or have a high need for social approval may imitate more than others.[15]

Curriculum implications of social learning theory Social learning theory has been successfully applied, according to research reports, to such learning objectives for young children as:

- delaying gratification;
- improving standards of achievement;
- developing productive self-reward patterns;
- improving cognitive style (from less impulsivity to more reflection);
- learning rule-governed responses;
- acquiring and using language;
- acquiring grammatical rules;
- making conceptual distinctions, such as same versus different;
- achieving conservation of amount, for example, in clay;
- acquiring problem-solving strategies;
- increasing creativity;
- developing moral judgment;
- increasing sharing;
- increasing altruism, or helping others.

Attitudes, skills, social behaviors, and cognitive learning have all been included in research studies of social learning theory. Their data challenge the premises of all types of early childhood curriculum developers, especially those most wary of manipulating children, that is, educators using child development and

---

14. Albert Bandura, *Social Learning Theory* (New York: General Learning Press, 1971).

15. Barry J. Zimmerman, "Modeling," in Harry L. Hom, Jr., and Paul A. Robinson, eds., *Psychological Processes in Early Education* (New York: Academic Press, 1977), pp. 37–70.

Piagetian-based models. Many nonbehaviorists who abhor learning theory accept its offshoot, social learning theory. When teachers themselves model, or use the behavior of more advanced children as models, the behaviorist base is subtle but nevertheless provides the framework for the theory. It should be noted that the Kamii-DeVries Piagetian-based model, in a pragmatic classroom-based series of tryouts, selected modeling as a very effective teaching strategy when children could not otherwise be encouraged to initiate some goal-oriented activities.[16]

If children can learn so many different kinds of content through imitation or observational learning, some content may be included that would otherwise be considered desirable but not teachable. For example, consideration of others through empathy and sympathy has been thought to be too sophisticated for young children to learn, but indicators of these feelings have been observed in behaviors of very young children. Altruism, moral judgment, and improved cognitive style are other examples of content regarded as being difficult or impossible to teach young children.

It is exciting to open new prospects for teaching content viewed as desirable by all criteria except the young child's ability to learn it or the teacher's improbable success in teaching it. Modeling seems to offer the teacher a new route to content the young child might encounter successfully.

Social-Developmental View

Robert Havighurst formalized his social-developmental approach by defining seven stages of life that coordinate social expectations and the results of success or failure at each level.[17]

16. Kamii and DeVries, *Physical Knowledge*, pp. 56–57.
17. Robert Havighurst, *Developmental Tasks and Education* (New York: Longman Green, 1952).

As in stage-development theory, just as stages of development cannot be skipped, so uncompleted social-development tasks seriously interfere with growth through subsequent stages. Table 5–2, listing the tasks of the stages of life, illustrates this dependency of one task on another in the sequence of sexual development. At stage one the task is to identify one's own sex; stage two includes the appropriate sex role; and stage three builds on these two earlier stages with the acquisition of sexual interests. The mature stage is finding and living with a mate in early adulthood.

Curriculum implications of social-developmental view In a world of changing social values, Havighurst's specification of social expectations may be subject to modification, but the idea of developmental tasks as influential in planning curriculum remains important. It should be noted that for each stage of development theory—whether cognitive, psychosocial, or social—curriculum implications necessarily converge on goals and activities that enhance the growth within a specific stage. In theory, only when the tasks from one stage are completed can the child move on to the next one. Havighurst's list, by specifying the social learning that belongs to each stage, can guide both the maturationist and the behaviorist toward selecting appropriate social goals for preschoolers and primary graders. For the interactionists, an open-ended approach to these goals would be logical.

SUMMARY

Concepts of child development and learning were discussed in terms of Kohlberg's three categories of theories, which govern the wide range of early childhood programs: maturationist, cultural training, and cognitive-developmental. The maturationist views are closely related to the normative approach to child development, most closely associated

TABLE 5.2. Havighurst's developmental tasks of life

Stage One: Birth to Six Years—Infancy, Toddlerhood, and Early Childhood
- Learning to take solid foods
- Learning to walk, talk, and control elimination of wastes
- Developing trust in oneself and others
- Exploring the environment
- Learning to identify with one's own sex
- Learning to relate socially and emotionally to others
- Learning to distinguish right from wrong

Stage Two: Six to Twelve Years—Middle Childhood
- Expanding knowledge of physical and social world
- Learning appropriate sex role
- Acquiring academic skills, reasoning, and judgment

Stage Three: Twelve to Eighteen Years—Adolescence
- Developing self-assurance and sense of identity
- Acquiring sexual interests and more mature relationships with peers

Stage Four: Eighteen to Thirty-five Years—Early Adulthood
- Finding and learning to live with a mate
- Developing responsibility to care for family needs

Stage Five: Thirty-five to Sixty Years—Middle Age
- Accepting greater social responsibility
- Adjusting to aging parents

Stage Six: Later Life—Aging
- Accepting retirement

with Gesell. In this view, readiness is a natural occurrence in the process of growth, and the school environment is therefore similar to a greenhouse, offering the best conditions for development by providing appropriate materials and nurturant people.

Opposite to the maturationist is the cultural training theorist, who sees the forces for development and learning as being largely external to the child, found in environmental factors. In this behavioristic view, learning accumulates in small steps achieved through reinforcement, with learning accumulating over a period of time. We noted that reinforcement is an integral part of teaching, whether planned or spontaneous. Behavior-modification theory, which has sparked considerable controversy among early childhood educators, was discussed in terms of procedures and differing views.

The cognitive-developmental theory of Piaget was summarized in terms of the four Piagetian stages and the curricular approaches this view of development generates. Piagetian programs, which are relatively new, raise may questions about teaching methods and curriculum, while the physical environment tends to be indistinguishable from that provided by the maturationist.

Briefly reviewed were Erikson's psychosocial, Bandura's social learning, and Havighurst's social-developmental theories.

Teachers might wish to analyze theories of child development and learning in terms of how the theories might complement rather than contradict each other. Motor learning may best be facilitated by reinforcement, while conceptual learning may require a Piagetian view to understand the child's potential at each developmental stage and the ways independent thinking develops. Theorists may begin to find overlapping areas of agreement as curriculum developers explore different approaches in practice.

The next chapter will deal with ideas about how content in the curriculum can be sequenced.

EXERCISES

1. Define in your own words:
    accommodation
    attention
    autonomy
    behavior shaping
    conservation
    cues
    delayed gratification
    equilibration
    errorless learning
    intuitive intelligence
    maturation
    modeling (social learning theory)
    reinforcement
2. Interview a teacher about her or his use of such behaviorist devices as reinforcement, small steps in learning, cues, prompts, and errorless learning. Request examples of use of these devices and reasons.

BIBLIOGRAPHY

Bandura, Albert. *Social Learning Theory*. New York: General Learning Press, 1971.

Biber, Barbara. "A Developmental-Interaction Approach." In Mary Carol Day and Ronald K. Parker, eds., *The Preschool in Action*, 2nd ed. Boston: Allyn and Bacon, 1977.

Elkind, David. *Children and Adolescents*. New York: Oxford University Press, 1970.

Erikson, Erik. *Childhood and Society*, 2nd ed. New York: Norton, 1963.

Evans, Ellis D. *Contemporary Influences in Early Childhood Education*. New York: Holt, Rinehart & Winston, 1975.

Forman, George E., and Kuschner, David S. *The Child's Construction of Knowledge: Piaget for Teaching Children*. Monterey, Calif.: Brooks/Cole, 1977.

Gesell, Arnold, and Ilg, Frances. *Infant and Child in the Culture of Today*. New York: Harper & Brothers, 1943.

Havighurst, Robert. *Developmental Tasks and Education*. New York: Longmans Green, 1952.

Kamii, Constance, and DeVries, Rheta. *Physical Knowledge in Preschool Education: Implications of Piaget's Theory*. Englewood Cliffs, N.J.: Prentice-Hall, 1978.

Kohlberg, Lawrence. "Early Education: A Cognitive-Developmental View." *Child Development* 39 (1968): 1013–1062.

Piaget, Jean. *The Psychology of Intelligence*. New York: Harcourt, Brace & World, 1962.

Resnick, Lauren B.; Wang, Margaret C.; and Rosner, Jerome. "Adaptive Education for Young Children: Primary Education Project." In Mary Carol Day and Ronald K. Parker, eds., *The Preschool in Action*, 2nd ed. Boston: Allyn and Bacon, 1977.

Zimmerman, Barry J. "Modeling." In Harry L. Hom, Jr., and Paul A. Robinson, eds., *Psychological Processes in Early Education*. New York: Academic Press, 1977.

6 Sequencing Curriculum

Making new connections depends on knowing enough about something in the first place to be able to think of other things to do, of other questions to ask, which demand the more complex connections in order to make sense of it all. The more ideas a person already has at his disposal, the more new ideas occur, and the more he can coordinate to build up still more complicated schemes.[1]

Sequencing curriculum requires using some logical basis for deciding what comes next. It means that the teacher provides a series of learning activities based on some idea of order. The following vignettes typify the kind of problems that result when teachers we have worked with did not deal with sequencing considerations adequately.

> When an urban kindergarten class visited a large airline terminal, the plan was to observe the process of baggage handling. Instead, the children noted with delight a large number of telephone booths. Turning their backs on the luggage-handling operation, they entered the telephone booths and excitedly engaged in dialing and carrying on make-believe conversations with family and friends.

> A teacher of three-year-olds, seeking to demonstrate the effect of heat on snow, placed a snowball in a toaster oven and watched with the children as the snowball melted. The teacher was unprepared for the children's observation that the snow "disappeared." Although she told them, as well as showed them, that "snow turns to water when heated," the children seemed content with their magical explanation.

> After several weeks of experimenting with magnets, the four-year-olds continued to talk about their "magic" sticks and "superpower" weapons. The teacher's encouragement to find out more about the magnets failed to alter the children's conclusions or the focus of their experimentation.

> The teacher in the four-year-old group decided to initiate a discussion period to focus on sharing nonschool experiences with families and friends. His goal was to improve communication skills, both listening and speaking. Despite the fact that the children really "knew" they had to wait their turn to speak, there was chaos during each discussion period. The children began by competing to talk and eventually turned to their neighbors to find a listener. This meant that there were a dozen small group interactions going on instead of the planned conversation in the total group. After a number of attempts to focus the children's attention on the assigned speaker of the moment, the teacher finally abandoned the idea.

All four experiences may be analyzed as having some form of sequencing problem. When the kindergarten children at the airport preferred the telephones to the baggage handling, it may be inferred that:

---

1. Eleanor Duckworth, "The Having of Wonderful Ideas," *Harvard Education Review*, 42 (1972): 231.

- Children learn by doing, not by watching, and that is why they turned to something they could manipulate.

  or

- Children relate more to the familiar than to the unfamiliar, and telephones were familiar, while baggage handling systems were not.

  or

- The children did not have sufficient prior learning to give meaning to their observations of baggage handling so they could not gain much from continued observation.

Similarly, explanations for the three-year-olds' misunderstanding of melting snow may also vary:

- Young children's explanations of events are determined by what they understand of what they see, rather than by causal relationships. Magical thinking is common at this age.

  or

- The children did not know enough about cold snow and the hot oven to give meaning to what they saw.

The sequencing problems identified above tend to fall into three categories—the sequence is wrong or the activity is developed too soon because:

1. Children need more experiences or greater familiarity with parts of the new experience so that the total activity will not be completely new. *The activity is unfamiliar due to insufficient prior experience.*
2. Children need more knowledge to bring to the new experience to make sense out of what they are seeing. *They have insufficient prior knowledge.*
3. The children's stage of cognitive development is not at the level required by the goals of the activity. Specifically, they cannot relate the actions of the baggage handlers putting luggage on moving belts to a process they could neither see nor imagine—that is, loading the bags inside the airplane to accompany the travelers. *Their cognitive stage of development is not sufficiently advanced for the selected goals.*

In the example with the magnets, the children's apparent lack of growth in their conception of the magnet and its power can also be explained in these terms—insufficient experience, limited knowledge, inappropriate match with the children's level of cognitive development, or some combination of the three. In the example of the group discussion period, one can say that the children's level or stage of social-emotional development does not conform with the requirements of waiting to talk or being interested in another's experiences different from their own. That is, they cannot tune in, or stay tuned in, to their classmates' descriptions of personal experience, nor can they delay their own desire to talk about their own experiences.

Early childhood teachers, no matter what their views on knowledge, child development, and program form, face unique challenges in sequencing curriculum. One major reason for the difficulty in selecting an order for teaching-learning interactions rests on the immaturity of preschool children. In terms of content and developmental concerns, curriculum for three- to six-year-olds can include almost anything; they have almost everything to learn! In many areas of this broad scope of curriculum, however, it seems possible to construct order by applying rules of sequencing.

Most teachers approach the task of deciding what to teach next with an unconscious idea that an absolute sequence exists somewhere, if only they could find it. As they grow in knowledge and professional experience, they learn that this idea of an absolute order is a mirage. In reality, different sequences of instruction or curriculum content grow out of differing approaches to both knowledge and developmental theory. A teacher who views knowledge as essentially memorized information or an accumulation of facts will order curriculum sequences in a way quite different from one who defines knowledge as key concepts.

Programs that are process oriented—that is, concerned primarily with how children learn, not with products or outcomes—are often thought to free the teacher of the need to select knowledge or to sequence it in some way. Even though knowledge acquisition and skill development are not high-priority objectives in process-oriented programs, they must be approached in one way or another. In practice, the approach has tended to be pragmatic and intuitive, without too much concern for how selections were made.

You should note that, when adopting instead of constructing a curriculum package, teachers often assume there is no need to deal with sequencing problems since these decisions are already made by the curriculum designer. The teacher's role, in fact, is to judge whether the designer did a good job. Since there are few if any packaged curricula that are comprehensive for early childhood classrooms, teachers of young children are challenged to develop a basic understanding of how to sequence teaching plans and how to judge the usefulness of plans they are expected to follow.

Discussions of what to teach next and what order of instruction to follow in early childhood programs readily provoke confusion. Professionals hold different views of child development and learning, as we discussed in preceding chapters, and the implications for curriculum development are not always apparent. However, the task of making decisions about sequencing, while initially confusing, tends to highlight some aspects common to all views of development and content.

The next section will review some of the commonly accepted guidelines for sequencing, with illustrations from different perspectives. Sequencing guidelines generally require moving from concrete to abstract learning, from the simple to the complex, from facts to concepts, and from the known to the unknown.

Additionally, sequencing rules include progressing from imitation to creation, from exploration to problem solving, and from self-concentration to social skills.

CONTENT ORDER VERSUS DEVELOPMENTAL ORDER

Different views about what comes next in a program activity or instructional sequence can often be traced to the dilemma of logical content order versus developmental psychological order. Does the logic for sequencing stem from the apparent steps in the subject matter to be learned or from the order in which children develop understanding and build knowledge? While it is possible that sequences developed from the two perspectives may appear to be the same, it is not likely.

Take, for example, the content of geometry. In early childhood programs, the recognition of standard geometric shapes as being circular, rectangular, or triangular is a popular curriculum topic. Lines, spatial relationships, and directions are additional geometric concepts for young children. From the logic of the subject matter, geometric form begins with a point or position in space and proceeds to a connection of dots to create a line. The classes and subclasses of two-dimensional shapes are shown in Figure 6–1, illustrating the logical sequence of the content. From this perspective, the logic of the content would dictate starting from the initial dot, then proceeding to line, then to open and closed curves, and finally to standard geometric shapes.

From a developmental perspective, however, children seem to acquire concepts of shape by developing awareness of the attributes of similarities and differences in closed-curve forms. A developmental sequence for geometric shapes begins with comparing and matching circles and rectangles. First the children match identical shapes; then they sort varied shapes; finally they classify the shapes into categories.

FIGURE 6.1. Sequencing content by logical order: Geometric shapes

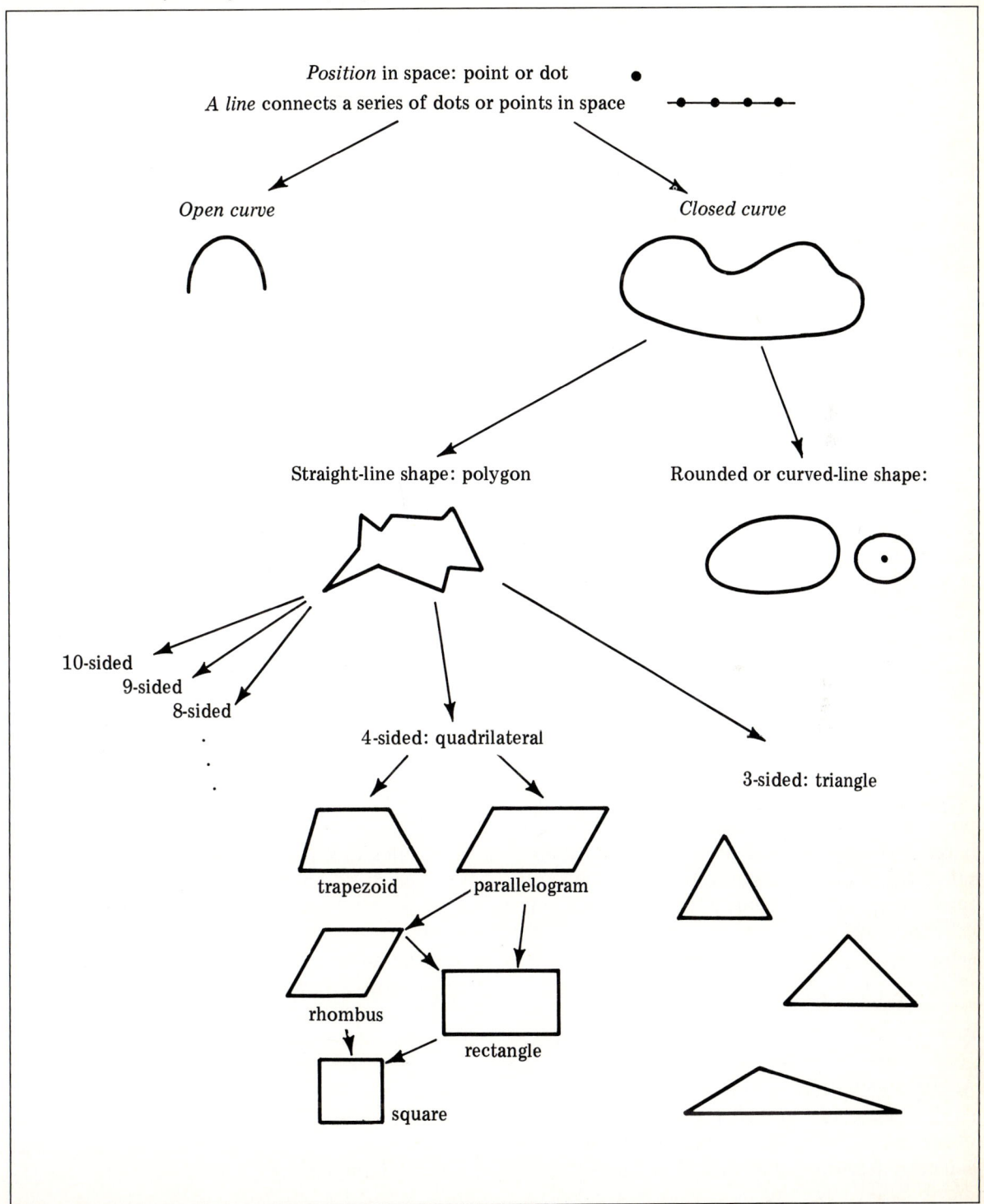

It is unlikely that any experienced early childhood teacher would teach young children geometry following the content sequence beginning with the dot. Nevertheless, the logical order of the content guides teaching decisions in many ways. For example, as shown in Figure 6–1, the class of four-sided figures is divided into subclasses. Square-shaped figures constitute the last subgroup in the sequence. This means that a square fits the definitions of rectangle, parallelogram, and quadrilateral. Since by definition a square is also a rectangle, these two shapes should be presented in an order that allows children to understand the relationship between the two and later to differentiate them. In the instance of geometry, developmental order guides the teacher in making appropriate selections from the content order.

In contrast, the order of number concepts for developing counting skills directly depends on numerical order. Children tackle counting tasks beginning with sets of one, then two, and so forth. Mastery of each successive counting task leads to the next larger set size.

The mathematics curriculum thus offers clear examples of sequence decisions that are dependent on both developmental and content concerns. Decisions in other curriculum areas pose the same challenges to the teacher, but since other subject areas are not as precise as mathematics, teachers need to find further guidelines to facilitate the decision-making process. A set of commonly used guidelines, based on research in learning theory, is usually taken for granted without much discussion and forms the basis for teachers' perceptions of the difference between "easier" and "harder," or sequence.

COMMON GUIDELINES FOR SEQUENCING

All approaches to teaching and learning require some review of children's progress and prior experiences to ascertain their readiness for selected learning activities and goals. Such review may be casual or formal. When children fail in a learning activity, the teacher inevitably considers whether there was a lack of interest or of prior experiences and understanding. This leads to a decision about which of the following to do and in what order: redesign the teaching-learning task, offer background experiences, revise the content, or wait for a more advanced cognitive stage. Diagnostic information is a key factor in ordering activities and content for almost all types of programs.

The idea of beginning where the child "is" implies movement from some specific point in a selected direction or sequence. There is no approach to curriculum that does not assume or follow some rules about starting where the child is and going on from that point. Such rules universally help teachers decide how to proceed from easier to harder learning tasks or activities. You are reminded that such decisions can be applied to a variety of curriculum forms, ranging from a happening to a planned program, in which specific kinds of learnings are identified at regular intervals, as described in Chapter 2.

The following rules apply whether the teachers choose the developmental view of the maturationist, the behaviorist, or the interactionist (as described in Chapter 5). To facilitate conceptualizing this group of rules, we have divided them into content and process, although most learning experiences deal with both, as indicated below in the following list. The rules that relate to content, or *what* children are to learn, are that:

1. Learning progresses from the concrete to the abstract. Concrete refers to the world of things and events, present and in view, while abstract refers to the world of symbols that stand for the real things, and ideas that represent or suggest things and events. It is easier to compare hardness and softness by touching a sponge and a block than by remembering things that are hard and soft.

2. Learning progresses from the simple to the complex. Complexity increases as the number of items, variables, or events increase. It is easier to work with five items than with fifteen. Complexity also increases as the difference between the variables reduces and becomes more subtle. It is easier to see the difference between a yardstick and a foot ruler than between two sticks 14 and 12 inches long.
3. Learning progresses from facts to concepts. Experiences challenge children to reconstruct concepts that no longer serve. Children's concepts grow as they understand relationships between objects or events. The concept of vehicles grows after the child has experienced different kinds of vehicles and as the range of images of objects considered to be vehicles increases.
4. Learning progresses from the known to the unknown. Experiences that are familiar and those that include only a few unknown facts accompanied by known facts are easier to process than experiences in which almost everything is new. New learning "hooks" onto what is known. In the airport experience described earlier, the children's preference for the telephones emphasized the need to start with familiar activities before introducing them to new, unfamiliar ones.

Rules that relate to processes, or *how* children learn, are that:

1. The learner progresses from exploration, to experimentation and hypothesis testing, and then to problem solving. New materials are examined to identify familiar and unfamiliar qualities before additional experimentation is developed to find out more. Ultimately the new knowledge is used to solve problems involving additional elements. After discovering how to hammer a nail into wood, a child can use this knowledge to solve a problem of attaching two pieces of wood.
2. The learner progresses from (1) imitation or copying observed objects and events, to (2) replication from memory, to (3) creation of new sets of objects or events. Imitation of observed events is easier than replication of events described but not seen.
3. The learner progresses from self-identity to perception of others. Experiences are processed first in terms of one's own feelings, perceptions, and understandings. How others might view the same experiences is more difficult to understand. Possessing before sharing is often seen at the clay table where the younger children monopolize all the tools before perceiving others' needs and desires for the same object.
4. The child is more likely to learn selected material if principles of practice are followed. Learning object labels, counting words, buttoning a coat, learning the lyrics and melody of a song, and learning a musical game are increasingly mastered through practice under conditions that produce success.
5. The learner is more likely to select and sustain practice activities when they are accompanied by reinforcement, either from internal or external sources. Children will choose to practice bouncing a ball, cutting with a scissors, and rolling up their blankets when such activities give them pleasure; that is, they are rewarded with a sense of accomplishment, mastery, and competence that results from internal satisfaction or external praise.
6. The child is more likely to learn selected material if there is variety in the tasks, methods, and materials. Using skills under more than one condition serves to stabilize the learning. For example, scissors mastery includes not only successful use of the tool with different materials but also appropriate selection of the tool for the task: a pair of scissors is not used to cut wood.

The following discussion of these rules illustrates how they affect the order of activities or of presenting curriculum content.

Concrete to Abstract

Focusing on concrete objects and actions before moving to symbols is a guideline followed almost automatically when teaching others. Classrooms for young children are filled with concrete materials, but the number of such materials is successively decreased for older pupils.

It should be especially emphasized that Piagetian developmental theory, behaviorist theory, and maturational theory are in accord on the young child's need to learn first from concrete objects before abstract forms of learning are introduced. However, each theory suggests different ways, ranging from child manipulation to adult demonstration with concrete objects. Piagetian theory requires the child to manipulate and experiment with concrete objects, while other approaches may require only teacher demonstration, object exhibits, or other uses for concrete materials.

Degrees to abstractness can be listed to guide the planning of instructional sequences. These levels, as listed in Table 6–1 indicate increasing distance between the concrete object and its symbolic forms. Some points identified on the continuum are the concrete level, such as a live dog; a life-sized replica, such as a stuffed dog; the representative symbol, such as the picture of the real thing; and the language symbol.

TABLE 6.1. Sequencing from concrete to abstract

Level	Example
Concrete: real objects in close proximity, to be touched and manipulated	Live dog[a]
Semi-concrete: three-dimensional representation	
• an object representing the real object, same size;	Life-size, realistic, stuffed dog, similar in color and texture
• miniature replica of real object;	Miniature dog—stuffed, plastic, or ceramic
• one object without visual similarity standing for another object.	Stuffed sock representing a dog.[b]
Symbolic:	
• two-dimensional, realistic representation of real object;	Photograph, picture, or drawing
• representative picture image;	Silhouette or similar image
• partial image evoking image of the object;	Drawing of tail suggesting a dog
• characteristic of object suggesting its image;	Imitation of movement or bark suggesting dog
• written language.	Manuscript for word *dog*

[a]This table does not attempt to reflect growth in classification thinking from a specific dog to the class of all dogs.

[b]By this point, the word *dog* is likely to be acquired but this form of abstraction is dependent also on language experiences and cognitive development.

As noted in Table 6–1 additional sequencing steps defining the movement from concrete to abstract include increasing the difference between the representation and the original object. With three-dimensional representation, this includes changing the size, color, texture, and degree of detail. With two-dimensional representation, the same pattern of movement from maximum detail, as in a photograph, to minimum as in a silhouette can be noted.

This sequence can be applied to children's growth from the action mode of learning, to working with representations, and finally to symbolization. That is, the easiest form of action to learn is one that is provided immediately in the present environment, such as demonstration. Increasing the distance from the concrete leads to verbal directions without a demonstration, illustrating a more abstract mode of learning.

Simple to Complex

Simple means having only one variable or one item to deal with at a time. *Complex* means having several factors to keep in mind simultaneously. When older children challenge each other to "pat the head and rub the stomach" at the same time, the participants are always surprised at the difficulty they have trying to do two simple actions simultaneously. The simplicity of each separate action does not diminish the difficulty that arises when focusing on both actions at the same time, which becomes a more complex task.

For young children, the example is equivalent to the difference between hopping on one foot and the more complex act of skipping. Hopping requires keeping one foot off the ground while bouncing the body up and down. Children need to focus on maintaining balance, keeping one foot up, and on producing the bouncing motion. This is a relatively difficult set of coordinated tasks for most three-year-olds. Skipping adds the variables of alternating the down foot, keeping one alternation to each bounce, and sliding with each bounce. A teacher who takes into account the simple-to-complex rule will plan developmental activities that add new variables only after the children have mastered the variables already presented. Three- and four-year-olds who cannot hop or who have yet to master the task of alternating their focus from one side of the body to the other, would not be asked to skip. If three-year-olds are still mastering the pattern of alternating feet when climbing stairs, the introduction of skipping activities would not offer an appropriate sequence. When appropriately sequenced, either by the children or the adults, growth in coordination is relatively rapid, as indicated by the fact that many primary children have developed so much physical coordination that they can ride two-wheel bicycles, a real achievement in balancing.

In contrast to the physical motor activity just described is the cognitive activity of patterning with concrete objects and symbols. Patterning activities that illustrate the simple-to-complex progression begin with one variable, for example, two different sets, each with identical objects that can be lined up in a single alternating pattern such as spoons and forks. When young children make bead necklaces, the simplest pattern emerges as two alternating colors: one yellow, one blue, one yellow, one blue, and so forth. The variable is color; the pattern is single alternation. Increasing complexity may include another color, producing a 1-by-1-by-1 pattern, such as red, white, and blue; red, white, and blue; and so on. There is still one variable—color—but now there are three dimensions of color. Or increasing complexity may include changing the number of items in the basic pattern, for example two yellow followed by two blue. The more variables the child has to keep in mind and the more dimensions of each variable, the more complex the task. Sequencing decisions require adding more variables *one at a time* as children demonstrate their ability and interest in new challenges.

Copying to Creating

Children perform many spontaneous behaviors that adults consider creative. This includes creating language, songs, and structures. It should be noted that many forms of simple activity, such as moving spontaneously to music or rhythm or creating pictures in any media, are easier for a child to create than to copy. However, these tend to be exploratory and personal, not instructional, tasks.

Children copy and create in the domains of (1) *physical actions*, such as hopping or washing a table with a sponge; (2) *manipulation and organization* of a set of materials to make a pattern or construct an object; and (3) *replication* of geometric forms, symbols, and pictures using plastic and graphic materials. While imitating and copying are vital activities for learning many behaviors, some actions are easier to copy than others. The task of successfully copying a simple arm swing, which is a two-part motion, is considerably easier than attaching a hinge to two pieces of wood, a multi-step process based on a conception that may not be understood by a young child.

This rule of copying-to-creating as a guide to sequencing learning almost always combines with other rules in process. For example, in developing competence with linear patterns, as previously discussed, the rule of *copying-to-creating* is combined with the rules of *simple-to-complex* and *concrete-to-abstract*, leading to the order outlined in Table 6-2. The first level of the task is to copy the pattern exactly, using concrete materials for both the model and the copy. Note that playful, exploratory activities in which children participate voluntarily and make their own tasks and discoveries would *precede* level one in most early childhood classrooms. This self-instructional form of playful activity is usually a necessary prerequisite to successful task completion in instructional sequences. Following self-directed manipulation of beads, the child might copy a bead-stringing pattern presented as a model at the table. The next level of the task is to copy a bead-stringing pattern from a picture of a pattern of beads. At this point, the task is made more *abstract* by the use of the picture to replace the concrete model. It is made more *complex* by the introduction of the picture as an additional variable, since the child needs to keep in mind that the items in the picture stand for the real objects. The child must also relate a two-dimensional picture to the three-dimensional beads.

There are many ways to increase the difficulty of the patterning activities, gradually moving to increasingly more complex patterns, toward more abstract patterns, or toward the creation of similar or analogous patterns. After the first step, a child may create a single alternating pattern with materials of his or her own choosing. Or the teacher may suggest changing the number of the units in the pattern from two to three. Sequencing considerations require that the introduction of new variables—such as number of items, level of abstractness, and the challenges of moving from copying to creating—be carefully paced in terms of children's mastery of simpler levels of the patterning activity. The child who creates a pattern demonstrates understanding of the concept of patterning.

A copying activity often developed in early childhood classrooms is setting the table for lunch. The major task of table setting is to distribute the same set of materials to all children or places at the table. The model to be copied is the complete set. Interestingly, teachers rarely view this as a copying activity because the model is assumed to be memorized. Unless a model is provided, such as one on a tray, there is none in view until the first setting is com-

SEQUENCING CURRICULUM

TABLE 6.2. Examples of sequences in linear patterning

Linear Patterning: Using rule of simple-to-complex, increase the number of variables, number of items, and the differences in variables.
Using rule of copying-to-creating, proceed from direct copying to copying from memory, to creating.
Using rule of concrete-to-abstract, provide a model pattern of objects, then a picture pattern.

Level of difficulty	Task
1 set of tongue depressors and 1 set of cotton balls *for model* and *for copy of model*	Make a two-item pattern (single alternation): • stick, ball; stick, ball Next make a three-item pattern: • stick, stick, ball; stick, stick, ball
Increase complexity: • by adding another set of objects; • or by using different-sized sticks, decreasing difference in variables; • or by increasing physical distance between the model and the place to copy the model.	Make a three-item pattern: • block, stick, ball Alternate the pattern: • big stick, little stick; big stick, little stick Place pattern on one tray at side of table, with copy to be made on another tray on other side of table.
Increase complexity: • by increasing size of pattern unit or length of pattern; • or by decreasing differences in variables; • or by increasing distance between model and copy; • or by using pictorial representation for the model; • or by using word symbols	Use three objects in a four-item pattern: • ball, block, ball, stick; ball, block, ball, stick Use three shades of red strips of paper or fabric. Cover model with cloth or tray before making copy. Provide a picture of a pattern to be copied with objects. Use word cards to describe patterns: • dog, man, clog, man

plete. Identifying a logical sequence for developing children's competence in table setting also requires combining the copying rule with the simple-to-complex rule.

The simplest activity in table setting is dealing with only one variable; consequently, the procedure of having one child distribute napkins while another child distributes cups maintains the basic simplicity, with children copying the actions of distributing one object for one person. At the other end of the continuum, the most complex level of table setting is replicating a series of place settings from memory, including being accurate in the number of items and the position of items. Here the table setter places napkins, forks, and spoons in prescribed positions related to the plate, left and right, from memory. The sequence of learning—from the simple, repetitive behavior of handing out one item to each person to the more complex behavior of replicating an ordered set of five or six items from memory—obviously requires activities that allow steady growth in table-setting skills. There is need to plan for increasing the difficulty of the tasks at a pace at which children will succeed.

One suggested sequence for table setting, as shown in Table 6-3, features balancing the increase in number of items, position of items, and distance from the model. Note that the sequence from close proximity to the model to no visible model is an important step in moving from copying to replicating from memory.

Teaching Suggestions Using Common Guidelines

Teachers have ideas that are often assumed but not stated about the differences between *easier* and *harder*. These ideas are frequently used in planning selected segments of the program but are rarely applied as a continuing guide for selecting content.

Ideas of progressions of difficulty such as *concrete-to-abstract*, *simple-to-complex* and *copying-to-creating* can be applied more easily to specifically planned instructional periods that occur daily than to unique classroom situations. It is difficult to use these rules when interacting with children "on one's feet" during free-choice activity periods or when the children are "doing their own thing." Programs in which these activity or play periods constitute a major portion of the daily schedule pose the greatest challenge to teachers to remember or reconstruct the rules defining logical sequences in learning processes and tasks. However, teachers who systematically follow these rules find that more and more "instant responses" will embody them.

TABLE 6.3. Sequencing tasks for table setting

Distribute *one item*, napkins or cups, to *two to four children, at one table*, after teacher distributes the first item as a model.

Increase the *number of items* or the *number of children* to be served:
- Examples: two tables and one item, such as napkins for twelve children, *or* one table and two items, such as napkins and cups for six children

Teacher gives verbal directions.

Table setter matches items at each chair without children present at the table.
- Example: one napkin at one chair

Teacher places first item as model at one table.

Increase the *number of tables* or *the number of items*.
- Examples: with model only at first table, napkins placed at chairs of two tables *or* napkins and cups placed at each setting of one table with model of setting given by teacher and order of setting unimportant

Increase *number of items in set*, and *establish some order*, by model.
- Example: one plate with napkins and utensils on plate
  Later: one plate with napkin next to plate and utensils on napkins

Create ordered set, first following verbal instructions and then responding from memory and without instructions.
- Examples: as above.

Increase detail of position to include standard table setting as desired. Copy model, then reproduce from memory.

The same challenge to sequence systematically exists with the daily routines of the classroom. Since sequencing requires identifying the child's level of development, achievement, or both to select the next steps, decisions for children must vary with individual differences. Procedures for routines based on one standard for all children ignore such individual differences. For example, if a classroom rule requires instantly ceasing all activity at a given signal, such as a piano chord, several children will usually be out of bounds because of their developmentally slower pace of achieving so much self-control.

Using the classes of content from Chapter 4 as a framework, illustrative applications of these guidelines will be discussed in the next section. You might keep in mind that teaching skills for coordinating both content and process guidelines grow with practice in sequencing and in observing the outcomes and comparing them to expectations. The final section of this chapter will review the implications developmental stages have for sequencing decisions.

SEQUENCING FACT ACCUMULATION

Fact accumulation content features specific and describable learning. Typically, such learning includes colors, seasonal weather information, facts about animals, vehicles, and growing things. The task of sequencing fact accumulation appears self-evident at first, since children seem merely to be collecting facts for later use. In reality, choosing an order for fact aquisition raises the question of what distinguishes facts from concepts. A concept is more complex than a fact and may occur later in the learning sequence. Logic, psychological theory, and research all suggest that it is best to sequence instruction from facts to concepts.

An excellent sample of the fact-concept relationship, which is often omitted in curriculum decisions, is found in teaching colors. As Table 6–4 shows, naming an object *red* is factual learning. Labeling as red a set of objects having many shades of red requires a concept of redness more complex than knowing a single shade of red. Sequencing considerations would require that children know many different shades of red to succeed in sorting a mixed-color collection.

Teaching Implications of Fact Accumulation

Some of the popular color-learning activities in early childhood classrooms include:

1. Making color books or collages by pasting different samples of the same color on a page. These samples may come from pre-cut shapes, collections of fabric, paper, cardboard, or magazine clippings.
2. Using color as a cue for games or for transitional periods in the program. This includes lotto-type games and other board games that use color markings. In transitions, clothing colors are used as cues to control the number of children moving from one space to another.

Using *content* as a basis for ordering as described in Table 6–4 the arts-and-craft activity requires beginning with a preselected set of swatches of one primary color. Then later other colors are added one at a time until the primary colors (red, blue, and yellow) and black and white are learned. Complementary colors come next. Finally, different shades of a color may be introduced uniformly by using pastel shades, primary colors plus white; then primary colors plus black. In this case, *simple-to-complex* means increasing the number of colors, then adding mixed colors in measured steps.

TABLE 6.4. Sequencing fact accumulation: Colors

Based on logic of the content	Based on logic of how children process learning
Name and use one color at a time, primary colors first, one hue for each color.	With two colors of objects or swatches for comparison and contrast, match same and different colors. Use primary and complementary colors with vibrant hues first. Labels are acquired in use.
Name and use different hues of same color, using only primary colors.	Sort by colors, first one hue of each color and then different hues of same color, using objects or color swatches. Then label them.
Name and mix complementary colors. Learn how to make complementary colors by applying rules of color mixing, for example, mix red and yellow to make orange.	Classify colors based on primary color and hues and then label them.
	Generate rules by creating or mixing colors.

Using *process* as a basis for ordering, the learning activity begins with *matching* objects for color value. *Simple-to-complex* in this case means beginning with easily matched colors, having little variation in hue and a limited number of sets. Later, the number of colors increases and more variation in color and hue is included. Matching is followed by *sorting* tasks, using first identical colors and then similar colors. *Classifying*, or *grouping*, many shades of the same color is the most advanced level. The use of magazine clippings and color cues that are available by chance such as on clothing, is only appropriate at this advanced level.

How can teachers tell which children have mastered one level and are ready for the next step in the sequence? The following indicators differentiate the children's level of learning about color:

- When color, such as redness, is used as a cue for children to move for a particular purpose, some children respond immediately, while others, who should move, sit waiting for further information.

- When color is used as a cue for a game, some children claim incorrectly that somebody moved who was not wearing the "right" color. This reaction suggests the color of the clothing did not match some notion they had about the color.

These informal indicators flag children who may not be ready for the next step in the sequence. Of course, teachers can always make more systematic evaluations at major decision points in sequencing.

SEQUENCING SKILL ACCUMULATION

The variety of skills that teachers of young children value fall primarily into three categories: psychomotor, academic, and social skills. The *motor skills* include *gross motor control*, as in the physical activities of running, jumping, skipping; and *fine motor control*, as in using tools for crafts, drawing, and writing, and in constructing with interlocking toys and small building units. The *academic skills*, while often dependent on the motor skills, include such familiar school learning as reading, writing, arithmetic, and oral language skills. The *social skills* include not only taking turns, sharing, respecting the rights of others, and sharing in group responsibilities, but also those skills of personal grooming and care such as dressing, toileting, and personal cleanliness.

The primary goal in skill accumulation is acquiring automatic performance; that is, developing the skill so well as to perform it without thinking, as if it were a habit. This accomplishment, often labeled *overlearning*, is exemplified when a child writes his name while continuing to talk to his friend, or when a child ties her shoes while continuing to look at a picture in a book, glancing at the shoe-tying task only periodically. Although skills tend to be categorized as motor, social, or academic, all skill development encompasses some mastery of body movement, some understanding of the elements of the skill, and the ability to relate the steps in the skill to the total process. Perception, cognition, physical development, and motor coordination are interlocked in skill mastery. To illustrate this, we will examine the sequence considerations of cutting with a pair of scissors (primarily a motor task) and name writing (an academic skill).

Scissors Skills

The skill of cutting with a pair of scissors is usually considered a motor skill. However, an analysis of this skill reveals that there are important cognitive components to this learning task. The motor task of manipulating the tool is combined with the cognitive task of identifying how the movement of the scissors affects the direction of the cuts on the paper.

The simple-to-complex guideline is not confined to the motor-coordination task. It can also apply to helping children understand the relationship between how the scissors handles are moved and what paper cuts result. For example, making a right-angle cut requires combining the two motions of cutting and turning while controlling the direction of the turn.

The sequence of developing scissors skills begins with the open-close motor task: the child must first grasp the relationship between the tool and the snip cuts that result from opening and closing it. Watch a young child who is first discovering how scissors work, and you will realize how complicated the task is. Note how slowly beginning cutters adjust the way they hold the pair of scissors and the process by which they figure out how to manipulate it. Between the first step and the more complex task of cutting out a picture requiring frequent changes in direction, curves, and angle cuts are a series of steps, outlined in Table 6–5. Complexity is increased by adding other motor tasks and cognitive tasks for the child to control simultaneously. For example, step two combines the cutting movement with the task of severing a piece of paper. The third step adds the variable of following a drawn line.

Often children's understanding of a process exceeds the required motor skill. Varying responses then occur, ranging from task perseveration in practice activities to avoidance of frustration by asking others to do it for them or by discarding the task. Sequencing motor-skill mastery usually reduces such avoidance behaviors.

In an urban kindergarten class, where a group of four children were drawing and cutting independently of the teachers, the task the children identified for themselves included drawing human figures and then cutting them out. Two of the four children were unsuccessful in the task, always failing to meet their own standards for cutting out the figures. Within a ten-minute period, these two children threw away at least five "failures" without ever discovering how to adapt their drawings, simplify the cutting task, or cut around the figure as if it were framed. A teacher

TABLE 6.5. Sequencing scissors skills

Motor skills *Logic of action sequences*	*Cognitive skills* *Logical sequence of processing*
1. Snips of paper: simple open-close movement of scissors on paper.	1. Concept of relationship between snipping motions and cutting process.
2. Repeated snips: severing a paper segment of random shape.	2. Concept of the severed paper as a product of the cutting motions.
3. Cutting on a short line (a) requiring two to three snips, (b) gradually cutting on a longer line requiring seven to eight cuts. Motor control is required to stay on line.	3. Concept of direction of cuts, and need to follow the line for straight cutting.
4. Cutting a corner: (a) making two cuts at 90° angle; (b) cutting a simple curved, continuous line such as a circle. Motor control is required to change direction.	4. Concept of following a line and change of direction of cutting, as line changes direction.
5. Cutting a simple geometric figure: three straight lines and three corners, or four lines and corners, or a circle, or an oval. Motor control combines following a line and changing direction.	5. Concept of a geometric shape and the perimeter line, and of directionality.
6. Cutting simple figure with both curved and straight lines. Motor control involves changing from curved-line cutting to straight-line cutting.	6. Concept of nonstandard as well as standard geometric shapes. Concept of boundary lines and directionality.
7. Cutting interior angles (inside angle less than 90°). Motor control requires direction of change and acute angles.	7. Concept of interior and exterior. Concepts of shape, boundary lines, directionality.
8. Cutting complex figures with curves, straight lines, obtuse and acute angles. Motor control includes all cutting skills.	8. Concepts of outline of familiar objects, of boundary lines and interior and exterior, and of directionality.

helping these two children to succeed would need to know first where in the developmental sequence the children were before matching instructional steps to their needs.

Early childhood curriculum activities ordered in terms of difficulty in cutting skills are:

1. making collages and carrying out activities in which children choose materials for cutting, pasting, or both, without a predetermined end-product;
2. decorating craft projects by cutting and pasting, similar to collage making but decorating a specific object;
3. cutting predrawn shapes such as hearts, triangles, and circles for class projects and seasonal activities;
4. making picture books by cutting out pictures from magazines.

Making collages usually offers children the most opportunity to function at their own level with a pair of scissors. Decorating craft projects, depending on the degree of teacher direction and the variety of materials provided, may also permit children to use a pair of scissors at their own level and to develop skills at their own pace.

It is more difficult to follow a line made by another person than it is to make cutting decisions as you go. Consequently, the task of cutting out shapes is more likely to challenge developmental levels. Magazine cutting poses the most difficult challenge because there is no control over the shape of the picture the children may select for cutting. If one child chooses to cut out a picture of a giraffe, his or her potential for failure is as great as it is for those kindergarten children described above who were unable to cut out their own drawings. To succeed in this task, the child needs to be at level seven on Table 6–5, able to cut interior angles less than 90 degrees.

Teachers wishing to use increasingly complex cutting tasks as a means of encouraging children to progress through a sequence can provide measured steps, adding difficulty or complexity when children can handle it. Teachers who do not wish to prescribe cutting activities have the same need to understand the sequence to help children to find tasks at which they can succeed.

Name Writing Skills

Writing one's name is an academic skill often highly valued in programs for five-year-olds (and sometimes younger children) and primary-grade children are expected to master it well. As a skill, it clearly includes more than the motor skill of holding and moving the writing tool. As shown in Table 6–6, there are at least five separate skills and levels of understanding used in the task of writing words, specifically one's name. Identifying the necessary prerequisites for learning serves to guide decisions on timing the introduction of name writing. Reviewing children's progress in terms of the prerequisite skills and comprehension often helps the teacher discover children who may have learning disabilities due to perceptual distortions, insufficient development of orientation in space, psychomotor control, or some combination of the three. While teachers may not be specialists in diagnosing learning disabilities, the practice of reviewing does help the teacher find those tasks at which the children can succeed. If the child fails to develop the necessary prerequisite skills, the teacher is alerted to seek expert evaluation.

Prerequisite skill and understanding often identified for name writing include concepts of directionality, ordered relationships of items in a series along a horizontal plane, positional concepts such as "next to," the distinction between open and closed curves, and perceptual clarity of letter and word forms. Also included are those skills related to tool control, such as small-muscle and eye-hand coordination sufficiently developed to hold the writing tool and produce the basic strokes.

Using the child's name as the first experience in writing features the rules of moving from self-identity to awareness of others. Two perspectives on the order of difficulty from easiest to hardest reflect the content and process approaches discussed earlier. In this instance, the content approach involves recognizing and naming the alphabet letters before learning to write them. The process approach features matching like letters; matching like sets of letters, as in one's name; copying simple circle and like shapes; and then copying letters. Ultimately, in the process approach, the letters are copied in order from a model and finally from memory.

Methods of teaching writing skills range from formal practice periods to spontaneous acquisition through children's choices or self-imposed tasks. Each extreme on the continuum poses problems for sequencing. The formalized practice periods tend to ignore the sequences noted in Table 6–6 that offer logical steps to letter formation and word writing. On the other hand, the naturalistic approach fails

TABLE 6.6. Sequencing skill development in name writing

Prerequisite learning: Direction	
Directionality in two-dimensional space: *top to bottom, left to right*	
Positional terms in two-dimensional space: *next to, first, last, in-between*	
Distinction between *open and closed curves, straight and curved lines.*	

Name-writing sequences	
Content base	*Process base*
Recognize and label alphabet letters, learning one letter at a time.	Match individual letters, using letters of one's name, order of matching irrelevant.
Distinguish one's own written name from others in a set of written names.	Match a set of letters to a name card using same-size script.
Write letters of a name, learning one at a time.	Copy letters of name from name card.
Master each letter before adding the next letter. Letters are copied from a model.	Practice writing letters of one's name.
Write name from memory.	Write name from memory.

to identify steps the children have omitted that are likely to help them write their names successfully.

Indicators during formal practice that children are skipping some steps or are moving to successive steps too soon are that they:

1. disregard the line,
2. shape letters incorrectly,
3. write letters out of order,
4. omit some letters.

For each one of these errors, children lack necessary prior skills and concepts. For example, when the letter *P* is formed by placing a circle at the bottom of the line rather than at the top and an *H* is formed by placing the crossing line at the top of the two parallel lines, the positional concepts of top and bottom have not been mastered. Children need to develop these missing concepts *prior* to name-writing practice. Without such prior learning, children may be seriously overloaded with too many instructions to follow at the same time.

Similarly, in a naturalistic or informal approach to name writing, in which teachers expect children's awareness and interest to guide self-teaching, indicators of the need for foundational learning activities can also be noted. These include:

1. children who persistently avoid name writing by requesting that the teacher "write my name because I can't";
2. children who over a period of time fail to recognize that they are leaving out letters of their name or are forming letters incorrectly or out of order;
3. children who seem to believe that any symbols stand for any name.

For the very young, name writing is not a natural activity, if you consider the conceptual and motor skills required, as well as their interests or needs. When awareness and interest begin, concerns for sequencing are appropriate.

Try to imagine the young child's puzzlement during an instructional activity, when, faced with a horizontal page on a desk or floor, the teacher says:

1. "Put your pencil at the top of the page." *Where is the top of a flat surface?*
2. "Start at the left and then move to the right." *Am I sure which is left?*
3. "Be sure to hold your paper straight." *How do I know if it's straight?*
4. "Some letters are small and some are tall. Be sure to write them that way."*What way?*
5. "Stay on the line." *How?*

These are all positional concepts young children have to learn to write legibly. When needed concepts are learned and motor skills are developed through successful practice, children enjoy feelings of achievement.

SEQUENCING IN SUBJECT AREAS AND ACADEMIC DISCIPLINES

Subject areas and academic disciplines pose many sequencing challenges. Subjects, which are convenient ways to organize content for teaching, may overlap with disciplines, as for example when arithmetic changed to the "new mathematics." Arithmetic is now viewed in two ways: (1) the traditional subject that includes such operations as addition and subtraction, or (2) a branch of mathematics, an academic discipline in which the concepts of the discipline are the foundations for mastering arithmetic procedures.

In early childhood, the subject of reading usually begins with prereading skills, such as visual and auditory discrimination, vocabulary, language meanings, perceptual-motor skills, picture reading, and symbol reading. The sequence of instructional activities for these prereading skills requires application of the simple-to-complex and concrete-to-abstract rules.

Auditory discrimination depends on the ability to discriminate likenesses and differences in sounds. Textbooks on teaching reading feature phonics or discrimination of word and letter sounds as the primary task in auditory discrimination. However, reading readiness texts also include discrimination of environmental sounds.

One exhaustive list of targeted, or desired, auditory discrimination skills, for a reading readiness program summarized by Marion Monroe, includes the following qualities of sound:[2]

1. Intensity: changes in loudness and softness of sounds help children become aware of meanings that can be acquired from varying intensity.
2. Pitch: High and low changes contribute to meanings of language.
3. Timbre: The ability to distinguish one source of sound from another helps screen out unimportant sounds.
4. Duration and sequence: Meaning grows out of sequence of sounds within a word and words within a sentence.

Monroe emphasizes the importance of sequencing from natural, or environmental, sounds; to vocal sounds; and finally, to word sounds.

Other sequences identified in the literature feature awareness or reception of sound, producing sound or motor responses to specific sound cues, reproducing sound patterns from memory, and finally, discriminating word and letter sounds.[3] Still other writers advocate a sequence that begins with phonics.

A sequence of activities for increasing auditory discrimination, beginning with natural sounds in the environment and culminating with language sounds, might be designed as follows:

2. Marion Monroe, *Growing into Reading* (New York: Scott, Foresman, 1951), pp. 110–139.
3. George Spache, *The Teaching of Reading* (Bloomington, Ind.: Phi Delta Kappa, 1972), pp. 24–25.

Activity Sequence	Explanation

1. Given a sound made by objects from a small collection, the child produces the same sound with similar objects:
  a. striking two wooden blocks;
  b. rubbing two pieces of sandpaper together;
  c. shaking two bell bracelets.
	All information is sensory and present. Object labels are not necessary when they are presented concretely. However, use of concrete objects greatly facilitates naming.

2. Add objects to the collection and maintain the matching task:
  a. striking: add two metal rods;
  b. rubbing: add two pieces of aluminum foil;
  c. shaking: add two small shaker cans containing sand or rocks.
	Increasing complexity in only one area by adding items and maintaining gross differences in sounds.

3. Continue the matching task, incorporating labels as an intervening step to word matching sounds: offer the cue sound, predict which object will match the sound, and then test the prediction.	Moving along the continuum from the concrete to the abstract; encouraging use of images of objects; making sounds.
4. Continue the matching task, placing the cue object out of view when providing the sound to be matched. Maintain labeling procedure.	Moving toward abstract when image is to be recalled from memory and labeled.
5. Use tape recording of sounds made by objects in the collection, as for steps 1 and 2 above. Match recorded sound with sound of object selected from the collection.	Transferring focus from objects to sounds through use of recordings; subordinating visual to auditory stimuli.

6. Introduce games using paired sound cues, same and different, such as in physical games in which the players "run if the sounds are the same," and "jump if the sounds are different."
  a. use familiar objects for cues,
  b. use unfamiliar objects,
  c. use words,
  d. use nonsense sounds,
  e. use phonic sounds.
	Adding the negative variable of "not-the same"; adding language sounds from words to phonics.

This sequence applies the simple-to-complex rule through (1) increasing the number of items, (2) decreasing the difference between the sound cues, (3) expanding the variables to include "not the same," and finally, (4) introducing physical responses to the cues. The concrete-to-abstract rule is applied as the cues are moved farther away from the child—at first in view, then hidden from view, and finally not present.

Auditory discrimination activities occur in spontaneous and planned ways almost daily in early childhood classrooms. Teachers may use spontaneous occurrences, such as the sounds of a fire engine siren, for further auditory discrimination. Where the cues are not present, such as the fire engine that is heard but not seen and that cannot be returned to view, the children who cannot distinguish fire engine sirens from other similar sounds (essentially at level one or two) are dependent on the adult's identification. Good sequencing should serve to reduce children's need to accept what the adult says is "right." Children can test their own hunches as they develop reliable skills of auditory discrimination.

KEY CONCEPTS AS A BASIS FOR SEQUENCING

The key concepts or big ideas in each discipline may be another way to organize instructional sequences. Jerome Bruner, who popularized this view in the early sixties, also proposed a spiral approach to these big ideas, coordinating the knowledge or content sequences with cognitive stages, so that at each successive stage the child would be dealing with concepts she or he could understand, but in greater complexity than before.[4] The key concepts do not change, but the child's development permits learning to proceed at a more advanced, challenging, or complex level than before. The disciplines are studied in increasingly greater detail and depth, using more sophisticated procedures of inquiry.

Each body of knowledge is regarded as having key concepts that give it its identifiable structure, together with distinctive forms of inquiry or ways of knowing. Relationships, laws, principles governing the key concepts are also included.

---

4. Jerome Bruner, *The Process of Education* (Cambridge, Mass.: Harvard University Press, 1966).

Key ideas, arranged in terms of curriculum order and structure, are the basis for sequencing learning activities. One example of sequencing a key idea is suggested below. The next section will suggest some ways of developing these key ideas.

Topics: Force, motion, speed, and distance on an inclined plane.

Key Idea 1: Some objects move down an inclined plane without a push or observable force, while others require force.
Speed of movement varies.
Distance of movement varies.

Key Idea 2: There are identifiable attributes of objects and planes that affect speed and distance.
- Attributes of the object include movable parts with curved or straight edges, the shape of wheels, and the surface texture of wheels.
- Attributes of the plane include the angle of the plane and the surface texture of the plane.

Key Idea 3: The degree of starting force affects speed and distance of movement.

Key Idea 4: The speed and distance of movement can be altered by changing any of the attributes of the object or the plane or by changing the intensity of the starting force.

Teaching Key Concepts in Physics

Sequencing content as key concepts is first a matter of finding learning activities that are developmentally appropriate for the concepts to be learned. Next comes identifying steps of increasing complexity. An activity sequence that might develop from the listing of key ideas concerning force, motion, speed, and distance is as follows:

1. In the block area, as children construct inclined planes, provide a collection of objects to "go down the plane," including some with wheels, curved edges (like a paper towel roll), flat edges (like small blocks or boxes), and balls. Encourage children to compare the way the objects move, how fast, and how far.
2. Select two different objects, one with wheels and one with straight edges, and place them at the top of the inclined plane together. Watch the movement.
3. Encourage children to test objects to find which move at the same speed, different speeds, the same distance, or different distances with additional force.
4. Invite children to sort the objects tested in terms of whether they move fast or slow, whether they need starting force or not, and how far they move beyond the base of the plane.
5. Try to find a way to make objects stop at a specific mark on the plane, at the foot of the plane, and at a distance from the plane. Experiment with starting force.
6. Experiment with different planes, using different materials and changing the angles.
7. Find real-life planes such as park slides, ramps, and sloped street curbs.

In each of these instances, the teacher-initiated activity is dependent on two factors—the interest of the children in the targeted learning activity, and the observed developmental capacity to deal with the cognitive task offered. The key-concept approach to defining next steps in the sequence requires close coordination with children's activity interests and cognitive functioning. If, for example, children are stacking blocks and exploring weight and balance, it would be inappropriate to initiate the activities previously listed that relate to force, speed, distance, and motion. Instead, a series of explorations centering on key ideas of weight and balance would be in order.

Teachers who choose to develop key ideas through a series of daily teacher-initiated activities, without waiting until children spontaneously demonstrate interest, are bound by the rules of simple-to-complex and concrete-to-abstract. The following section lists key ideas in music and illustrates a model sequence that occurs when teachers plan regular instructional periods for cumulative learning.

Sequence of Key Ideas in Music

Some key concepts for early childhood learning in music are:[5]

Rhythm:	Beat
	Parts of a beat
	Accent
	Meter
	Shape
	Patterns
	Rests
Tempo:	Fast-slow
	Same-different
Design:	Repetition
	Contrast
Melody:	Pitch
	Direction
	Shape
	Parts
Dynamics:	Soft-loud
	Accent
	Changes
Tone Quality:	Raw sounds
	Nonpitched percussion
	Pitched percussion
	String instruments
	Winds
	Brasses
	Piano, organ

Applying child development theory to this key-concepts approach might yield the following sequence of learning activities over a period of weeks and months:

1. Echo the child's chant and rhythmic movement.
2. Follow the child's beat and rhythm on a drum or other rhythm instrument.
3. Offer a beat or rhythm for the child to follow with movement, song, or other rhythm instruments.
4. Select songs in the C to G range in the middle of the piano.
5. Accept singing at any level of skill, working for even closer approximations of the melody; that is, up, down, or flat on the scale.
6. Sing songs the child knows and likes.
7. Introduce new songs in a narrow, middle range and repeat often.
8. Introduce new songs in slightly wider range—from one note below middle C to one note above G above middle C.
9. Initiate clapping the beat or rhythm of songs, musical selections, or dances.
10. Initiate differentiating the rhythm of the melody from the basic beat.
11. Initiate rhythm band control: starting and stopping, entering on cue; waiting for the downbeat; stopping on signal; playing or beating in the requested rhythm.
12. Initiate child-controlled creative rhythms in movement and dance.
13. Play recorded or live music for musically controlled rhythm for movement and dance.
14. Request elaborated movement to musically controlled rhythm.
15. Help children sing well-known songs on pitch, in rhythm, and with the correct words.

A coordinated sequence emerges that builds slowly on both developmental progress and processes and on music concept development and that reflects the child's growing ability to penetrate musical knowledge.

THEMES AS A BASIS FOR CURRICULUM SEQUENCING

As a class of content, themes pose some difficulty in making sequence decisions, since themes include a wide variety of curriculum activities that integrate or alternate focus on classes of content. Consequently, the teacher needs to apply the rules to each activity included in the theme and be aware of the range of content classes already discussed. The application of sequencing principles to theme activities leads to a diagnostic overview of children's prior experiences, their fact accumulation, skill development, and concept acquisition.

The seasons in temperate climates often serve as a basis for themes in early childhood classrooms. Autumn themes include a variety of activities related to collecting and studying leaves and their color change, observing animal behavior outdoors, and discovering the meaning of the harvest season. Spring themes include the renewal of the growth cycle, the change in the landscape, and related changes in people's lifestyles to include outdoor living. Planting activities are traditional within the context of this theme. The analysis of two seasonal activities—planting seeds and preserving leaves by storing them in waxed-paper frames—illustrate an approach to sequencing through the review of prerequisite knowledge. Note that the first activity, leaf preserving, is very popular in five-year-old classrooms, although we, along with many teachers, might prefer other, less hazardous tasks (this one requires a hot iron) and with more possibilities for children's choices. This review should serve to warn teachers that this activity could be dropped for a different one if the children's readiness is not apparent.

The following analysis has two parts. The first part reviews the many mistaken notions children may develop during an activity if the teaching does not take into consideration their prior experiences. The second part details learning sequences that build in the necessary prerequisite learning before initiating the activity in question.

Example of a Thematic Activity: Preserving Leaves

A walking trip in the neighborhood or to the local park to collect leaves during the fall season is usually prerequisite for this activity. A series of classroom experiences often follows the initial trip in which the children examine the leaves, grouping and regrouping the collection according to identified properties. The culminating activity involves ironing the leaves between sheets of waxed paper.

Prerequisite activities, experiences, and understanding No matter what perspective on sequencing is taken, a prior series of activities related to the properties of (1) wax and waxed paper, (2) leaves, and (3) heat transformations is indicated. Ironing on waxed paper without understanding the relationships between electric iron, wax, and heat can lead to a variety of mistaken notions. Such mistaken notions might be:

1. The iron is magic.
2. All paper, not just waxed paper, sticks together when ironed.
3. All leaves get sticky when ironed.
4. A tree will grow between the pieces of waxed paper where the leaf is kept.

Prior experiences are required for this new experience to be understandable and the causal relationships to become clear:

1. *Changes in wax.* The waxed paper will be transformed by heat. The heat source will be an iron. When the waxed paper is transformed, the changes children can see are restricted to the adherence of the two pieces of paper. They do not see the melting and resolidification of the wax since the iron blocks the view. The teacher may seek to explain this phenomenon but the explanation is likely to have little meaning.
2. *The iron.* For a young child, prior experience with an iron is usually confined to watching an adult at home use one to smooth out wrinkles in clothes. If this prior experience is used as a basis for understanding the present activity, the child will attempt to focus on smoothness after ironing. The waxed paper is very smooth after ironing, but it also was smooth before ironing. The meaning to the child is thus elusive.
3. *Preservation of objects.* The idea of encasing a leaf between two pieces of paper to preserve it introduces an experience of preserving things that is quite foreign to most young children. The use of food wraps to protect food from drying out or becoming stale may be the closest experience they have to preserving. However, the leaf is already dry, and the similarity of preserving by reducing contact with the air is not likely to be understood.

This analysis reveals that there is a series of experiences needed for foundational learning prior to introducing this activity. Planning for learning sequences removes this activity from the realm of entertainment and places it within a scheme of orderly development of learning based on content order, learning theory, and developmental stages. Table 6–7 defines an order or sequence. Variations occur as the teacher emphasizes one basis of sequencing over others. You should note that a hot iron is a source of danger with young children, especially those who have difficulty conforming to safety rules.

TABLE 6.7. Activity sequences leading to preserving leaves in waxed paper

There are three streams of activity that precede preserving leaves by ironing between two pieces of waxed paper: each stream is independent.

Wax	Leaves	Heat transformations
1. Melt wax candle by heating in a saucepan, dripping wax into non-uniform shape. • *Learning*: Wax turns to liquid when heated by fire and solidifies when heat is removed. It returns to original state but not original shape.	1. Collect leaves and let them stand at room temperature. Note drying out, brittleness, and cracking of leaves. • *Learning*: When leaves fall off the trees, they dry out and become brittle.	1. Identify sources of heat. Sort or group those sources that people can control. • *Learning*: Heat comes from a number of sources.
2. Melt wax candle and drop an object into the liquid wax before it solidifies. Examine wax with encased object. Immerse waxed object and experiment for wetness. • *Learning*: Wax protects an object from becoming wet.	2. Try storing leaves under different conditions to delay or inhibit drying out for example, in a paper bag, plastic bag, plastic food wrap, or aluminum foil. • *Learning*: Drying of leaves varies under different conditions.	2. Experiment with heat transformations of solid to liquid, using such materials as ice, butter or margarine, and jello. • *Learning*: Heat transforms some objects from solid to liquid.
3. Apply heat to waxed paper by ironing two pieces together. Compare product to original material. • *Learning*: Waxed paper reacts to heat by clinging. The wax melts and then solidifies.		

Target activity

Place leaf between two pieces of wax paper, waxed sides facing. Apply heated iron to wax paper. *Optional*: the leaf may be ironed within the wax paper or the ironing may be confined to the area that does not touch the leaf but merely surrounds it.

Example of a Thematic Activity: Planting

Planting activities may include:

1. germinating seeds,
2. caring for growing plants,
3. comparing and contrasting plants,
4. experimenting with germination and growth conditions.

Activities with plant growth described in the literature seldom specify learning goals or prerequisite learning.

The activity in which the goal is to identify the differences among plants in their needs for water, sunlight, and temperature control suggests the following analysis, using the principles of concrete-to-abstract, fact-to-concept, and known-to-unknown. If the learner is just beginning to conclude that there is a set of things in the environment called plants, then study of difference in plants begins at the perceptual level, comparing and contrasting how plants look. If all plants look alike to the young child, the first step is to find out how they differ in appearance, not how they differ in needs for survival. Comparisons start with color, shape of leaves, thickness of stems, surface texture of different parts of the plant, and distinctive attributes such as flowers, thorns, and runners. Other forms of differentiation come next.

Subect matter approach Using the logic of the subject matter, a sequence for planting activities might be the following:

1. *Start new plants*, first in soil and then under nonsoil conditions. Use:
   a. germinating seeds,
   b. bulbs,
   c. cuttings, leaf, and stem,
   d. root splitting,
   e. runners.
2. *Maintain plants* with proper control for light, water, heat, and nourishment.
3. *Experiment with plants*, deliberately withholding light, water, or another critical need.

Key concepts approach Teachers who prefer themes to other classes of content often find that identifying key concepts will suggest sequences that can be developed through a variety of activities. Such a sequence for planting might be:

1. There are a variety of objects in the environment called plants.
2. Plants with the same labels have the same characteristics. Radish plants have radishes. Rosebushes bear roses. Simple sorting and classifying precedes multiple classification.
3. Over a period of time, changes occur in color, size, shape, and leaf texture, and in number of leaves, branches, stems, and flowers. Changes differ in pace and form.
4. People can influence changes in plants considerably. But there is a limit to how much change will occur in rate of growth and in other plant attributes.

Adding considerations of children's developmental stages alerts the teacher to individual differences in learning among children experiencing the same activities. Basing curriculum on themes challenges teachers to review the prior experiences and understanding children bring to the planned activities. It also requires use of such principles as concrete-to-abstract, fact-to-concept, and known-to-unknown.

TASK ANALYSIS AS A TOOL OF SEQUENCING

Robert Gagné and other learning theorists who stress the need to sequence activities based on prerequisite learning offer a tool known as task analysis to identify the understandings required.[5] *Task analysis* is a technique for specifying the skills, facts, and concepts the child must have to succeed in a planned activity.

5. Robert M. Gagné, *The Conditions of Learning* (New York: Holt, Rinehart, & Winston), 1972.

Once prerequisite learning is known, teachers can assess children's acquisition of it. If the teacher discovers that a child or several children lack some prerequisite understanding, the necessary activities can be provided. Advocates of task analysis say it supports children's growth, "a singularly human process," in which teachers do not "inadvertently punish children for not performing according to . . . expectations."[6] Analysis of an activity in this way can be regarded as planning in reverse since one starts with the desired outcome and charts the route backward to where the child is.

Task analysis is a procedure for outlining and sequencing an activity, unit, or theme. For each point in the sequence, the teacher identifies what the child is expected to know. For example, if the teacher expects to say, "Fold your paper in half lengthwise," the child needs to know how to fold, and what *half* and *lengthwise* mean.

A teacher who had just graduated from one of our programs was stimulated to use task analysis when a child came in one day proudly displaying his sixth birthday present, a real wristwatch. Suddenly, a whole group of children were struggling to "tell time." At first the teacher worked with a group on time concepts, making simple clocks out of paper plates with crayonned faces. In a very warm, informal discussion, she elicited from the children what meanings time had for them. One child decided to copy the numbers and hand positions from the nearby wall clock. Another child crayonned rough circles on a paper plate to represent the numbers, finishing up with thirteen circles for hours.

This teacher's review of the initial activity included various ways to restructure it by making a task analysis of time concepts. This helped the teacher choose steps for the sequence and learning activities and materials for helping children learn to read time. A first analysis produced a list of time concepts such as these:

seconds	before-after
minutes	during
hours	at the same time
days	daytime-nighttime
today	dusk
yesterday	morning-afternoon-evening
tomorrow	noon-midnight

More thought produced these:

quarter hours	fast-slow clocks
half hours	timepieces, such as
before the hour	timers, clocks, and
after the hour	watches
a.m.-p.m.	

The teacher noted that, in addition to time concepts, math concepts were needed, and she added these:

Number
- relationship of seconds to minutes—60 to 1
- relationship of minutes to hours—60 to 1
- simple counting—to 60
- relationship of hours to day—24 to 1
- interval counting—by 5s
- ordinality of clock numbers
- fractions of hours—¼, ½, ¾

Geometry and Measurement
- positional terms—long hand (minute hand) *over* short hand (hour hand) at 12 o'clock;
- directional terms—pointing up, down, right, left; moving clockwise;
- halfway around the circle.

After the teacher analyzed the concepts required for reading time, she consulted texts on early childhood mathematics and began to list possible activities. From her list of ten activities, she selected "making simple egg timers."

---

6. Mary Budd Rowe, *Teaching Science as Continuous Inquiry*, 2nd ed. (New York: McGraw-Hill, 1978), p. 495.

To implement the activity, ordering based on the simple-to-complex rule suggested this sequence:

1. Children construct timers by making paper cones to set in jars to hold a given amount of sand to drip through.
2. Children compare with each other the time it takes for the sand to drip through, as faster or slower. Direct comparison between two events is the simplest form of time comparison.
3. Children seek to change the duration of their timers. The children have the option of changing the amount of sand or the size of the opening of the paper cone.
4. Children match the duration of their timers to a standard unit of time measurement, such as a three-minute eggtimer or a mechanical timer that rings.
5. Children use timers they have made in play and games.

This example of thoughtful reflection on a teaching plan sparked by a classroom event indicates how a framework begins to form that can help assure continuity and individual competence and sustain children's interest in learning.

To summarize, task analysis—used *for whatever purposes and methods the teacher chooses*—helps to:

1. identify a desired learning objective specifically;
2. identify prior skills or concepts required;
3. determine the probable order of prior learning required, which will suggest a useful sequence;
4. flag activities or learning objectives that are not developmentally appropriate and that should be eliminated;
5. indicate the kinds of materials needed;
6. spur children's personal application of learning activities;
7. serve as a basis for assessment of progress.

DEVELOPMENTAL THEORY AND SEQUENCING

The idea that children proceed through developmental stages is fairly universal, as mentioned earlier. For generations, parents and teachers have talked about children's behavior as "just a stage." The concept of a *stage of development* has grown out of accumulated years of seeing the same sequence of maturity repeated by successive groups of children. Research has documented scientifically how development proceeds through stages.

Studies of developmental stages now provide teachers with descriptions of social-emotional, moral, physical, perceptual-motor, and cognitive development. Each stage takes its own form, as noted in Chapter 5, in characteristic ways of thinking and behaving that reflect the stage. Further, a stage is an integral part of a complex network, following in regular order from the prior stage and building the basis for the next stage. Stages do not end abruptly but blend gradually with each succeeding one. No stage can be skipped, however.

The idea of developmental stages strongly influences long-term decisions about sequencing. Knowledge of stages and the related clusters of behaviors helps the teacher to anticipate changes in the way children deal with experiences. For example, Piaget's cognitive stage of intuitive intelligence or the preoperational period (ages two to six or seven) leads to curriculum planning that respects the characteristics of this stage—egocentrism, dominance of perception over logic, precausal reasoning, and impulsivity. However, as children approach the next stage of concrete operations, curriculum sequences can take account of the child's growing ability to *decenter*, or differentiate personal perspective from that of the other person, and to *reason logically*, or use logic to override sensory information when necessary and classify objects and experiences using more than one variable at the same time. Chapter 5 contains a summary of Piaget's cognitive stages. Stage-development theory not only provides guidelines for identifying the potentials and limits of learning, but also helps in ordering activities as children show evidence of moving to the next stage.

In a Piagetian curriculum, sequencing in terms of thought processes is more important than content selection. The child's ability to reason at a more complex level gradually generalizes to all types of content.

George Forman and David Kuschner illustrate one kind of sequencing in a constructivist view. Applying a Piagetian approach with very young children, they identify two guidelines for sequencing:

1. Repetitive activity precedes experimenting.
2. In psychomotor activity, the order of increasing task complexity is:
   a. changing target direction,
   b. changing force,
   c. changing content,
   d. changing product.[7]

Based on Forman and Kuschner's description of sequencing, Table 6-8 shows the order of complexity in a psychomotor activity with a cylinder block. Using a general goal—"to explore the limits of the self as an agent of change and relate movement of the self to movement of objects"—the chart shows movement from the simple task of changing the target to the complex task of changing the product or outcome. This order is a fine example of integrating developmental theory, learning theory, and key concepts of a discipline. From develop-

---

7. From *The Child's Construction of Knowledge: Piaget for Teaching Children* by George E. Forman and David S. Kuschner. Copyright © 1977 by Wadsworth, Inc. Reprinted by permission of the publisher, Brooks/Cole Publishing Company, Monterey, California.

TABLE 6.8. Sequencing considerations: Preoperational stage

Sample: Increasing complexity in the psychomotor activity of using one object to affect another object.

Task	Activity
1. Change target: Child engages in directional thinking.	As child engages in repetitive rolling of a cylinder block across a surface, establish a target, for example, by standing another cylinder block at one end of the surface. The task for child is to reach or touch the target with the rolling cylinder. Place targets at each end of the surface area if desired.
2. Change force: Child engages in thinking about both direction and force.	Knock over the target by rolling the cylinder across the surface until it hits.
3. Change content: Child engages in thinking about starting points and pathways, dealing with obstacles.	Place obstacles between the target and the starting point.
4. Change product or outcome.	Change task to one of moving the target, for example, causing the target—a car or ball—to roll in a specific direction.

mental theory comes the focus on the needs of the cognitive stage to act on objects and observe effects. From learning theory comes the sequence in the direction of increasing complexity by adding new variables. From the key concepts of the discipline, in this case physics, come the variables required to affect the movement of objects, or direction, force, speed, and distance. All of these separate components are well coordinated in this example.

Developmental Stages of Classification

Generally, knowledge about cognitive stages and their relationship to other aspects of development has already influenced much of the thinking about sequencing activities for sorting and classification. For example, Piaget's developmental sequence in sorting skills serves as a basis for ordering early childhood activities in both mathematics and science. Ronald Good's review of Piagetian order of acquisition of classification ability suggested the summary in Table 6-9, which reflects a clustering of skills as classification ability develops for young children. There are eight levels collapsed here into five.[8] For example, the simplest sorting level is *resemblance sorting*, which groups two objects that look alike. This level clearly precedes *exhaustive sorting*, where the child groups together all the objects having a particular characteristic. The highest levels listed, hierarchical classification and class inclusion, generally do not occur in early childhood stages but begin to appear at ages nine to ten.

8. Ronald Good, *How Children Learn Science: Conceptual Development and Implications for Teaching* (New York: Macmillan, 1977), pp. 37–55.

TABLE 6.9. Hierarchy of sorting and classification skills

1.	Resemblance sorting	Grouping two objects together that look alike.
	Consistent sorting	Grouping more than two objects together based on similar properties.
	Exhaustive sorting	Grouping together all things that possess a particular attribute.
2.	Some-all classification	Objects can belong to more than one set, and subsets can be formed from a more inclusive set.
	Part-whole relationships	Similar to "some-all," but now the words *some* and *all* are used in joining subsets to form a larger set.
3.	Multiple-class membership	Elements of a set might also belong to other classes if a reclassification occurred.
4.	Hierarchical classification	Attributes are combined into nested combinations in constructing successively larger classes.
5.	Class inclusion	A realization that a class identified by certain criteria is always larger than its subclass.

Note: This table is based on Good's listing of Piagetian stages in classification and Kofsky's study of children's classification skills. It covers only eight of Good's listing of eleven stages (condensed here to five) and applies only to ages three to eight years.

Source: Reprinted with permission of Macmillan Publishing Co., Inc. from *How Children Learn Science: Conceptual Development and Implications for Teaching*, by Ronald G. Good. Copyright © 1977 by Ronald G. Good.

Very young children manipulate materials collections they find in their immediate environment. They tend to group objects in terms of their personal experiences rather than the objective properties. The sorting base, which is personal-functional, is clearer to the child than to the observer. For example, a functional sorting might include "my bath toys." Since this class is not necessarily known to others, it tends to be unique to the child. Gradually, children establish perceptual bases for sorting, such as shape or color. The classification stages identified in Tables 6–9 and 6–10 omit this beginning level, since it does not reflect genuine classification thinking. However, since personal-functional sorting precedes sorting based on perceptual properties, it is necessary to select objects for initial sorting that foster focus on perceptual properties of the objects. Collections of objects with several variables may be sorted and resorted, first using one such as shape, and then adding others, perhaps color or size. The number of objects the child can handle is limited at first. As children master sorting small sets, the number that can be sorted increases.

The next major change in sorting ability, which usually appears by ages six to seven, is multiple classification. At this level, the child is able to keep in mind two variables and to understand that an object can simultaneously be a member of two sets, such as square objects and blue objects. The teacher is likely to be successful in sequencing sorting activities by following the child's demonstrated level and challenging the child only at that level or toward the next level. Another advanced level is *relational sorting*, or classifying objects that are functionally related, such as hardware tools.

Several ways in which the teacher may be misled in sequencing sorting should be noted:

1. Collections too large in size may falsely suggest that the child cannot do simple sorting.
2. Directing the child in detail to collect specific objects may falsely suggest that the child understands the base for sorting, when the child is only following directions.

TABLE 6.10. Sample sequence of sorting activities

Task	Activity materials
Matching identical objects	Two identical sets with two objects in each set. Example: two red blocks of same size and shape and two blue straws of same length. Gross differences between sets.
Consistent sorting, identical sets	Increase number of objects in sets, three to four, then six to eight, and then eight to twelve. Gross difference between sets, such as between cotton balls and plastic spoons.
Multiple classification possibilities	Collections, varying on two dimensions, can be sorted and resorted. Examples: styrofoam balls, two sizes and two colors; attribute blocks, two shapes and two sizes. Eight to twelve objects in each. Sorting collections varying on three dimensions. Example: two sizes, two shapes, and two colors. Up to twenty objects.

3. Rushing the progression to relational sorting before the child is ready tends to drive the child to personal-functional sorting, rather than to relational class.
4. Relational sorting requires not only the cognitive thought, but also sufficient experience with the objects that are to be classified.

The sequence of sorting activities outlined in Table 6–10 provides a fairly reliable base for sequencing learning goals. Complexity increases in both attributes of objects and number of objects. While the order of sequencing suggested here for sorting is functional generally, readers should remember that research studies constantly offer new perspectives.

SUMMARY

In this chapter we have identified principles and procedures for sequencing instructional plans. Principles of progression include the universal requirements of moving from simple to complex, from concrete to abstract, from facts to concepts and from known to unknown. They also include understanding the stages of learning modes from imitation to creation, from exploration to problem-solving, and from self-identity to perception of others. Distinctions have been made between basing sequencing on content or on learning processes, on logic or on psychological processes. Teachers, no matter what their commitment to curriculum form or program, make decisions on both content and process sequence.

Illustrative application of these principles to classes of content featured examples of curriculum sequencing in a broad range of curriculum areas—from routines such as table-setting to various types of standard curriculum content.

Sequencing procedures for early childhood teaching and learning requires continuously filtering through developmental theory to identify children's current functioning and insure that teaching plans do not outrun their reasoning capacity or experiential base for learning. Sensible and well-tested sequencing principles help teachers maintain children's interest and achievement in school.

EXERCISES

1. List and illustrate four sequencing principles that help teachers plan content sequences.
2. List and illustrate six sequencing principles that guide the design of instructional processes or learning activities.
3. Write a lesson plan for a specific group of children and a selected topic:
   a. Complete a task analysis, indicating the prerequisite learning required.
   b. Order the prerequisite learning from simple to complex.
   c. Design an assessment instrument to determine children's readiness to participate.
   d. Indicate next steps for children who have mastered your intended learning.

BIBLIOGRAPHY

Aronoff, Frances W. *Music and Young Children*, Expanded Edition. New York: Turning Wheel Press, 1979.

Bruner, Jerome. *The Process of Education*. Cambridge, Mass.: Harvard University Press, 1966.

Duckworth, Eleanor. "The Having of Wonderful Ideas." *Harvard Educational Review*, 42 (1972): 231.

Forman, George E. and Kuschner, David S. *The Child's Construction of Knowledge: Piaget for Teaching Children*. Monterey, Calif.: Brooks/Cole, 1977.

Gagné, Robert M. *The Conditions of Learning*. New York: Holt, Rinehart & Winston, 1972.

Good, Ronald. *How Children Learn Science: Conceptual Development and Implications for Teaching.* New York: Macmillan, 1977.

Kofsky, Ellin. "A Scalagram Study of Classificatory Development." *Child Development,* 37, no. 1 (1966): 191–204.

Monroe, Marion. *Growing into Reading.* New York: Scott, Foresman, 1951.

Rowe, Mary Budd. *Teaching Science as Continuous Inquiry,* 2nd ed. New York: McGraw-Hill, 1978.

Spache, George. *The Teaching of Reading.* Bloomington, Ind.: Phi Delta Kappa, 1972.

7 Designing Curriculum: Putting Components Together

Having reviewed the major variables in curriculum design, we now make suggestions for selecting and integrating these variables. The selection may be made for one or more of the following reasons:

1. to facilitate construction of a new design;
2. to practice curricular designing;
3. to create a list of criteria for reviewing and evaluating programs in use by student teachers, inservice teachers, or others;
4. to select criteria against which to evaluate, for possible purchase, various available packaged curricula;
5. to assess the logic and congruency of curriculum designs encountered in the literature, in classroom visits, or in descriptions by classroom teachers and school administrators.

Our first suggestion is to review the options listed for each major variable. Secondly, you are encouraged to add other options you may know, have heard, or read about, since there are many subcategories of each major variable. Third, using a grid such as Figure 7–1, make a tentative selection for the first empty column. Following this figure, decide on curricular *form*, *purpose*, views of *content*, views of *development* and *learning*, and *curriculum sequences*, as follows:

1. *Form.* Shall it be a happening, a written syllabus, or another form? Review Chapter 2.
2. *Purpose or objectives.* What are long-term purposes? When long-term goals are detailed into a set of short-term objectives are there any contradictions? No program can serve all objectives. Review Chapter 3.
3. *Views of Knowledge or Content.* Here there are usually more choices than might appear, for almost any curriculum design, although some views of content have traditionally been associated with one kind of design more than another. Review Chapter 4.
4. *Views of Child Development and Learning.* Views on these two areas, *development* and *learning*, must be harmonious. If development is chosen to mean primarily *learning* then learning theory or behaviorist theory offers the most helpful and congruent concepts. If development is viewed as maturation or as an interaction between the individual at a developmental stage and the individual's experience, then knowledge of stage-related characteristics is critical to program planning. Well-established principles of learning should not be disregarded in any design, since they usually point to a more effective design. Review Chapters 5 and 6.

FIGURE 7.1. Curriculum designing

Major variables	Tentative selection 1	Tentative selection 2
1. Form		
2. Purpose or objectives		
3. Views of content		
4. Views of development and learning		
5. Examples of content sequence		

ANALYSIS OF SELECTION

Having made a first tentative selection on a grid similar to Figure 7-1, among the choices for each major variable, you now need to take several additional steps:

1. Analyze the selected purposes or objectives for:
    a. *Consistency.* Do they contradict each other, as for example, obedience and autonomy? (See Chapter 5, Erikson's psychosocial stages.)
    b. *Cruciality.* John McNeil suggests that how crucial or important a school objective is depends on three factors:[1]
        1. expectation that the child will need this;
        2. expectation that the child will accomplish this;
        3. expectation that the child will have accomplished it outside of school. For different kinds of schools, the answer to this question for an objective may be different. In day care centers, where children spend more of their waking hours than at home, most objectives will be accomplished within the program, if at all. In other words, you do not need objectives that the school cannot accomplish or that the child will accomplish anyway without the school's help.
    c. *Realistic orientation.* Could a curriculum for children under eight realistically expect to provide, for example, vocational background experiences in today's world? With rapid changes in the job market, there are no sure predictions of which kinds of jobs will be in demand in another decade or two.
    d. *Adaptability to range of children.* For example, if the objectives selected apply only to the brightest children without any handicapping conditions, how will a random group of children with a range of abilities accomplish them? Even for schools with selective entry requirements, unpredictable problems may surface for any child, and this makes one set of standards irrelevant. No matter how children are selected or admitted to a program, growth and developmental patterns require some elasticity and adaptability.
    e. *Ethical acceptability.* Ethical questions arise concerning acceptability of the objectives to the teacher, and ultimately, to the hiring group that makes policy for a school and to the community. This can be resolved by applying one's own ethical standards, and if one knows these are not shared by the local community, this gap should be recognized. Some teachers have refused to teach in early childhood centers that clearly required pursuit of objectives not ethically acceptable to them, such as an unreasonably high degree of conformity and obedience on the part of the children.
    f. *Usefulness.* Does the selection of objectives serve to create a clear boundary for curriculum design? Is it clear what should be omitted and what included? Or does the boundary need further specification? If coping skills are among the objectives, which ones are included?
2. Compare views of learning and of development and resolve any contradictions, since this is where many curriculum designs tend to introduce variables that seem to defeat each other.
3. Apply some rules of sequencing to a set of short-term goals that are intended to achieve a long-term one. Do the rules sustain an order?

---

1. John D. McNeil, *Designing Curriculum, Self-Instructional Modules* (Boston: Little, Brown, 1976), p. 80.

4. To test your logic and congruence, complete the second column in Figure 7-1, but this time, select for each variable the option you really *don't* like. In the process, you will find it necessary to clarify your true preferences.
5. Compare the two selections. Are they really in opposition to each other, or is one a minor variation of the other?

Hold onto this figure so you can add other preferences for kinds of learning activities and teaching strategies that support these selections for curriculum design, as will be reviewed in Section Two. The rest of this chapter discusses some universal concerns of early childhood curriculum design.

PROBLEMS IN CURRICULUM DESIGN FOR THE YOUNG

Problems in early childhood curriculum design range from selecting content, to setting comprehensive and specific goals, to choosing methodology. As noted in Table 7-1, goal selection includes a variety of related problems, most of which have already been discussed in earlier chapters. A brief summary of these problems follows.

Articulation

When the kindergarten teacher says, "These children didn't learn *anything* in Head Start, nursery school, or day care," the teacher is exposing a problem of *articulation*. It means that the program in the prior school year does not appear to fit current program expectations.

Typically, it is the kindergarten that comes under attack for not conforming to expectations of first-grade teachers. In public school classes for young children, there is often a tendency to view curriculum needs from the perspective of the school's requirements for later grades. For a long time, "readiness" was regarded as being the purpose of kindergarten. Extended daily periods of sitting for assigned instructional tasks and teacher-directed instruction in the kindergarten were often justified as preparing the child for first grade.

These articulation problems between kindergarten and first grade are so well publicized that one can easily miss the fact that articulation concerns are pervasive throughout nursery school, day care, and Head Start and in the primary grades where children move from one classroom to another, even in small schools. Since teachers vary in curriculum goals, methodology, and related classroom programs, the philosophical distance between one classroom program and the next directly determines the degree of adjustment required of children. Articulation problems in curriculum design include how to identify children's prior experiences and how to help children move into the current program. Ideally, each year of schooling builds on prior years, and to do so, some form of articulation is required. When children move from an academically oriented classroom of four-year-olds to a "readiness," maturation-based kindergarten, there will be great discontinuity in learning experiences.

Five suggested ways continuity may be built between preprimary and primary programs are:

1. using an outside sponsor to establish program continuity;
2. selecting a unified program to serve preschool and primary classes;
3. assigning teachers to groups for more than one year (continuity of staff);
4. maintaining classes intact from preschool into primary (continuity of peers);
5. establishing parental training programs (continuity through parents).

School staffs are challenged to coordinate programs within and among their centers.

TABLE 7.1. Problems in curriculum design for young children

Problem area	Sample decisions
General curriculum	
1. Articulation	How to smooth the child's school experiences from one age or grade level to the next?
2. Knowledge of content	Available and useful content? Classes of content that should dominate the curriculum?
3. Curriculum roots	National traditions? Concerns of local or national community? Bilingual education? Cultural heritage? Parent involvement in curriculum? Minority group traditions? Current social issues? Contemporary views of knowledge? Contemporary views of child development and learning? Minimum competency?
4. Universal or individualized curriculum	Whether to individualize curriculum, to what degree, and how?
5. Criteria for achieving balance	Experiences in school? Access to types of knowledge? Breadth of content? Activities—content—process?
Objectives	
6. Establishing objectives	Social utility? Social responsibility? Knowledge and skills? Special culture? Common culture? Personal development?
7. Process-product arguments	Process? Product? Process and product?
Methodology	
8. Methodology	(See Section Two, "Teachers and Teaching")
9. Teacher role	Construct a curriculum? Adopt a curriculum? Improve curriculum? Change curriculum?

Knowledge of Content

Novice early childhood teachers learn how much knowledge young children seek as they pursue different activities. Nathan Isaacs referred to this as the "illimitable subject of the world" to which young children attend, and he follows this observation with a staggering list of content needed by the teacher of young children.[2] No teacher can expect to master such a list. Consequently, problems in designing curriculum include: (1) knowing the volume of knowledge available, (2) selecting from that volume to fit the design, (3) tapping into that knowledge when interests emerge. Curriculum resources, discussed in Section Four, suggest ways of making selections.

It is appropriate that teachers emphasize what they know best—their own experience and knowledge. However, teachers maintain vitality in teaching through excitement in acquiring new knowledge. Hence, leading from known strengths means leading into new strengths.

Curriculum Roots

Some groups seeking to develop pride in their heritage have designed unique curricula to teach native languages, religions, values, and ways of life. American Indian groups and some black groups, among others, have designed the kind of curricula intended to transmit selected values and learning.

Early childhood programs in the United States are generally responsive to community needs and aspirations. Day care center boards, on which parents are often the majority, hire directors, as do governing boards of most nonprofit early childhood facilities. In preferring one candidate for director over another, the boards can suggest, require, monitor, evaluate, or otherwise influence the curriculum to reflect the special interests of parents and community. In some centers, community pressure requires bilingual or multicultural components for curriculum design.

Reflecting the distinctiveness of a community or responding to its special needs need not deprive a curriculum design of national and international values and concerns. For example, as discussed in Chapters 16 and 17, including values of energy conservation, which represent local, national, and international values, would not conflict with almost any type of design one could imagine.

Giving dignity to a child with handicapping conditions or from a poor family is simply a special case of the need to give dignity and respect to every child. For the handicapped child, giving respect may sometimes mean letting the child take a long time to complete a self-help routine and enjoy the satisfaction of achievement without unnecessary assistance. It may mean adding some forms of self-help supports or modifying equipment for special use. Poor children vary as much as any other group—some are shy, verbal, very active, quiet, or ingenious in solving problems; others are not. Those who have special needs will be identified by alert, observant, and sensitive teachers, who may decide special learning for selected purposes is required, as it is for other children. The community may collaborate to help give dignity to a child and her family.

Changes in the education of the handicapped impose new demands on all teachers. *Mainstreaming* increases classroom observations and interactions among children with and without handicaps. Educating children with handicaps in the least restrictive environment greatly increases children's opportunities to observe and to interact with children, with multiple handicapping conditions as well as those with single or minimal handicaps. Respect for all children must specifically include children with unfamiliar forms of handicap.

---

2. Mildred Hardeman, ed., *Children's Ways of Knowing: Nathan Isaacs on Education, Psychology, and Piaget* (New York: Teachers College Press, 1974), pp. 71–75.

Objectives will require overcoming reactions of fear or rejection through becoming familiar with and accepting others who are different.

Universal or Individualized Curriculum

Universal means "for everyone." When talking about curriculum, the usual image is one of everybody doing the same thing at the same time, whether in small groups or as one large class group. However, the timing, pacing, and grouping for children's experiences are not necessarily tied to the curriculum package.

In most settings, there is some universal learning that is valued and required. Teachers who plan for all children to use all areas for the same approximate time during a week, month, or season value a balanced experience. Essentially, the question to be answered is, What objectives, if any, are for all children? To answer this question, teachers can list those activities they expect of all children.

Balance

Balance in curriculum means different things to different people. To some, it refers to the children's ebb and flow of energy and their needs for food, rest, spontaneity, and social activities. This kind of balance is achieved through the daily schedule of activities, alternating passive with active periods, and group times with independent activities.

Another meaning of balance is access to all kinds of knowledge. Some critics of open classrooms, for example, point to the preponderance of craft activities and the absence of certain cognitive challenges. Critics of many public school kindergartens deplore lack of access to learnings outside of language arts and beginning number work. Some programs are criticized for lack of play opportunities, others for the predominance of play. Many primary programs are criticized for having too narrow a focus on reading instruction.

A recurrent criticism of many early childhood programs today is that they lack concern for the major modes of thought and don't provide learning experiences that stimulate the different kinds of thinking.

Establishing Objectives

Establishing objectives provokes controversy in early childhood programs. Objectives relating to behaviors are easy to formulate. Such objectives as personal grooming and academic skills are readily stated. It is more difficult to articulate process objectives, such as developing and using concepts of balance in block construction.

Common problems in stating objectives include:

1. the tendency to be over-inclusive and therefore contradictory;
2. finding solutions to the process-product dilemma;
3. setting long-term versus short-term objectives;
4. making statements that are too abstract and ambiguous.

Solving problems in selecting objectives sets the stage for curriculum design. Solutions to these problems directly affects the outcomes of problems mentioned previously, such as articulation, universality, and community values.

Process-Product Arguments

Within the range of beliefs and values for the young child's curriculum, process-product arguments are common. Process is concerned with children's experiences, not with the end-products. Product emphasizes results—what did the children accomplish, or learn? Most teachers of young children are middle-of-the-road on this issue. They are often hard-pressed by supervisors, directors, principals, parents, and the local educational administration to be "accountable," to show results. But in closest interaction with young children, teachers often choose activities that stimulate children, considering the objective of *involvement* to be more important than products or skills.

Product emphasis has as many options as process. Featuring process may mean stressing expressive, creative forms of activity, or it may involve problem solving, discoveries, problem choosing, self-valuing, and many more. Product emphasis may feature selected degrees of skill mastery, accumulation of knowledge, academic achievement of a reading level or mathematics goals, or satisfactory completion of a specific program or workbook materials.

Problems in stressing either process or product concern degrees of clarity, predictability, and prescription. How much is possible, or desirable; how much must be decided and what kind? If all goals or objectives must be clear, predictable, and prescriptive, then flexibility will have to be built into pacing, instructional materials, practice opportunities, learning style, and duration and type of instructional activities.

SUMMARY

Many teachers inherit a curriculum. They are hired to implement a particular kind of program, learning environment, or curriculum. Directors, school principals, and local school boards frequently interview candidates for teaching positions to find out their preferences and experiences. When a specific program has been selected for a group of children, ethics requires a teacher either to be able to find merit in it and follow it or to refuse a position that offers no alternative. Sometimes a particularly articulate candidate can convince a hiring official that an alternative approach is just as good or better than the officially preferred one.

Inheriting a curriculum does not preclude improving it by broadening or adapting it to the particular children in the group or by obtaining agreement to change it. One curriculum seldom looks the same in any two teachers' classrooms. For this reason, many hiring officials concentrate less on curricular preferences than on experience with young children. They look for sympathy for and understanding of children in the age range involved and for the personal qualities that attract observers to one teacher more than another—sincerity, humor, and warmth, combined with professional skills.

Constructing a curriculum from scratch is another matter. It usually requires deliberate decisions about *what*, *why*, and *how*. It must have struck you that many arguments are made for or against curriculum approaches that would in practice complement each other in many ways. It is suggested that a more fruitful analysis could indicate suggested combinations of various types.

EXERCISES

1. After completing Figure 7-1, discuss your choices with a colleague or fellow student.
2. Summarize the reasons for your partner's choices.

BIBLIOGRAPHY

Hardeman, Mildred, ed. *Children's Ways of Knowing: Nathan Isaacs on Education, Psychology, and Piaget.* New York: Teachers College Press, 1974.

McNeil, John D. *Designing Curriculum, Self-Instructional Modules.* Boston: Little, Brown, 1976.

II Teachers and Teaching

Researchers point out that teaching is a complex set of activities, influenced not only by the dynamics of personal interaction, but also by what each teacher brings to the educational setting. We are alerted to the ecology of the classroom, which affects and is affected by the attitudes, values, style, and unique characteristics of each member. The ecological factors are:

1. the social system teachers and children create;
2. the curriculum activities designed by teachers and children;
3. the physical setting provided and the materials and space organized by teachers and children.

These factors interact to have notable impact on the experiences children have in the classroom, that is, on the curriculum as it is realized.

Not only do teachers communicate expectations, but peers establish relationships and roles based on personality, preferences, and personal needs. Chapter 8 considers children's self-concepts, the ways children learn from others, and how their social-emotional needs are met. Chapter 9 focuses on the organization of the physical space and the development of program activities. Chapter 10 considers teaching roles and strategies, identifying major functions, strategies, and roles. Diagnostic assessment follows in Chapter 11, summarizing the many ways teachers can find out what children need and what kind of progress they are making.

8 Meeting Children's Social-Emotional Needs

Children learn a broad range of information, ideas, values, attitudes and skills from others. They learn who they are and where they fit in the world of people. They learn endless how-to behaviors, such as how to throw a ball, express anger, use a spoon, greet people, or describe an object. They learn how to earn approval and admiration and avoid punishment and rejection. Much of this learning occurs with limited awareness on their part of being taught. It occurs daily through interaction, observation, practice, and feedback from others. What is learned through formal teaching is a small part of what young children learn. Since many studies confirm the difficulty of changing a self-concept once it has become established, it cannot be overemphasized that teachers' contributions are extremely important during the formative period.

Children learn from others as they observe first the important persons in their lives and then others. They copy what they think they have seen and heard. Through observation and interaction, they develop attitudes and values:

- toward *activities*, such as, "House cleaning is unpleasant" and "Biking is fun";
- toward *other people*, such as, "The neighbors are nice people," "The gas station attendant is a crook," "The police officer will *catch* you" or "The policeman will *help* you";
- toward *themselves*, such as being smart or dumb; ugly, handsome, or pretty; sweet, unpleasant, or nasty; clumsy, or an agile, fast runner, able climber, and high jumper; sloppy, dirty, or neat; orderly or clean.

They develop ways to express emotion through approved behaviors. Sometimes this requires remembering not to copy some behaviors, such as an adult who swears when angry. Instead, approval may follow if the child takes the advice of an adult who says, "When you are angry, go kick the ball outside," which means "Express it elsewhere." Or the adult may say, "When you are angry, go to your room," which means "Isolate yourself and spare others." Attitudes toward winning and losing are also generated by observation and interaction, in addition to the influence of internal needs. These few samples suggest the many aspects of learning and growing in children's expanding experiences with others.

As children grow, they meet new models and attitudes, many of them contradictory. They see a broad range of social behaviors, many of which are unfamiliar. One major determinant of how new experiences with people foster healthy development is the view of the self and the degree of self-esteem the child has learned.

THE DEVELOPMENT OF THE SELF-CONCEPT[1]

It is generally accepted that important people in the child's world powerfully affect the child's growing self-concept. The self has been defined as an "abstraction that an individual develops about the attributes, capacities, objects and activities which he possesses and pursues."[2] The abstraction takes form in the symbol *me*, a symbol that represents self. Designating the self as an abstraction highlights the likelihood that young children's concepts of self are not well defined because of their limited capacity to abstract. This may account for the apparent lack of continuity in the way young children view themselves, one moment as strong and powerful, a "can do" person, and another moment as dependent, tentative, and "no can do."

Agreement that children's self-concepts are influenced by the quality of interactions with others does not preclude considerable disagreement about how this occurs. Views of personality development stem from three major theories—behaviorist theory, featuring environmental determinants; psychoanalytic theory, with internal needs as major but not sole determinants; and humanist-field theory, in which the individual functions as an active agent in her or his own personality formation.[3]

---

1. For a more extensive review of views of the self-concept, see child development texts such as Donald Dinkmeyer, *Child Development: The Emerging Self* (Englewood Cliffs, N.J.: Prentice-Hall, 1965); special topic texts such as Kaoru Yamamoto, *The Child and His Image: Self-Concept in the Early Years* (New York: Houghton Mifflin, 1972); and readings such as Arthur Combs, ed., *Perceiving, Behaving and Becoming* (Washington, D.C.: ASCD Yearbook, 1962).

2. Stanley Coopersmith, *The Antecedents of Self-Esteem* (San Francisco: W.H. Freeman, 1967), p. 20.

3. Cecil H. Patterson, "Insights about Persons: Psychological Foundations of Humanistic and Affective Education," in Louise Berman and Jessie Roderick, eds., *Feeling, Valuing and the Art of Growing: Insights in the Affective* (Washington, D.C.: Association for Supervision and Curriculum Development, 1977 Yearbook), pp. 145–175.

As indicated previously in this text, concepts of development, learning, curriculum, and program are rarely translated in the pure form into practice. Most teachers are eclectic and use procedures that they think are effective.

Behaviorist Approach to Self-Concept

Behaviorists claim that if people could control *all* the stimuli in the environment of an individual, they could produce any kind of person they choose. Since such control is not possible, the behaviorist is concerned with controlling those stimuli needed to assure desired learning. This means setting objectives for the child based on diagnosis of progress or prior learning, defining steps of learning, and specifying reinforcement to achieve objectives (as outlined in Chapter 5). Ultimately, the child acquires the selected knowledge, behavior, attitude, or value.

Using a behaviorist approach, teachers develop desirable social actions by controlling environmental stimuli. For example, sharing, a valued behavior in preschool settings, is achieved through a series of steps in which the teacher:

1. communicates verbally or by modeling what sharing behaviors are expected;
2. sets up situations to elicit and increase practice of sharing, such as providing *one* rolling pin at the play-dough table so they will "learn to share";
3. praises or otherwise reinforces the child who demonstrates sharing behavior;
4. labels the successful child a "good sharer" in some way.

This sequence illustrates the relationship between the goal and the final behavior. Note that praise, if publicly given, takes on some of the attributes of social learning theory, in which children acquire values and attitudes from observing others without direct reinforcement.

Remember that Bandura's social learning theory, described in Chapter 5 as an offshoot of behaviorism, features learning by imitation. Accordingly, to become successful imitators, children have to observe, remember, and be able to and want to copy others' behaviors.

Cognitive and motor development influence what children actually see and understand of what is to be imitated. For example, a very young child who had observed an adult express affecton to a dog by a multiple set of actions such as patting, kissing, and hugging, in that order, copied only one behavior, the patting action. Having little sense of the intensity of the patting, and limited motor ability to control it, the child hit the dog repeatedly, provoking a snapping response from the dog. The interactions between the child and the dog took on a quality of conflict that was not present in the model. Bandura reminds us that the child's use of imitation is limited by her or his understanding of the total meaning of the behaviors observed and by the motor skill to reproduce it. This suggests that there are very real limits to the potential of modeling as an instructional strategy.

Social learning theory also alerts us to the need to conform the behavior of adults to what is expected of children. If you want children to reduce temperamental outbursts and use more socially acceptable methods, then teacher modeling of yelling and emotional distress provides the wrong model. Social learning theory further requires consistency of the model so that children have sufficient experience to observe and understand what is to be copied. This theory clearly places responsibility on the teacher to identify steps toward learning goals and to diagnose each child's capacity to attend, retain, reproduce motorically, and become interested in the learning to be imitated.

Psychodynamic Approach to Self-Concept

Psychoanalytic theory views the self as a "complex mental system acting upon experience, reacting to experience, adapting, storing, integrating in a continuous effort to maintain balance between inner needs and outer demands."[4] Mental health depends on the "maintenance of balance within the personality between the basic human urges and egocentric wishes on the one hand and the demands of conscience and society on the other hand."[5] The constant struggle between meeting internal demands and accommodating to external realities establishes the arena within which the concept of self develops. Tension, anxiety, pleasure, and pain are continual internal pressures, as the young child adapts behavior to fulfill urges, where possible, or redirects actions to satisfy needs where impulsive actions are perceived as prohibited.

With increased awareness of the conflicts between impulsive behavior and the expectations of important adults, the young child adapts behavior toward more realistic possibilities. Selma Fraiberg defines the ego as the mediator between the demands of the two worlds, inner needs and external expectations. The ego, then, is a major determinant of self-concept, judging and assigning both guilt and responsibility.[6]

According to psychoanalytic theory, teachers contribute to the development of a healthy self-concept by rejecting impulsive behaviors that do not conform to expectations and by providing acceptable alternatives. Children may be encouraged to use puppets and dolls, for example, as an alternate target for aggression to redirect unsocial impulses into

---

4. Selma Fraiberg, *The Magic Years* (New York: Charles Scribners, 1959), p. 7.
5. Ibid., p. 9.
6. Ibid., p. 4.

acceptable actions. The former deflects aggression to an acceptable target, while the latter permits action in fantasy, allowing a painful experience to be controlled. Unacceptable behavior persists when a child cannot find acceptable substitutes. Phobias, irrational fears, or withdrawal from interaction are considered symptoms of the child's inability to resolve conflict.

Psychoanalytic theory has stressed the need to treat the causes, not the symptoms. Otherwise the child can easily substitute one symptom for another if basic causes persist. Making the child aware of successful use of previously unacceptable behavior, as with punching bags, is a reminder to maintain the alternate pattern. This helps the child understand ways to meet needs wthout getting into trouble.

Humanist Theory

Humanist theory stresses understanding the whole before understanding the parts, placing the self in a central position to coordinate internal and external conditions. The whole field includes the self and others in their natural contexts of family, school, community, and church or temple. The individual decides how to behave to meet both social demands and internal needs. This dynamic view of the self-concept stresses the importance of self-actualization, on the one hand, and approval, valuing, and caring, on the other.[7]

According to the phenomenological view, one of the humanist theories, changes in the self-concept can only occur when perceptions change or when needs change.[8] An example of changing perceptions might be:

Given a child's self-perception as being "ugly," attempts to change this concept with generalized praise such as "How pretty you look!" will be rejected as *not true*, contrary to perceptions. Changes in perception might occur as the child is helped to focus on parts of the self, such as hands, feet, hair, eyes. This allows the perception of "ugly" to filter through changing perceptions of one item at a time.

One writer, recalling her childhood, related that as she continued to try new things she received conflicting messages about herself as bright and dumb, smart and silly or stupid. Her reflection of this was, "How could I be smart when it came out one way, and silly when it came out another? I was the same both ways."[9] These observations, from the holistic view, alert us to the fact that a child's experiences are patterned from within. The child either has to ignore responses that cannot be fitted into an existing pattern or change the pattern to accommodate unexpected responses.

In teaching, it is important to provide continuity of experience. Visible and tangible daily interactions that stress attributes of children's selves that are repeatedly successful foster their sense of having permanent qualities not dependent on feedback from others. Research supports teaching that helps children value themselves because they can do more.[10] A child who has often poured her own juice successfully, will be more stable in her view of self as a successful pourer. Such a child is likely to reject contradictory judgments from others, such as "You're too young to pour your own juice."

---

7. Dinkmeyer, *Child Development* pp. 185–187.
8. Arthur Combs and Donald Snygg, *Individual Behavior: A Perceptual Approach to Behavior*, rev. ed. (New York: Harper & Row, 1959).
9. Carl Rogers and Barry Stevens, with Eugene Gendlin, John Shlien, and Wilson Van Dusen, *Person to Person: The Problem of Being Human*. Lafayette, Calif.: Real People Press, 1967), p. 34.
10. Lorrie Shepard, "Self-Acceptance: The Evaluative Component of the Self-Concept Construct," *American Educational Research Journal*, 16, no. 2 (Spring 1979): 139–160.

Children learn a great deal about themselves as they relate to larger numbers of people. To each new set of relationships, children bring views of themselves that are reinforced, expanded, or changed by the nature of the new relationships. As they confront new situations requiring adaptation and acquisition of social skills, their estimates of themselves may change. The self-concept filters new experiences, which may require a change in the self-concept.

Each of the three approaches to self-concept development—behaviorist, psychoanalytic, and humanist—implies different teaching behaviors and places different emphases on how children learn about the self. The stable school group is likely to have greater impact on learning about one's self than other occasional experiences. Therefore, the classroom's social environment is an important influence on achieving curriculum goals.

TEACHING STRATEGIES TO MEET CHILDREN'S SOCIAL-EMOTIONAL NEEDS

When young children enter school groups, they meet expectations for social-emotional behavior that are often different from the home. The greater the differences, the more difficult the adjustment. Teachers help children meet the social demands of early childhood programs by supporting children's feelings of individuality, importance, and competence. If teachers are to meet children's social-emotional needs, they must first decide what the children need—initial instruction, relearning, or help to resolve emotional confusion.[11]

As children learn more about themselves and their capacities through new situations making unexpected demands on them, they are required to:

1. *learn new social skills*, such as waiting in line to wash their hands, or waiting for a turn on a tricycle;
2. *revise or adapt social skills* that were useful but no longer serve, such as taking toys when desired, irrespective of whether others were using them;
3. *deal with inner feelings* related to new experiences, such as containing or channeling frustration that results from waiting to use desired equipment.

If new learning is required, the question is how to teach it. For example, if a three-year-old is unaware of the expectation to take turns at school, teaching this procedure under the least stressful conditions will lead to successful learning. Behaviorists call this *training*, while developmentalists consider this *facilitating learning*.

If the child needs to replace certain habits with more socially approved behaviors, the behavior-modification approach requires that the teacher select strategies to reinforce new behaviors. In this way the child is expected to increase approved behaviors and drop out those that are not reinforced. From a psychoanalytic perspective, the child learns to choose the behavior to fit specific conditions, adjusting to external realities. For example, children learn when to use different language styles, such as "school" language or "playground" language, indoor voice levels or outdoor ones.

Teachers often find it difficult to help children cope with strong feelings. An angry child, spilling rage by hitting, kicking, and screaming, is not likely to respond to any direct teaching approach until the outpouring diminishes. The child who is expressing strong, overpowering emotion cannot simultaneously receive messages. The child's communication channels are fully committed to sending, there-

---

11. James L. Hymes, *Behavior and Misbehavior: A Teacher's Guide to Action* (Englewood Cliffs, N.J.: Prentice-Hall, 1955), pp. 13, 76–135.

by blocking receiving. When the child can begin receiving messages, the teacher is challenged to select among several options, such as:

1. exploring feelings and causes with the child—a psychoanalytic view;
2. accepting feelings as expressed—a humanistic view—which assumes that the discharge and expression of feeling is therapeutic;
3. acknowledging behavior and teaching more acceptable ways of coping by reinforcing or shaping desired behaviors—a behavioristic view.

The one procedure unacceptable in all approaches is punishment. All three approaches assume responsibility for teaching the child to control or deal with frustration. The psychoanalytic approach also alerts the teacher to the negative effects excessive guilt has on one's capacity to function.[12]

Exploring Feelings and Causes with the Child

Exploring feelings and causes with the child can take several forms. The teacher may ask the child directly what his or her feelings are and what events provoked them. Another approach is for the teacher to talk about personal experiences that have caused strong emotional responses in the teacher as a way of encouraging a child to follow suit. A third way is to engage another child in the discussion of feelings. A fourth is to tell a story or read a book about a similar set of feelings.

From the psychoanalytic view, young children figuring out what causes them to become distressed serves two purposes. First, it establishes a pattern of trying to work through emotional frustrations instead of exploding. Secondly, it provides a basis for anticipating problems in the future, thereby avoiding some of them. If teachers prefer to help children understand what causes negative feelings, they can provide support and guidance to avoid or defuse the provocations. Teachers and parents quickly learn, however, that children do not know what caused their distress. Young children find it difficult to recall incidents that provoked emotional conflict. Sensing threat, the child fends off the threat in many ways, often without conscious realization of doing this. Piaget's work emphasizes that young children are now-oriented people, bound by their perceptions of the moment. Therefore, if they are required to explain what caused a fight, they are likely to focus on the most recent event—the fight—rather than on its cause. Thus, while the children's fight from the adult view resulted from conflict over a toy, the child may explain, "He hit me." If forced to try to recall the incidents prior to the actual fight, the young child's response, "I don't know," is honest, since the vivid event of the fight overshadows the prior causes.

A teacher who has observed a conflict may be able to help recapitulate events, thus encouraging children to examine causes of their defensive behavior. However, when the teacher has not observed the conflict or when there was no overt conflict, only a sensitive relationship with the child is likely to yield the necessary information to help the child develop coping behaviors through exploring feelings.

Accepting Feelings as Expressed

The nondirective approach features (1) accepting feelings as expressed, as a way of helping the child distinguish between feelings and actions, and (2) organizing perceptions of feelings or emotional events.[13] The central thesis of this approach is to help the child identify real

---

12. Fraiberg, *The Magic Years*, pp. 242–265, especially p. 246.

13. Virginia Axline, *Dibs, in Search of Self* (New York: Ballantine Books, 1964).

conflicts to decide what are the possible behavior choices and select one as needed. Play therapists have uncovered many ways in which overpowering emotions block successful coping.[14] While strong claims are made for the nondirective, accepting stance in helping children cope in brief therapy sessions, school and home settings require more limits on behavior than a therapy context. Although the school setting lacks the privacy of the therapist's office, relationships between children and caring teachers can include the accepting, respecting, and trusting emphasized in this approach.

James Hymes reminds us that what the world considers misbehavior is the child's notion of behavior, that is, the child behaves in terms of how she perceives herself in the situation.[15] If she finds the situation challenging and yet accepting, she responds in ways adults call *behaving*. If, on the other hand, the situation makes no sense, or presents frustrations beyond her limits of tolerance or control, the child behaves in ways that defend against the threat, often in unapproved ways.

Dr. Haim Ginott, in his book *Between Parent and Child*, encourages teachers and nurturing adults to maintain conditions for accepting children's feelings and helping them find ways to work through their more destructive emotions. Teachers can do this by using the following guidelines:[16]

1. Conversations between parents and children should protect the self-respect of both child and parent or teacher.
2. Before giving advice or direction, it is important to let the other person know your impression of what they feel.

---

14. Axline, *Dibs*; and Clark Moustakas, *Psychotherapy with Children: The Living Relationship* (New York: Ballantine Books, 1959).
15. Hymes, *Behavior and Misbehavior*, pp. 18–19.
16. Haim Ginott, *Between Parent and Child: New Solutions to Old Problems* (New York: Avon (paperback), 1969) p. 21.

His principles of relationship are that one should:[17]

1. respond to children who appear to have negative feelings about events by accepting their feelings;
2. respond to children's statements of poor self-concept in specific ways: that is, avoid giving general praise, reassurance or pep talks, since these are likely to be ineffective;
3. help children become aware of ambivalent feelings, especially toward significant adults; that is, encourage their self-awareness.

Ginott's further recommendations sound like a handbook for teachers and parents on ways to praise and criticize, reward and punish, and generally live with growing children. An adult can model the roles of authority, companion, and independent person. The "do's" and "don'ts" represent an eclectic view, melding behaviorist, psychoanalytic, and humanist theories.

Teaching Procedures According to Three Theories

Common guidelines for dealing with children's behavior include:

1. establishing logical consequences of social-emotional behavior;
2. avoiding punitiveness and personal rejection;
3. providing guidance to change annoying or negative behavior;
4. increasing the child's sense of worth by providing opportunities for success;
5. featuring the child's strengths instead of her or his weaknesses;
6. praising the child's actions, not endowments or physical characteristics;
7. using meaningful rewards that are not dependent on adult moods.

---

17. Ginott, *Between Parent and Child*, p. 27.

It should be noted that three of these guidelines deal with misbehavior, two with success conditions and two with rewards.

Table 8-1 lists interpretations of these common guidelines for dealing with children's behavior from three different perspectives. For example, guideline two, avoiding punitiveness, finds three justifications. Behaviorists have established the power of positive reinforcement without emotional overtones. Psychoanalytical theorists contend that, while a little guilt contributes to developing moral behavior, excessive guilt is dysfunctional. Humanists view the child as the agent of his or her own actions and find no justification for external judgments or impositions. So for at least three different reasons, theorists of different persuasions all deny punishment is a functional strategy for learning. Similarly, other commonly accepted guidelines receive different justifications from each perspective.

In summary, children's needs for guidance may be viewed as requiring one of three forms of learning:

1. learning new behaviors,
2. relearning behaviors not in current use but previously learned,
3. learning to cope with emotional confusion.

Three different theoretical approaches to personality development agree on common guidelines, but offer different justifications. Behaviorists, psychoanalytic theorists, and humanist theorists agree on the need for procedures that (1) respect the child, (2) are consistent, and (3) set logical outcomes for behaviors, as shown in Table 8-1.

LEARNING FROM CHILDREN WITH HANDICAPS

As federal legislation on mainstreaming is implemented throughout the country, concern is mounting for the self-esteem of children who have various forms of handicaps. Young children deal with differences they perceive in others without using the social restraints they will have as adults. Parents are continually embarrassed by young children's spontaneous remarks about the physical attributes of others. For example:

- "Why does he walk so funny?" (disabled leg)
- "Look at those funny red spots on her face." (disfigurement)
- "Ugh! I don't like the way she looks." (cerebral palsy victim)
- "What's the matter with his eyes?" (different racial group)
- "She doesn't know how to talk." (stutterer)

Such responses usually provoke adults to silence the child in embarrassment, postponing discussion for later. Then, either the "do's" and "don'ts" of social convention are discussed, or the reality of physical differences in people, or both. Using Stanley Coopersmith's theory that young children's self-concepts are tied to their physical attributes poses some interesting challenges in working with handicapped children.[18] Teaching young children sensitivity to another person's feelings requires procedures that conform to ideas about one's sense of self-esteem. It means expanding the base on which children build self-esteem to include more than physical attributes. The Piagetian ideas of the young child's inability to view a situation from more than one position explains why preschoolers rarely respond as expected to when asked, "How would you feel if you were André and heard what you said about him?" Piaget demonstrated that the child cannot see himself in two places at the same time, both as the producer of the behavior and as the receiver.

Teachers can influence children to copy adult accepting behavior when a particular child is not accepted by the peer group.[19]

---

18. Coopersmith, *The Antecedents of Self-Esteem*.
19. Joan Swift, "Effects of Early Group Exerience: The Nursery School and Day Nursery," in Martin L. Hoffman and Lois W. Hoffman, eds., *Review of Child Development Research*, vol. 1 (New York: Russell Sage Foundation, 1964), pp. 249–282, especially 270–280.

TABLE 8.1. Justifications of common guidelines

Common guidelines	Justifications		
	Behaviorist theory	Psychoanalytic theory	Humanist theory
1. Establish logical consequences of social behavior.	This is a reinforcement technique: proximity of reinforcement to behavior establishes desired behavior.	Reality demands exert control on impulsive need behavior, establishing the necessary level of guilt to assure inner controls.	As the child discovers consequences, choices become available and the child can act to change the causes or more effectively deal with consequences.
2. Avoid punitiveness and personal rejection.	This maintains clarity of desired behaviors without confusing reinforcement with personal-emotional reactions.	Guilt, while a necessary emotion to assure continued adjustments to reality, must be manageable to serve personality development. Harsh or punitive procedures produce excessive guilt, which is dysfunctional.	Increasingly more effective choices require identifying feelings and accepting feelings to deal with them.
3. Provide guidance for youngsters producing annoying or negative behavior.	Behavior training or modification techniques are most effective to change behavior.	An expression of psychological need requires teacher guidance to help child develop control.	If the child's best response to the situation is insufficient, the child needs help in seeing the situation differently.
4. Increase the child's sense of self-worth.	Well-paced training in small steps ensures success with appropriate reinforcers. Self-worth is built on successful experiences.	Sufficient adult controls to assure that children's internal drives do not overtake reality of external conditions is required. Accepting negative emotion and channeling expressions of aggression are tools of guidance.	Encourage child to identify how she or he sees the world and feature options and decisions on ways for child to retain, modify, or change conditions.

TABLE 8.1.   (continued)

| | Justifications | | |
Common guidelines	Behaviorist theory	Psychoanalytic theory	Humanist theory
5. Feature the child's strengths instead of weaknesses.	Failure is avoided by clear, well-paced expectations and by reinforcers to assure success.	Inferiority feelings are diminished as child successfully balances internal needs and external reality. An adult monitors external reality to avoid excessive stress and regression.	Inferiority feelings reflect differences between (1) perception of expectation and ability to produce desired behavior and (2) a fault in logic.
6. Praise the child's actions, not endowments or physical characteristics.	This reinforces behaviors that are desired.	Reality orientation, is encouraged through discussions of feelings of competence as well as feelings of incompetence.	Focus on child's ability to control his or her world by perceiving more clearly, knowing more options, and learning to make good choices.
7. Use meaningful rewards that are not dependent on adult moods.	Clear shaping and reinforcement of selected behaviors provides objective rewards that are consistent and do not depend on people's moods.	For the child to mediate effectively between internal drives and reality conditions, the external conditions must be visible and consistent and the maturity of the teacher must assure objective support to achieve desired rewards.	When expectations are clear, the child can learn to make decisions that become increasingly constructive with experience and maturity.

Working directly with the handicapped child is also recommended to strengthen self-esteem and to develop needed social skills. Mainstreaming gives urgency to the need to expand the base on which all children build self-esteem.

The experience of one class will illustrate this. When a hydrocephalic child was enrolled in a day care center, neither the teachers nor the children had had prior experience with this kind of handicap. The four-year-old was placed in a group of three-year-olds because prolonged hospital stays had limited both social and motor development. The teachers worried about the child's safety and were notably over-anxious at first. One teacher expressed concern by avoiding the child and the other chose to supervise the child closely. The children were curious about why the child tilted his head in an unfamiliar way, but they otherwise seemed oblivious to other attributes of this condition. As the staff in team meetings began to work through ways to encourage the child's growth, they identified his strengths, capacities, and needs, as they had for other children in the group. They agreed to teach the child at each incident of difficulty as though he had never been taught before. To the teachers' surprise and pleasure, the child responded to each new learning experience like a thirsty sponge. Initially, he whined when in trouble, but teachers helped him and explained how to ask for help without whining. He began to use other ways, but often he did not realize he was in trouble. Then the teachers began to help him identify his problems. Soon, the teachers' responses to queries from visiting professionals about the child's progress reflected normal concerns—they viewed him as one child among others, with unique needs. The children, in keeping with social learning theory, copied the teacher models, sometimes helping and sometimes ignoring the child's problems. The tilt of the head became familiar enough to be taken for granted.

Other situations including children with special needs or handicapping conditions may require more extended efforts to absorb the child successfully into the social setting and the program. What is significant in this situation is the team approach to specifying the needs for teaching and guidance that will apply in each instance.

Including a child with handicapping conditions in a group highlights all children's needs for a broad base for building self-esteem. The broad base requires identifying strengths and providing experiences of success. Teaching plans must be specific and well designed. Teacher modeling of respect for individual differences and increased familiarity with a handicapped child in a setting where strengths are emphasized both contribute to successful mainstreaming.

THE TEACHING TEAM

Early childhood programs have a long tradition of teaching teams because of the urgent physical and emotional needs of young children. In classrooms with teaching teams, the presence of more than one authority figure for children requires team cooperation. *Differentiated staffing* generally means a group with varying credentials working in one classroom, for example a head teacher, one or more assistant teachers, a parent volunteer, and a student teacher. Effective use of differentiated staffing depends on respecting and emphasizing their individual differences without breaching consistency in general classroom procedures and expectations. Attributes of effective teamwork include:

1. agreement on the roles to be filled by each member of the team;
2. agreement on the responsibilities of each member;
3. procedures for redistribution of roles and responsibilities when necessary.

Since every member of the team affects the quality of the children's experience, teams require ways to reach agreement on all points of decision. Such decision points include classroom schedule, room arrangement, activities to be developed, distribution of teaching roles among the members of the team, disposition of materials and equipment, evaluation of children's progress, needs for program changes, and ways of working with parents.

The relationships of the classroom teaching staff with each other directly affect their relationships with the children. For example, lack of agreement on classroom schedule will result in teachers communicating different expectations to children about the expected sequence of activities. Thus, team relationships have direct impact on classroom atmosphere. These relationships affect continuity in teacher-child relationships; levels of warmth, spontaneity, and humor; involvement of children with adults; and ambience of tension or relaxation.

The teaching team may agree on major program features even though they expect to operate individually within the agreed-on program structure. To use the resources of the teachers to the maximum, a team approach should not suppress personality differences or style. One of the team's strongest assets may be that children with different emotional needs, interests, skills, and ideas can interact with more than one mature personality. Hence, a functional teaching team probably requires more personal variety rather than less, if the adults are to complement each other in different ways that benefit children.

Optimal involvement of each member of the teaching team may be limited by ineffective procedures for agreeing on roles and responsibilities. In such cases, members become frustrated and divert teaching energy away from their relationships with the children. A teaching team can obviously contain a broad range of personalities and styles of classroom interaction. Unity is required, however, in decisions about schedule, rules, classroom limits, program development, and distribution of roles and responsibilities.

Part-time Members of the Teaching Team

Part-time members of the teaching team include students, volunteers, and older school children who work in the classroom on a regular basis. The same consideration for roles, responsibilities, and procedures is required for part-time as for full-time members of the team. Persons who come and go during a week often prove to be unexpected resources for initiating new curriculum activities. Their role in the program has some of the attributes of the visitor, and visitors, by virtue of novelty, tend to spark new interests. Additionally, temporary or intermittent members of the team may offer supportive services to the program by helping maintain records on children's progress. See Chapter 11 for further discussion of record-keeping procedures.

SUMMARY

In the early years, the effects of teachers on children's developing self-concepts are of great importance. Once formed, self-concepts tend to resist change.

Differing views on how self-concepts develop grow out of behaviorist, psychoanalytic, and humanist (or phenomenological) theories. All unite to bar the use of punishment and all support positive approaches to self-concept development.

In the classroom, children are challenged to learn new behaviors, suppress unsocial impulses, and adapt behaviors to new demands. There are some common guidelines that support children's positive self-concept formation and that are upheld by all theoretical approaches.

Assimilating children with handicaps challenges teachers to maintain an environment that features children's strengths and respects each child's limitations. For children whose handicaps are visibly different, teacher modeling of accepting differences and reinforcing strengths sets the pattern for peer relationships.

Teaching teams provide personal variety for children with differing emotional needs, interests, skills and ideas. However, planning and cooperation are required to realize the potential contribution of members of the teaching team.

EXERCISES

1. List at least five common behaviors that are universally rejected for teaching.
2. Complete at least three anecdotal recordings of your own dissatisfactions in initiating or responding to young children's social-emotional needs.
    a. Review the guidelines summarized on Table 8-1 and identify the approach you took.
    b. Write a brief description of an alternative approach.

BIBLIOGRAPHY

Axline, Virginia. *Dibs, in Search of Self.* New York: Ballantine Books, 1964.

Combs, Arthur, ed. *Perceiving, Behaving and Becoming.* Washington, D.C.: ASCD Yearbook, 1962.

Combs, Arthur, and Snygg, Donald. *Individual Behavior: A Perceptual Approach to Behavior.* Rev. ed. New York: Harper & Row, 1959.

Coopersmith, Stanley. *The Antecedents of Self-Esteem.* San Francisco: W.H. Freeman, 1967.

Dinkmeyer, Donald. *Child Development: The Emerging Self.* Englewood Cliffs, N.J.: Prentice-Hall, 1965.

Fraiberg, Selma. *The Magic Years.* New York: Charles Scribners, 1959.

Ginott, Haim. *Between Parent and Child: New Solutions to Old Problems.* New York: Macmillan, 1965; Avon, 1969 (paperback).

Hymes, James L. *Behavior and Misbehavior: A Teacher's Guide to Action.* Englewood Cliffs, N.J.: Prentice-Hall, 1955.

Moustakas, Clark. *Psychotherapy with Children: The Living Relationship.* New York: Ballantine Books, 1959.

Patterson, Cecil H. "Insights about Persons: Psychological Foundations of Humanistic and Affective Education." In Louise Berman and Jessie Roderick, eds., *Feeling, Valuing and the Art of Growing: Insights in the Affective.* Washington, D.C.: Association for Supervision and Curriculum Development, 1977 Yearbook.

Rogers, Carl; and Stevens, Barry; Gendlin, Eugene; Schlien, John; and Van Dusen, Wilson. *Person to Person: The Problem of Being Human.* Lafayette, Calif.: Real People Press, 1967.

Shepard, Lorrie. "Self-Acceptance: The Evaluative Component of the Self-Concept Construct." *American Educational Research Journal,* 16, no. 2 (Spring 1979): 139–160.

Swift, Joan. "Effects of Early Group Experience: The Nursery School and Day Nursery." In Martin L. Hoffman and Lois W. Hoffman, eds., *Review of Child Development Research.* Vol. 1. New York: Russell Sage Foundation, 1964.

Yamamoto, Kaoru. *The Child and His Image: Self-Concept in the Early Years.* New York: Houghton Mifflin, 1972.

9 Design of Space and Activities

Teachers develop curriculum in the context of the school environment—the classroom and outdoor space—and through the activities that occur. How does the arrangement of the furniture and materials affect the program? Is one arrangement more supportive of curriculum goals than others? If one or two types of instructional activities are preferred, how do they support valued outcomes? Since research does not document the value of one instructional activity or one form of room arrangement over another, the teacher is challenged to design the use of space and select instructional activities that conform with the teacher's curriculum framework. This framework, you will recall, includes curriculum form, goals and purposes, classes of content, views of development, and principles of sequencing. Criteria for designing and evaluating room arrangement and use of outdoor space are discussed in the next section. Next we will discuss criteria for evaluating the effectiveness of rules and routines. In the final section of the chapter, we will analyze types of instructional activities in terms of the teacher's role, the child's role, and forms of learning. As the teacher makes successive decisions on each curriculum component, the preferred solution emerges to the many questions of design.

USE OF SPACE

Early childhood teachers have always recognized the importance of planning good use of space. Room-arrangement decisions include placement of materials, centers of interest, traffic patterns, accessibility of materials, and a decorator's eye for such characteristics as neatness, balance, interest, and attractiveness. Since early childhood programs require many materials, their optimum arrangement is vital to smooth program development.[1]

The way teachers arrange their rooms reflects values and expected outcomes. A kindergarten teacher who values a teacher-directed, academically oriented program of specific reading and mathematics skills will arrange a room to provide space for group instruction and practice periods. Play centers, for dramatic play, and block construction, for example, would be separated from the areas intended for academic instruction. In contrast, if a kindergarten program gives high priority to children's active involvement with materials and with each other, well-equipped interest centers would be provided throughout the room.

Regardless of program goals, there are some guidelines for arranging classrooms and outdoor play areas. In all programs, spatial arrangements can facilitate smooth scheduling, reduce distractions or confusions, emphasize

1. Association for Childhood Education International, *Space Arrangement, Beauty in School*, pub. no. 101 (Washington, D.C.: ACEI, n.d.); Minnie P. Berson and William W. Chase, "Planning Preschool Facilities," in Joe L. Frost, ed., *Early Childhood Education Rediscovered, Readings* (New York: Holt, Rinehart & Winston, 1968), pp. 547–555; William Fowler, *Infant and Child Care* (Boston: Allyn and Bacon, 1980), especially chap. 4, "The Physical Environment," pp. 84–108.

traffic lanes, and diminish conflicts concerning materials and equipment. In essence, guidelines for arrangement of space feature visible orderliness, visual cues, and self-evident procedures. Furniture is grouped as it is intended to be used, and materials are stored in logical order. Traffic patterns are distinctive. Orderliness reduces the need for verbal rules and corrective teaching, although even the best physical arrangement cannot eliminate this need completely. Order is both perceptual and conceptual. The test of how well the order is communicated to children is how they use and maintain it.

Guidelines for the arrangement of physical space include:[2]

1. *Clarity.* Establishment of clearly defined interest centers or work areas helps children know what materials to use, and how much space is available. Boundaries of an area are identified by placement of furniture, floor tape strips, or other visual indicators. For example, the indoor area available for block construction may be indicated by either of the visual cues just mentioned or by a carpet. The outdoor area for ball playing may be designated by a chalk line.
2. *Visible order.* Provision for storage, with space to remove and return materials without spilling others, helps children to maintain the desired order. Teachers can monitor this quickly if storage is open and visible. Indoors, marking shelves and containers with picture cues facilitates the maintenance of order. Outdoors, "parking spaces" for vehicles guides efficient storage of tricycles and wagons, and painted or chalked lines divide ball games from other types of physical activity.
3. *Clearly defined pathways.* Arrangement of access to all centers, avoiding traffic through a center, both indoors and out, diminishes confusion and conflicts.
4. *Placement of centers.* Generally, centers with high activity are placed at a distance from those requiring quiet. Indoors, for example, a block area would be placed next to a dramatic play area rather than next to a library center. Outdoors, swings or climbing bars are placed well away from ball playing.

A brief, efficient checklist for evaluating room arrangement may include a list of children's behaviors that are valued and those that are not. Thelma Harmes suggests an evaluation checklist of questions to help the teacher view the environment from the child's perspective. She arranges about forty questions into four categories: the physical environment, the interpersonal environment, activities to stimulate development, and the schedule.[3]

Some indicators of a need to reorganize the use of space in any program design are:

1. *Space conflicts.* Too many children gather in an area, causing overcrowding and disrupting the activity. Options include:
   a. expanding the space provided;
   b. reducing the amount of materials available for use in the area;
   c. finding a more efficient way to monitor group size.
2. *Materials conflicts.* Insufficient materials are provided for the number of children involved in the activity. Options include:
   a. reducing the size of the space available in the area to lower the number of children competing for the materials;
   b. increasing the quantity of materials provided;
   c. instituting procedures for sharing and taking turns.

---

2. Helen F. Robison and Sydney L. Schwartz, *Learning at an Early Age*, vol. 1 (Englewood Cliffs, N.J.: Prentice-Hall, 1972), pp. 197–216.

3. Thelma Harmes, "Evaluating Settings for Learning," in Judy Spitler McKee, ed., *Early Childhood Education 80/81*, Annual Editions (Guilford, Conn.: Dushkin, 1980), art. 64, pp. 256–257.

3. *Traffic collisions.* As children move from one area to another, activities are interrupted because of collisions. Options include:
   a. redesigning the traffic lanes by changing the placement of activity centers;
   b. marking traffic lanes more clearly with tape or other marking materials.

Although there has been little research on the effects of physical environment on classroom climate and activities for young children, positive effects on task involvement have been documented for older children in open classrooms when the organization of space and materials was improved.[4]

Indoor Space

It is usually easy to identify which interest centers are most valued and which least valued in a classroom by noting location, size, accessibility, and lighting. Block areas located in small entryways that have high levels of traffic and poor lighting reflect the low value placed on this activity. Similarly, library areas—designated solely by a bookshelf placed against a wall near the bathroom or in other traffic lanes without a chair or table—discourage children's enjoyment of books.

Children respond to teacher expectations communicated through the physical arrangement of the room. Accessible materials communicate "help yourself." Clearly marked storage areas encourage children to put things away. Where there are mixed messages about children's use of materials, ambiguous communication generates confusion. For example, when children are grouped for a story in an area with open shelves of manipulative materials, the mixed messages are "Listen to the story," or, "Choose a play material from the shelf." Some children are bound to respond to the implicit invitation to play with materials rather than the stated request to listen to the story. Where overcrowed shelves are coded for materials placement, the message to put the materials away in specific spaces is contradicted by the invitation to be disorderly.

Boundaries and traffic lanes or pathways pose similar challenges for room organization. Furniture and such visible markings as floor tape and rugs identify clear boundaries for interest centers. Such boundaries define work/play spaces and determine traffic lanes in the classrooms as well. Children tend to follow traffic lanes marked off for specific use. When boundaries are invisible, it is easy to ignore or forget them or not even realize they exist. As teachers examine room arrangements, they are often surprised at the number of boundaries that are assumed but not visible. The clearer the demarcations of space, the less need there is to rely on verbal rules and reminders.

We suggest that you draw scale maps of the classroom to review boundaries, traffic lanes, location of interest centers, and proximity of materials to areas of use.

Outdoor Space

The same considerations listed for indoor space apply to the organization of outdoor space. However, the high degree of physical movement outdoors—running, riding tricycles, using wagons, playing ball, and jumping rope—poses more challenge to establishing boundaries, traffic patterns, and space use than do indoor areas. Curriculum goals, of course, provide the basis for decisions on the design of the outdoor play area. Boundary needs depend primarily on expectations for activities, independence, and care of equipment and materials.

Typically, tricycle riders who see no limits may collide with each other and interfere with block builders, ball players, and climbers.

---

4. Carol Weinstein, "Modifying Student Behavior in an Open Classroom through Changes in the Physical Design," *American Educational Research Journal*, 14, no. 3 (Summer 1977): 249–262.

Problems that result from poor use of outdoor space can lead to a review of curriculum goals, which will have implications for changing the space design. For example a day care teacher with whom we worked was observing children's use of outdoor space and realized that the children were confused about where to use materials and what pathways to follow. There were frequent collisions, conflicts, and interruptions of activities. After planning with other teachers who used the same outdoor space at different times, she introduced tricycle pathways by taped "roadways" in one area, away from climbing gyms and ball playing. She also placed related materials along the path to encourage dramatic play, such as "gassing up." She monitored her new arrangement to make sure it worked. In this instance, the teacher found a desirable decrease in conflict and an increase in task-oriented play related to thoughtful reorganization of outdoor space.

RULES AND ROUTINES

Essentially, effective rules and procedures free adults and children to relate to each other and to the program, minimizing confusion and conflict. The necessity of rules and procedures, therefore, is assumed. The number of rules needed is a matter of the teacher's personal preference, the type of curriculum and the age of the children.

In some classrooms, children seem to know the rules and routines and follow them automatically. In other rooms, every rule becomes a battleground for power between teachers and children. These battles can so dominate the climate of a classroom that they interfere with orderly programs.

Rules

Rules and procedures are intended to channel behavior and to set limits. A rule that children take turns to clean the snack tables clearly indicates that children, not adults, will do the job. The tighter, more restrictive rule that each person throw away her or his own cup and napkin leaves no choices.

Children acquire information and instruction on rules under two types of conditions—in advance, and in process. Answers to the question of when to advise children of rules and procedures favor these two conditions: wait until needed or anticipate and give advance information.

TABLE 9.1. Views on when to teach rules

Wait until rules are needed	*Anticipate need with advance teaching*
Children can generate their own rules if given an opportunity.	Children need information on rules and procedures before an activity, or they will get into trouble.
If children are given a battery of rules in the beginning, it will frighten them since they cannot deal with a large number of rules at once. They may also forget most of the rules.	Corrective teaching tends to build guilt, unnecessarily penalizing children for not knowing rules that have never been taught.
The most effective time to give rules is in context, when they are obviously needed and have meaning.	Rules taught "properly," in advance, reduce chaos and avoid conflict.

As noted in Table 9-1, advocates of "wait until needed" focus on the timeliness of rule learning and the importance of giving children the opportunity to establish their own rules. In contrast, advocates of advance teaching cite the values of emotional and physical safety. When children know what is expected, they can adjust their behavior, avoiding conflict and anxiety. The reasons for waiting are essentially those of the child development–maturationist point of view, and the reasons for advance teaching stem from either a behaviorist or psychodynamic perspective.

In reality, teachers who anticipate needs for rules and procedures still find it necessary to generate more rules in process. Those who prefer the in-process approach find that some procedures, such as fire drills, require advance information and practice. A few rules can only be generated after the fact because nobody expected to need them. These are likely to be unpredictable health and safety features that occur during a disaster, such as power failure or unusual weather effects.

Routines

Teachers tend to think of routines as necessary care-taking procedures unrelated to curriculum. Consequently, procedures for routines may be different from the major curriculum approach. Examples of variations in approaches to routines are illustrated in Table 9-2, showing procedures ranging from maximum independence of children to maximum teacher control. Behaviorists claim that children can achieve maximum independence if they are taught the procedures in sufficiently small steps to assure mastery of each step and ulti-

TABLE 9.2. Approaches to routines

Routine	Maximum child independence	Shared responsibility	Maximum teacher control
Cleanup	Teacher walks around the room advising children of impending end to the work period; then requests children to begin cleanup.	Teacher announces cleanup and assigns or solicits one child in each area to monitor task.	Teacher gathers children in a circle and assigns cleanup tasks.
Eating	Each child sets own place, serves self, and cleans up.	Children take turns setting tables, serving, and cleaning up.	Teacher sets tables, serves children, and cleans up.
Attendance	Without teacher help, children record their own attendance as they arrive.	Children record their own attendance during teacher-supervised attendance period.	Teacher takes attendance by calling names and having children respond.
Toileting	Each child monitors own toileting needs without direction from teacher.	Teacher periodically reminds children to use toilet as needed.	Teacher terminates all classroom activities for bathroom period, with children in line for turns.

mately of all steps. Under such guidelines, routines may be analyzed for component parts so that teachers can direct children through each step of the ladder. For example, in cleaning up, the component parts might be:

1. terminating play,
2. selecting a cleanup task,
3. performing the cleanup task.
4. signaling readiness for the next activity,
5. moving to the expected station or area.

To teach children to terminate play, the teacher may begin by using a distinctive signal that becomes automatically associated with the end of play. Subsequent steps include providing each child with a choice between two specific tasks, followed by return to the group. Later, as children develop skill in making a choice between two tasks, the choices are expanded and, in addition, a series of tasks may be undertaken, such as putting away all the table toys after completing unfinished puzzles and finding containers for each set of materials. Ultimately, the children begin and complete cleanup without teacher direction.

Teachers preferring more child independence add such personal touches as advising individuals of impending cleanup, discussing with children their activities and the need for rules, or considering requests for exemption from rules. In some programs, the process of carrying out routines is designed to further curriculum goals. For example, mathematics and beginning reading are supplemented through the use of helper charts that designate job assignments and keep tallies on the frequency of turns.

Some teachers prefer routines that do not require monitoring. This means that skill practice is embedded in the procedure. For example, one kindergarten teacher designed a procedure for self-monitoring the limits on number of children in interest centers during the activity period. She set up an "interest center activity board" with a designated number of slots along a line for each center. Children placed discs containing their photographs in slots to signal where they would be playing. When changing interest centers, they went to the chart first to switch their picture discs. If no slots were vacant in the area they desired, either they selected a different center or arranged a trade of places. You might note the social skill practice in trading that is built into this procedure.

Another design for controlling the numbers of children in interest centers used neck chains or wrist chains specifically designating centers by color. Limited numbers of chains were available for each center. Both procedures require some mathematical skills, but the chain procedure is more suitable to younger children unable to read charts.

The productive arrangement of the classroom and playground, including provision of space and materials for learning centers and smooth-flowing traffic patterns, help to create the conditions needed for curriculum development. Active use of children's knowledge and skills may be featured in the design of rules and routines. Additionally, curriculum goals can be advanced by the rules and routines requiring mastery of skills, application of understanding, and problem solving.

INSTRUCTIONAL ACTIVITIES

Plans for instructional activities, like designs for routines, range from maximum teacher control and child dependency to the opposite. A pattern of maximum teacher control puts the child at the receiving end of the spectrum, where she is expected to take in information passively without acting on it at the time. Maximum independence occurs when the child is pursuing her or his own learning and the teacher's role is almost invisible.

Seven distinct types of teaching-learning activities, ranging from most to least teacher control, include:

1. structured information-giving activities;
2. structured skill-acquisition activities;
3. structured presentation of experiences;
4. structured review of school and nonschool experiences;
5. directed practice activities for recall of information, use of information, and skills repetition;
6. problem-solving activities: games, projects and structured problems;
7. problem setting by children.

Table 9–3 identifies the relationship between the teacher's role and the child's role in the activity. The form of children's involvement varies from passive reception to active production as the teaching influence diminishes from direct toward indirect teaching.

The seven variations in teacher-child role relationships shown on Table 9–3 illustrate the major options.

1. *Structured information-giving activities* involve the standard didactic pattern of instruction in which the teacher provides information and the child's energy is directed to attending and receiving the information. If concrete materials are included in the activity, the teacher uses them for demonstration and illustration.

This type of instruction is frequently selected to anticipate new experiences, such as describing the details of a forthcoming trip or associating a consonant sound with its symbol. Often, didactic presentation is used for new content, such as "how to brush your teeth," "eating a healthy breakfast," and "how to use the nature book to identify trees." In this mode, teachers often use informational books and demonstration materials.

2. *Structured skill-acquisition activities* require the teacher to model the new skills, using materials if necessary. Children observe or receive the information and are expected to imitate or copy the skill immediately.

Using scissors, writing one's name in manuscript, and learning new sight-word vocabulary are activities representative of this category. The Montessori program utilizes this approach extensively.

3. *Structured experiences through language* occur in story reading and comprehensive discussions after a reading lesson. Listening to records and viewing television typically place the child in a passive, receptive role.

4. *Structured review of both school and nonschool experiences* includes retelling stories, describing a cooking activity, and reporting on a family visit to an amusement park. The major difference between the in-school base and the out-of-school bases for review is the teacher's access to verification. When children report on home experiences, the child is in control of the content since the teacher was not present.

5. *Directed practice activities for recall or use of information and skill practice* occur in many popular games such as lotto, bingo, teacher-made games, and board games. In playful activities, the teacher reviews children's knowledge of such facts as name labels, counting skills, or geometric shapes and then initiates practice activities, checking for accuracy of children's responses. Using a game-like format, the teacher retains control by being the leader or monitoring the leader. Independent games are included in the next category.

6. *Project and problem-solving activities and independent games* are generally, but not necessarily, structured by the teacher. However, children control their participation in the activity and in the outcomes. Teacher-made and commercial materials may be used, but children pursue their games with little or no need for teacher guidance.

7. *Problem-setting* gives children maximum control. Teacher entry into the children's activity is determined by the child. Typically, the teacher provides the materials and the setting and postpones participation until children indicate a need for help or a desire to share. At this point, if entry is accepted, the teacher may question, suggest, probe, challenge, or even participate.

TABLE 9.3. Teacher-child roles in instructional activities

Type of activity	Teacher's role	Child's role	Sample activities
1. Structured information giving	be didactic lecture demonstrate read	be receptive: visual and auditory	new information on health, transportation, or weather directions for fire drills information on trips and what to look for
2. Structured skill development	be didactic lecture demonstrate model	be receptive: visual and auditory be productive: motor and oral	manuscript practice and name writing counting labeling geometric shapes donning outer clothing using a tape recorder
3. Structured presentation of experiences	read or narrate story	be receptive	story reading and storytelling showing filmstrips, films, or slides hearing a tape or watching television
4. Structured review of school and nonschool experiences	select topic and control review by questions and validation where possible	recapitulate experiences according to teacher-imposed guidelines	retelling a familiar story reviewing events of a trip reviewing a sequence of cooking activity narrating a family trip recapitulating a story dramatization
5. Directed practice for recall and use of information; skills repetition	explain activity procedures lead activity monitor child's response for accuracy	respond to cues repeat behavior as required	lotto games teacher-made game-like activities counting using color names tracing shapes songs, movement, chants, and poems rules

TABLE 9.3. (continued)

Type of activity	Teacher's role	Child's role	Sample activities
6. Problem solving in projects and independent games	pose the task present materials act as resource monitor outcomes	utilize knowledge and skills to produce teacher-defined project	art and craft projects games (as in 5 above but without teacher monitoring) construction and carpentry projects
7. Problem setting	provide materials value activity, outcomes, and processes enhance child's understanding through probes and challenges	set own task identify and solve own problems verbalize understanding defend own point of view	constructing with blocks recreating a puzzle mixing own colors inventing games designing projects coping with environmental problems identifying problems in social skills development

Craft projects can be designed to fit anywhere within this range of activities from teacher control to total child independence. Musical games, songs, and chants can also be adapted to the range of possibilities, as well as motoric and circle games, although such activities tend to be more teacher dominated. Other activities, such as cooking, papier mâché, finger painting, playdough, and paint mixing can lead toward independence but usually represent more teacher control rather than less.

Selection of instructional activities grows out of decisions about the framework components, discussed in Section One. Since all programs are likely to include some activities reflecting each of the seven forms discussed, the teaching decisions of necessity relate to immediate goals. For example, if children in a classroom emphasizing curriculum as a happening need to learn the school fire-drill procedures, a structured information-giving and skill-practice activity is indicated. While this teacher may not choose such an activity for most of the program, it is appropriate to train children for fire drills. In an academically oriented program featuring more teacher-directed skill practice, open periods for child-selected games and activities are often required for balance and relaxation. Whether instructional activities will be more active or passive depends on the teacher's view of child development.

SUMMARY

The classroom climate is affected by the arrangement of the physical environment, procedures for routines, and teachers' roles in instructional activities. Well-planned room arrangements foster involvement in learning without distractions due to conflicts over space and materials. Well-planned routines function smoothly, avoiding unnecessary waiting time and frustration. Instructional activities ranging from high teacher domination to high child control of materials, tasks, and outcomes are selected in terms of activity goals, program objectives, and views of child development and learning.

EXERCISES

1. Make a map of your own classroom or one where you are having field experiences.
2. Analyze your map for:
   a. traffic-lane effectiveness,
   b. space allocation for centers related to learning activities,
   c. values indicated,
   d. materials—organization, availability, and storage.
3. Make a new map to solve the problems identified or to emphasize other values, indoors or outdoors.

BIBLIOGRAPHY

Association for Childhood Education International. "Space, Arrangement, Beauty in School." Pub. no. 101 Washington, D.C.: ACEI, n.d.

Berson, Minnie P., and Chase, William W. "Planning Preschool Facilities. In Joe L. Frost, ed., *Early Childhood Education Rediscovered, Readings.* New York: Holt, Rinehart & Winston, 1968.

Cherry, Clare. *Creative Play for the Developing Child.* Belmont, Calif.: Fearon Publishers, 1976.

Fowler, William. *Infant and Child Care.* Boston: Allyn and Bacon, 1980.

Harmes, Thelma. "Evaluating Settings for Learning." In Judy Spitler McKee, ed., *Early Childhood Education 80/81.* Annual Editions. Guilford, Conn.: Dushkin, 1980. Art. 64.

Robison, Helen F., and Schwartz, Sydney L. *Learning at an Early Age.* Vol. 1. Englewood Cliffs, N.J.: Prentice-Hall, 1972.

Weinstein, Carol. "Modifying Student Behavior in an Open Classroom through Changes in the Physical Design." *American Educational Research Journal*, 14, no. 3 (Summer 1977): 249–262.

10 Teaching Roles and Strategies

Teaching is a complex mix of feelings, intentions, actions, and interactions. Teaching comprises both action and thought, heart and mind, affect and cognition. Teaching behavior takes physical and visible forms and is therefore open to observation and study. To those who emphasize feeling and personality over actions and events, it is possible to say that teaching is more than a series of acts or interactions. Nevertheless, it seems likely that teachers pattern the expression of their feelings and intentions in observable forms of classroom behavior. What teachers do and say offers rich material for self-study, for analysis of teacher input patterns, and for help in developing self-awareness and desired skills.

Teachers can sort out the roles and strategies that make up teaching behavior to become clearer and more precise about their own teaching. We think that analysis of one's teaching helps teachers review their intentions compared with performance. It also contributes to a teacher's personal growth and stimulation. This chapter describes teaching roles and strategies and illustrates their relationship to curriculum components. As teachers clarify their values and goals, selecting roles and strategies will follow.

THE TEACHER AS A PERSON

A mother was driving by an elementary school during morning recess when her four-year-old remarked with intensity, "I wonder if those children love their teacher as much as I love Ms. S." Verbal four-year-olds serve notice that early childhood teachers are important persons in their lives. Teachers, however, vary considerably in teaching style, interests, skills, and experiences. They bring unique personal strengths, habits, and styles of teaching. Interests spill out in innumerable ways as teachers respond selectively to children's activities.

The following examples of classroom style dramatize vividly the impact of teachers on curriculum. In one two-classroom nursery school, where the rooms were equipped equivalently and programs followed similar schedules, the teachers were theoretically committed to the same program. However, the difference in interests and personality style of the head teachers led to remarkably different programs. One teacher's major strength was in the arts. He was an accomplished musician and oil painter and also a very gregarious person. The other teacher, with limited skills in the arts, featured nonverbal expressive modes and emphasized sympathy for and empathy between persons.

A visitor would be likely to conclude that either the basic programs of these two teachers were different or the two groups represented different backgrounds. Children in the artistic teacher's room used color, shape, and other visual language spontaneously. Their activities centered in the constructive and art-craft areas. Their limited dramatic play activities were re-enactments of performances, dance, singing, and drama. In the other room, the children's activities featured dramatic role play with considerable detail, such as playing a grocery clerk asking whether a customer wanted a large or small bag. The language of personal feelings permeated the classroom.

In these classrooms, the personality and interests of the teachers were clearly reflected in the children's learning activities. A periodic review of one's unique style increases the possibility that personal contributions will make their way into curriculum plans by design rather than by chance.

TEACHING ROLES

Teaching still connotes to many people a front-and-center individual lecturing to children or filling them with knowledge. More than any other teaching group, early childhood teachers have refused to maintain this stereotype. Young children invite spontaneity, warmth, humor, versatility, and flexibility. These qualities can be respected within many different teaching styles.

The demands of teaching in activity-based, materials-rich classrooms require teaching roles seldom found in the more sedentary classrooms of the upper grades. The teacher, like the actor, functions in roles when working with young children.[1] Commonly, these roles are played spontaneously rather than deliberately, they are selected intuitively rather than with conscious purpose, and the teacher is rarely able to recall what role was played to achieve successful learning with children. An exploration of role possibilities and alternatives may offer more options to the teacher in daily interaction with children and build more competence and skill in matching the role to the immediate goals.[2]

Several lists of teaching roles in early childhood have been suggested in the recent past.[3] Such lists have ranged from four broad categories to a dozen or more narrowly defined ones. One categorization developed by us in the sixties lists the many roles by function:[4]

- *Nurturer*—offering children acceptance and support through praise, affection, interest, and thoughtful attention. One example is cuddling a lonesome child or accepting expressions of unhappiness such as crying, noting to the child that "you must really be unhappy to cry."
- *Reinforcer*—using selective reinforcement techniques to feature desired forms of behavior and to discourage undesirable forms of behavior through nonreinforcement. One example is praising a child who returns play materials to the shelves and ignoring the behavior of the child who does not put materials away.
- *Information Giver*—supplying information verbally and by action or gesture to one or more children. Examples include telling two children the time of day, or telling the class the current date and day of the week; demonstrating how to use paste; and pointing to the position of a puzzle piece.
- *Challenger*—creating dissonance, puzzlement, curiosity, and expectation of competence. One example is, when children prematurely generalize that a magnet "sticks" to metal, offering them copper, lead, and aluminum to test.
- *Tutor*—active instruction of a child. One example is helping a child spell her or his name by matching flannel letters to the teacher-written model.

---

1. Bruce J. Biddle and Edwin J. Thomas, *Role Theory: Concepts and Research* (New York: Wiley & Sons, 1966).

2. Raymond S. Adams and Bruce J. Biddle, *Realities of Teaching* (New York: Holt, Rinehart & Winston, 1970).

3. Lillian Katz, "Teaching in Preschool: Roles and Goals," *Children*, 17 (1970):42–48.

4. Helen F. Robison and Sydney L. Schwartz, *Learning at an Early Age*, vol. 1. (Englewood Cliffs, N.J.: Prentice-Hall, 1972), pp. 79–88.

- *Observer*—watching children without interacting with them or with the material they are using. This may include note taking or active forms of record keeping.
- *Evaluator*—testing or assessing children's information, skills, or concepts. One example is asking a child to replicate in beads a color pattern offered in pegs. This role may also include recording children's performance or scores.
- *Participant*—active involvement with children in some form of activity, whether in the leadership role or as a member of the group. Examples include singing with children or playing a game.
- *Manager*—leadership in organizing the room, the materials, the equipment, and the auxiliary staff. Examples include setting out art materials, requesting an assistant to tutor a child, announcing snack time, and determining the temporal sequence of the program.
- *Caretaker*—providing physical care and safety and emotional security during the day away from home.

Although the roles as defined are essentially distinct, some roles tend to occur simultaneously. For instance, it is most likely that in the tutoring role, the teacher will also fill the roles of nurturer and reinforcer. On the other hand, the role of observer, by definition requiring noninvolvement, cannot encompass another role at the same time unless the teacher is relating selectively to two different children. In this case, the teacher could be an observer of one child while playing a nurturer or other role with another child.

CHILD DEVELOPMENT VIEWS AND TEACHER ROLES

The basic approaches to child development discussed in Chapter 5 include the views of the maturationist, behaviorist (or cultural training theorist), cognitive-developmentalist (or interactionist) and the psychoanalyst. A set of teaching roles can be derived from each of these views. The behaviorist, with emphasis on external influences, draws primarily on the roles of information giver, reinforcer, evaluator, and manager. From this perspective, the teacher establishes expectations for children's behavior through managing, clarifies what is to be learned by giving information, and reinforces the desired learning as it is acquired.

The maturationist view, in which the child's inborn capacities are allowed to flower, features the nurturing, managing, scheduling, observing, and caretaking roles. These roles meet affective concerns directly through nurturance and caretaking and indirectly through managing and scheduling.

The interactionist view gives weight to the challenging and observing roles, where teachers identify what ideas children are testing, and encourage further experimenting through challenging comments and questions. Management is an important role in arranging a challenging environment and scheduling time for exploration and discovery.

The psychodynamic, or psychoanalytic view, with major concern for children's inner feelings, tends to combine those roles which help children resolve inner conflicts, inhibit antisocial behaviors, and develop social skills. These roles include challenging in the realm of feelings and emotions, giving information about behavior options, and nurturing by supporting children so they can deal with anger, frustration, and self-destructive feelings.

Based on Kohlberg's three-way classification of early childhood programs into maturationist, cultural training, and cognitive-developmental groups (see Chapter 5), the major teaching behaviors for each can be summarized. The teaching roles are *instructor*, *facilitator*, and *teacher-director* for the cultural training, cognitive-developmental, and maturationist approaches, respectively.

The most specific behaviors can be identified for the cultural training type. Teaching activity is clearly defined—from selecting behavior goals and assessing entry behavior for that goal to the various steps in the instructional design, including the systematic use of selected reinforcers. The cultural training teacher is expected to reinforce, usually by praising a child; it may be assumed that a teacher providing a child reinforcers will be perceived very positively by the child.

Unlike cultural training programs, where teachers are actively involved in transmitting information and teaching children directly, the teacher in a cognitive-developmental program is generally regarded more as a facilitator, except for social forms of knowledge, such as the names of objects that cannot be derived from exploratory activity. The cognitive-developmental teacher can suggest activities but prefers the child to find her or his own involvement. In either case, the teacher's major role is to guide the child to discoveries, to follow up on the child's struggles to solve problems, and to help the child test his or her ideas. Errors in the child's findings are not corrected. Instead, the teacher's role is to help the child continue to deal with the problem; experiencing discrepant information, comparing findings with peers, and growing in maturity all help make corrections when the child understands enough to do so.

The least clear-cut of all teaching roles are those of the maturationist teachers. Since the maturationist teacher expects the child to unfold, in many ways the concept of teaching is simpler than for the other two types of curricula. The most useful roles for the maturationist teacher are:

1. *Observer*—Observe children closely or test them for readiness for various kinds of instruction.
2. *Evaluator*—Classifying children by their degree of readiness for various kinds of instruction or for types of activities.
3. *Nurturer*—Maintain good rapport with child to encourage unfolding.
4. *Manager*—Prepare a good environment for learning, with the selected materials and arrangements desired.
5. *Information giver*—Direct preplanned lessons or improvise lessons.
6. *Mixed roles*—Supervise play activities.

It should be noted that some behaviors are present for all types of curricula, especially close observation of children, didactic instruction (information giving), and preparing the environment for learning. This role of preparing the learning environment has different meanings in each program. In cultural training, it refers to a specific child and the need to maximize the learning situation for a particular objective, including motivation and reinforcement. In Montessori programs, the prepared environment refers to the well-ordered arrangement of Montessori materials in a classroom where the children have been taught the desired behaviors and the rules of acceptable classroom functioning. Cognitive-developmental curricula usually define this role as arranging an attractive classroom, well equipped with a wide variety of materials, so that young children have many choices for spontaneous play and manipulation and easily become involved in productive activities.

Remember that individual teachers have many different styles of teaching, varying with personality, prior teaching preparation, school preferences, and community influences, and these determine results as much as specific program requirements do. Teachers—being complex humans—are not easy to classify.

TEACHER STRATEGIES

Teaching strategies are distinguished from teaching roles in the same way that the individual parts of a garment are distinguished from the garment as a whole. Like teaching roles, strategies may be categorized in various ways. They take verbal and nonverbal forms and cluster around direct- and indirect-teaching behaviors. Direct-teaching behaviors involve teachers and children in interaction. Indirect-teaching behaviors are those that precede and follow direct interaction, such as taking out and putting away materials.

One system that features the kinds of strategies used by early childhood teachers, follows:[5]

1. *Information-giving strategies* include:
   a. *Modeling.* Verbal and nonverbal behavior—for example, writing a letter of the alphabet for a child to copy—is clearly designed for children to copy. Some forms of modeling are subtle. The teacher may not ask the child to copy the modeled behavior but expect the child to copy it sooner or later. For example, the teacher takes the Lotto game off the table and places it on the top shelf saying, "The Lotto game belongs on this top shelf." Or the teacher says, "I'm sorry," after accidently bumping into a child. Note that the potential and limits of this strategy, as discussed in Chapter 5, depend on the child's ability to understand the behavior observed and motivation to copy it.
   b. *Supplying information.* The teacher furnishes information verbally through labeling, lecturing, explaining, reading and nonverbally through gestures and facial expression. Information is supplied in response to children's requests, or is initiated by the teacher. The nonverbal information is provided, for example, by pointing to a position on a paper for namewriting, or nodding yes to a question.
   c. *Giving feedback.* The teacher gives a child factual information about some aspect of behavior. For example, the teacher tells one child that he has mixed red and yellow paints to get orange and another that she has written her name with only five letters instead of the six that she needs.

5. Ibid., pp. 89–101.

2. *Questioning strategies*, which are discussed in detail in the final section of this chapter, include:
   a. *Eliciting verbalization.* By using questions accompanied by materials and by demonstrating affection, interest, and concern, the teacher stimulates children to talk. For example, using a picture collection of foods, the teacher asks a child about his favorite food; the teacher asks another about her experience at the zoo the previous day.
   b. *Probing.* The teacher questions children to help clarify their thinking. For example, when a child overgeneralizes and says that all people who wear white shoes are nurses, the teacher asks whether he the teacher would also be a nurse if he wore white shoes.
3. *Strategies for stimulating children's activity involvement* include both direct interaction and management strategies:
   a. *Inviting to a task.* The teacher makes an attempt to involve the child in a task by explicit invitation, or makes a less specific offer of materials that suggest an activity. An example of direct invitation combined with an offer of materials is requesting a child to replicate a pattern on a set of beads.
   b. *Giving directions.* The teacher specifies behavior he or she expects to have followed. For example, the teacher tells children how to play a musical game.
   c. *Manipulating materials.* The teacher is actively involved with classroom materials commonly used by children. For example, the teacher cuts construction paper for children's use in collage pasting.
   d. *Running machines.* The teacher operates machines, such as a record player, tape recorder, or movie or slide projector.

4. *Strategies that serve planning needs* include:
   a. *Testing.* The teacher questions a child for recall, duplication, or performance of a skill or various forms of thinking. For example, children's skills in name writing may be tested by asking them to write their names on their pictures. The testing strategy provides the teacher with information for curriculum and activity planning.
   b. *Observing and recording.* The teacher makes a record or notation about a child or a group of children. For example, taking attendance provides information needed to plan snacks and lunch. Or, recording how many children can count past ten influences the kinds of counting tasks the teacher will encourage.
   c. *Designing lessons or activities.* The teacher sketches general or detailed plans for children's learning activities. For example, the teacher fashions a cooking experience.

Behavior control strategies include supplying information, giving directions, and reinforcement, as just cited. However, these strategies are directed specifically toward helping children to develop the necessary controls for successful social relationships in the class group and to conform with the basic rules and routines.

The strategy of giving affection serves all teaching functions and is often inseparable from other strategies. Voice tone when asking questions and giving feedback and body language when expressing actions are elements of the affective communication system.

Many teaching roles and strategies have been studied, but none in more detail than questioning strategies. In addition to giving information, teaching is often thought to consist of asking questions for children to answer. Since the questioning strategy is distinctive and serves many teaching purposes, study and control of questioning skills is a productive area for increasing teaching skills.

THE STRATEGY OF ASKING QUESTIONS

Asking questions has been a recognized teaching technique since at least the time of Socrates. As Michael Duncan and Bruce Biddle indicate, teachers have a commitment to question asking, a firm belief that such strategies are good.[6] This commitment accounts for the fact that some teachers do not examine the necessity for their own strategies. Since questioning seems to be an ongoing part of all teaching, it is generally accepted as useful. Researchers who have studied question strategies can contribute to teachers' examination of issues related to curriculum goals.

Queston asking serves two major functions: to contribute to instructional goals and to obtain diagnostic information. The diagnostic purpose of questions is to find out what children know and can do so that programs can be planned. In contrast, the instructional purposes of questions focus children's attention on the learning task. These questions fall into five groups:

1. Attention to known facts: what facts does the child know that are relevant to what the child is doing?
2. Relationship between objects, actions and events: what are the causative relationships?
3. Processes and sequences of events: in what order do the actions and events occur?
4. Alternative procedures and outcomes: how can the child change any or all of

---

6. Michael Dunkin and Bruce Biddle, *The Study of Teaching* (New York: Holt, Rinehart & Winston, 1974), p. 5.

what happens, the order in which things happen, and the outcomes?
5. Selection among alternatives and preferences: what does the child want to happen and how?

This variety of instructional purposes distinguishes instructional from diagnostic questions. In practice, however, teachers easily shift focus back and forth from diagnostic to instructional questions. The intermittent use of diagnostic questions in planned instructional episodes often interrupts the flow of the child's thought and shifts the child's focus from the ongoing task to the teacher's request for information. Following is a discussion of the use of instructional questions to encourage learning and thinking, organization of knowledge and understanding, and clarification of what is known.

Instructional Use of Questions

An important set of guidelines for viewing questioning is provided by Irving Sigel and Ruth Saunders. They suggest that

> a model for question-asking requires the consideration of . . . linguistic structure of a particular question, psychological function of the questioning process, cognitive processes activated by the particular question, teacher strategies in executing the model, and evaluations of children's responses to types of questions.[7]

That is, they emphasize the way a question is worded, the purpose of asking the question, the level of thinking the question taps, the teacher's methods in posing questions, and ways of judging children's responses.

7. Irving Sigel and Ruth Saunders, "An Inquiry in Inquiry: Question Asking as an Instructional Model," in Lillian Katz, ed., *Current Topics in Early Childhood Education*, vol. 2 (Norwood, N.J.: Ablex Publishing Corporation, 1979), p. 169.

Linguistic Structure of Questions

One of the most striking insights teachers develop as they study the kinds of questions that are asked is that they think of certain kinds of statements that grammatically are not questions as questions. The statement, "Tell me what you're going to do with this piece of wood," constitutes a command or direction to do something, rather than a question. However, such statements may be viewed as indirect questions, depending on tonality and inflection. Minimizing the "tell me" and emphasizing the "what, where, when, why, and who" communicates a questioning stance rather than a command. Since young children are particularly sensitive to the teacher's affect, the teacher's intonation cues children as to whether there is a command to answer correctly or an inquiry into the child's understanding. Linguistic analysis of questions can alert teachers to some attributes of questions that have particular significance in teaching the very young.

Simple questions   These are easily understood in terms of what is intended and thus are more suitable to the young learner than are complex questions or the even-more-difficult embedded question.[8] The simple questions avoid subclauses and distracting detail. Some examples follow:

Woodworking:	"Where are you going to start this nail?"
Art:	"What color do you want for your house?"
Puzzle task:	"Which piece are you going to put next?"
Dramatic play:	"When will the baby wake up?"
Blockbuilding:	"Which block do you need for the tower?"
Social conversation:	"Where did you get your new shoes?"

8. Ibid., pp. 170–172.

Complex questions These often include the *if-then*, or conditional clauses which help to clarify the question, adding detail that can distract a child, depending on the placement of the clause and the timeliness of the question. Examples of complex questions are:

Woodworking:	"If you want to attach these two pieces, where will you place the nail?"
Art:	"When you think about the color you want, which of these crayons will you select?"
Puzzle task:	"If you want to complete the red dress, which puzzle piece do you think you need?"
Dramatic play:	"If baby wakes up when she is hungry, how soon will that be?"
Block building:	"Which block do you want to place on top of the tower so it will not fall down?"
Social conversations:	"When you want to buy shoes, how do you know which store has the red shoes you like?"

In complex questions, the child is required to think about two things—the actual question and the conditions of the question. In woodworking, the sample question referred to the placement of the nail, and the condition might be "to attach the two pieces of wood." Teachers often use complex questions to help the children focus on points teachers have identified. The conditional clause gives clues, as, for example, in the puzzle task by specifying the color of the dress. However, the clues may mask the teacher's meaning if they confuse the child or divert attention from the question.

The embedded question In this instance, the question is buried within several other statements and thus is the most difficult and least recommended kind of question for young children. For example, in a group planning session, where the teacher is helping children think through necessary rules for a trip, an embedded question would be: "When we go to the farm and want to be sure that no one gets hurt, what rule can we develop about partners that will remind us to stay together?" Embedded questions often look as though there are several questions, and young children are easily misled. In the example just cited, the specific question is about the rule, but distracting elements indicate that the question may be, "How do we avoid getting hurt?" Typically, young children tune into the beginning or end of complex utterances; the embedded question example is likely to provoke unexpected suggestions about safety instead of the apparently desired answer, "hold on to your partner's hand."

Open- and close-ended questions Another aspect of linguistic analysis concerns the degree to which the responder is expected to elaborate or extend an answer. *Close-ended questions*, usually requiring only one answer, do not invite narrative extensions. Specific fact questions about color, object, or size elicit one-word answers. *Preference questions*, such as, "Which do you want, peas or carrots?," are also close-ended questions. In context, if teachers are involved in instructional interactions and not in testing, such close-ended questions serve to help the children focus on salient features of a situation. For example, if a child at the woodworking bench wants to attach a sail to a boat by using a nail for a hook, the teacher may encourage this with a close-ended question such as, "Does this nail have a head that will hold the end of the sail?" In contrast, an *open-ended* question on the same problem might be, "How are you going to know whether the nail will hold the sail?" Note that, as in the woodworking example, questions are not necessarily confined to verbal answers, since they may also provoke action answers.

Psychological Function

Intonation and inflection are attributes of teachers' talk, which can be analyzed for consistent and conflicting meanings. A harsh, rejecting tone distracts listeners from responding to the content and shifts them to dealing with the affect. Observers easily spot sarcasm or rhetorical questions that communicate criticisms rather than requests for information. Little needs to be said about avoiding use of questions that reject and demean children.

Less obvious psychological correlates of teacher questioning concern timing, pacing, and context of questions. In early childhood classrooms, instructional questions are asked throughout the program, focusing on children's selected tasks and teachers' selected tasks, in both didactic and action-based situations. Questions that intrude on children's self-selected tasks carry a different message than ones that are integral to the activity. For example, when a child is constructing a mobile and not seeking help, questions from the teacher may imply that the child is not meeting some unstated expectation or that the teacher does not value the activity. In a different situation, where the children are gathered with the teacher to make pudding, questions related to both process and product are a natural part of the activity and usually help maintain the learning focus and momentum. In essence, the appropriateness of teachers' questions to the learning activity is a strong indicator of the psychological effect of such questions.

Mary Rowe investigated teachers' questioning behavior and discovered powerful psychological messages, until then undocumented, that teachers communicate unconsciously through patterns of timing and pacing.[9] Rowe found that teachers wait longer, after asking a question, for answers from those children considered "smarter" than from those viewed less able. This means that the lower-achieving children were given less time to figure out an answer than those who were considered higher-achieving and thus more likely to answer, thus creating a situation in which only the successful *can* succeed. Equally distressing was her finding that the waiting time between asking a question and repeating it was usually one second, and that teachers produce approximately three questions per minute.[10] There are two psychological messages here. The first is that teachers do not expect answers from the poorer students, and therefore waiting is unnecessary. The second message is that teachers use questions to tap information and understanding children already have, not to provoke thinking about new information or new meanings. Why else would they expect instant responses?

Rowe also found that the waiting time between children's answers and the next questions from the teacher was equally short. As teachers developed the skill of waiting before proceeding with more questions, the children elaborated their answers, adding clarity and detail to the initial response. Additionally, more of the less-advanced children made responses.[11]

In a related finding, Rowe discovered that there were distinctive differences in the way teachers respond to the answers of poor students and achieving students. The poor students receive remarks that are evaluative and uninformative, such as "Great," while the higher-achieving students receive validating types of remarks, such as, "That's right."[12]

9. Mary Budd Rowe, *Teaching Science as Continuous Inquiry*, 2nd ed. (New York: McGraw-Hill, 1978), pp. 241–272.
10. Ibid., p. 242.
11. Ibid., pp. 244–250, 258–260.
12. Ibid., p. 250.

Rowe's work draws attention to the contradictions between planned and unrecognized influences. Her studies center on the science curriculum with the objective of stimulating more complex levels of thinking, such as comparing and contrasting, classifying, predicting, and problem solving. These studies indicate how dysfunctional some questioning techniques might be.

Cognitive Processes Activated by Questions

The most popular area of study in teachers' questioning is the level of cognitive challenge posed by the questions. Benjamin Bloom's taxonomy of educational objectives became the foundation for one of the best-known analyses of questions, which was made by Norris Sanders.[13] A *taxonomy* is a classification system in which items are ordered from lowest to highest in terms of complexity—in this case, in terms of the complexity of the thought processes activated.

13. Norris Sanders, *Classroom Questions: What Kinds?* (New York: Harper & Row, 1966), pp. 3–5.

Sanders identifies seven levels of thinking. The simplest level is direct memory, in which recall of information exactly as taught is requested. Increasing complexity occurs as the initial information is processed and transformed to other kinds of knowledge. As mentioned earlier, memory questions serve to remind children of usable knowledge they possess. If they are involved in a task such as making play-dough, remembering the measurements of two parts flour to one part salt helps them get started. Memory questions can be close- or open-ended, the former featuring facts and simple understanding, the latter dealing with narrative recall of experiences. A question such as "What did you see at the circus?" requires recall of experience but is open-ended in how much is recalled and reported.

As noted on Table 10-1, the next two levels of questioning after memory represent the kinds of questions that feature organizing perceptions and experiences and building concepts. Increasingly complex use of knowledge, understanding, and concepts is featured in the next three levels of questions. According to this taxonomy, the three levels of problem resolution range from simple application of

TABLE 10.1. Sanders's levels of questioning

Level	Description
Memory	Questions focusing on recall and recognition of information
Translation	Questions focusing on changing information into a different symbolic form
Interpretation	Questions focusing on discovering relationships between facts and on generalizations, definition, and values
Application	Questions focusing on solving lifelike problems, requiring identification of important features of the problem
Analysis	Questions focusing on solving a problem by reviewing parts
Synthesis	Questions focusing on solving a problem requiring creative thinking, putting parts together
Evaluation	Questions requiring judgments of good and bad, right and wrong

Source: From pp. 3–5, in *Classroom Questions: What Kinds?* by Norris Sanders. Copyright © 1966 by Norris M. Sanders. Reprinted by permission of Harper & Row, Publishers, Inc.

known facts and processes, to creating new solutions. With early childhood groups, teachers selecting from this end of the sequence are probably limited by the developmental level of the children, which excludes many complex types of questions.

The Piagetian perspective, which focuses on how questions challenge children's thinking, suggests a different kind of guideline, as outlined by Constance Kamii and Rheta DeVries. They suggest that, once children are engaged in some form of active manipulation and experimentation with physical objects, there are four types of questions that encourage children to think about the relationship between objects and events:[14]

1. "Acting on objects and *seeing how they react*" suggests questions that involve predictions, such as, "What do you think will happen if you do *X*?"
2. "Acting on objects *to produce a desired effect*" suggests questions of the type, "Can you do *X*?" and "Can you find anything else you can do with *X*?"
3. "Becoming aware of *how one produced the desired effect*" suggests questions such as, "How did you do *X*?" The teacher can also encourage comparisons by raising questions such as, "Which way works better (or is it easier)?" "How is so-and-so doing *X* differently?"
4. "*Explaining causes*" suggests asking, "Why does *X* happen?" or saying, "I wonder why *X* happened."

Kamii and DeVries' guidelines continually focus on the actions of the children, using only two cognitive levels. The first three questions represent one level and can be used in any activity. The "why" question representing the second cognitive level requires the children to think in a different way about the present experience, according to Kamii and DeVries.

14. Constance Kamii and Rheta DeVries, *Physical Knowledge in Preschool Education: Implications of Piaget's Theory* (Englewood Cliffs, N.J.: Prentice-Hall, 1978), pp. 48–52.

Sigel and Saunders suggest that a major task of the questioning strategy is to encourage the child to separate from the present and create a "representation of a past experience or a construction of an anticipated experience."[15] The authors discuss *distancing* as a primary goal of questioning for inquiry. The assumption is that the more objectivity the child can achieve, the more cognitive growth will result. The degree to which different kinds of questions stimulate distancing for the children constitutes the basis for this taxonomy, which is not very different from the Bloom and Sanders base. Labeling and reproducing questions are considered less distancing than those that feature classifying and generalizing.

Guidelines for Improving Questions

To teachers seeking to improve their questioning strategies for encouraging children's thinking, Sigel and Saunders make excellent recommendations no matter which hierarchy is selected. Their guidelines are:[16]

Ask questions	Maximize the use of open-ended questions, predictions questions, and relationship questions. Minimize close-ended, label, yes-no, and limited descriptive questions.
Give real choices	Encourage a child to weigh options. Choices must be mutually exclusive and there must be a consequence; if the child makes a prediction, results are examined in terms of that prediction.
Watch, wait and listen	Allow time for questions to provoke thought and for choices to be made. Avoid rushing their thought and approving only "right" answers.

15. Sigel and Saunders, "An Inquiry in Inquiry," p. 175.
16. Ibid., pp. 180–184.

Be responsive	Model thoughtfulness, value questions, and use questions to initiate dialogue and generate more questions.
Arrange the physical environment	See that "potentials for integration are obvious to the child," such as placing blocks near the dramatic play area to invite constructing furniture in house area. Select multiple-purpose material, and encourage multiple forms of expression.

SUMMARY

The ways in which teaching occurs are becoming easier to define and identify. It is now possible to improve one's teaching skills through self-study and plans for skills development. Teaching roles are conceived in many different ways but generally break down into the major functions of planning, implementing, and evaluating instruction; managing the classroom; and meeting children's affective, cognitive, physical, and social needs. Teaching strategies are defined in this chapter as specific teaching behaviors combined into functional roles. The range of strategies includes modeling, giving feedback, eliciting verbalization, and questioning, among others.

Because of the importance of questioning strategies in the teaching functions, we made detailed analyses of types of questions and their use in classrooms.

EXERCISES

1. Write an instructional activity plan, detailing intended teaching strategies.
    a. Write an alternative strategy.
    b. Compare values, advantages, and disadvantages of the two strategies.
2. Tape record a sample of your instructional interaction with two to five children.
    a. Transcribe all questions you asked of children. Include questions masked as directions or requests.
    b. Analyze the pattern of questioning for:
        i. your predominating view of knowledge,
        ii. proportion of memory questions to cognitive-process questions
    c. Rephrase at least three memory questions as cognitive-process questions.
    d. Rephrase close-ended questions as open-ended questions.

BIBLIOGRAPHY

Adams, Raymond S. and Biddle, Bruce J. *Realities of Teaching.* New York: Holt, Rinehart & Winston, 1970.

Biddle, Bruce J., and Thomas, Edwin J. *Role Theory: Concepts and Research.* New York: Wiley & Sons, 1966.

Dunkin, Michael, and Biddle, Bruce. *The Study of Teaching.* New York: Holt, Rinehart & Winston, 1974.

Kamii, Constance, and DeVries, Rheta. *Physical Knowledge in Preschool Education: Implications of Piaget's Theory.* Englewood Cliffs, N.J.: Prentice-Hall, 1978.

Katz, Lillian. "Teaching in Preschool: Roles and Goals." *Children*, 17(1970): 42–48.

Robison, Helen F., and Schwartz, Sydney L. *Learning at an Early Age.* Vol. 1. Englewood Cliffs, N.J.: Prentice-Hall, 1972.

Rowe, Mary Budd. *Teaching Science as Continuous Inquiry.* 2nd ed. New York: McGraw-Hill, 1978.

Sanders, Norris, *Classroom Questions: What Kinds?* New York: Harper & Row, 1966.

Sigel, Irving, and Saunders, Ruth. "An Inquiry in Inquiry: Question Asking as an Instructional Model." In Lillian Katz, ed., *Current Topics in Early Childhood Education.* Vol. 2. Norwood, N.J.: Ablex Publishing Corporation, 1979.

11 Diagnostic Teaching: Determining Children's Needs

As professionals, teachers want to know whether their curricular decisions are right for individual children in the group. The major questions teachers want to answer for this purpose is, "Where is *this* child now, and what is this child ready to learn?" Teachers need to determine not only what is developmentally appropriate, but also what is consistent with their program objectives. Another related question is, "What did this child learn? How do I determine the outcomes of the experiences and activities I provide?" This is the role of diagnostic teaching.

Diagnostic procedures vary widely, and many forms of assessment are available for general and specific purposes. As in all other aspects of curriculum development, diagnostic efforts relate to program objectives. Programs that stress academic achievement would use achievement-type assessments to show progress. Other programs should choose forms of assessment congruent with their purposes. A variety of goals in development and achievement areas serving as the basis for designing diagnostic procedures are listed in Table 3–1.

The gamut of diagnostic procedures that can be useful to teachers includes:

1. informal tests;
2. use of children's products;
3. observational procedures;
4. unobtrusive measures, including parental feedback;
5. formal tests, commercial and teacher-made.

Selection from these options depends on teacher purposes, on curriculum design needs, and especially on the goals of the program. It is important to note that diagnostic instruments that require less complexity in administration and interpretation are usually more suitable for classroom use.

Curriculum and program evaluation is distinguished from diagnostic teaching by its focus on more comprehensive concerns, such as whether one curriculum design produces better achievement, more creativity, or more of other desired outcomes than another.[1] Diagnostic information serves teachers' needs for program planning and teaching. This chapter deals with teachers' needs for guidelines, procedures, instruments, criteria for collecting and analyzing information on children's growth, development, and learning.

INFORMAL DIAGNOSTIC PROCEDURES

Informal diagnostic teaching can include (1) collections of children's work samples; (2) observations of children; (3) anecdotal recordings; (4) checklists and task-completion records; and (5) unobstrusive measures, such as parental feedback, library records of books withdrawn, or other forms of data not elicited directly from children.

Informality suggests for both teacher and child options in timing, pacing, form of re-

---

[1] See Bruce W. Tuckman, *A Guide to Instructional Program Evaluation* (Boston: Allyn and Bacon, 1979).

sponses, and ways of eliciting behavior samples. For example, one teacher related that a boy in a Head Start program in a formal test situation responded to a question about the color of grass that "Grass is yellow." Since this child was viewed as bright, the teacher was puzzled by this response and followed the test with an informal assessment. She asked the boy, "Is grass really yellow?" He took the teacher by the hand and led her outdoors to show her the yellow grass left by a prolonged drought. The teacher discovered that the child understood the question to be, "What color is the grass *now, here*?"—and not, "What color is grass generally?" This anecdote is an excellent example of informal, on-the-spot assessment, as distinguished from formal testing. It further illustrates some of the limits to formal testing with young children.

Work Samples

Work-sample collections need names, dates, and if possible explanatory notes. Such collections also need adequate shelves, drawers, or other forms of storage space. Ideally, children should have access to their own work-storage areas. For many children, a review of their own productivity serves to enhance self-identification and self-valuing. Children delight in showing off their work to friends, parents, and visitors. Easy access is also essential for teachers' use. For example, after comparing a child's latest easel painting to the five already stored, the teacher can write on the back of the new picture, "first representational effort—a house," or "beginning to mix colors with awareness of outcome." Teachers enjoy the progress children make and need as many ways as possible to note it and to reflect such enjoyment to children.

Work-sample folders are more useful if entries are made on the cover that list the contents. This need not become burdensome to the teacher, who can enlist the aid of other team members, or parent and community volunteers, or older children in a public school setting. The cover entries alert the teacher when work samples are accumulating more slowly for some children than for others; and the teacher can find out why this is so.

Work samples may include photographs of construction as well as paper products. Notes are needed for photographs to indicate the names of leaders, collaborators, problems, and methods of problem solving. Similarly, a tape recorder can preserve children's conversations in the housekeeping area or in the table-games center to indicate use of rules and ways of managing problems. Thus, work samples can be aural, visual, tactile, or verbal, or any combination of the four.

It is best to keep work sample collections representative rather than complete. Teachers have to decide how many samples to collect. The basic guide is to be sure that changes in performance and different kinds of products are represented.

Teachers often say they have no difficulty collecting work samples and storing them. The problem is the lack of time to review these products and to make diagnostic judgments about cirriculum possibilities. Suggestions for periodic review of these work samples might include:

1. Review at least two children's folders every day, preferably with the child; use a list of the names of the children in the group to aid review.
2. Review all folders at least once a month at a regular time, such as the last Thursday morning of the month. Plan the program for that time so that it will either be self-sustaining or supervised primarily by others—another member of the teaching team, a colleague, or parent or community volunteers.
3. Review all folders at least twice each semester with the parents, during planned parent conferences.

Since reviewing work-sample folders generates some judgments about learning opportunities for specific children in different work areas, it is advisable to record these judgments as they are made. Duplicated blank forms facilitate this procedure. Children could be listed by name vertically and learning centers or tasks horizontally, with dates of review included. An example of work-sample reviews of children's skill in writing their names would note omissions, reversals or distortions of letters, use of upper- and lower-case letters, regularity and size of letters, and spacing between letters. See Figure 11-1 for a sample recording form.

Collecting, storing, and reviewing children's work samples with recorded judgments on teaching needs give teachers secure diagnostic information on developmental progress, interests, problems, and possibilities, and they suggest teaching plans to reach program objectives. Follow-up of teaching plans, based on written reminders or charts, helps teachers realize well-based teaching intentions. As noted earlier, children also benefit from concrete evidence of their own capabilities and industry.

Observation of Children

Observation of children is stressed as a major diagnostic procedure in almost every type of early childhood program. Some programs rely almost entirely on close and intense observations to guide teaching decisions, while others use observation as one of several procedures. As a basis for making teaching decisions, observational procedures are probably the most widely used and useful means of determining children's needs and diagnosing their levels of functioning. Observations may be systematized or informal. Systematic observation, with planned procedures and formats, requires understanding of the limitations and values of the data. On-the-spot observations are always difficult to interpret, although such observations may help identify areas requiring more carefully planned observations. On-the-spot, informal observations seldom provide secure data about frequency or representativeness.

Reasons for observing children are legion. Examples are:

1. for physical health, especially to spot symptoms of disease, infection, illness, or disability, or child abuse;
2. for emotional health, usually to note behavioral clues to dysfunctional affect and to study a particular child who appears to be having unusual problems;
3. for safety, to prevent accidents and injuries and to monitor adherence to rules for safety;

FIGURE 11-1. Sample checklist: handwriting skills

				Name writing skills				
Child's name	Date	Some letters	Date	Most letters, no order	Date	Some reversals	Date	Mastery
Alicia	10/1	Ai	12/1	Aica	1/15	Alicie	3/1	√
Barlo	11/1	ARO	1/15	arBol		—	2/1	√
Sondra								
Peter								
Frank								
Andre								
Michelle								
Aisha								

4. for rapport, to find ways to establish personal, warm relationships with children based on detailed knowledge of the child's behavior and personality;
5. for balance, to insure that individual children's experiences in the group are balanced in terms of active-passive, noisy-quiet, group-indivdual activities, and similar attributes;
6. for making teaching decisions about when and how to enter into a child's activity, offer materials, make suggestions for re-direction, or use other teaching ideas or directions;
7. for identifying problems, such as unequal playmates in conflict, above-average forms of activity, aggression, passivity, nonverbal behavior, speech immaturities, or toileting or eating problems;
8. for identifying progress, such as increased social maturity, verbalization, vocabulary, skill development, problem-solving behavior, initiative, interests, curiosity, independence, attention span, and group participation;
9. for assessing achievement, as evidenced by children's mastery of such activities as jigsaw puzzles, constructions with blocks, reading signs, charts, books, and math skills;
10. for identifying interests to plan group projects, such as murals, constructions, stories, charts, experiments with materials, writing, reading, or work with numbers;
11. for collecting data for parent conferences, especially knowledge about individual children;
12. for collecting case history data, especially when a child has been or will be referred for psychological evaluation or therapy. Ideally, no such referrals should occur before detailed observational data are collected and analyzed, since such data often contradict casual judgments that a child's behavior is outside the limits of normality.

Many teachers who make detailed observations of individual children have limited written records. They rely on memory to make on-the-spot decisions or to refer a child to the nurse, speech specialist, or school psychologist. In small settings, much can be accomplished informally by professionals who meet face-to-face frequently. After a short period of time, however, memories falter and cease to be as accurate as they otherwise might be. Also, much useful information is unavailable to support staff who have neither the time nor the opportunity to be briefed orally. Written observations serve not only the teachers, but also their team, the administrators, those who provide special services, and teachers in subsequent grades. A major test of usefulness is the frequency with which teachers consult recordings before they make decisions on teaching plans.

When initiating or improving systematic recordings of observations, it is well to build in:[2]

1. *Ease of recording.* Prepared charts, checklists, and other forms greatly facilitate quick and regular recording.
2. *Representativeness of recordings.* For example, if observations focus on a behavior problem, recordings should show not only that a child bit a good friend during an angry dispute, but also that no bites were recorded at other times, or that more acceptable ways of resolving disputes were generally used by this child. One-time or occasional transgressions should not be taken as symptoms of gross maladjustment or pathology.
3. *Purposefulness of recordings.* Selectivity relates to the objectives and content of the curriculum and the unique characteristics of children in the group.

2. Murray Tillman, Donald Bersoff, and John Dolly, *Learning to Teach: A Decision-making System* (Lexington, Mass.: D.C. Heath, 1978), pp. 274–292.

4. *Objectivity.* A record of objective facts is more useful than deductions or judgments. "Bobby was mean today" is a judgment that describes the teacher's attitudes rather than the child's behavior. Factual statements about hitting or refusing to give turns on the bicycle, for example, keep their inherent informational value indefinitely. Objectivity is advanced when:
   a. facts are stated;
   b. more than one person contributes to the recordings, which lessens personal bias;
   c. records span sufficient time periods to allow for rapid growth and learning patterns;
   d. context information is included, such as a divorce or a death in the family.
5. *Clear focus.* Information is more pertinent when it focuses on a selected aspect of child development or behavior. Examples of clear focus include listing:
   a. favorite free-play activities, to locate points of entry for teaching objective;
   b. acceptance or challenge of magical explanations for physical or natural occurrences;
   c. social skills in making friends;
   d. samples of *decentering*—understanding or accepting another viewpoint or perspective;
   e. requests for help in deciphering words, to indicate interest in language arts and beginning reading;
   f. favorite songs or records.

Detailed and recorded observations of children often make formal testing unnecessary. Well-focused observations can reflect a child's way of functioning in different situations, with different materials or children, at different points in time.

6. *Validity and Reliability. Validity* means that the behavior you intended to observe is what you are observing, and *reliability* assures you of the accuracy of your data.

To improve reliability, two major procedures may be used, time sampling or event sampling. *Time sampling* requires using uniform observational intervals, such as every ten minutes, or every half hour, for selected forms of behavior, such as persevering on a task. Disruptive behaviors are commonly time sampled to note hitting, biting, kicking, and other forms of aggression or disruption. A whole class can be time sampled, for example, to find out which children are "on task" or "off task," or which learning centers are over- or underused. Clearly, another teaching team member has to be present during such time-sampling procedures.

Event sampling requires tallying or counting every time a selected behavior occurs. This yields frequency rates of occurrence. If a particular behavior, such as taking initiative to experiment with materials, is selected, a base line can be calculated by averaging the frequencies tallied per child, per group, or per class, for a one-week period. This is done before instituting teaching techniques designed to increase the rate. Continuing to record the event samplings gives the teacher regular information on whether the teaching techniques are working as desired. Similarly, this procedure can be used to measure decreasing rates of aggression, disruption, noninvolvement, solitary play, and other desired teaching objectives. It should be noted that behavioral events need to be clearly described if they are to be tallied. Many forms and simple methods of tallying are available for selection by teachers.

From detailed observations, teachers learn that a seemingly nonverbal child is really shy; or that a child who seems to be bilingual really understands only his or her first language, not English; or that a passive child may not feel ready for full participation in the group. To reach such vital conclusions, it would be difficult to find a better way than through intensive, focused, and systematic observations.

Anecdotal Recordings

Anecdotal observations are recorded narratives about specific incidents involving children in the group, or they may be descriptions of many different incidents concerning the same child. The purpose of anecdotal recordings is to preserve detailed observations of a child in one or more situations to reveal personality characteristics, characteristic ways of behaving, typical problems, or strengths. Some teachers use this procedure primarily to identify and record undesirable behaviors and the circumstances in which they occur. Over a period of time, the observations might indicate that problems are either increasing or decreasing, and details would be sought to help explain the direction of change.

Making anecdotal recordings systematic requires establishing some patterns, such as jotting down at least one record per child weekly and shuffling the cards to randomize the order in which children are observed. Randomizing avoids always observing a particular child at the beginning of a free play period when involvement may be high or another child later in the day when energy may be used up. If time-sampling or event-sampling systems are added to this procedure, the information would be regarded as more reliable.

In all observational systems, there is a problem of observer bias. Teachers should remember that they may unknowingly underplay the negative or poor performances of children they like and do the reverse for children they dislike. Again, objectivity is more likely if more than one person makes observations and if many observations are made.

Checklists and Records

Checklists and various other recording methods are available to reduce the burden of collecting observational data. It is essential that recording systems operate without interfering with teaching plans. Checklists are useful for recording events as they occur, for time and event sampling; or for recording selected behavior, such as task completion or task selection. If checklists are thoughtfully constructed and posted in convenient places for quick checkoff, much useful data are collected without interference to teaching. Some teachers like to post checklists in learning centers; others prefer to carry them in pockets or file them in desk drawers.

FIGURE 11-2. Sample checklist: children's development in blockbuilding

ENTER DATES OBSERVED					
Child's name	Manipulating, collecting, piling blocks	Simple horizontal structures, 3-10 blocks— no props	Horizontal and vertical enclosures— some props	Preplanned structures— props	Using structures to extend play

Checklists can be used in any type of program from the most formal to the most informal, from the least structured to the most, from the most traditional to the least. They are easily constructed for simple recording of information about children's interests, skill development, and developmental levels. Figure 11–2 illustrates a checklist for children's developmental level in block building. If the name or symbol of the interest center (in this case, block building) is clearly marked on the sheet with children's names listed, either children or teachers may take responsibility for making check marks. A child may check his or her name in every interest center used during the day or during the free play or work period. For some kinds of activities, children take pride in demonstrating their accomplishments by checking themselves off.

Teachers yearning for good data collection who have difficulty keeping a system going can enjoy the results of a child-maintained checklist system. It is important to avoid undue emphasis on record keeping at the expense of other important teaching tasks.

Unobtrusive Measures

Unobtrusive measures are indirect forms of data collection that do not require observing or testing a child. Parental reports, complaints, comments, and suggestions are some of the most important forms of unobtrusive measures. Parental reports are usually invaluable bases for planning home-school collaboration and relating general classroom goals to the real needs of individual children. In addition to parents, other sources of unobtrusive data are school records, school personnel such as bus drivers, and crossing guards, and other school staff.

Informal feedback is most easily secured from parents who regularly escort their children to the school or center and chat with the teacher before leaving. These brief, informal conversations are ideal for exchanging information, because they are frequent and usually not confined to problems and solutions. Teachers may have specific questions ready for certain parents so they can follow up on classroom occurrences, or they may pose the same general open-ended questions to all parents. Open-ended questions are general and give parents wide latitude for response. For example:

- "How is it going?"
- "What's new?"
- "Anything special today?"
- "Have you noticed anything lately?"
- "Anything to report?"

Examples of specific questions for the follow-up might be these:

- "Who is tying his shoelaces?"
- "Is she interested in your reading now?"
- "Does he want playmates after school these days?"
- "Do you notice any more tolerance for new foods?"
- "What signs of independence do you see at home?"

More formal procedures might include sending home questionnaires for parents to return or asking parents who come for conferences to complete a questionnaire. Questionnaires might deal with such topics as:

1. children's energy levels after school or problems in preparing for school in the morning;
2. aspects of parents' satisfaction or dissatisfaction with the child's school experience;
3. problems at home that parents wish to discuss with teachers, such as fears, eating difficulties, or toileting problems;
4. changes in the child's behavior at home in such developmental characteristics as self-help, sympathy, or empathy demonstrated;
5. parents' suggestions or expectations.

School records that include medical forms are often less complete than teachers would like, but occasionally they shed light on a child's behavior. These records may contribute to teachers' understanding of prior or current effects on children of such experiences as frequent family moves over wide geographic areas, family membership, and parental occupation.

DIAGNOSTIC TEACHING IN PIAGETIAN-BASED PROGRAMS

Piagetian-based programs offer rich examples of diagnostic teaching, which is individualized and entirely integrated with teaching strategies. A basic premise in this teaching style is the need to ascertain how a child conceptualizes and reasons.

According to Fredricka Reisman, "The meshing of the steps of the learning hierarchy into the developmental level at which the child is performing is the heart of diagnostic teaching."[3] Remember the child mentioned in Chapter 6, who proudly displayed the new watch he received as a birthday present? Assuming that learning to read clocks fits the curricular objectives of the program and that the child's motivation is strong due to the birthday gift, there are two pieces of information the teacher needs to make a decision about curriculum. (1) What is understandable or conceivable to this child? That is, what are the child's cognitive skills? (2) What is the hierarchy of concepts and facts required for clock reading? If the answers to these two questions can be mapped together, the teacher can feel secure with an on-the-spot curricular decision.

Since teachers need knowledge of sequential levels in math learning and in conceptualizing generally, it is best to know these in advance. Good math programs and textbooks furnish the sequential steps in math learning, which are well established. Workbooks do not necessarily follow such sequences and may not be authoritative. For sequential levels of concepts in math or in any other area, teachers are referred to some of the interpreters of Piaget's theories, as well as to Chapter 5 of this book.[4] Understanding the hierarchies of conceptualizing, the teacher can concentrate on finding the comfort level at which the child can function, where tasks are neither too easy nor too difficult.

For Kamii and DeVries, a major teaching principle is to, "figure out what the child is thinking and respond sparingly in his terms."[5] This requires close observation of and dialogue with individual children to try to "get inside their heads" and grasp what they are trying to do, according to these authors. In the Piagetian-based approach to teaching, this information guides the teacher to tune in to the child, and at the same time meet specific objectives, which include three social-emotional and two cognitive goals. The social-emotional objectives are:

For the child to
1. become increasingly more autonomous within a context of generally noncoercive relationships with adults;
2. respect the feelings and rights of others and begin to cooperate (through decentering and coordinating different points of view);
3. be alert and curious and use initiative in pursuing curiosities, to have confidence in his ability to figure things out for himself, and to speak his mind with conviction.

---

3. Fredricka K. Reisman, *A Guide to Diagnostic Teaching of Arithmetic*, 2nd ed. (Columbus, Ohio: Charles E. Merrill, 1978), p. 3

4. See especially Ronald Good, *How Children Learn Science* (New York: Macmillian, 1977); and Richard Copeland, *How Children Learn Mathematics*, 2nd ed. (New York: Macmillan, 1974).

5. Constance Kamii and Rheta DeVries, *Physical Knowledge in Preschool Education: Implications of Piaget's Theory* (Englewood Cliffs, N.J.: Prentice-Hall, 1978), p. 54.

The two cognitive objectives in this approach are:

For the child to
1. come up with a variety of ideas, problems, and questions;
2. put objects and events into relationships and notice similarities and differences.[6]

Kamii and DeVries note that teachers need to update their knowledge of physics, for example, if they are to help children test ideas in actions on objects that yield visible feedback on what happens. Following Piagetian theory and the general expectations for each stage of development, teachers pattern their work with individual children. For example, knowing that three to five-year-olds think in an egocentric fashion, the teacher seeks to help children pursue their ideas about how things work. But there would also be stress on *different* ideas expressed by various children, helping them to challenge each other. The child, hearing different ideas from others, is also expected to realize that ideas are not necessarily the same for everyone. Thus, children are not "corrected" and given "right" answers by teachers. Their "wrong" ideas are challenged by physical events that give visible feedback often contrary to their expectations.

Forman and Kuschner, using a Piagetian base for teaching young children and mixing it with behaviorist theory, are more explicit about their guidelines for observational processes. They state that teachers need to understand general dimensions of development to aid individual children to make progress in specific aspects of these general dimensions.[7] Thus, in this view, diagnostic procedures for teaching would be based on detailed theoretical knowledge of child development, especially Piagetian theory, with informed observation of a particular child, and on knowledge of methods that support development. These authors list four requirements for improving teaching:

1. clear specification of teaching objectives;
2. use of effective techniques to monitor teaching, by teachers and observers;
3. teacher openness to constructive criticism and willingness to change;
4. development of specific plans for change.[8]

Kamii and DeVries stress "a way of thinking about teaching that can provide a basis for making decisions from moment to moment in the course of an activity as well as in planning and evaluation."[9]

It should be noted that neither of the Piagetian-based approaches just mentioned requires recording observational data. Instead, these authors stress the observational needs of teachers who have to think on their feet while deciding how to guide particular learning situations. This reflects the particular focus of these two texts on the cognitive aspects of group learning situations. Both books are concerned with how young children learn physical knowledge, which is important but does not cover the total range of knowledge, attitudes, and experiences young children usually have in group settings or schools.

FORMAL DIAGNOSTIC PROCEDURES

There are numerous standardized tests for young children that teachers give for various purposes. The vast majority of such tests assess reading achievement. Others focus on

---

6. Ibid., p. 40.
7. George E. Forman and David S. Kuschner, *The Child's Construction of Knowledge: Piaget for Teaching Children* (Monterey, Calif.: Wadsworth, 1977), p. 128.
8. From p. 191 of *The Child's Construction of Knowledge: Piaget for Teaching Children* by Forman and Kuschner. Copyright © 1977 by Wadsworth, Inc. Reprinted by permission of the publisher, Brooks/Cole Publishing Company, Monterey, California.
9. Kamii and DeVries, *Physical Knowledge in Preschool Education*, p. 61.

concepts, basic skills, reasoning and thinking levels, sensory functioning, identification of learning disabilities, language dominance, motor skills or visual-motor skills, motivation, social competence, and self-concept.

In addition to these individual tests, there are also collections of tests, usually annotated for content, form, administration, and scoring; some provide evaluation analyses. Sources for such tests are listed in Appendix A. It should be noted that one of the great disadvantages of many tests for young children is the requirement of administering them to groups. Considering the egocentric responses young children make to many requests, the validity of a group test situation must always be questioned. However, many tests originally designed for group administration could be given to one child, if the instructions are improved.

Children's tests should always be given with thoughtful arrangement for comfort and reduction of fear and anxiety. Not all children respond to test situations the same way. Some are highly stimulated by the challenge; others freeze or try to fathom what "right" answers are sought. Many children interpret a question from a very personal perspective frequently at variance with the intention of the question maker. In our view, tests should *never* be the sole basis of any important decision about curriculum selection, placement, or promotion. Test results should always be evaluated in the light of observational and recorded data about a child's functioning. Furthermore, any *one* test should never be regarded as more than an inadequate sampling of the child's performance. Finally, a child who is unwilling should not be forced to take a test—no useful data are likely to result.

A selected listing of popular early childhood tests in Appendix A runs the gamut of test content previously noted. All of these tests have been, and often are, administered by teachers; many of these tests are given most often by psychologists or specialists in special education. Tests that must be given by qualified psychologists because of complexity of administration or interpretation have been omitted from this list, such as the Illinois Test for Psycholinguistic Abilities.

Some of the tests listed are widely used as either achievement or reading readiness tests. The Metropolitan Readiness Test is one of the most popular tests of this type. It is often given toward the close of the kindergarten year to help determine whether a child should be promoted to first grade, held in a kindergarten for a second year, or placed in a transitional kindergarten–first grade class. The test may also be used to form seemingly homogeneous first-grade classes, assuming that high scorers will be more advanced than low scorers.

Critics of the use of readiness tests for placement or promotion purposes point out that this penalizes the slower-maturing child, especially boys, whose physical and social development is on the average slower than girls during the first six years. Socially immature children are usually the ones most disadvantaged by these tests. Some of them may be unwilling or unable to sit still for the time required to complete the test. Some children may be less test-wise than others; they may be non-English-speaking; or they may have other characteristics that dilute the value of the test results. Furthermore, a child tested in April or May, who will be about six months older when actually entering first grade, is being tested on many aspects that change very quickly in these years of rapid growth. Obsolescence is one of the problems with these test results. Another is the labeling of children that results from the placements based on test scores. Labeling is always insidious and has great potential for real harm in a child's aspirations, self-concept, and self-valuing. This harm can be compounded if the family conveys feelings of disappointment and chagrin at the child's tested functioning.

Other problems with teacher responsibility for test administration, scoring, and analysis include:

1. reduction of teaching time;
2. undue teacher concern for results, expecting to be held accountable for scores, for which teachers actually have little control or responsibility;
3. viewing diagnostic tests as teaching tests, instead of clues for children's teaching needs;
4. lack of standardization in teachers' administration of tests, giving some classes apparent advantages over others—such test features as timing, tension, explanation, or answers to children's questions for clarification, giving hints, clues, or outright answers are some of the ways that standardization is compromised;
5. lack of relationship between test results and program objectives—teachers resent what they see as time-wasting, child-intimidating and labeling test procedures, which result in no useful clues for teaching.
6. low validity of many tests—a low score on some reading readiness tests may be quite irrelevant to the specific reading methods in use in the classroom or school.

However, there may be tests listed which teachers can find useful in individual cases when they need data to confirm or disprove hunches difficult to document in other ways. Tests may be helpful to identify possible learning disabilities, handicapping conditions, sensory malfunctioning, or giftedness. Where the purpose to be served clearly relates to teaching decisions, placement, or promotion, it may be in the child's best interest and worth the time and trouble to give a well-selected test to a specific child or group.

Another problem with teacher administration of tests is the difficulty teachers have in suppressing teaching while testing. If tests are needed, it is important to administer the test without influencing the results. There can be no objection to teachers using tests as teaching instruments if testing results are not desired.

In deciding to use tests instructionally, teachers are challenged to create a relaxed context in which children are stimulated to think through problems without becoming fearful or overanxious. This may be an excellent way to build children's skill in test taking.

Teacher-made Tests

Teacher-made tests can overcome many of the disadvantages of standardized tests. Teachers can formulate their tests to assess classroom-related learning within the objectives of their own programs. The major purpose of teacher-made tests, aside from teaching children how to take tests without anxiety, is to assess the outcomes of teaching. What did children learn from a planned instructional project? This, of course, provides the necessary relationship between teaching and testing that seems to merit the time required. Such tests need not be formally administered nor given to large groups. One child can be tested at a time, or a few children may be grouped for a test.

Criterion-referenced test data, which compare a child's performance with preselected criteria are easily checked on a checklist. These tend to be yes-no tests—that is, "yes" if the performance meets the criteria, "no" if not. Such yes-no testing may refer to writing one's name acceptably, conserving quantity, taking initiative, or following instructions.

Tests can be culled from any available sources that serve the teacher's purpose. Or the teacher can construct a test. Teachers often collect many test items to have a good pool of questions and problems from which to draw. Testing young children requires collecting interesting materials and active tasks that can stimulate the child to attack the problem and persevere and maintaining good rapport with the child to reveal the child's real understanding and knowledge.

In making their own tests, teachers need to be as systematic as they can. Test making requires answers to such questions as:

1. What outcomes are required by my objectives?
2. What forms of behavior can I accept as evidence of such outcomes?
3. What context for the test is appropriate?
4. What criteria for success are useful?
5. How can I insure that no child will be harmed by the process?

The answers to questions one to three refer to conditions of testing, such as informal versus formal, group size, control of tension and anxiety levels, children's willingness to participate, and avoiding distraction. Above all, the teacher must maximize the child's opportunities to be successful and to feel good about his or her work. In planning the test, the teacher must look candidly and objectively at the content taught and methods used. If the test is truly diagnostic, the teacher really wants to know how much has been learned or accomplished and what level of accuracy and completion will be appropriate criteria.

Examples can be found in Appendix B of the kind of teacher-made tests that are easily constructed for specific purposes. It should be noted that, while these tests are formally written, there is no requirement that they be formally administered. Many of these tests could readily be converted to observational recordings, so that in a context of well-constructed activity, the teacher could reliably gauge children's responses.

Readers should note that some of the test items in Appendix B serve as check points in sequencing learning. Test items refer to such mathematical skills as patterning and counting, reading and writing skills, and cognitive skills of sorting and classifying. Diagnostic teaching requires individualizing the schedule of tests to assure appropriate timing for each child.

SUMMARY

Diagnostic teaching identifies what children are learning in the program and guides teaching plans for individuals and groups. Diagnostic procedures include informal and formal tests, planned and incidental observations, review of samples of children's work, reports from parents and others, as well as unobtrusive measures.

A systematic approach to diagnostic procedures is viewed as a necessary condition for effective curricular development. There are many observation guides, checklist formats, criterion-referenced tests, and standardized tests that teachers may use. Additionally, teacher-designed procedures may provide more disired inforamtion.

EXERCISES

1. From Appendix B, select diagnostic procedures for two different content areas.
   a. Try these out with several children.
   b. Analyze your results for effectivness in identifying learning needs.
2. Develop a recording form to reflect children's interests and analyze the results for the adequacy of your form. Identify any changes in form indicated.

BIBLIOGRAPHY

Boyer, E. Gil; Simon, Anita; and Karafin, Gail, eds., *Measures of Maturation: An Anthology of Early Childhood Education Instruments.* Vols. 1–3. Philadelphia: Research for Better Schools, 1973.

Cartwright, Carol A. and Cartwright, George P. *Developing Observational Skills.* New York: McGraw-Hill, 1974.

Center for the Study of Evaluation, and the Early Childhood Research Center, UCLA Graduate School of Education. *Preschool/Kindergarten Test Evaluations.* Los Angeles, Calif.: CSE-ECRC, 1971.

Cooper, James M. et al. *Measuring Concept Learning: A Handbook.* Lexington, Mass.: D.C. Heath, 1977.

Copeland, Richard. *How Children Learn Mathematics.* 2nd ed. New York: Macmillan, 1974.

Educational Testing Service. "An Annotated Bibliography of References to Tests and Assessment Devices." Princeton, N.J.: Educational Testing Service, undated.

Educational Testing Service. *Head Start Test Collection.* Princeton, N.J.: Educational Testing Service, 1971.

Engel, B.S. *A Handbook on Documentation.* North Dakota Study Group on Evaluation. Monograph Series. Grand Forks, N.D.: University of North Dakota Press, 1975.

Forman, George E., and Kuschner, David S. *The Child's Construction of Knowledge: Piaget for Teaching Children.* Monterey, Calif.: Wadsworth, 1977.

Good, Ronald. *How Children Learn Science.* New York: Macmillan, 1977.

Gordan, Ira. *Studying the Child in School.* New York: Wiley & Sons, 1966.

Hoepfner, Ralph; Stern, C.; and Nummedal, S. G., eds. *CSE-ECRC Preschool/Kindergarten Test Evaluators.* Los Angeles, Calif.: Center for the Study of Evaluation, UCLA, 1972.

Johnson, Orval G. and Bommarito, James N. *Tests and Measurements in Child Development: A Handbook.* San Francisco: Jossey-Bass, 1971.

Kamii, Constance, and DeVries, Rheta. *Physical Knowledge in Preschool Education: Implications of Piaget's Theory.* Englewood Cliffs, N.J.: Prentice-Hall, 1978.

Mager, Robert. *Goal Analysis.* Belmont, Calif.: Fearon Publishers, 1972.

Reisman, Fredricka K. *A Guide to Diagnostic Teaching of Arithmetic.* 2nd ed. Columbus, Ohio: Charles E. Merrill, 1978.

Steenburgen, Frances. *A Practical Guide to Writing Goals and Objectives.* San Rafael, Calif.: Academic Therapy Publishers, 1973.

Tillman, Murray; Bersoff, Donald; and Dolly, John. *Learning to Teach: A Decision-making System.* Lexington, Mass.: D.C. Heath, 1978.

Tuckman, Bruce W. *A Guide to Instructional Program Evaluation.* Boston: Allyn and Bacon, 1979.

Walker, Deborah Klein. *Socioemotional Measures for Preschool and Kindergarten Children.* San Francisco: Jossey-Bass, 1973.

III A Prototype Curriculum

Section One of this book reviewed curriculum options and emphasized selecting a curriculum framework, developing a context for teaching and learning, and identifying sequencing principles. Teaching procedures dominate the second section, stressing the central place for theories about children's social-emotional needs in decisions about teaching responses. Teaching roles include organizing the environment, selecting activity designs, choosing teaching strategies, and devising diagnostic procedures.

This section describes a prototype curriculum as an example of how curriculum design translates into learning activities. The design of this prototype evolved from specific selections of major components of curriculum identified in the earlier chapters. The prototype curriculum, originally developed with the cooperation of early childhood teachers, had extensive testing and redesign in more than a decade of use by preservice and inservice teachers. In this section, we will specify how we transposed theory into practice.

12 Framework for a Prototype Curriculum

A prototype curriculum is a model of how theory will look in practice; it translates specific ideas into reality. The function of a prototype in industry is to try out an experimental design that can, if successful, be produced in quantity, such as a new car design. In human service fields such as teaching, a prototype is illustrative and cannot be exactly reproduced in quantity. It serves to describe how ideas might be realized. Therefore, a curriculum prototype suggests how to develop program activities from a design that has been specified in writing.

The prototype to be described is constructed from choices made for each of the components discussed in Section One. The philosophy of the curriculum becomes visible through this selection. Types of learning activities and teaching roles, described in Section Two, are presented here as *instructional models*. You are encouraged to study the prototype described in Chapters 13 to 15 to determine how the selected components are reflected in the program design. For example, this program's view of development is that children learn through experiences that have meaning to them. Hence, the design of language activities is based primarily on children's actions and interactions, not on lecture-drill activities. After considering the internal consistency of this program design, you may review your own preferences for each component.

The specific views on form, goals, knowledge, development and learning, and sequencing and methodology for this prototype, which are detailed later, can be summarized here:

1. The *form* is a total program, not a selected part of the curriculum. However, it is not possible to include the total curriculum in this book. The program is written for maximum clarity, transportability, and sharing with others such as teaching team members, parents, administrators, and visitors.
2. The *long-term objectives* include learning that is the hallmark of a self-confident and caring individual, who has the skills of acquiring and using knowledge effectively in a rapidly changing world. Such learning is viewed as being forever in process. Mastery of language, symbol systems, and social skills is included.
3. The *short-term objectives* reflect content and process goals for learning concepts, skills, and information; these goals are keyed to fields of knowledge and stages of development. The attempt is always to integrate the logical and psychological properties of curriculum.
4. *Knowledge* primarily features key concepts drawn from the structure of the disciplines.

5. The views on *child development* are most closely associated with the developmental theories of Piaget and Erikson.
6. The *instructional sequences* grow out of universally accepted rules of learning applied to the logic of the content and the stages of psychological development.
7. The *methodology* is based on the premise that children give their attention and learning energy to those experiences in which they become most deeply involved. The program features children's choices of involvement with people, activities, and materials. Children's choices are made within the context of a well-equipped environment that provides options for independent, constructive, expressive, and social activity, as well as participation in teacher-designed and teacher-guided activity.

These selections of curriculum components are translated into program design in the following section.

CURRICULUM FORM

In this prototype, the curriculum form is a *program* in which a coordinated set of plans are related to program goals. The plans encompass all aspects of the program, the design of the environment, the schedule, the routines, and the instructional design. Decisions are programmatic, reflecting long- and short-term goals. These grew out of choices about what is worth knowing, how it is learned, and what learning is appropriate for the current stage of development. Teachers with whom we worked contributed much detail about what content is learnable and teachable.

The programmatic approach to a curriculum design suggests teaching plans sufficiently detailed to give genuine guidance to teaching decisions. This includes guidance for on-the-spot decisions needed in dynamic classroom situations and for detailed advanced planning. The degree to which detailed plans guide or bind the teacher depends on the individual. A curriculum plan that does not shape teaching interactions is meaningless, while a plan that restricts meaningful guidance is mindless. We perceive a useful curriculum design as a flexible instrument a teacher uses with increasing skill and with limitless opportunities for improvisation.

When working with a new program, teachers at first tend to follow designs literally to find out how they work. Then they make adaptations. As teachers become more secure with a basic design, they generate new activities that respond to the interests and capabilities of the children. However, to improvise without a framework or clear program objectives is to flounder at the mercy of chance. This ignores the need to know one's destination. To teach "by the book" without flexible adaptation is equally unproductive, for it ignores the individual differences of the learners. With practice in developing a curriculum, teachers find opportunities in the naturally occurring events of the classroom to pursue the same goals that are the basis of careful plans.

GOALS AND VALUES

A distinctive feature of this prototype is the clarity and sequence of goals. The goals, stated in terms of children's learning outcomes, are organized in familiar curriculum areas with pervasive and overriding emphases on affective goals, cognitive skills, and language development. Long-term goals guide the identification of short-term goals.

Long-term goals are those toward which the program seeks continual progress. These goals are developmental. That is, children are expected to show progress and growth but not necessarily total mastery during the early years. In this prototype, the following affective, cognitive, and language goals are featured:

1. Personal development
    a. intellectual stimulation and language development
    b. independence and autonomy
    c. playfulness and expressiveness
    d. self-valuing
2. Social utility
    a. competence in symbolic forms of learning
    b. self-discipline
3. Social responsibility
    a. care about people and living things
    b. nonstereotyping of others
    c. moral development
4. Skills
    a. cognitive skills
    b. arts-and-crafts skills
    c. social skills
    d. beginning reading and mathematics skills
    e. physical skills
5. Common culture and special culture
    a. understanding of one's world
    b. entering the world of school learning
    c. value and use of first dialect or language as well as standard English
    d. equal valuing of all cultures

Readers will find that these objectives have formed a framework for the content selection as well as the methodology. This is the high-priority list of goals. Teaching children to say *please* and *thank you* would be low-priority goals compared with encouraging children to help others, share, collaborate, and respect others' rights.

Since long-term goals tend to be global, it is short-term goals that shape decisions on daily and weekly bases. These short-term goals feature primarily concepts and skills appropriate to defined developmental stages, which are related to the fields of knowledge.

Affective Goals

Affective goals are long-term since they deal with children's perceptions about themselves as worthwhile and competent individuals who are valued contributing members of a group. Evaluation research on Follow-Through shows that those programs emphasizing achievement have done more to increase children's self-valuing than those trying to improve self-valuing directly.[1] This confirms the hunch on which our prototype is built; that is, children feel worthy if they know they have achieved and if those close to them communicate approval of such achievements. For young children, achievement grows out of their voluntary involvement in activities and daily experiences at which they are likely to be successful. Children's success experiences require the following features of school atmosphere, attitudes, and procedures:

1. Encouraging children's autonomy and independence by honoring their right of choice or refusal.
2. Providing visible structure in the program so children are not dependent on others to know what is expected.
3. Interacting with children to convey affection and confidence in their ability to learn.
4. Preparing the classroom for easy access to and maintenance of materials. Children's selection and care of equipment and their independent activity generate as much autonomy as possible.
5. Providing enough time for each element in the program so that progress can be made toward all valued goals.

1. *The Follow-Through Planned Variation Experiment*, Vol. IV-A, An Evaluation of Follow Through (Washington, D.C.: U.S. Department of Health, Education, and Welfare, 1977) pp. 147-148.

6. Valuing each child's uniqueness by featuring the evidence of her or his personal attributes, such as name, photograph, voice, artwork, preferences, skill achievement, and social interaction style.
7. Fostering children's sense of membership in such groups as the family, the school, and the community through orientation to physical space and to human relationships. Orientation to physical space includes learning the way around the school and the route to and from home. Human relationships include classroom, school, and community roles and responsibilities.
8. Stimulating progress in cognitive skills in specific instances, which give children feedback about achievement.

In addition to shaping classroom procedures, affective goals translate into specific activities that support self-valuing, self-expression, and a sense of belonging to family, community, and school groups. Table 12-1 lists affective goals, the first of which is to increase self-recognition. Photographs, mirrors, and recording devices and physical activities are primary sources for developing familiarity with the physical self.

Self-valuing follows self-knowing. Some activities that feature self-knowing are:

1. musical and physical action games using children's names;
2. attendance taking by children using photographs on a chart;
3. use of mirrors in a follow-the-leader game;
4. use of tape recorder to dictate stories about personal experiences and recognition of voices and accomplishments on replay;
5. physical activities accompanying chants and music and using round-robin leadership: a child selects a physical motion for others to copy, leads the group action, and enjoys being in control.

These activities suggest the variety available for developing self-knowing and self-valuing.

Cognitive Goals

Cognitive goals include both cognitive processing and outcomes of knowledge and skill. The cognitive process goals permeate all curriculum areas in the form of cognitive skills, as children sort, classify, and generalize their experiences; predict outcomes; and solve problems. Processing skills include:

1. comparing and contrasting objects and events,
2. ordering and patterning sets of objects and events,
3. sorting and classifying,
4. generalizing,
5. problem solving,
6. giving personal meaning to words and ideas.

Since cognitive skills cannot be isolated for instructional purposes, our prototype curriculum features developmental aspects of cognitive activity in all content areas. These cognitive expectations are based on the Piagetian stage of intuitive thinking (ages three to seven or eight), with the beginning of concrete operations showing up in the older ages.

Cognitive processing requires having content "to chew on." Fact accumulation fills this need. If children need to understand the concept of heat as energy, cooking activities provide specific facts from which this concept can take shape. As children manipulate physical objects, note outcomes, and try to figure out why or how things happen, cognitive goals are advanced. This is what cognitive process is —arranging one's understanding into some pattern that satisfies the questions that either preceded or will follow the activities.

In cooking experiences, children notice that foods may harden or soften, depending on cooking method and characteristics of the food. Eggs, for example, are an ideal food for contriving almost any result intended. Cooking methods, temperature, utensils, and food processing—all contribute to massive accumu-

TABLE 12.1. Long-term and short-term affective goals

Long-term goals	Short-term goals
SELF-KNOWING AND SELF-VALUING	
1. Recognition of one's own physical attributes and possessions; pride in oneself.	a. Respond to one's own name when spoken. b. Recognize images of oneself in photograph, mirror, film, and videotape recording. c. Recognize one's own recorded voice. d. Develop competence in physical actions. e. Recognize and care for personal possessions such as clothing and playthings.
2. Awareness and expression of feelings.	a. Express oneself in artwork, in other expressive activities such as music, dance, movement, in construction activities, and in language, including poetry, stories, chants, and word games. b. Express feelings of love, happiness and joy, excitement and anticipation, fear and confusion, disappointment and grief, anger and frustration, and likes and dislikes, verbally or in specific styles of movement, music, or art.
3. Awareness of skills and abilities, valuing those already acquired and those in the process of being acquired.	a. Over a period of time, choose to engage in a variety of activities, familiar and unfamiliar. b. Use skills to help others. c. Accept help when needed and refuse help otherwise. d. Recognize and take pride in one's own art and craft work, and in achieving cognitive, language, affective, physical, and social skills.
GROUP MEMBERSHIP	
1. Recognition and sense of membership in a family group.	a. Know the members of one's family and their relationships. b. Identify some attributes of family membership, such as adult responsibility for child welfare and individual responsibility for each other. c. Identify unique characteristics of home and family, such as dwelling, family history, family rules, family recreation, and mutual responsibilities.

Note: Affective goals are integrally combined with cognitive goals of perceiving and processing experiences and are not pursued in isolation.

TABLE 12.1. (continued)

Long-term goals	Short-term goals
GROUP MEMBERSHIP	
2. Recognition and sense of membership in the class group and in the school.	a. Identify the characteristics of the class group, such as members of the group, favorite games and activities, special trips or projects, birthdays, ethnic holidays, and other languages.
	b. Name one's school and classroom, and find one's way in school to key locations.
	c. Contribute to and support class rules and routines.
	d. Know the class schedule, recapitulating and anticipating the sequence of program activities.
	e. Take responsibility to help the class stay on schedule through cleanup, demonstrating self-discipline and cooperation.
3. Recognition and sense of membership in a community.	a. Identify important ideas and celebrate some cultural holidays of national and local interest through craft production, music, and other activities.
	b. Describe a route from home to school or to another important community location.
	c. Identify characteristics of the community, including *physical characteristics*, such as structures, transportation centers, and commercial centers; and *social and cultural events*, such as street craft show, community sing, and recycling collection in community.

lation of facts about heat as energy. Out of these experiences, impressions, perceptions, and feelings, concepts are shaped and reshaped where found wanting.

Language Goals

More language development can be stimulated in an on-going program than could possibly occur in separate language lessons. We do not conclude from this that there is no need to specify language development plans; rather that language learning is included as part of all curriculum areas. Related language learning is listed with goals in each area for emphasis, as shown in Chapters 13 and 14. The approach to language development and beginning reading will be described in Chapter 15.

Goal Specification

Goals focus on practicing, applying, and extending knowledge and skills. New learning is viewed as an extension or expansion of what children already know and can do. Actually, all three types of goals—new learning, practice, and application—occur in most activities, although one is usually featured in a specific instructional interaction.

Essentially, the goals in this prototype serve two major areas of decision making. One area encompasses the procedures required for managing the program, such as organizing the classroom, establishing routines and schedules, observing and recording, and assigning roles and responsibilities to members of the teaching team. The other area includes program activities and teaching interactions—or what is usually thought of as *the curriculum*.

Goals within the curriculum areas are content-specific rather than activity-specific. They refer to learning outcomes rather than to learning activities. In this way, the goals may be developed through many different activities. Although a specific activity is offered to illustrate each goal, the teacher is free to choose or construct other activities. For example, one beginning goal in geography is that "Children move in space avoiding collision with people and things." While the instructional model of a sample activity may suggest an obstacle game arranged by the teacher, other options are available, such as:

1. extending children's spontaneous exploration of space in the classroom or on the playground by adding new space-exploration tasks;
2. having children find new challenges for moving in space through musical, rhythmic, and physical activities;
3. initiating a game utilizing pathways and obstacles that the child can pursue without teacher guidance.

Activities designed to meet goals are not necessarily confined to the instructional program. Teachers involve children in such management decisions as how to rearrange a classroom or playground area. Such an activity engages children in solving the problem of moving about in space without colliding with objects and people. It requires thinking about pathways for traffic and boundaries for interest centers. It requires making and testing hypotheses. The activities through which the teacher seeks to achieve goals are viewed as only some of many learning activities teachers might design.

KNOWLEDGE SELECTION

The selection of knowledge in our prototype is based on an integration of separate curriculum areas, chiefly in terms of key concepts taken from the disciplines approach to knowledge selection. The separate areas of curriculum content serve as the "bins" from which to choose. Once selected, however, it is necessary to coordinate, integrate, amalgamate, or otherwise combine the content to feature cognitive processes and skills in productive ways. Keeping separate "bins" of content serves to guide sequencing needs when order is required and to maintain the clear detail needed in planning. These "bins" also indicate the diagnostic testing needs, to plan for children's learning. The separateness of the content areas is especially useful in updating content to eliminate obsolescence, restructure where it seems productive, and add new detail when it becomes available. Thus, one could update the science "bin" without disturbing the language "bin" in the process.

Content areas include (1) music and arts, (2) science, (3) mathematics, (4) geography, (5) economics, and (6) beginning reading. Important learning in each area is identified by key concepts, cognitive process skills, subject matter skills, and related vocabulary.

Key concepts from the curriculum areas provide the basis for defining what process skills and subject matter skills are needed. For example, a set of key concepts in economics includes:

1. Production, distribution, and consumption of goods and services are the major economic functions performed in our country's system.
2. Economics is concerned with studying *what* shall be produced to meet fundamental needs for food, shelter, and clothing as well as other needs; *by whom*, that is, who shall be the producers; and *for whom*, that is, who shall receive these goods and services. It is the study of exchange transactions, most of which require use of money in our system.
3. Production includes growing agricultural products of every kind and all forms of extracting or collecting such raw materials as coal, oil, minerals, metals, wood, and the like. Production covers all forms of processing and manufacturing, including construction of houses, roads, bridges, and highways.
4. Distribution is the vital function of linking goods and services to possible consumers, who are, of course, on the receiving end of all these transactions.
5. Scarcity is the major economic theme, since all economic goods, by definition, are not free but limited or scarce. At any one time, there is a limited supply of land, labor, and capital and of goods and services available for distribution.
6. The laws of supply and demand are supposed to set prices through the mechanism of the market place and to determine how goods and services are distributed. While these laws seem to work imperfectly and with many constraints, they do in a general way account for the pricing structure.

From the economic concepts, we derived a variety of cognitive and subject matter skills that are involved in the growth of the key concepts by young children. All of the possible emphases just listed require the cognitive processing skills of observing, sorting, classifying, and finding patterns of relationship. Vocabulary, communication, and language interaction needs are apparent. Symbol learning could include any level of reading or mathematics with which children can deal, either orally or in writing. The content of economic concepts gives teachers wide latitude for choices of activities, tasks, trips, and cognitive skill practice.

VIEWS OF DEVELOPMENT AND LEARNING

Our views on development flow from stage theory, and since no single theory accounts for the totality of the child's development, for our prototype curriculum we have drawn freely on Piaget for intellectual development and on Erikson for psychosocial development. Gesell's normative data chiefly guide placement and sequencing of content. Learning theory provides important guidelines for sequencing as well as for setting up routines. Our use of social learning theory, or learning by imitation, centers on modeling concepts. We made the usual assumptions that, while stages of development are universal, each child has a unique pace of traversing these stages.

Children's play is regarded as fundamental to the child's development. It helps the child achieve personal meaningfulness, to engage in spontaneous forms of verbal and physical expressiveness, and to meet such psychosocial needs as fantasy and discharge of tension. Play activities make it unnecessary to teach children many facts they can pick up by themselves, or to encourage them to shape concepts they can develop by themselves. Teaching roles to stimulate play are important in all of the teaching plans. For example, in the use of any material with which a child is not familiar, exploratory play precedes planned interaction. Thus, teacher plans to stimulate children's play serve major objectives for physical, social, emotional, and intellectual development.

Children's interests lead to many learning activities during the free-choice activity period, since this is a classroom with varied interest centers. Large blocks of time allow for exploratory, constructive, creative, and social-interaction purposes. Teachers open new activities to children to broaden their interest. Introducing children to a wider world than they otherwise encounter means providing many kinds of learning that do not occur outside of school.

While learning flows from the child's active manipulation of the environment, views of teaching are definite and specific. Teaching includes certain roles in guidance, direction, redirection, challenge, and modeling valued ways of using materials and skills. Thus, social learning theory indicates that much learning occurs with very little direct teaching if modeling procedures are used appropriately. For example, while autonomy in making choices is always respected, children who show interest in hearing storybooks read automatically become models for other children, if the conditions for *voluntary* imitation are present.

With a developmental base and an interactive approach to children's learning, our prototype curriculum starts with their interest and voluntary involvement in activities. The teacher plans specific curriculum sequences for small groups and individuals. As in many early childhood programs, the teachers set up special activities during the multiple-activity period, and they interact with children selectively. Tasks or challenges are offered to children who seem likely to need them, but refusals are respectfully accepted.

Action-based learning activities indoors and outdoors serve as the primary basis of this program, in which all children's play is valued as a learning tool in all domains of development and learning. First-hand experiences for observation, manipulation, sorting, and problem solving stimulate children's construction and skill practice. Knowledge and skills naturally integrate content areas.

SEQUENCING THE CURRICULUM

Criteria for sequencing include the universal guidelines of moving from simple to complex, concrete to abstract, known to unknown, and facts to concepts. When selecting the instructional activities and teaching strategies in the program, these guidelines are applied to curriculum content, skill development, and problem setting. Sequencing decisions determine the order of goals in curriculum areas, as well as the provision of materials for children's self-directed use and the content of informal interactions.

Cognitive stage theory establishes the limits of curriculum sequences. Other criteria contribute to sequencing within the context of the stage. These include the knowledge area, and the academic and psychomotor skills required to pursue the activity goals.

Sequences are more easily defined in mathematics than in the social sciences. Fields that have an order based on a skill-concept sequence provide more obvious guidelines. The general order for beginning number learning proceeds as follows:

1. basic set identification;
2. concepts of *more than*, *less than*, and *equivalent to*;
3. matching one to one;
4. counting;
5. simple addition and subtraction or combining and partitioning sets under ten;
6. concepts of zero;
7. addition and subtraction with sets of ten to twenty;
8. repeated sets, multiplication, and division under twenty.

This general sequence provides the order for teaching or encouraging number learning, and for integrating these instructional activities with others. These number concepts can be fostered in games on the playground or in the classroom, in cooking and eating experiences, and in arts-and-crafts activities, among others.

This program values children's sense of competence, which builds self-valuing. Consequently, when children do not succeed in an activity, the responsibility rests with the teacher to review sequencing needs. For example, a child who has chosen to sort a collection of objects but walks away from the task in frustration is signaling a need for help. Teacher review may indicate that failure could be prevented by changing the size of the collection, the contrastive features, or the materials. Calling a child to complete a task that is too difficult encourages failure, so teachers are cautioned to avoid this. Lack of challenge to a child is also avoidable. The many examples of sequencing cited in Chapter 6 illustrate the way in which sequencing rules are applied in this prototype program.

CHILDREN'S SOCIAL-EMOTIONAL NEEDS

Meeting children's social-emotional needs was described in the earlier subsection, "Affective Goals." Sensitivity to children's individual differences in affective needs grows with general teaching experience and with increasing understanding of each child. As previously indicated, procedures are stressed that meet individual needs in pacing and development, as well as children's universal needs for stimulation, acceptance, interaction, and autonomy. Designing learning activities for individuals and small groups is another way to stress affective goals. Children's choices to participate or observe activities are respected.

Affective development is increased through acccepting children's feelings, channeling aggression positively, and fostering autonomy in specific ways. Children's feelings of competence achieved through mastering various tasks and their awareness of family approval of these achievements are the two main sources of continued motivation. This requires that teachers collaborate with families to unify feedback to children in terms of their self-worth as well as their accomplishments.

THE ENVIRONMENT AND LEARNING ACTIVITIES

This prototype curriculum requires an early childhood classroom organized into centers of interest and equipped with a variety of manipulative materials. Children have generous periods of time to use the materials for exploratory, constructive, creative, and social-interaction purposes. Open activity periods are balanced with routines of group living such as clean up, quiet activities, and eating periods. Total group activities, generally very few, are designed to increase exposure to new stimuli and to enhance group interaction.

Learning activities range from spontaneous, self-chosen play situations to specific structured tasks, games, and construction projects. Informality and individual choices within well-defined limits prevail throughout the program. Individual or tutorial instruction is stressed. Social development is emphasized through procedures of classroom management, encouragement of independence, and self-regulation, with teacher guidance provided in conflict situations.

Just as children have choices, so do the teachers. While children are engaged in interest centers of their own choosing, the teacher may select a learning task that matches the learning level of the child or children the teacher plans to work with. As the members of the group pursue their interests, the teacher may extend an invitation to one or a few to join.

One important requirement of this prototype is to avoid large group or total class teaching whenever possible. When a teacher is working with a child, other children may watch, since it so often happens that children learn this way. When music activities run parallel with other activities in a self-contained classroom, unrealistic compromises are demanded of the participants in other activities. Consequently, total group activities are indicated when they are not practical for small groups, and alternate choices are made available to those children who might not choose to join.

In most activities, the teaching role moves from active leadership and instruction toward the roles of resource person and facilitator. The children's actions move from exploration to expression and construction, and to increasing control of their behavior and their learning outcomes.

VIEWS OF TEACHING

Within this program, teachers fulfill many roles and selectively use all the basic strategies listed in Chapter 10. You are reminded that *teaching roles* refer to a function encompassing a set of behaviors; *teaching strategies* are behaviors that combine to make up a role. Selections vary with the nature of the content and the characteristics of the children.

Teaching Roles

Theories of development, in our view, do not offer much guidance in designing teaching roles. From developmental theory comes the assumption that effective teaching of young children, irrespective of program preferences, requires nurturance. We further assume that the roles of reinforcer and manager contribute to a stable and secure environment. These three roles—*nurturer*, *reinforcer* and *manager*—provide the affective climate for safety, acceptance, and support for children as they engage in program activities.

Other featured teaching roles depend on the specific program goals and activities. For example, where children are engaged in activities of their own choosing and a program goal is "fostering independence," the role of observer is called for and the reinforcing role is minimized so children can experience their autonomy. When children apply what they know to construction projects and solving problems, the teaching roles featured are likely to be those of *challenger* and, less visibly, *manager*.

The direct teaching roles of *information giver* and *tutor* in planned instructional activities involve introducing new knowledge, and initiating skill practice. An example of the first is when the teacher, introducing a new song or musical game, provides the necessary information, that is, the melody and words, or the steps in the game. An example of the second—the tutoring role—is when the teacher works with one child in a planned interaction featuring copying a color pattern with poker chips and other materials.

The role of *participant* allows the teacher to join with children in their activities for brief periods to enrich the play. This may occur as the teacher role plays a visitor in the housekeeping area or works with clay along with a small group of children. As a participant, the teacher contributes to the play through modeling and interaction without assuming the position of leadership or authority. Appropriate use of the participant role means that the flow of children's activity is not interrupted as the teacher enters or leaves.

Teaching Strategies

The goals of an activity determine the selection and coordination of strategies. In this program, instructional models have been developed to illustrate how strategies can be used. That is, strategies are viewed as the means by which the teacher implements program goals. These strategies are pervasive and occur in all program activities.

Teaching strategies follow a consistent sequence in all instructional models:

1. The teacher offers choices with selected materials for self-directed play or self-chosen task.
2. The child manipulates materials as a first step in the development of the play or task.
3. The teacher introduces a structure for play with materials that promotes a series of inputs by the teacher with children contributing and responding spontaneously as they perceive the task. These inputs generally follow a fixed sequence:
   a. The teacher introduces verbal labels of materials and actions while both teacher and child manipulate the materials.
   b. The teacher specifies a task, based on observed capabilities of the child.
   c. The teacher transforms the task, if necessary, to make it simpler or more complex.
   d. The teacher varies the task to extend the child's interest as mastery is achieved.

As we worked with teachers to develop this prototype, we noted that there are certain teaching habits or conventions that interfere with this program design. Specifically, common patterns of questioning and reinforcement pose the most difficult problems. See Chapter 10 for a discussion of the different functions of questioning. In this program, testing children follows rather than precedes teaching sequences. For example, in a cooking activity in which the goals are to identify changes in food materials, questions are designed to focus on observation and on comparison and contrast. A strategy of testing for stored information contradicts this goal. The pattern of asking children about what they already know rather than what they are currently learning serves diagnostic rather than teaching purposes. In this prototype, evaluation is usually completed as an activity distinct from instruction.

A similar problem relates to the teacher's approval of children's work. Teacher approval of "right" answers distracts children from processing the experience their own way and leads them to accepting a universal right answer. Affective reinforcement—through smiles, nods, and touch—or cognitive reinforcement are preferred when children are developing skills, concepts, or logical reasoning. Children's attention to the activity is reinforced through an ambience of teacher support, acceptance, and interest. Approval of right answers is appropriate in teaching names, labels, or factual content children need for the task in hand.

PROTOTYPE FORM

The detailed prototype is summarized in charts for each topic within the area. The charts include specific learning goals and sequencing order, which when necessary are based on increasing complexity or challenge. Chapters 13 to 15 describe the program areas of science and mathematics, music and the expressive arts, and language development and beginning reading, respectively. These constitute the heart of the program, but because of space limitations, only a few sample instructional models are included for each area. However, we think these samples are sufficiently detailed to suggest ways teachers can construct others.

For each curriculum area, the content is summarized and the teaching approach is defined. Next, the goals are outlined, accompanied by some illustrative activities. That is, the tables in each curriculum area list learning goals, suggested planned activities, and some of the many naturally occurring program activities by which the teacher may pursue these goals. These activities are listed to remind the teacher that there are many different ways to reach desired goals and that on-the-spot decisions are often ideal for achieving more than one goal at a time. Since spontaneous events are not predictable, it generally requires familiarity with the full range of program goals to capitalize on the unexpected.

The sample instructional models following the tables offer specific examples, including:

1. selecting and organizing materials;
2. inviting children to participate;
3. presenting the task by verbal and nonverbal means;
4. guiding interaction with children to foster interest and involvement, and to promote the learning goals;
5. variations for increasing children's independence and decreasing teacher involvement in the activity.

Summary of Prototype Features

This curriculum is based on a developmental view of the young child's progress in interrelated physical, social, emotional, and cognitive growth. Young children are expected to learn through intensive sensorimotor activity and manipulation of objects, as well as from each other. They also learn much from the language of the adults with whom they work, from the behavior of these adults, and from their expectations. Our prototype assumes that children are continuously learning, and the task of the school is to channel this learning energy toward increased competence in understanding and skills of interaction with the physical and social environment. Channeling learning energy means pursuing activities that capture interest and capitalize on what children already know and can do.

For the six- to eight-year-olds, maintaining action-based learning means including more symbol learning, language arts, and reading skill development. The same integration of goals and content areas is emphasized for primary grades as for pregrade children, although some tasks and activities become more structured. Different reading programs can be accommodated in the same general activity designs.

The assumptions in this curriculum about children as learners, the organization and administration of the classroom learning environment, and strategies for teaching include:

1. The teacher's expectations for children's activity and progress are conveyed through the clarity, selectivity, and attractiveness of the arrangement of materials. Rules and procedures for classroom management facilitate children's growth toward independence. The physical environment includes interest centers where children choose to engage in learning activities and acquire increasing independence in pursuing their interests.
2. The scheduling of the program minimizes the time required for making transitions and managing routines and thus maximizes the time for teacher instruction and children's involvement in the program.
3. Goals are sequenced in the content area where appropriate. Instructional models suggest order for both parallel learning goals and sequential goals for each content area.
4. Diagnostic activities precede instructional planning for each child, and individual progress records are maintained that note which goals have been mastered.
5. Teachers establish relationships with children on a one-to-one basis and value individual differences in interests, maturation, and life experiences.
6. Social-emotional and physical learning, which constitute major goals of early childhood programs, are developed within the context of meaningful activities.

The curriculum design places social-emotional and physical learning within the context of specific activities in content areas or in the routines of daily classroom life.

7. Though teaching styles are expected to be unique, teaching procedures have some common features:
   a. Testing children follows rather than precedes teaching sequences.
   b. Diagnostic testing and instructional teaching are completed as distinct and separate.
   c. Demonstration is offered simultaneously with verbalization whenever possible, until there is clear evidence that verbalization alone is sufficient.
8. Language development is maximized when children produce speech spontaneously and extensively during activities and conversations with their peers and teachers. Language learning is fostered as teachers elaborate and expand children's utterances appropriately and in context, as suggested in many of the instructional models. This curriculum design assumes that children's speech learning depends to a great extent on their spontaneous generation of speech forms heard within the context of activities in which they are genuinely interested.
9. Most curriculum content is interdependent and overlapping. This makes it possible for teachers to identify multiple learning goals for each activity.
10. Only when children take over the learning activity and practice on their own is it clear that they are stabilizing the desired learning. When children indicate readiness to direct their own learning activity, they are encouraged to do so. Rapid learners are often encouraged to reinforce their own learning by working with other children who desire guided practice in a task.

The teacher is expected to be sensitive to the individual child's unique needs and to be flexible in planning to meet these needs. Individualizing the curriculum includes simplifying or introducing complexity as the situation warrants and letting the child take the lead in demonstrating preferences for materials, activities, and play content.

SUMMARY

This chapter describes a prototype curriculum, defined as a model of a design, which suggests how to develop the intended program. Written as a total program with long-and short-term objectives, each program component, as identified in Section One, includes selections from the options available. A knowledge base is drawn from key concepts in the disciplines, or fields of knowledge. Views on child development, based chiefly on Piaget and Erikson, also use Gesell's norms to place and sequence content, and social learning theory, or learning by imitation, as theoretical bases for teaching.

Other features of this prototype include integrated views of the child's physical, social, emotional, cognitive, and moral development and sequencing principles that integrate content logic and psychological development views. Methodology focuses on children's activity and interests in well-equipped environments, with wide latitude given for children's choices and teacher's guidance placed at strategic moments when success is most likely.

Teaching strategies are identified, along with specific instructional goals and teachers' roles, although teachers' options for applying these guidelines are unlimited.

Play is a valued activity for children in this design, and children's self-knowing and self-valuing are regarded as major desired outcomes of successful learning activities. Language and affective and cognitive goals are pervasive in all learning activities. Their universal inclusion in instructional models, or written teaching plans, is explicit and never left to chance.

The three following chapters show how this prototype translates into teaching plans for many forms of activity and most kinds of content or knowledge.

EXERCISES

1. Write a brief analysis of the prototype curriculum described in this chapter.

2. Indicate where you agree and disagree with the major features of the prototype, and explain why.

BIBLIOGRAPHY

Abt Associates. *The Follow-Through Planned Variation Experiment.* Vol. IV–A, *An Evaluation of Follow Through.* Washington, D.C.: U.S. Department of Health, Education and Welfare, 1977.

13 Prototype Curriculum: Science and Mathematics

This chapter describes the science and mathematics content in our prototype curriculum. Science and mathematics have common bonds. Webster's Dictionary defines *science* as "systematized knowledge derived from observation, study and experimentation carried on in order to determine the nature or principles of what is being studied."[1] Mathematics, which deals with quantities, operations, and fractions, provides the working tools for scientific study. Understanding number, measurement, and geometric form offers ways to compare objects and events to generate principles of relationships, the outcomes of many scientific investigations. Consequently, in this prototype, mathematics and science are viewed as interdependent curriculum areas with similar beginning goals.

The common starting point for both the mathematics and science curriculum is the *creation of sets*, putting objects together into collections that go together in some way. The identification of similarity and difference grows out of manipulating and experimenting with objects, observing, comparing, and contrasting their properties. Making sets requires excluding objects that do not belong as well as grouping together those that do.

Initial learning in science and mathematics focuses on finding out about the properties of objects and the construction of sets. Classifications grow out of many experiences of manipulating and sorting objects according to their properties.

Following the beginning goals that science and mathematics hold in common, the two areas branch, although they continue to overlap.[2] Subsequent goals in science involve the development of concepts about the properties of objects and how changes occur. Natural materials, natural phenomena, and man-made materials help children build concepts in:

1. the life sciences, including plants and animals;
2. the physical sciences, including aspects of motion, weight, balance, gravity, buoyancy, and temperature;
3. the earth and environmental sciences, including such areas as weather, geology, erosion, and pollution.

Scientific inquiry and the use of mathematical measuring skills and recording procedures combine with the cognitive skills of comparing, contrasting, classifying, and problem solving to comprise the activities in science. Con-

---

1. *Webster's New Collegiate Dictionary*, 8th ed., S.V. Science.

2. For views on how children develop science and mathematical knowledge, skills, and understanding, see especially Ronald Good, *How Children Learn Science* (New York: Macmillan, 1977); and Richard Copeland, *How Children Learn Mathematics*, 2nd ed. (New York: Macmillan, 1974). For further resources, see bibliography.

ventional content areas such as botany, physics, and chemistry are included whenever these are suitable for young children's manipulation and study.

In mathematics, manipulation of sets helps to develop ideas about number, geometry, and measurement. Recognizing and creating patterns within sets and between sets of objects and events lead to increasing mathematical understanding and skills.

INSTRUCTIONAL APPROACH: BEGINNING SORTING AND CLASSIFICATION

The essential activity in the beginning science and mathematics curriculum is active manipulation and exporation of solid objects and fluid materials. This occurs in the daily program with all kinds of classroom and outdoor materials in creative play, project activity, and routines. Collections of materials are provided that stimulate sorting and classification thinking, such as mixed collections of textured materials, of standard shapes, and nonstandard shapes. Different types of materials are combined for exploration and experimentation, such as a water table with absorbent and nonabsorbent materials, or hollow and solid objects. Collage collections, woodworking materials, clay, and paints are additional materials that stimulate sorting and classifying activity.

Challenging materials such as a magnifying glass, magnets, and mirrors are provided; repeated use helps children discover various physical properties. Table 13–1 gives an extensive list of suitable materials and popular classroom activities in which the materials are frequently used.

TABLE 13.1. Materials resources

Physical property	Activity	Materials	Key language
1. Rigidity	crafts: collages, books, mobiles, woodworking.	wood, metal cotton balls, plush fabrics, pipe cleaners rigid plastic spoons and forks tongue depressors steel rod paper, washers copper wire	hard, soft fluid, freeze frozen, melt pour, firm flexible, inflexible bend, twist straight, crooked break, fold squeeze, solid stiff
	water play	sponge, foam rubber, water, rock assortment	pliant, unyielding
2. Surface texture	crafts (as above)	wood, sandpaper, marble, rope, styrofoam, wire, corrugated paper, yarn, aluminum foil	hairy, smooth rough, flat bumpy, shaggy slippery, nap scratchy, porous

TABLE 13.1. (continued)

Physical property	Activity	Materials	Key language
3. Heat	cooking freezing and melting water	food materials water, ice cubes, glass tumblers, hot plate, refrigerator	*icy, freeze* *frozen, melt* *heat, cool* *steam, boiling*
4. Size, shape and color	sorting objects in collections and in crafts block building	assorted balls: ping pong, tennis, hard rubber, soft rubber, cotton, styrofoam, plastic assorted paper, fabric, and yarn and string collections assorted lengths of material unit blocks attribute blocks counting cubes logic blocks	*round, flat* *fat, thin* *big, little* *roll, bounce* *color names* *long, longer, longest* *short, shorter, shortest* *heavy, light* *stretch, knot* *bend, tie* *longer, shorter* *rounded edge* *cylinder, curved* *thicker, thinner* *hard* *round, square* *triangular* *fat, thin* *color names* *little, big*
5. Consistency	play-dough cooking finger painting arts and crafts	salt, flour, water, food coloring, colors cooking ingredients soap flakes, liquid starch colors and poster paints clay, chalk, crayons, paste	*sticky, crumbly* *lumpy, smooth* *thin and watery* *thick, thicker* *pasty, creamy* *jellied, fluid* *solidified* *clear, muddy* *vivid, hazy* *powdery*
6. Buoyancy	water play	water variety of objects that sink or float	*float, sink* *quickly, slowly* *suspend* *surface*

TABLE 13.1. (continued)

Physical property	Activity	Materials	Key language
7. Odor	cooking and eating growing plants	fruits (such as oranges, cantaloupe, watermelon, lemon) vinegar herbs spices cheeses planting materials	*smell, fragrance pleasant, unpleasant odor, fumes fruity, scorched, sharp, spicy aroma It smells like . . .*
8. Taste	cooking and transforming food materials	cooking ingredients stove, refrigerator	*sweet, sour sweeter, more sour bitter salty, sugary It tastes like . . .*
9. Auditory properties	playing with musical instruments experimenting with sounds using a collection of objects	musical instruments, bells varied objects such as balls, boxes, plastic jars, buzzer, rattles	*hollow, solid rattle, ring, buzz soft, loud striker, chime* names of instruments
10. Absorbency	experimenting with materials	blotters, sponges, fabric, wood, wax paper, food coloring, towels	*absorbs, squeezing dry, damp, wet waxy, evaporates*

Key language is suggested to facilitate the way teachers and children talk about the experiences. As noted in Chapter 12, teachers are expected to use language in the context of the child's activity to expand vocabulary without interrupting the flow of the child's exploration, experimentation, or construction. Teachers know that children pick up new vocabulary in activities they are interested in. As children try out new words, meanings grow in action.

Planned activities focus children's attention (1) on selected attributes of objects and (2) on event phenomena, especially steps in an event, when the action and the consequence can be related. Children discover that blowing through a straw in water produces water bubbles or that pouring food coloring into clear water changes the color of the water. As exploration changes to experimentation after repeated experiences, children begin to organize their experiences as a basis for prediction and problem solving. For example, after many opportunities to make play-dough, children may plan and test ways to reduce its "stickiness" after overnight storage.

Projects concerned with changes in objects are activities such as cooking, germinating seeds and planting, making play-dough, finger-paint, paste and papier mâché. Children are natural scientists, exploring and experimenting, hypothesizing and testing, predicting and finding out. Capitalizing on this natural curiosity, the science and mathematics program provides activities that evoke the children's use of their growing skills of inquiry. The teacher's role balances between (1) planning the environment, including provision of materials; (2) responding to and extending children's spontaneous exploration; and (3) planning experiences that encourage use of the skills of inquiry.

Sorting and categorizing depend on each child's understanding of materials and events. Therefore, it is important that teachers refrain from imposing their own organizing concepts on children as they work. Teachers' corrections of children's groupings interfere with growing concepts of set and do not necessarily change a child's view. For example, if a child sorting materials based on their hardness or softness places a harder object in the softer pile, she may move the object from the softer to the harder group if the teacher insists. However, there is no assurance that the child will agree with the teacher's way of thinking.

In the sequence of sorting tasks, identical objects are grouped first, then similar objects, and finally related objects. *Identical* objects are exactly the same in all dimensions or attributes. *Similar* objects vary in one dimension only, such as color or size, but not both. *Related* objects belong to a class, such as "three-dimensional geometric forms" or "cooking utensils."

Simple tasks use small collections of two sets of distinctively different objects, such as red pegs and blue wooden cubes. Interesting materials invite manipulation and sustain children's interest in exploring properties and sorting. Table 13-2 lists sample materials for identical, similar, and related categories, as well as props enhancing sorting activity.

The criteria for materials and designing sorting activities are:

1. *Developmental cognitive levels of the children:* will the children be able to make sense out of their manipulations and experimentations?
2. The degree of *direct involvement* of the children: will the children have an opportunity to see the results of their own actions on objects and to control results?
3. *The concepts:* what concepts have appropriate activities that can be developed?
4. *Safety:* can the materials be used without danger?

CHARTING THE MATHEMATICS AND SCIENCE AREAS

A series of tables in this section provides an overview of the science and mathematics curriculum goals and related activities. The teacher can use these tables in several ways. The goal statements in each table are placed in a sequence of increasing complexity, against which the teacher may check children's spontaneous activities in the program. The suggested list of planned activities offers guidelines for appropriate sequencing. Activities that grow out of spontaneous events are indicated so teachers may capitalize on teachable moments.

Table 13-3, the first table in the series, deals with the common goals of science and mathematics. These goals require extensive manipulation of objects for stimulating comparison and contrast that leads to sorting and classifying. Using the full range of sensorimotor actions, children continually organize and reconstruct their perceptions and concepts. The table lists goals of sorting and classifying, indicating not only the usual classroom materials, but also teacher-prepared activities that target timeliness, variety, and the unique interests of

TABLE 13.2. Sorting materials

Identical materials: any item can be substituted for any other item of the same kind

kidney beans	dry macaroni
milk cartons	napkins
tongue depressors	tissues
cookies	plastic bottles
spring clothespins	white pipe cleaners
rubberbands	large paper clips
dry cereals	

Similar materials: (items in each collection) vary only in one dimension, such as color, length, or size

new crayons	pegs
checkers	pipe cleaners
poker chips	multicolored toothpicks
shoelaces	straws
counting cubes	beads
buttons	

Related materials: classes of things

paper flowers	buttons
miniature cars and trucks	shells
plastic bottle caps	hardboard geometric shapes
colored yarns and threads	property blocks
plastic forks and spoons	felt shapes
unit blocks	plastic fruits and vegetables
balls—pingpong, rubber, styrofoam	

Props for sorting

Containers
    hoops or loops, using shoelaces, ribbon, rope, plastic covered wire, ordinary string
    containers, paper plates, trays or pieces of construction paper, muffin tins, plastic cutlery trays, boxes

Measuring Materials

rulers	quart measures
tape measures	funnels
yardsticks	measured containers
measuring cups	teacher-made cardboard lengths

Additional Materials

magnets	symbol cards
magnetic objects	numeral stamps
teacher-made number cards	precut numerals
teacher-made numeral cards	chalk and chalkboard
spinners	dice
foam rubber cubes	paper cups

TABLE 13.3. Science and mathematics: common beginnings—sorting and classifying

	Goal	Teacher-prepared activities	Naturally occurring program activities
*1.	Compare and contrast concrete objects based on multisensory perceptions of size, shape, color, structural detail, texture, density, taste, pitch, and so forth. Sequence of complexity: a. matching objects, pairing identical objects; b. simple sorting; c. resorting, leading to simple classification. *Related language goal:* acquire object labels and descriptive language in process. Example: as a child manipulates a cotton ball by squeezing it and says, "Look," the labels for the squeezing action are supplied in context by the teacher: "You're *sqeezing* the *cotton ball.*"	*Making collections* of interesting materials appropriate for sorting using such criteria as size, shape, color, density, or texture (as with leaves, rocks, or seeds). Use sorting trays, sorting bins, and boxes. *Providing collections* of paired objects. Example: two identical miniature thumb dolls, two identical bottle caps. May include smelling jars, sound cylinders of very distinctive differences easily contrasted, or use of attribute blocks (kits of blocks in two sizes, three to four shapes and colors, and two thicknesses) for sorting and classifying. Preparing glasses with water at different levels to compare and contrast pitch. Making simplet plucking instruments with rubber-band strings or simple drums to compare pitch and timbre. Reorganizing classroom materials based on discussion and decisions of children. *Taking trips* for collecting natural material. *Playful sensory activities*, such as "mystery" bag with objects or "match" game for matching a model.	*Block building* and block clean up, requiring matching identical shapes. *Play in the housekeeping area:* dramatizations; "cooking," manipulating "foods" and materials; sorting dishes, cutlery, and pots and pans. Collections of rocks, leaves, nuts, seeds, pine cones gathered by the children. *Water table and sand table:* manipulating water, sand, and various containers and utensils; classifying them by function. *Manipulating materials*, such as interlocking objects of plastic and wood; sorting them by size, shape, and color. *Routines:* Manipulating and sorting cleanup tools such as sponge, broom, dustpan; grouping waste materials for discard. *Craft activities:* classifying attaching materials (such as paste, staplers, and fasteners) and tools (such as scissors and paint brushes). *Sorting* woodworking tools and materials, such as nails, screws, washers. *Snack and lunch:* tasting, smelling, and manipulating food. Sorting and pairing foods such as cookies or vegetables. Categorizing foods such as fruits, desserts, or beverages.

TABLE 13.3. (continued)

	Goal	Teacher-prepared activities	Naturally occurring program activities
*2.	Experiment to identify additional properties of objects. Identify physical changes and the processes of interaction.	The degree to which teachers provide any of the materials listed below for free selection by children determines whether an activity is listed as naturally occurring or teacher-prepared. Teacher-planned activities and naturally occurring activities may be identical, differing only in the teacher's anticipation and follow-through. In all activities in which changes are being produced, help children focus on the process of change as it occurs, as well as on the outcome at the end of the process. Where possible, retain samples of original ingredients to foster increasingly accurate comparison of properties before and after changes are produced.	
*3.	Identify changes in properties of objects under selected conditions: a. mixing fluids, b. adding fluids to dry material, c. mixing dry materials, d. heating materials, e. cooling materials, f. light exposure/darkness.	Making and/or using play-dough. Making and/or using finger paint. Making and/or using flour and water paste. Making and/or using papier mâché. Preparing painting activities and mixing colors. Using a magnet on collection of magnetic and non-magnetic materials. *Experimenting with absorbency* of different materials. *Blowing* soap bubbles, finding out how to blow bigger bubbles. *Making and flying* paper airplanes and kites. *Breaking open* rocks by force. Experimenting with rolling objects in the *block area*, finding out which objects roll and which do not. Experimenting with water absorbency in different kinds of soil. Observing properties of wood at the *woodworking table*, sawing wood and making sawdust.	Painting at the easel. *Crayoning:* wearing down of crayon, wax scraps occurring in use, changing texture of surface. Working with clay and plasticene. *Eating periods:* food dries out, mixes by chance, spills, and changes color. Hand washing: soap bubbles and cleansing effects. *Music area:* experimenting with sounds of instruments. *Cleanup:* washing tables, washing paint brushes and paint spills. *Wetting paper goods,* such as cleansing tissues and paper towels, and observing accompanying shredding. Noticing the stiffening of drying finger-painted paper. Observing condensation on windows on cool days. *Sand table:* experimenting with water trails. Blowing soap bubbles.

TABLE 13.3. (continued)

Goal	Teacher-prepared activities	Naturally occurring program activities
*4. Predict changes and test predictions.		All of the above
5. Use knowledge of changes in planning and developing a class activity or project.		All of the above

Note: Goals 1, 2, and 3 are overlapping; a clear delineation between them is neither necessary nor recommended.

the children in the class. Sorting requires manipulation to discover properties and experimentation to produce changes in properties.

The sample instructional models following Table 13-3 are provided to help you visualize how the activities might develop. However, it is important to keep in mind that these samples illustrate only *some* of the many possibilities for translating curriculum ideas into curriculum practice. Explanatory notes in Instructional Model 13-1 (righthand column) give the guidelines that were used, based on the views of teaching, learning, development, and content identified in Chapter 12.

Instructional Model 13-1 (based on goal one of Table 13-3[3]) concerns sorting skills according to hardness and softness. The suggested activity is structured to foster organization of perceptions. Such structuring appropriately follows activities of open exploration without formalizing children's findings. The sequence of activities—from exploring, to organizing, then classifying, and finally to generalizing—is honored throughout the program.

Instructional Model 13-2 (based on goal two of Table 13-3) describes the teaching approach for focusing children's attention on observing

---

3. Throughout the tables in Chapters 13-15, asterisks (*) indicate goals on which the instructional models that follow are based.

changes. Instructional Model 13-3 (for goal three of Table 13-3) extends such observations to selected activities. Preparing food provides an excellent opportunity for comparing objects before and after changes have occurred. Retaining samples of original ingredients is essential for young children who find it difficult to recall original properties after changes have occurred.

Instructional Model 13-4 focuses on procedures to encourage prediction, in which children use their knowledge of changing properties to anticipate what will happen under selected conditions. Note that children's arguments are valued throughout this process. These experiments, featuring a single attribute such as buoyancy (floating or sinking) or friction (rolling or not rolling), provide the information for sorting objects into groups of like properties.

Following Table 13-3 and its accompanying instructional models, which outline the beginnings science and mathematics have in common, the two areas are discussed in terms of the content unique to each.

MATHEMATICS

For each of the mathematics topics—number, geometry, and measurement—goals are identified. However, the many ways children

INSTRUCTIONAL MODEL 13.1
Science and Mathematics:
Sorting Based on Multisensory Manipulation of Objects
(From Table 13.3, Goal One)

Model	Explanation of teaching decision
Goals: Children use their five senses—auditory, gustatory, olfactory, tactile, and visual—to identify the observable properties of concrete objects and to group identical and/or similar materials.	*Goals:* Language goals are always present in all activities. In this activity, communication skills are fostered as children use language to describe experiences of finding properties of objects. New vocabulary words are acquired in context as needed. Use of symbols is encouraged when children's language and concept development indicates readiness and when children show interest.
Related Goals in Language Development and Reading Readiness: 1. Children use language to share experiences, ideas, and feelings. 2. Children acquire and use, in context, object names and descriptive terms as needed. 3. Children write numerals, words, and sentences.	
Group Size: 1, 2, 5	*Group Size:* All activities occur with small groups. If more children are interested, they are included as openings occur, *or* two separate groups may work simultaneously.

Materials:
  2 trays   scissors
  paper   crayons
  2 boxes   letter stamps
  paste   numeral stamps
  tape   stamp pad
  stapler   pencils
• Hard materials:
  buttons   sticks
  wood   bolts
  plastic discs washers
  paper clips   nuts
• Soft materials:
  cotton cloth rayon
  cotton batting yarn
  sponges   string
  velvet   silk
  wool cloth   plush
	Materials: Select primarily familiar objects but include a few unfamiliar or high-interest objects in the beginning. This assures a level of comfort with the task. If *too many* new or high-interest objects are selected, the sorting may not occur until a later time. If *no* new or high-interest materials are included, the children may not respond to the invitation or sustain interest.

INSTRUCTIONAL MODEL 13.1   (continued)

Procedure:

1. Invite children to make a "hard-soft book" or to make two collages, one of hard materials, the other of soft.
2. Encourage children to sort and label materials, classifying objects as hard or soft. Use sorting props, such as two trays or two pieces of paper. Teacher supplies name labels that may be new.
3. Encourage children to review their decisions before pasting, taping, or stapling, as a way of promoting self-checking. Accept their decisions on grouping.
4. After pasting, help children who are interested and can handle the task without excessive help or frustration to write or use letter stamps or numbers, to number the pages, to head pages "hard things," "soft things," or to write their names on their work.
5. Let children solve problems, such as how to make some objects adhere to the paper, how to fasten a book, and how to find additional items for a class of subjects. If needed, review the options with a child as a problem is identified but refrain from offering a solution.

Variations:

1. Select other properties and materials that can be used for projects of this type.
2. Additional projects may be designed that use contrasting mobiles, bulletin board exhibits, classroom collection boxes, and mystery bags.
3. Change project format. For example, suggest a "find it" activity: give each child an object, with the task of finding another object in the classroom that resembles it in some way. Suggest children check each other's discoveries.

---

1. Children choose to participate.
2. Set the task by initiating the first step in the procedure.
3. Language accompanies action. Self-checking is promoted in contrast to teacher approval or validation. The process of sorting is valued. Any lack of clarity in sorting is silently noted for future planning.
4. When interested and ready, children are encouraged to use symbols to signify an order, such as page numbers or page titles.
5. Problem solving is valued as a process. To avoid failure, a review of the options helps the child to select a procedure likely to succeed.

Variations: Add complexity by increasing the number of objects, changing the form of the task to include more problem solving, and expanding the "world" from which selections are made.

INSTRUCTIONAL MODEL 13.2
Science and Mathematics:
Sorting Based on Experiments with Objects
(From Table 13.3, Goal Two)

Goals:
1. Children experiment to identify properties of concrete objects.
2. Children sort objects by properties.

Related Goals in Language Development:
1. Children use language to share experiences, ideas and feelings.
2. Children use new language labels in context.
3. Children write numerals, words and sentences (older children).

Group Size: 1, 2, 5
Sample model for contrasting: things that roll with things that do not roll.

Materials:
- boxes;
- inclined plane made of wood strip with an upright, or use two long blocks;
- collection of materials such as wheels, paper clips, balls, hardware nuts, blocks, plastic plate, pencils, and ruler. (For additional collections, see Table 13-1.)

Procedure:
1. Invite children to make collection boxes, mobiles, exhibits, collages, or books based on experiments with things that roll and things that do not roll.
2. Provide an inclined plane or invite children to make one at the carpentry bench or with blocks to experiment with objects that roll and those that do not.
3. Offer children boxes and a tray of objects, some of which are round and some of which are not.
4. Ask children to sort objects into two boxes labeled "Things That Roll" and "Things That Do Not Roll." Let children write or letter stamp these labels if they wish.
5. Suggest to the children that they find additional objects in the classroom to sort into these two boxes.

Variations:
1. After a number of experiences, help children use the contents of each box to make an exhibit, a book, a collage, a mobile, or other end-product.
2. Contrast other properties such as:

    light/heavy   magnetic/nonmagnetic
    sink/float   compressible/noncompressible
    absorption/nonabsorption of liquids   bounce/nonbounceable
    rigidity/nonrigidity   rattle/ring/no vibration
    elasticity/nonelasticity   low pitch/high pitch

INSTRUCTIONAL MODEL 13.3
Science and Mathematics:
Changing Properties of Objects
(From Table 13.3, Goal Three)

Goals:
1. Children identify and label changes in food materials as evidence of interaction.
2. Children use hindsight to compare changes in food materials after interaction.
3. Children match one set of objects to a duplicate set.

Related Goals in Language Development and Reading Readiness:
1. Children use descriptive language in context.
2. Children narrate classroom experiences in sequence.
3. Children read and write sentences.

Group Size: 2, 5

Materials: Two sets of any of the following:
- fresh oranges and orange squeezer to make orange juice;
- apples, water, sugar, and hot plate to make applesauce;
- pancake mix, butter, eggs, milk, and a waffle iron to make waffles or pancakes;
- cranberries, sugar, and blender to make cranberry sauce;
- fresh heavy cream and closed jar to make butter;
- instant pudding or gelatin mix;
- frozen fruit juice, water, spoon, and jar to make juice drink;
- confectioner's sugar, water, bowl, and spoon to make icing for cookies or cake.

Procedure:
1. Assemble two sets of ingredients, each on a separate tray.
2. Help children label materials on one tray, providing vocabulary words as needed in context.
3. Encourage children to identify properties of the objects by such activities as tasting, touching, looking, smelling, lifting, shaking, tapping, and rolling.
4. Ask children to match objects on the reference tray to the duplicate set to establish the equivalence of the two sets.
5. An example of a teaching sequence:
    a. Invite a small group of two to five children to make orange juice from fresh juice oranges.
    b. Help children cut and squeeze the oranges. (For younger children, precut at least two to five oranges to diminish waiting time for children not yet ready to use knives.)
    c. In the process of making the juice, elicit observations and interject vocabulary without slowing the activity.
    d. Encourage children to compare the used ingredients and the end product with the duplicate set of unused materials to identify and label differences between original food materials and final product.

Follow-up Activity:
1. Invite children to compose a story about the activity for a duplicated booklet.
2. Invite children to tape record a narration of the experience.
3. Invite children to make grapefruit juice or another kind of juice from fresh fruit.

INSTRUCTIONAL MODEL 13.4
Science and Mathematics:
Predicting Changes in Properties
(From Table 13.3, Goal Four)

Goals:
1. Children make changes in properties of familiar objects and predict outcomes.
2. Children compare changes to original predictions.

Group Size: 1, 2, 5

Materials: water tumblers   water   detergent
           cooking oil   salt   talcum powder
           food coloring   sugar   string
           paper towel   yarn   straws

Procedure:
1. Invite children to experiment with materials.
2. Before they experiment, ask children to predict what will happen. Accept any prediction.
3. Ask children to tell you whether their predictions are borne out.
4. An example of a teaching sequence follows:
    a. Give a child water, tumblers, and a collection of materials such as those listed above.
    b. Tell the child to select one material from the collection to put in the water. Ask the child to predict what will happen to the material and to the water.
    c. Check the prediction with the child.
    d. Or ask several children to replicate one child's choice of material. Encourage them to discuss or argue about what happened. If they agree, suggest taking turns to pick out the next material to be tested.

---

achieve these goals reflect considerable interdependence among goals, as shown in the curriculum tables. In the primary grades, children progress from simple number concepts to mathematical operations, including double digits, exchange, operants and tens, regrouping, and other decimal concepts.

Number

The abstract concept of number is developed through extensive experience with sets of concrete objects (see Instructional Model 13-5). Number learning is featured during repetitive classroom activities as children set the table, serve food, distribute objects, collect materials, and generally use quantifying terms to communicate their experiences. Collections of materials are organized for playful activities to engage children in creating, comparing, and analyzing sets and in using number and numeration in context.

After initial understanding, skill with numbers becomes a function of practice. Practice occurs more frequently, for longer periods, and with greater payoff when it is embedded in an activity that is inherently interesting. *Teacher-imposed drill—compared with self-initiated practice—is viewed as being relatively wasteful of energy of both teacher and children*, especially younger children. Therefore, drill for its own sake is avoided unless children spontaneously initiate repetitive practice.

Number activities are sequenced as follows:

1. identifying sets;
2. matching one-for-one and pairing, which lead to ideas of *more than*, *less than*, and *the same number as*;
3. ordering objects within sets;
4. simple counting—first one to five, then six to nine, and finally, double digits;
5. analyzing sets—first for subset relationships with up to ten items, then over ten items;
6. understanding the empty set, or zero;
7. sequencing sets.

INSTRUCTIONAL MODEL 13.5
Mathematics:
Copy Model Sets and Make Equivalent Sets
(From Table 13.4, Goal Two)

Goals:
1. Copy a model set.
2. Make equivalent sets.

Group Size: 1, 2, 5

A.   COPY MODEL SETS
Use Figure 13-1 at the end of this instructional model as a guide for sequencing the complexity of the tasks.

Materials: Box or tray containing eight pairs of objects and two pieces of construction paper on which objects will be placed (see Figure 13-1).

Procedure:
1. Invite child to play by saying, "Let's play. This is a follow-the-leader activity. Here is my paper and here's your paper."
2. Select five different objects from the box, placing them on your paper in a row. Say, "This is my set of objects. Now you copy and make a set on your paper that is just like mine."
3. Use checking procedures as follows:
   a. Leave each set on its own paper.
   b. Slide the two pieces of paper next to each other.
   c. Say, "Let's check. I have a cow." Move the cow to the edge of the paper.
   d. Say, "Where is your cow?" Point to where the child should place his/her cow on the paper.
   e. Check remaining objects in the same way. Maintain as brisk a pace as possible. When checked, the two sets look like this:

cow	0	0	cow
truck	0	0	truck
crayon	0	0	crayon
fork	0	0	fork
cup	0	0	cup

INSTRUCTIONAL MODEL 13.5   (continued)

Variations: (See Figure 13-1, items 1b, 2a, and 2b)

1. Repeat with different sets of objects.
2. Reverse roles with child. Child becomes the leader, creates the model set, and leads the checking procedure.
3. Reverse roles and make errors for child to correct.
4. Children make sets for each other to copy.
5. Vary the sets using different materials and more than one of a kind. Increase the number of objects in a set.

Evaluation: Check children's mastery of copying model sets by bunching objects listed in items 2a or 2b of Figure 13-1. Children who show mastery move to item 4 and match color and number of objects.

B.   MATCH SETS FOR EQUIVALENCY

Materials:
- two coffee cans or two identical-size boxes with lids marked for identification.
- counting cubes
- marbles
- corks
- two low-rimmed, rectangular trays or two hoops.

Procedure:
1. Place one to three yellow cubes in one can and eight to nine black cubes in another can with a matching color top.
2. Invite a child to figure out (not guess) which can has more cubes. Say, "These cans have some blocks in them, just like this block." Show the sample block. "Without looking inside which can do you think has more blocks?" Hand the cans to the child.
3. After the child selects one can, say, "Let's find out. You say the black-topped can has more blocks than the yellow-topped can." Pour blocks from one can on one tray, placing cap of can on the tray as marker. Invite the child to do same with the other can on the other tray.
4. Say, "Let's check," using the same procedure as for copying model sets.

C.   MAKE EQUIVALENT SETS

Materials:
- bean sticks, with one to nine beans glued on;
- shoebox with an opening on side large enough to reach in with hand;
- poker chips.

INSTRUCTIONAL MODEL 13.5 (continued)

Procedure:
1. Invite two to three children to play a game with bean sticks.
2. Show sticks and explain that in this game the player collects poker chips using the bean stick to mark how many.
3. Place the sticks in the box. In turn, children draw sticks from the box and make a matching set of chips.
4. When sticks are gone from the box, return all materials to original positions and begin again.

FIGURE 13.1. Copying model sets

	Teacher prepares		Teacher presents model set A	Child constructs matching set B	Task
1.	a box or tray containing 8 pairs of objects 2 pieces of construction paper	a. b.	1 cow, 1 truck, 1 crayon, 1 fork, and 1 cup *in a row* vary objects and size of sets	same as set A same as set A	identical copy of mixed objects—1 each of 5 objects
2.	2 boxes, each containing no more than 12 objects, such as 3 cows, 3 forks, 2 trucks, 4 red pegs 2 pieces of construction paper	a. b.	2 cows, 1 truck, 1 crayon, 2 forks, and 1 cup, or similar mixture *in a row* vary objects and size of sets—*in a row*	same as set A same as set A	identical copy of mixed objects—with 1 or more of a kind
3.	evaluation: repeat item 2—*bunching objects*		same as item 2—*bunch objects*	same as item 2	same as item 2
4.	2 boxes, each containing 5 each of 4 colors of cubes 2 pieces of construction paper		2 red, 3 yellow, 3 green colored cubes, *row or bunch*	same as set A	identical copy of similar objects, more than 1 of each

The use of symbols for notation may parallel goals from beginning counting onward. However, using a notational system is not an independent goal but intended for representing what is already understood. In this curriculum, understanding precedes drill and symbol learning.

Ordering objects within sets, the third goal in Table 13-4 takes the form of patterning (see Instructional Model 13-6). The skill of organizing perceptions into patterned relationships is promoted in mathematics and science, but is also basic to reading, music, and other curriculum areas.

TABLE 13.4. Mathematics—number

	Goals	Teacher-prepared activities	Naturally occurring program activities
1.	Identify sets, distinguishing members of sets from nonmembers.	Provide attractive sorting sets, for a simple sorting task—to note gross differences in properties of the objects.	*Cleanup of manipulative materials:* Sorting puzzles, Tinker Toys, plastic interlocking blocks, collage materials.
*2.	Match sets one-for-one. Ideas of *more than*, *less than*, *same number as* achieved without counting, through matching objects one-for-one. Includes: a. Copying model set, equal sets, identical objects in sets. b. Matching sets for "*more than*," "*less than*," "*same number as.*" c. Making equivalent sets: same number of objects, but objects are not identical (for example, straws for milk containers).	Provide two identical sets of mixed objects, such as red-colored cube, black button, miniature car, tongue depressor, and empty thread spool. Child copies teacher's model set by creating an identical set and checking for accuracy. Use separate trays or mats for each set. Add complexity to task by reducing difference in items and using two of an item. Alternate leadership with children. As skill develops, encourage children to play with each other. Estimate and check the contents of two closed boxes, for *more-than/less-than* comparisons. Use grossly different sized sets, such as two beads in one box and eight beads in another. Use identical materials and identical containers. Add complexity later by reducing difference in size of sets and by varying materials.	*Table setting for snack:* one straw for each milk container; one cookie, one cup, and one napkin to each placemat. *Distribution of craft materials:* one crayon, one piece of paper, and one pair of scissors to each child. *Circle time:* one chair to each child *Lotto game:* one card per child.
3.	Order objects within a set: • patterning • serial order • spatial order	Patterning. *Decorative crafts:* children create border designs for a project such as placemats or gift-wrap paper, pasting a selected set of materials in a selected order.	Making spontaneous pegboard patterns. Stacking interlocking blocks in a pattern. Using pattern blocks. Constructing with blocks. Painting a pattern with color dots or lines. Pasting a pattern of precut shapes.

TABLE 13.4. (continued)

Goals	Teacher-prepared activities	Naturally occurring program activities
4. Count and apply number names to a set of objects in an orderly way, using one-to-one matching to find out how many objects are in the set.	Active, meaningful use of counting as children begin to understand it. The use of counting for classroom purposes is the most important ongoing activity at this stage of mathematics learning. Continued use of playful activities of matching sets may now include counting. *Picture card games*, in which pictures are cues for creating sets of concrete objects. *Craft activities*: number mobiles and number collages. *Simple board games* on which markers move along a track and which use picture dice or picture cards with simple sets to count.	Distribution of craft materials for collages, mobiles, bracelets, necklaces, number booklets, belts. Materials may include such items as buttons, pipe cleaners, gummed shapes, sheets of colored paper, cotton balls, popsicle sticks, tongue depressors, beans, toothpicks, feathers, springs, beads, paper clips, string, yarn, rubber bands, straws, sticks, bottle caps.
*5. Analyze sets: take a set apart to create subsets; then recombine subsets to form original set.	Provide sets of similar objects, such as red and white counting cubes. Make equivalent sets of mixed colors, such as sets of six cubes: one red, five white; two red, four white; three red, three white. Make sets of identical objects: partition and recombine groups of objects to find out size of subsets. Grouping objects: See Instructional Model 13–8.	Craft activities. Organizing and using small collections of similar or identical objects: at woodwork bench with nails, ordered sets of nails representing subsets of collection; collage, pasting sets of identical and similar materials.
6. Identify empty set as having *no objects* in set.	Provide a covered box with beans or small rocks with one partition. Shake and find out how the set divides into the two partitioned areas.	Sorting and resorting, creating different subsets with collections such as rocks, buttons, leaves, or blocks.

TABLE 13.4. (continued)

	Goals	Teacher-prepared activities	Naturally occurring program activities
7.	Sequence sets: order the relationship of sets based on number, with each set larger than the previous set by one more (1, 2, 3 . . .). Count in intervals, such as by twos, threes, and fives.	Picture-set cards to be ordered by number.	Stacking collections of chips or counting cubes, each stack having one more or two more than the last stack.
8.	Apply numerals to the sets. (*Note:* this goal can be initiated at step 4, but the focus is on understanding number relationships before emphasizing written symbols. Writing numerals is optional.)	Add numerals to existing games and activities with sets of objects and pictures of sets. As children indicate they are reading numerals, develop games that require matching a numeral card to a card of a pictured set and convert dice games to numeral signals. Play physical games with numeral recording procedures, such as bowling. Many playful activities offer practice in set and numeral matching, making drill activities unnecessary.	*Noticing number labels in the environment:* on schoolroom door, houses or apartments, mailboxes, and elevator buttons. Attendance records for setting up snack, lunch, and cots.
*9.	Add and subtract using symbols: Use numerals to label two sets and then the third set created when the first two sets are joined. Write equations. Understand concepts of equivalence.	Using sets of materials and numeral cards, build number statements of equivalency, such as "2 + 2 = 4." See Instructional Model 13–1 and add numerals to activity. Use worksheets with number sentences or equations.	Applying numeral writing to children's helper activities: serving milk and cookies, distributing supplies, and counting heads.
10.	Understand zero as the empty set.	Add the zero symbol to the numerals and include zero in the numbers used to designate numerosity of sets.	Adding zero to numeral-writing activities in progress.

TABLE 13.4. (continued)

	Goals	Teacher-prepared activities	Naturally occurring program activities
11.	Be able to exchange units and tens.	Exchange beans or popsicle sticks: compare fixed sets of ten units with unpackaged collections of ten units.	Encouraging exchange of units and tens when children use play money.
12.	Perform addition and subtraction using double digits, regrouping, and decomposition. Be able to do repeated addition or beginning multiplication. Be able to do repeated subtraction or beginning division.	Use abacus, button collections, beans, or sticks to establish decimal concepts, followed by worksheets to practice written problem solutions.	

With materials, children organize their perceptions, first by grouping and then by establishing order within and between groups. Sorting based on simple comparison and contrast precedes patterning in any activity area. Visual patterns are created with color, shape, size, and distance using objects, pictures, and symbols. Other kinds of patterns use sounds, actions, and events.

As indicated in the list of naturally occurring activities on Table 13–4, children often initiate their own patterning practice by arranging and rearranging sets of classroom materials into linear and spatial patterns. Although such child-selected patterning tasks are ideal for building teaching sequences, caution is advised to maintain a balance between child-selected and teacher-directed practice. When children are extending their own patterning skills, teachers need not intrude, interrupt, or distract.

Teachers can plan brief instructional periods in patterning for beginning learners. As children build their skills, they tend to sustain interest longer. Patterning goals deal specifically with single-line or linear patterns, which are recommended for early skill development. Instructional Model 13–6 illustrates activities for initiating patterning with individual children. Note that it involves not only the process of reproducing patterns, but also checking the completed pattern. Language goals of vocabulary expansion and communication fit naturally into the activity.

The next two instructional models illustrate activities for analyzing sets (Instructional Model 13–7), taking sets apart to create subsets, and then recombining sets, leading to beginning concepts in addition and subtraction. (Instructional Model 13–8).

Geometry

Geometric shapes include three-dimensional solids (such as spheres, cubes, cones, rectangular solids, and cylinders) and two-dimensional geometric figures (such as circles, rectangles, and triangles). Identifying the attributes of two-dimensional and three-dimensional shapes

INSTRUCTIONAL MODEL 13.6
Linear Patterning
(From Table 13.4, Goal Three)

Goals:
1. Children copy object patterns.
2. Children copy color, shape, size, or other attribute pattern.

Related Language Goals:
1. Children respond to and use such key language as color names, object labels, positional terms (*first, next, last*), row, and pattern.
2. Children practice following left-to-right reading direction.

Group Size: one to two children

A. OBJECT PATTERN

Materials:
- sheet of construction paper;
- eight to ten plastic spoons, all one color;
- nine to ten plastic forks, same color as spoons.

Procedure:
1. Invite a child to sit next to you on the same side of the table.
2. Make a row of alternating spoons and forks on a piece of paper and slide it in front of the child, leaving a workspace directly in front of the child.
3. Say, "I made a row with my materials. Now you make a row just like mine on your paper." (The task is to use the same number of objects as are in the teacher's row.)
4. If the child appears confused, say, "My row is spoon, fork, spoon, fork, spoon, fork," pointing to each object, always from left to right.
5. Check the child's copy. Point to the first object on the left in your row. Say, "Let's check. My first one is a spoon. Show me the first one on your row. Is it a spoon?" After the child answers, say, "Next comes a fork. Is your next one a fork?" Continue this until the last one. For the last one say, "My last one is a fork."
6. If the child loses his or her place in checking, begin again and help the child point or touch each item in the sequence.
7. After checking, say, "This is a spoon-fork pattern. Let's try another pattern."
8. Repeat steps 1 through 7 following the suggested order of patterns, as follows:
    a. Reverse single alternation pattern from spoon-fork to fork-spoon.
    b. Change to a double alternational pattern, such as fork, fork, spoon, spoon.
    c. Reverse the double alternation to a spoon-spoon-fork-fork pattern.
    d. Use three objects. For example, add straws to make a fork-straw-spoon pattern.
    e. Vary the order of three objects.
    f. Change to a two-item alternating pattern and double one item (for example, spoon, spoon, fork, spoon, spoon, fork).
    Note: With each model, always state the pattern from left to right.

INSTRUCTIONAL MODEL 13.6 (continued)

B. COLOR PATTERN

Materials:
- poker chips, two colors
- cubes, two to three colors
- pegs and pegboards, two to three colors of pegs
- beads and pipe cleaners, two to three colors
- two or three colors

Procedure: After children demonstrate mastery of tasks with object patterns, change tasks, as follows:
1. Make a color pattern using cubes. For example: red, white, red, white, red, white, red, white.
2. Offer the child a box of cubes. Say, "I made a pattern with my cubes. Now you make a row just like mine." The task is to use the same number of cubes as in the teacher's row.
3. Follow checking procedure by saying, "My first one is red. What color is your first one?" Continue checking from left to right across the row.
4. Have the child touch each item. If the child's row is a different length from the model row, say, "Your row is shorter (longer) than mine." Help the child correct the length only if the child wants to do so.
5. Say, "This is a red-white pattern. Let's do another one."
6. Vary colors and number of cubes.

---

includes comparing and contrasting surfaces, sides, angles, straight-line forms, and curved-line forms. To locate objects spatially requires understanding positional relationships such as *up-down, over-under, next to* and *inside-outside*.

The following four steps reflect the sequence of goals:

1. manipulating;
2. matching concrete shapes through comparison and contrast to find identical shapes;
3. sorting concrete shapes based on similarity;
4. creating shapes.

Table 13-5 suggests playful activities, using props such as a mystery bag and arts-and-crafts materials, as the primary contexts in which geometric concepts are developed.

Names of shapes accompany manipulation and playful use. The teacher supplies the names without stopping the flow of activity. Since shape and color names are easily overemphasized at the expense of constructing and comparison-contrast activities, the teacher is cautioned to avoid interrupting spontaneous activities. Using shapes as cues in action games is one way to use labels purposefully. Words, as Piaget reminds us, do not structure thought, but they do facilitate communication of thought.

INSTRUCTIONAL MODEL 13.7
Mathematics: Analyzing Sets
(From Table 13.4, Goal Five)

Goal: Children regroup sets of objects.

Materials:
- counting cubes or wooden beads;
- papers with line drawn down center, or paper plates;
- numeral cards four through ten

Group Size: 1,2

Procedure:
1. Invite a child to work with beads or cubes and a set of paper plates.
2. Ask the child to pick a numeral card, collect the same number of paper plates plus one more plate, and place that number of cubes on each plate.
3. Encourage the child to find out how many different ways the cubes can be arranged on the plates, varying the size of the groups placed on each side of the line. For the numeral four, a complete set of groupings on the paper plates would look like this:

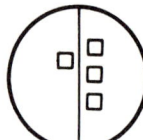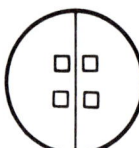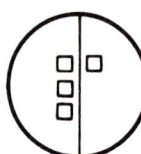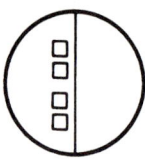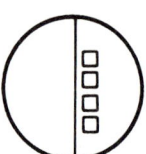

4. Accept what the child does even though the child may not make all the possible combinations.

Variation: Craft activity—grouping booklet.

Materials:
- sheets of paper folded in half, gummed circles, or other shapes for pasting;
- sets of identical objects;
- wet sponge or paste.

Procedure:
1. Invite a child to copy the groupings that have been made on plates (in the above acivity) by pasting gummed circles on each half of the folded paper.
2. Encourage the child to check the pasted groupings with those on plates to find out if all variations have been made.
3. Staple or otherwise fasten the papers together to make a booklet.
4. Add written numerals, stamps, or precut numerals, as children acquire numeral-reading skills.

INSTRUCTIONAL MODEL 13.8
Mathematics: Addition Using Symbols
(From Table 13.4, Goal Nine)

Goals:
1. Children associate a numeral with the number of objects in a set.
2. Children join sets and apply a number to the newly created set.
3. Children use the symbols plus (+) and equals (=) to make an addition equation.
4. Children partition a set into two groups and identify the number in each subset.

Group Size: 2, 5

Materials:
- deck of numeral cards *1* through *4*
- deck of numeral cards *1* through *5*
- deck of numeral cards *1* through *9*
- Symbol cards for "+" and "="
- two plates
- tray
- box of fifteen attractive objects

Procedure:
1. Invite two children to play who have shown mastery of counting and of numerals through 9.
2. Ask one child to pick a numeral card from the *1-through-4* deck. Ask the other child to pick a card from the *1-through-5* deck.
3. Tell each child to put her or his card on a paper plate and to put that number of objects on the plate.
4. Ask each child to check by counting aloud.
5. Say, "We are going to do some addition. We are going to join this set of three things with this set of five things. This "plus" sign means to put things together."
6. Start an equation with the cards: 3 + 5.
7. Point to the cards and say, "This means we take three things and put them together with five things."
8. Ask children to combine their sets. Say, "You put your three things together with your five things on the tray.'
9. Ask one child to "count these things and find out how many things there are altogether."
10. Ask the child to check the count and find the numeral card for this number.
11. Place this card to the right of the other cards, leaving a space for the equals sign: 3 + 5   8.
12. Summarize the procedure so far by saying, "This means that when you put three things together with five things, you have eight things. We need one more card. This is an equals sign." Point to the blank space between the "3 + 5" and the "8." Say, "This is where we put the 'equals' sign."
13. Put the equals sign in place in the equation: 3 + 5 = 8. Point to each card in turn and say, "Three things together with five things gives us eight things."
14. Repeat steps 1 through 13 several times for practice, using different numbers.
15. Give the teaching role to a child who shows mastery of the addition operation.

INSTRUCTIONAL MODEL 13.8   (continued)

INDEPENDENT ACTIVITY: "Banker" Addition Game

Materials:
- spinner
- die
- play-money dollar bills

Procedure:
1. Invite a small group of children to play the game and appoint one child as banker.
2. Demonstrate the rules of the game:
   a. Each player spins the spinner (numerals *1* through *6*), and the die (numerals 1 through 6)
   b. The player tells the banker, "I have a *3* and a *4*. Pay me seven dollars."
   c. Banker counts out two piles of dollars, three in one and four in the other, and checks by counting. If the count is correct, the banker pays money. If not, the banker says, "Add again."
3. *Variation:* Add zero to die and spinner. Key language: *zero* means *No dollars.*

Measurement

Measurement includes linear (distance along a line), volume, and weight measures. Measurement provides a way of describing selected attributes of objects, especially their size and weight and the space they occupy. It can be made with arbitrary units and with standard units. Measuring skills are dependent on growing *concepts of conservation*, that is, understanding that the measured information remains the same despite changes in the appearance of the measured material. Conservation of length is more rapidly acquired than conservation of volume and weight. Since measurement is a tool used for construction, arts and crafts, cooking, and exploration of properies of objects, planned measuring activities are included with other tasks. Planned tasks are:

1. *measuring games,* such as drawing sticks from a box to find two of the same length.
2. *action games,* such as rubber horseshoes, in which the players measure distances from the target;
3. *craft activities,* such as using strips of paper to border or frame a picture for a present;
4. *problem-solving activities,* such as figuring out how to determine the length of construction paper needed to cover a wall area being readied for a new exhibit.

Note that all the measuring tasks in this list can and should be performed with arbitrary measures, which precede standard measurement in children's development. Before children can grasp the idea of standard measurement, they have to understand the need for a standard unit and how it differs from any arbitrary object, such as a crayon or a strip of ribbon.

As illustrated in Table 13–6, measuring activities are sequenced toward increasing dif-

TABLE 13.5. Mathematics—geometry

Goals	Teacher-prepared activities	Naturally occurring program activities
Plane Geometry		
1. Distinguish between open and closed curves and between straight and curved lines.	Use yarn or string playfully to make open and closed curves in craft activities. Play a game of open and closed curves, in which the goal of the game is to have the figure closed at the end of the game.	Spontaneously producing open and closed curves in collage, finger painting and other craft activities, and deliberately seeking to close a curve while manipulating sticks, pipe cleaners, and string.
2. Match standard plane shapes or figures: a. identical shapes, b. similar shapes.	Play lotto and other matching games with pairs of standard plane figures. Later use similar shapes and vary the color.	Craft activities: pasting precut shapes. Matching shapes found in books. Matching surfaces of solid objects while manipulating blocks and other classroom materials.
3. Match simple, nonstandard, plane shapes, by distinguishing curved-line edges, straight-line edges, and angles.	Provide precut, standard plane shapes and simple nonstandard shapes to be combined by pasting or otherwise connected; discuss newly created shapes.	Manipulating puzzle pieces to complete classroom puzzles. Using property blocks or other sets of plane geometric shapes.
4. Create plane figures, tracing and freehand. Combine figures to create new figures. Partition figures to create other figures.	Make tracing plates, first for inside trace, later for outside trace. *Note:* these need to be a minimum of 4 inches on a side for beginners.	Arts-and-crafts activities as children create their own shapes. Block building. During eating periods, arranging food, such as cookies, to create new shapes and breaking bread in half diagonally to create triangles from a rectangle.
Solid Geometry		
1. Distinguish between flat and curved surfaces. 2. Match solid figures first identical, then similar shapes. 3. Create similar solid geometric figures.	Provide sets of paired solid figures for simple matching activity, focusing on straight or flat and curved surfaces. Create a game with the set. Organize a craft project requiring a set of identical figures, such as spheres or balls of clay.	Matching solid figures in block building constructions. In water play, matching containers based on exterior dimensions or how they look. Making figures out of clay and play-dough to match ones made by others or themselves.

TABLE 13.6. Mathematics–measurement

	Goals	Teacher-prepared activities	Naturally occurring program activities
1.	*Linear Measure:* Match one item to another item by length.	Play a matching game with sticks or pipe cleaners to find the sticks that are the same length. Extend activity to include longer and shorter lengths.	In block building, matching length of roads or height of buildings. In craft activities, using materials of different lengths. Making "snakes" in clay and play-dough activity and matching the "snakes" for length.
a.	Match a length with: • an equivalent length • a longer item, a shorter item		
b.	Compare lengths, ordering them from longest to shortest.		
c.	Find congruent (same) lengths.		
d.	Line up a collection of lengths along the side of a table or box for repeated measure, *using arbitrary units.*	Collect paper clips or counting cubes. Line up items to match a length of stick, rope, or other object. Compare set of clips to cubes that represent the length of an item.	
e.	Use *standard units*, such as meter, decimeter, and centimeter; inches and feet.	Same as above using Cuisinaire rods, one centimeter base, or inch cubes, tape measures, rulers, metersticks	
2.	*Liquid measure:*	Use unified sets of containers conforming in shape, varying in depth or diameter, in direct proportion, so that there is an exact serial relationship in quantity of two to one, or four to one.	At water table and sand table. (*Note:* use standard sets of containers for exact ratios of two-to-one.) During eating periods, pouring milk or juice from container into glasses. *Note:* children need to develop concepts of "fullness" by overfilling. The sand table and water table are ideal places for such practice.
a.	Match one container's volume to another container's volume to see if it has more, less, or the same amount of fluid as the other.		
b.	Measure volume by counting repeated use of a measuring unit.	Use for making play-dough, cooking, or other mixing activities, as well as for planting. Transparent containers are recommended.	
c.	Use standard measures, including ounces, pints, quarts, and liters.	Record measurement using bar graphs, line graphs, tallies, and other pictorial forms, beginning with a record of comparison between two or more objects.	

TABLE 13.6. (continued)

Goals	Teacher-prepared activities	Naturally occurring program activities
3. *Time measurement:* Identify time units and clock time	Chart changes in an object occurring over time as children are developmentally ready. Use timers, stopwatches, and clocks to time various classroom events. Make timers using rice or water or sand.	Encouraging children's spontaneous clock reading.

ference or distance between the objects to be measured:

1. Match two quantities by direct comparison.
2. Use an arbitrary objective measure for comparing two quantities.
3. Use an objective measure repeatedly to measure a quantity.
4. Repeat, but this time use a standard measure, such as a ruler, yardstick, or meterstick, to measure a quantity.
5. Use tables and graphs to record measurements, for example, pictorial representations.

This sequence also reflects movement from the concrete to the abstract.

SCIENCE

As discussed at the beginning of this chapter, using the skills of inquiry with all environmental materials constitutes the heart of the science curriculum. Key concepts about objects, events, energy, and matter develop as children manipulate, experiment with, compare, contrast, and organize their understanding. Since the environment offers an endless array of objects and events (interactions between objects), further detailing of the science curriculum is only suggestive. The three areas outlined (see Tables 13-7 to 13-9) are those most popular and familiar in early childhood programs: (1) plants, (Table 13-7), (2) animals (Table 13-8), and (3) physical laws (Table 13-9). The sequences usually feature exploration and examination of existing properties, attributes, and conditions, followed by some controlled experimentation. Ultimately, prediction and problem solving call forth children's use of acquired knowledge. Instructional Model 13-9, which derives from Table 13-8, features caring for animals. Note that curriculum goals in geography, economics, mathematics and beginning reading are incorporated. Geography goals are furthered as children follow pathways on a walk to buy materials; understanding of economics grows out of experiences with buying; and mathematics and beginning reading skills are both drawn on with the use of helper charts. Finally, experience booklets (with simple narrations of children's experiences) highlight beginning reading experiences.

TABLE 13.7. Science—plants

Goals	Teacher-prepared activities	Naturally occurring program activities
1. Compare and contrast properties of plants, including such things as seeds, leaves, stem, roots, texture of soil in which plant grows, size of plant, growth pattern, and light sensitivity. *Related goals in language and reading:* Vocabulary word meanings, labels, and descriptions in context.	Collect leaves found on the ground from different trees. Compare leaf shapes by manipulating them directly, outlining them, mounting them in order on a line for easy contrast, or preserving them within food wrap. Where possible, without injuring plant, collect leaves and continue as above. Collect seeds from fruits and sort collection of mixed seeds based on properties of size, color, shape, texture, and weight.	On class walks or during outdoor activity periods, as children collect plant waste from ground, encouraging comparison to the "mother" plant. During eating periods as children discard seeds, teacher comparing and contrasting discarded seeds for size, shape, color, texture, and weight.

2. Observe and identify changes in seeds and plants and identify some conditions of the process.
Related goal in mathematics: use picture graphs, tallies, or other form to record growth at regular intervals.
Related goals in language and reading:
  a. Understand word meanings in context.
  b. Read signs and symbols on charts.
  c. Read informational books about planting.
	Germinate seeds in transparent plastic glasses, or in beds of cotton or paper towels, or in soil. Compare with unsprouted seeds.
	Explore variety of ways of starting new plants: through cuttings, runners (spider plant), root splitting, bulbs, and leaf germination (jade plant).
	Prune classroom plants as needed and observe new growth following pruning.
	Compare two plants of same species, one inside a terrarium and the other outside.
	Compare germinating pattern and duration:
	  a. different seeds, of the same species,
	  b. seeds of different species.
	Plant a garden in season, in the yard or in outdoor planters. Plant vegetables and flowering plants. Set up terrarium.
		Watering a wilted plant and observing change at intervals following addition of water.
		Discovering spontaneous generation of new plants.
		Observing bending of light-sensitive (heliotropic) plants toward light sources.
		Observing cycle of flowering plants.
		Observing growth pattern in a terrarium.
		Observing change in outdoor plants during weather cycle.
		Finding evidence of erosion by water and wind.
		Children bringing plants and flowers to the classroom as presents for the teacher.
		Parents' association holding a plant sale to raise funds during school hours; children visiting and buying plants.

TABLE 13.8. Science—animals

	Goals	Teacher-planned activities	Naturally occurring program activities
1.	Compare and contrast the attributes of different animals.	*Visit zoo:* Identify differences in such physical attributes as	As children spontaneously imitate sound and movement patterns of familiar animals, such as a dog or cat, teacher encouraging comparison and contrast of such characteristics as speed, noise quality, and size.
*2.	Identify animal survival needs.	a. size of parts of the body;	
		b. skin and/or hair color, thickness, length, and texture;	
3.	Classify survival needs.	c. movement styles, walking, running, jumping, sitting, and changing from sitting to standing;	
		d. obtaining and chewing food;	
		e. forms of communication: tone, quality, and pattern of noises produced.	
		Identify differences in needs for food, shelter, and protection.	
		Adopt a class pet: Select a suitable animal, based on classroom facilities, children's maturity, and teacher's preference. Set up appropriate living conditions for the animal to thrive in. Establish routines for care of animal and guidelines for handling and playing with animal.	
		Make a bird feeder and install within view of classroom. Attach a bell to the feeder that rings in the classroom whenever a bird lights on the feeder.	As children begin to point out small ground animals, teacher initiating comparison and contrast.
		Find small ground animals, such as worms, ants, and beetles. Compare their attributes. House them in the classroom temporarily if possible.	

TABLE 13.9. Science—physical laws

Goals	Teacher-prepared activities	Naturally occurring program activities

1. Identify physical phenomena related to physical laws of:
  a. movement, force, speed, distance;
  b. temperature, forces of change;
  c. buoyancy;
  d. gravity.
2. Use laws to predict outcomes of physical interactions.
3. Use laws to solve problems.
	Movement: experiment with rolling objects down an inclined plane in playful ways. Encourage finding relationships between the angle of plane, the intensity of the starting force, and the type of surfaces in contact between object and plane. Design a game to feature one of the attributes, such as speed. Play ten pins, using ball to knock down pins. Play a marble rolling game; on a track, on an open surface with contrasting surfaces of rug and smooth floor, or on another polished surface.
	Temperature: cooking activities featuring heating and cooling, using natural and manmade heat sources.
	Buoyancy: experiment with floating and sinking. Sort objects by their buoyancy. Predict which objects will be buoyant and which not.
	Gravity: experiment with construction materials, such as a domino game of adding objects to a structure one-by-one without toppling it.
		Using wagons, bikes, tires, balls, and other rolling objects outdoors.
		Using cylinders and cars in block area.
		Using rolling objects in collage collections and in manipulative materials.
		At lunch, contrasting rolling of peas on a plate to mashed potatoes.
		In temperate climates, exploring and experimenting with ice and snow.
		Playing at the water table.
		Cleaning up: washing classroom materials and furniture.
		Block-building activities, focusing on balance and height. Ball playing and other forms of outdoor play requiring body movement in vertical space.

SUMMARY

The science and mathematics in our prototype curriculum are viewed as interdependent curriculum areas that promote the skills of inquiry as a common beginning. Sorting and classifying, based on comparing and contrasting the properties of objects, occur through manipulating, experimenting, and acting on the objects. Creating sets initiates thinking about the mathematical concepts of *number*, *geometry*, and *measurement*, as well as scien-

INSTRUCTIONAL MODEL 13.9
Science—Animals: Caring for Animals
(From Table 13.8, Goal Two)

Goals:
1. Children identify attributes of animals by caring for them in the classroom.
2. Children label animal needs while caring for animals.
3. Children classify the survival needs of animals while caring for them.
4. Children acquire respect for animals' autonomy needs by providing basic care and by avoiding teasing, overstimulating, or unnecessarily imposing on them.

Group Size: 1, 5

Materials:
- various small, hardy animals that can be cared for in the classroom, such as:
  gerbils   white mice
  rabbits   turtles
  hamsters   chameleons
  (Less-hardy animals may be cared for with special equipment and the required environment, such as temperature or noise control. This includes tropical fish, tadpoles, and chicks.)
- cages, or other housing
- animal food
- cleaning equipment
- feeding equipment

Procedure:
1. If walks are planned to acquire an animal, food, or other equipment, highlight the geography goals of following walking pathways, mapping routes, and coping with intersections of people paths and vehicular paths. If you have planned to have children participate in making purchases at a pet shop or other store, promote the economic goals of identifying roles of buyers and sellers and of exchanging money for goods.
2. Through stories, discussion, and photographs, involve children in planning to acquire a classroom pet. The extent of the preparation is dependent on the age of the group and on their prior experiences with classroom pets. For children who have had no experience with classroom pets, preparation time is kept to a minimum so that children will not become discouraged by their own ignorance of the preparation needs. As their experience increases, you can devote more time to preparation, since they will draw on prior experience to identify preparation tasks.
3. Involve children in preparing the living conditions for a classroom pet before its acquisition.
4. After the classroom pet is acquired, demonstrate care of the pet, verbalizing your action.
5. Feature the animal's needs for protection against overstimulation, too much noise, and rough handling.

INSTRUCTIONAL MODEL 13.9 (continued)

6. Rotate the responsibilities for pet care among the helping chores as listed on a helper chart.
7. Encourage children to discuss your classroom pet's attributes, such as mode of locomotion, eating, elimination habits, visual and tactile properties, and reactions to being held.
8. Encourage children to raise questions about the classroom pet that require observation and experimentation (but only what will be safe and not discomforting for the pet). For example, encourage children to find out what kinds of food the pet will eat, whether it can hear or see, what noises it can make, and what kinds of responses it can make.
9. Invite children to tape record their experiences with the pet.
10. Prepare a series of booklets based on children's tape-recorded experiences of purchasing and caring for the pet.
11. If there is more than one kind of classroom pet, for example, gerbils and tropical fish, encourage children to identify similarities and differences among them.
12. Encourage children to make simple classifications of animals, using their experience with their own pets and the classroom pets. For example, classification may simply be based on whether the pet is fur-bearing or not, its food habits, patterns of locomotion, or sleeping habits.

tific classification. Further experiments with sets leads to subsets, subclasses, and class inclusion in science.

These two content areas diverge to meet goals reflecting concepts and skills associated with each discipline. Goals in number learning are sequenced for increasing complexity—from simple matching of objects through beginning arithmetic. Addition, subtraction, simple fractions, and beginning decimal concepts are included in the primary grades. Physical laws and plant and animal life concepts form the major substance of the science program.

The teaching approach in both the mathematics and science areas promotes active manipulation of materials by children, which calls for planned activities preceded by exploration and manipulation. Related language goals feature increasing vocabulary and oral language skills in process. Since children participate by choice, planned activities are designed to conform to their natural interests, learning capacity, and learning styles.

EXERCISES

1. Based on diagnostic checks in Appendix B, select and use one of the instructional models in mathematics presented in this chapter.
2. Evaluate outcomes in terms of:
    a. consistency in following the model;
    b. results in children's participation and learning;
    c. your reaction to the instructional approach used.
3. Select a science activity you can try out with a group of children.
    a. Complete a task analysis before initiating the activity.
    b. Evaluate outcomes.

BIBLIOGRAPHY

Copeland, Richard. *How Children Learn Mathematics.* New York: Macmillan, 1974.

Donaldson, Margaret. *Children's Minds.* New York: Norton, 1978.

Good, Ronald. *How Children Learn Science.* New York: Macmillan, 1977.

Harlan, Jean Curgin. *Science Experiences for the Early Childhood Years.* Columbus, Ohio: Charles E. Merrill, 1976.

Harms, Thelma. *Maximizing Learning from Cooking Experiences.* Chapel Hill, N.C.: Frank Porter Graham Child Development Center, University of North Carolina at Chapel Hill, 1977.

Holt, Bess-Gene. *Science with Young Children.* Washington, D.C.: National Association for the Education of Young Children, 1977.

Kamii, Constance. *Piaget, Children and Number.* Washington, D.C.: National Association for the Education of Young Children, 1975.

Kamii, Constance, and DeVries, Rheta. *Physical Knowledge in Preschool Education: Implications of Piaget's Theory.* Englewood Cliffs, N.J.: Prentice-Hall, 1978.

Laurendeau, Monique, and Pinard, Adrien. *Causal Thinking in the Child.* New York: International Universities Press, 1962.

Lovell, Kenneth. *The Growth of Basic Mathematical and Scientific Concepts in Children.* 5th ed. London: University of London Press, 1968.

National Council of Teachers of Mathematics. *Mathematics Learning in Early Childhood.* Reston, Va.: NCTM, 1975.

Nickelsburg, Janet. *Nature Activities for Early Childhood.* Reading, Mass.: Addison-Wesley, 1976.

Nuffield Mathematics Project. Teacher Guides: *Beginnings, I Do and I Understand, Pictorial Representation, Computation and Structure, Shape and Size, Graphs.* New York: Wiley, 1967.

Renner, John, and Stafford, Don. *Teaching Science in the Elementary School.* 3rd ed. New York: Harper & Row, 1979.

Robison, Helen F. *Exploring Teaching in Early Childhood Education.* Boston, Mass.: Allyn and Bacon, 1977.

Webster's New Collegiate Dictionary. Springfield, Mass.: Merriam Co., 1979.

Yardley, Alice. *Discovering the Physical World.* New York: Citation Press, 1973.

———. *Senses and Sensitivity.* New York: Citation Press, 1973.

14 Prototype Curriculum: Music and the Arts

The material included in the prototype music and art curriculum serves important long-term goals listed in Chapter 12, especially personal development, specific skills, common culture, and special-culture goals. In addition, this content is of primary importance in meeting such affective goals as emphasizing the child's autonomy, uniqueness, self-valuing, and self-expressiveness. Short-term goals are easily identified in this content area, notably self-knowing, self-valuing, and nonverbal expressiveness, as well as specific skills in singing, dance, music making, and the arts.

In this chapter, overall program goals are analyzed for the specific skills, concepts, and goals of the content areas of music and art. Goals in art deal with progress in self-knowing and self-valuing through the specific developmental art skills of representing three-dimensional objects in two-dimensional space; understanding grouping, unity and variety; and using color, balance, movement, and aesthetic judgment. In music, specific goals require similar developmental progress in rhythm, tempo, pitch, timbre, dynamics, and melody.

The music and art area is singled out for promoting the goals of self-knowing and self-valuing because of the emphasis in this area on spontaneity, uniqueness, and personal ways to shape concepts, feelings, and knowledge. Children can be themselves most completely when painting or dancing. The product or the action serves as self-affirmation. The child who says, "That's my picture," needs little feedback to know she has the competence to produce a picture unlike anyone else's. Similarly, children are able to express their feelings and ideas through songs, rhythms, and dances without the burden of verbalization. The child's expressiveness is accepted and valued as it is offered, and every child can feel, "I do and therefore I am worthy of respect."

Since self-knowing through action and products is the major goal, all other goals involve specific ways to build the child's self-awareness and self-appreciation. Skills in any area contribute to self-valuing, as do reflections of valuing by parents, other children, and teachers. The emphasis in skills is always developmental. That is, each child's progress is appropriately valued without regard to the accomplishments of others. Some children attain goals sooner than others, as in any content area. Teachers look for forward movement and not for absolute achievement standards.

In art, many materials feed children's imaginative and expressive needs. Products range from the most personal forms of expression, such as abstract shapes, to conventional types of useful objects, such as placemats or baskets.[1] In music, listening, singing, dancing, and using rhythm instruments are the activities usually developed. And to serve major affective goals, both music and art activities need to be fun.

1. Edmund B. Feldman, *Becoming Human through Art: Aesthetic Experience in the School.* (Englewood Cliffs, N.J.: Prentice-Hall, 1970).

In the following description of the music and art content area, the purpose is not to present a complete section of the curriculum but to suggest the ways concepts are developed, the types of activities found useful, and the flavor of this part of the prototype curriculum.

MUSIC

Children learn musical concepts through frequent participation in musical activities, since they delight in repetition and mastery. Building on children's enjoyment of their own competence, teachers offer increasing complexity, finer discrimination tasks, and new challenges within the developmental framework.

Music concepts for young children include:

Rhythm: steady beat and melodic pattern,
Tempo: fast—slow,
Pitch: high—low,
Timbre: tone quality of different instruments,
Dynamics: loud—soft,
Melody: musical melody and related words, phrasing, accent, and mood of musical selections.

These concepts develop through singing and chanting, moving to music, playing musical instruments, listening to music, and composing music. The order of acquiring the concepts is not predetermined, and consequently they may develop simultaneously. However, for each concept there is an order of complexity that guides the teacher in matching the child and the activity.

Instructional Approach

Young children's spontaneous enjoyment of music and movement is the base on which music concepts are build. This joy is enhanced as children begin to acquire some of the concepts listed above. While music learning is usually developed within the total group, a primary condition for learning is that children choose to participate in musical activities. Therefore, music experiences can be limited to one child, to a small group, or open to all. In music and art, as in most content areas, teachers are cautioned to respect the wishes of children not ready to participate who prefer to watch.

The musical program develops in two ways. First, the planned music periods actively engage children in singing, movement, and playing instruments and listening to music. Second, during naturally occurring activities, children often spontaneously engage in rhythmic movement, chanting, or singing. Music goals can guide teachers in both types of experiences.

Frequent group singing for enjoyment, without much emphasis on the words of the songs, soon builds a good song repertoire. Movement experiences feature selected activities such as walking, running, or sliding before promoting individualized interpretative or creative movement. Playing with rhythm instruments encourages children to explore the range of tone and pitch and the timbre unique to each instrument. Planned instrumental activities include rhythm bands and movement to music.

Movement to Music

Table 14-1 shows how specific music concept goals in movement generate music activities. It also specifies how the same music goals are incorporated into activities that develop naturally throughout the day. The two are called, respectively, *planned* and *emerging* activities, the latter being generally unplanned. For example, the first music goal in Table 14-1 identifies planned activities stressing rhythm through structured experiences. The same goal is also stressed in rhythmic chanting at clean-up time or in outdoor physical activities such as seesawing. (As indicated previously in this content-specific prototype, suggested activities

TABLE 14.1. Music: movement

Goals	Teacher-prepared activities	Naturally occurring program activities
*1. Respond with movement to the rhythm of familiar language patterns, names, and chants.	Jumping, clapping, and slapping thighs to the rhythm of children's names, teachers' names, and familiar chants.	*Arrival*: using clapping chants as greetings. *Cleanup*: chanting and stacking blocks. *Outdoors*: repetitive rhythmic activities, such as biking and seesawing

Respond with movement to the rhythm of music, both steady beat and melodic pattern.	Marching, jumping, clapping, fingersnapping, hand shaking to steady beat or melodic pattern, and using different kinds of music (modern, popular, folk, or classical).
	Examples of a steady beat:
	  "Shoo-Fly, Don't Bother Me"
	  "Drill Ye Tarriers, Drill"
	Examples of a melodic pattern:
	  "I Could Have Danced All Night" (from *My Fair Lady*)
	  "Shall We Dance?" (from *The King and I*)
	  Strauss waltzes
	  Mozart minuets
	  Grieg Norwegian dances
	  "As I Walked Out in the Streets of Laredo" (folk song)
		Singing, humming, or whistling in natural settings: moving to the rhythm of the music.

*2. Copy and produce rhythmic patterns without music.	*Echo* clapping (copying the clapping pattern of a leader). Change leadership from teacher to child.	*Waiting periods*: converting uninvolved or inappropriate behavior to instructional activities.
3. Transform rhythm patterns from one action to another.	Clapping or drumming a pattern for children to copy by jumping. Singing a pattern such as "la, la-la, la" for children to copy by clapping. Encourage children to take leadership role.	*When children are spontaneously producing rhythm*: encouraging alternate ways to express the rhythm.

TABLE 14.1. (continued)

	Goals	Teacher-prepared activities	Naturally occurring program activities
*4.	Respond with movement to selected musical patterns: 　dynamics: loud and soft 　tempo: fast and slow 　pitch: high and low	Featuring change in dynamics, tempo, form, and pitch, one activity at a time, as children adapt movement responses to musical change.	*On the playground or local walking trip:* singing, walking, changing tempo.
*5.	Respond by different actions to two-part musical form. *Related Cognitive Skills:* understanding *same* and *different* in music and actions. *Related Language Learning:* understanding word meanings in context— labels, such as *finger, foot*; action terms; positional terms; descriptive terms, such as *hard*; music terms, such as *pitch, tempo*	Musical games, action songs, and musical dances. Examples: 　"Did You Ever See a Lassie?" 　"Hokey Pokey" 　"Looby Loo" 　"If You're Happy and You Know It" Encourage children to make up stanzas to songs to indicate actions.	*Outdoors on playground or on walks and indoors during activity periods:* supporting children's initiation of songs, games and actions.
6.	Use creative music: 　a. Create movements to music. 　b. Create lyrics to songs. 　c. Create melodies. 　d. Create dance dramatizations.	Playing selected records or tapes and encouraging creative movement to music without words. Encouraging creative movement for expression of moods, feelings or ideas. Encouraging creation of lyrics to rhythmic patterns, creative movements, or to well-known songs. Encouraging dance dramatizations of stories, poems, or programmatic music.	*When children create rhythms outdoors:* encouraging further development of lyrics, rhythms, chants, or movement to accompany play activities by participating or guiding the children.

indicate some of the ways teachers may choose to use the content. Teachers decide which activities they prefer for any content or process goal.)

Note that the movement activities develop from simple rhythmic actions—such as jumping or clapping to the rhythm of children's or teachers' names—to eventually moving in time to the steady beat of music. Five-year-olds learn quickly to distinguish the steady beat, which is invariant, from the rhythmic pattern of a melody. They can even maintain a steady beat by clapping as a group while another group is clapping the melody. They feel very competent and sophisticated when they find they can do this. Thus, the skill building in movement is continuous, progressing to actions associated with dynamics (loud and soft), tempo (fast and slow), and pitch (high and low).[2] Six- and seven-year-olds show increased control in all music areas, and they have a wider singing range.

This curriculum area is extremely active. Children are not learning about music. They are very busy *making music.* Yet, note the integration of language goals into this content area, as shown in Table 14–1. Vocabulary is used in context, and children pick up exact names of objects and actions in the natural way that word meanings grow. Challenge to cognitive skills produces delight in creating patterns of rhythm, melody, and instrumental ensemble, after many types of exploration and practice.

Instructional Model 14–1 (based on goal one of Table 14–1) sketches a design for a basic lesson in using a steady beat through chants and jumping actions. In addition to the music goals, this instructional model specifies the affective, social, and cognitive goals of the activity. Comparison and contrast of the sound patterns is a clear application of a cognitive skill and appears frequently in other curriculum areas. Note also that this is not a "one shot" lesson, but a procedure teachers develop over several months, accepting and adapting the rate at which children develop these skills. Repetitive practice, done by choice in response to frequent opportunities and with purposeful teacher guidance, is the major form of learning stressed here.

Goals in clapping rhythms (goal two from Table 14–1) are developed in Instructional Model 14–2. In this activity, children learn clapping rhythms just by copying the teacher's brief patterns. As skill develops, the child is encouraged to create patterns for others to copy. With increasing skill, interesting variations are suggested, such as transforming action to chant or other verbal patterns. The increasing complexity of goals helps teachers plan new cognitive and musical challenges for the group or individuals, as children show sufficient progress for "next steps."

Let us review two more sample instructional models (14–3 and 14–4). Instructional Model 14–3 uses a "Jack-in-the-box" metaphor to crouch low for low pitch and stand up tall for high pitch. Similarly, children adjust their movement as the tempo changes from slow to fast to slow. The Dalcroze method uses similar means to teach children as young as three to adjust movement to major and minor modes, as well as to these simple pitch and tempo changes. Emile Jaques-Dalcroze originated this method in late nineteenth-century France, and music is taught in many countries by this method today.[3] The teacher who maintains children's enjoyment of these movement activities finds it easy to increase the challenge from gross to finer distinctions. Thus, ear training proceeds painlessly, based on the fun of action and group-movement experiences. Most important, children are neither graded nor judged; they are simply encouraged to enjoy the activities. Note that a goal in geogra-

---

2. Layne C. Hackett and Robert G. Jensen, *A Guide to Movement Exploration* (Palo Alto, Calif.: Peek Publications, 1961).

3. Emile Jaques-Dalcroze, *Rhythm, Music and Education.* Translated from the French by Harold F. Rubenstein (New York: Putnam's Sons, 1921).

INSTRUCTIONAL MODEL 14.1
Music: Steady Beat of a Chant
(From Table 14.1, Goal One)

Goals:
1. Children jump rhythmically to a drum downbeat or to a clapped pattern of names.
2. Children relate jumping to the soft-loud dynamics of a drumbeat.
3. Children control physical movement in response to such signals as a drumbeat and a verbal signal.

Related Goals:
1. *Affective:* self-knowing and self-valuing.
2. *Social:* knowing members of class group.
3. *Cognitive skills:* comparison and contrast of sound patterns.

Group Size: small or total group

Materials: drum and beater

Procedure:
1. Demonstrate the procedure: Beat the drum rhythmically and jump while chanting your own name several times, for example, "Ms. Brown, Ms. Brown, Ms. Brown."
2. Ask one child at a time to jump to his or her name. When you stop beating the drum, add a verbal signal: "Now sit down."
3. Adjust the drumbeat to the child's jumping rhythm, whether fast or slow.
4. Slowly adjust the beat to the rhythm of the name as the child begins to follow the drumbeat.
5. Vary the drumbeat's dynamics (loud and soft) and the tempo (fast and slow).
6. Emphasize physical control with positive comments, such as, "You sat down when I sang "Now sit down."
7. Later omit the verbal signal of "Now sit down." Offer feedback to children, such as "You stopped jumping when the drum stopped," "You jumped faster than my drum."

Variations: Develop these procedures slowly over a period of several months, accepting and adapting to the rate at which children develop these skills.
1. When chanting and beating the rhythm of your own name, have all the children jump with you. Otherwise have only one jump at a time (as before) when that child's name is being chanted.
2. Give more advanced children turns controlling the drum and calling names of the other children.
3. As more children show control, allow children to pass the drum around the circle after each child completes a turn as the caller.
4. *In the first and second grades,* emphasize more precision of starting and stopping, more contrast between group and individual responses, and fewer distinctions in tempo and dynamics. Also, using different instruments, associate each with a different signal for action. For example: marching to the drum, skipping to the triangle, clapping to the rhythm sticks, and dancing to the tambourine. Give more leadership roles to children, rotating leadership frequently.

INSTRUCTIONAL MODEL 14.2
Music: Clapping Rhythms
(From Table 14.1, Goal Two)

Goals:
1. Children copy and produce rhythmic patterns by clapping.
2. Children transform rhythmic patterns from one action to another and from action to language.

Group Size: 5 to all

Procedure:
1. Invite several children to join in a clapping game.
2. Produce simple, brief rhythmic patterns having no more than five claps, for example, two long and two short claps.
3. Repeat the pattern several times, inviting children through gesture rather than words to join you, maintaining a brisk pace.
4. Try out a variety of patterns, such as:
    long, short, short
    long, long, short, short
    short, short, short, long, long
5. Invite each child to reproduce a pattern individually.
6. As children demonstrate skill in copying patterns, encourage them to produce their own patterns.
7. Invite children to lead clapping patterns by producing a pattern for other children to copy.

Variations:
1. Repeat the preceding procedures, adding a percussion instrument to accompany or lead the clapping activity.
2. Substitute for hand clapping such actions as foot tapping, finger snapping, *patschen* (thigh slapping), or stamping.
3. Transformation 1: Demonstrate a transformation from one action to another by clapping a rhythmic pattern and then foot tapping the same pattern or by making mouth noises in the same pattern.
4. Transformation 2: Demonstrate a transformation from an action to a chanting pattern, for example, by foot tapping a pattern and then chanting it, singing "la-la-la." Invite children to make similar transformations.
5. Transformation 3: Demonstrate a transformation from an action or chant to a verbal pattern. For example, chant "la-la-la"; then chant a sentence to the same rhythmic pattern, such as, "I can dance." Invite children to make similar transformations.
6. Primary grade children select their own transformation patterns and create variations on each other's patterns.

INSTRUCTIONAL MODEL 14.2   (continued)

7. For six-, seven-, and eight-year-olds, give children the initiative to create two or more groups to clap complementary rhythms together or different rhythms in a question-and-response pattern.
    a. Example of a question-and-response pattern: One group of children agrees on a question pattern, clapping four even beats. The other group finds an agreeable response pattern of a series of three uneven or syncopated beats. After several performances, each group tries out the other group's rhythmic clapping pattern.
    b. Example of a complementary clapping pattern: One group agrees to clap the basic beat. A second group claps twice as fast. A third group emphasizes the first beat of the basic beat pattern, clapping only once in four-quarter time.

INSTRUCTIONAL MODEL 14.3
Relating Movement to Pitch and Tempo
(From Table 14.1, Goal Four)

Goals:
1. Children relate movement to low and high pitch.
2. Children adjust movement to changes in tempo.

Related Goal in Geography: Children respond first to positional terms, later to directional terms (right and left).

Group size: 5 to all

Materials: drum; bells or triangle

Procedure:
1. Describe the game of Jack-in-the-box: "When I play the drum, see how low on the floor you can get. Keep your head down low while I play the drum. When I play the bells, jump up or dance any way you like. As soon as I play the drum again, get down on the floor just as low as you can get."
2. Play the drum, chanting, "Jack-in-the-box, you're down so low, you're asleep in your box when I tell you so." Maintain a distinct rhythm.
3. Play the bells, chanting, "Jack go fly, up high, in the sky, so high."
4. Repeat steps two and three.
5. Later, play the drum and bells without chanting, relying on musical signals alone.
6. Change tempo to slower and faster.
7. Later, ask a child to play the instrument and be the caller.

INSTRUCTIONAL MODEL 14.3   (continued)

Variations:
1. Use the same instruments. Associate the drum sound with an airplane motor warming up on the ground and the bell with an airplane flying in the air. Ask children to make appropriate movements as you gradually change tempo and instrument use.
2. Use different instruments for such actions as climbing a ladder, walking upstairs, climbing a mountain, or ascending in an elevator. Always associate the higher pitch with physical height.
3. Drop verbal signals as soon as children appear ready to respond to musical signals alone.
4. Use the piano, associating the upper registers with height. Vary the tempo and dynamics, associating loud and soft, fast and slow with specific movements suggested by you or the children.
5. With primary-grade children, use major and minor keys to contrast two types of action, such as circling to the right or the left.

INSTRUCTIONAL MODEL 14.4
Movement: Same and Different Motions
(From Table 14.1, Goal Five)

Goals:
1. Children produce appropriate movements to words of song, and match and contrast other children's movements.
2. Children copy movements, make same motion, or produce different movement upon request.

Related Language Learning:
1. Children use word meanings in context, especially *same* and *different*. Also use nouns, verbs, pronouns, adjectives, and adverbs.
2. Children use positional terms, such as *up*, *down*, *back*, and *beside*.
3. Children use directional terms, such as *left* and *right*.

Procedure:

Materials: None, unless teacher wishes to play a recording or instrument.
1. Teacher sings "If You're Happy and You Know It" or "Did You Ever See a Lassie?"
2. Ask the group to make the same motions as you. Help children if necessary.
3. As children learn the words, call on each child to make a motion. Ask the group to copy the same movement.
4. Gradually emphasize a change, saying, "John made this motion," then demonstrating it. "Now Sharon, show us a different one."
5. Use other songs, such as "The Mulberry Bush," "All around the Kitchen," or "Let Everyone Clap Hands Like Me."

phy—responding to positional terms, with directional terms in a later sequence—is integrated into the instructional model. Learning is greatly facilitated by the actions that the music experiences offer to children.

Instructional Model 14-4 stresses using same and different motions, another important cognitive goal for young children. Again, while the sample describes a very simple musical lesson, challenge and complexity are readily added as children are able to handle them.

Singing and Using Instruments

Goals and activities in singing are listed on Table 14-2. While teachers often chime in or initiate songs or chants on walks or outdoors, these goals help the teacher plan or use teachable moments to advance specific goals. Once children get the idea of contrasting rather than matching tones, for example, practice can occur almost anywhere, and children become more skillful and secure about their skills.

TABLE 14.2. Music: singing

Goals	Teacher-prepared activities	Naturally occurring program activities
1. Sing new and familiar songs and sing songs to accompany movement.	Singing familiar songs suggested by children. Introducing new songs through voice, piano, records, initiated by adults and children. Seek variety from popular, folk, classical, foreign language styles; try light opera, dance, songs, actions, and finger plays. (See Bibliography for suggested sources; also refer to Table 14-1.)	High-action activities: spontaneous chants of rhythmic and melodic patterns and use of familiar songs to accompany the actions. On the playground or walking trips. In the class, for woodworking, dramatic activities. During transitions to accompany cleanup or convert waiting time to purposeful activity. During activity periods, extending child-initiated singing, or chanting, or singing tones by participating with the child.
2. Children match singing tones with teacher and each other.	Introducing the task of matching singing tones: encourage children to try them, one at a time.	
3. Produce contrasting singing tones on request, both higher and lower than given tones, and identify singing tones as matching (same) or different (higher or lower).	Singing a chant for children to copy: descending- or ascending-scale chant, monotone, or any simple melodic line. Use familiar content in chant, such as children's clothes color, a recent class activity, or a special event. Encourage children to make up a chant for others to copy.	

The terrible noises children tend to make when they have access to quantities of rhythm instruments can be avoided by following the suggestions given in Table 14–3. Purposeful or spontaneous activities create the base for learning the different sounds instruments make (timbre) and their names. Exploration of instruments, for limited numbers of children, leads to disciplined efforts to coordinate ensemble playing and to produce selected effects in rhythm, dynamics, and tempo. Children also learn to "conduct." Instead of uncontrolled noise, everyone finds satisfaction in skills of self-discipline and in purposeful use of instruments.

Summary of Music Area

While the foregoing discussion of music goals and activities is far from exhaustive, it describes a content area with specific goals, from simple to more complex, sophisticated learning, all of which can be developed with any size of group. For each music area—listening, singing, movement, and instrumental playing—learning may build on well-planned activities and on spontaneous, child-generated efforts. Self-knowing and self-valuing are major affective goals, but language and cognitive skills are always integrated with music goals. A basic premise of this curriculum content use is its value in building feelings of competence and achievement; it also provides a great deal of action, humor, and fun.

ART

As an expressive and aesthetic activity, art is certainly different from other forms of school learning that use chiefly verbal or mathematical symbolism. As a personal form for expressing feelings or ideas, art must not be shackled by other people's criteria for such expression.

Nor should taste be formed by others. Yet developmental patterns in art activity are sufficiently universal and well understood that teachers can identify, from the characteristics of the work itself, a child's stage of art development. This, along with the child's own mode of expression, gives knowledgeable teachers clues to next steps or comfortable challenges.

Children's developmental stages in art have been studied and analyzed by many researchers.[4] It is generally agreed that the first art activity is *scribbling*, random actions with a pencil, crayon, or brush. According to Viktor Lowenfeld, scribbling, which occurs usually from ages two to four, gives way to preschematic drawings at ages four to seven.[5] During the *preschematic* stage, children become purposeful in the use of art materials, although what they are able to produce is usually far from their intentions. The *schematic* stage follows during ages seven to nine, with increasing skill in representation and other art values. According to this analysis, further stages include *dawning realism* and *pseudorealism* at about ages nine to eleven. From stages eleven to thirteen, more sophisticated concepts and skills are developed.

Other researchers have analyzed early artwork of children in terms of the universal shapes that can be seen in any environment, such as circles, lines, corners, sunburst patterns, and incomplete curves of many kinds.[6]

---

4. See especially Rhoda Kellogg, *Analyzing Children's Art* (Palo Alto, Calif.: National Press Books, 1970); Rudolf Arnheim, *Art and Visual Perception: A Psychology of the Creative Eye* (Berkeley, Calif.: University of California Press, 1969); Arnheim, *Visual Thinking* (Berkeley, Calif.: University of California Press, 1969); Victor Lowenfeld and W. Lambert Brittain, *Creative and Mental Growth*, 5th ed. (New York: Macmillan, 1970), and Elliott Eisner, *Educating Artistic Vision* (New York: Macmillan, 1972).

5. Lowenfeld and Brittain, *Creative and Mental Growth*, pp. 91–164.

6. Kellogg, *Analyzing Children's Art*.

TABLE 14.3. Music: instruments

	Goals	Teacher-prepared activities	Naturally occurring program activities
1.	Distinguish timbre of different instruments by matching.	Using three to five instruments, having children match the instruments by timbre first when model to be matched is in view, and then when not in view. Model may be the instrument itself, a photograph, or the instrument name with or without the picture.	Children spontaneously experimenting with striking sounds of blocks or other classroom material. Encourage finding matching and nonmatching sounds and higher or lower sounds.
2.	Respond with instruments to two-part musical form, such as bells for first part and rhythm sticks for second part.	Singing or playing music on record, tape recorder, guitar, or piano, with simple, two-part musical form. Encourage children to respond with different instruments to each part.	Children spontaneously producing rhythmic patterns with hands, tapping tables or other materials. Encourage changing tempo and dynamics.
3.	Play instruments rhythmically in a steady beat with melodic pattern as accompaniment, responding to change in dynamics and tempo.	Rhythm band activity, which may include jumping or other movement forms. Use piano, tape recorder, records, or voice to establish the pattern.	Introducing selected instruments as part of exploring musical sounds.
4.	Produce rhythmic patterns on instruments, improvising and copying another's pattern. *Related Cognitive Skills:* a. comparison and contrast of musical sounds and timbre of instruments; b. identifying, copying, and creating patterns or clusters of sounds, changing tempo, accent, and dynamics. *Related Language Goals:* using word meanings in context.	Using different kinds of instruments, inviting children to produce rhythmic patterns for others to hear and copy.	

Many observers note young children's tendency to depict what they know, rather than what they see; this is usually called a cognitive theory of child art. A child, knowing a table has four legs, will draw it with all four legs stretched out, although these are seldom visible from any perspective.

Rudolf Arnheim, fundamentally Piagetian in his approach, applies a Gestalt view of perception to developmental growth in art. Using the Gestalt point of view, which stresses unity and wholes, Arnheim explains that the child tends to see the large shape and to ignore parts. Thus, a head without ears, neck, or even a nose makes good sense to a young child if a more-or-less-circular line suggests the shape of a head. It is the shape of the head that is important to the child, not the details of neck, ears, chin, or eyebrows. As the child moves into more advanced stages and copes with problems in perspective, overlapping figures and time sequences and spatial relationships begin to be understood.[7] This is when the child seeks to show relative size or distance, for example.

Another major approach to child art development takes a psychodynamic, mainly Freudian view. Art values for young children are viewed primarily as means of coping with emotions or of projecting universal images. Art symbols, for the mature artist as well as for the child, derive from the unconscious. Much material is worked through with little awareness on the part of the child or artist of the source.[8]

In our prototype program, an eclectic integration of these theories supports the curriculum in art and music. These various theories can be viewed as pieces of a puzzle, all of which are required to account for the complex functions of art in our culture and in education. Thus, children are seen as working through unconscious emotions and drives, (psychodynamic view), drawing what they know (cognitive view), perceiving wholes and subordinating details for unity and completeness (Gestalt view), and at the same time depicting the universal shapes available in all environments (developmental view).

In artwork, it is helpful for the teacher to know that young children have to struggle to learn how to deal with such concepts as:

1. *Three-dimensional objects represented in two-dimensional space:*
    a. Young children tend to represent *what they know, rather than what they see;* they are satisfied to draw a fetus inside the pregnant mother, even though they know it cannot be seen.
    b. *Perspective* is not required or understood until later in the stage of concrete operations, at about ages nine to eleven.
    c. *Relative size* of objects may be determined on the basis of personal significance rather than objective fact. In a family picture, the baby may be the largest object for emotional reasons.
    d. *Distortions in space relationships and proportions* are frequent. Forms take up space without regard to other objects nearby, with each form existing in its own space.
    e. *Disregard of the need to signify distance* is due to the lack of conception of perspective.
    f. Lack of ways to represent action usually account for *static scenes.*
    g. *Selectivity* in realistic detail accounts for representation of curly hair or a pipe, even though neck, ears, or arms may be omitted.
2. *Grouping of forms.* Young children's artwork sometimes presents breathtakingly lovely groupings, when children work quickly and intuitively, but representational and realistic art present great problems in arranging elements to appear to belong together.

---

7. Arnheim, *Art and Visual Perception,* and *Visual Thinking.*
8. Kellogg, *Analyzing Children's Art.*

3. *Unity.* Relationships among form, space, color, balance, shape, rhythm, pattern, and size all contribute to a unified work with visual bonds, suggestions, and directions.
4. *Variety.* Young children slowly develop the ability to create interest by varying shape, size, color, shades, movement, or other visual values.
5. *Color.* Relationships of colors to each other and to the theme or intent of the work are sophisticated concepts that grow out of guided experiences.
6. *Balance.* A concept of visual equilibrium is required, to balance the size and relationships of objects in space. This is a complex art value that grows slowly.
7. *Movement.* Lines or patterns that move the eye and suggest actions to the viewer are subtle and are seldom noticed or created by the young artist.
8. *Aesthetic judgment.* Which forms are more pleasing, which are flat and uninteresting, what constitutes excitement that compels renewed viewing, what is banal, what is original and fresh—these aesthetic judgments form long-term objectives as all become judges of visual beauty. Teachers preserve their own humility about aesthetic judgment when they remember that art critics differ with one another and that tastes change with fashions.

If the concepts listed above (or a similar list), were regarded as the specific long-term goals of the art program, sequencing expressive activities and instructional guidance could be largely based on children's developmental characteristics. Children's progress could be stimulated individually as art understanding grows with performance skills and cognitive capability.

Art is an *integrating experience* that children use to construct or express ideas and feelings in nonverbal forms.[9] Children often paint pictures that perplex adults. Yet teachers can see that the children are constructing images and concepts they probably could not verbalize or communicate. Following exciting trips, children in their artwork often communicate moods, concepts, or relationships they do not express in other ways.

Instructional Approach

In art, as in music, children's work is accepted nonjudgmentally. Enjoyment, expression, release of feelings, shaping of ideas and of taste, and repeated practice are the major features of children's artwork. Self-satisfaction and self-valuing develop from this acceptance of one's work by others, and of gradual progress in specific skills.

Learning one's common culture develops from craft activities associated with historical holidays and cultural events. Valuing cultural pluralism comes through art activities that feature the holidays, traditions, and history of special culture groups. Art activities for Puerto Rican Discovery Week, Martin Luther King Day, or the Chinese New Year, for example, serve to dramatize cultural uniqueness and equal valuing. Skills include eye-hand control, use of tools, achievement of specific skills in shapes, or other art values listed in this art section. Language and cognitive skills are, as usual, integrated with affective and aesthetic goals. Children's growth is individual in pace, unique in its various manifestations, and extremely variable in outcomes.

Variety is featured in arts-and-crafts work because initial capabilities and interests vary. Some children are drawn to tools, especially hole punchers, scissors, staplers, or fasteners. Others like free action with fingers and paint.

9. B. Lark-Horovitz, *The Art of the Very Young: An Indicator of Individuality.* Columbus, Ohio: Charles E. Merrill, 1976.

Some children doubt their ability to use arts-and-crafts materials well, fearing criticism or perhaps punishment. The atmosphere of acceptance and adventuring is therefore crucial to progress with arts and crafts. Motor skills, especially small muscle control, are easily achieved with arts-and-crafts work, and they transfer immediately to controlling the pencil in writing and making visual distinctions in reading. We stress artwork for its own values. But it is fortunate that what children achieve in art they can usually achieve in language arts, science, math, and other content areas as well.

The messiness of much arts-and-crafts work deters some teachers from using it as often as possible. This messiness may be therapeutic for some children and challenging to others. Preparation and cleanup of artwork is a productive way to develop skills of self-management, work through feelings about messiness, and deal with group rules and projects. Social skills, as well as personal development skills, are directly derived from frequent experiences with arts and crafts.

Art Activities and Projects

Art media that children use without much direction or guidance include pencils, crayons, finger paint, tempera paint, collage pasting, and clay. Play-dough and plasticene are substitute materials or occasional novelties for these basic art media.

Children use art materials because they are available, because other children participate and socialize while they work, and because teachers value the activity, the process, and the product. For younger children, teachers are encouraged to stress the process far above the product. But when children feel pride in their work, it is only natural for teachers to support and nurture satisfaction in accomplishment, especially for children ages five to eight. When teachers plan carefully for artwork activities, children find materials readily available. They know where to work, how to protect their clothes and their workspaces, and how to clean up. Children also need shelves, drying racks, and other ways to store work in process and protect fragile products. Aprons, clay boards, accessory tools, water, sponges, paper towels, cleaning cloths, mop, broom, dust pan, or similar cleaning tools are needed, in place everyday.

Teachers usually offer a selection of art media daily, although clay may be withheld on days when other demanding projects diminish supervisory opportunities. In many classes, children can manage their clay modeling with remarkable independence, both in process and in cleanup, because of effective teaching.

Explorations of art media are continually encouraged. Occasionally excitement climbs when sponge prints or junk printing gives a new twist to tempera paint. Or a child discovers the wax-resist quality of crayons applied underneath paint. Or children discover pastel tints, mixing colors with white paint.

Teachers try to:

1. encourage continuous art explorations;
2. avoid judgments and comparisons of one child's work with another's;
3. keep samples of each child's work and date them so that the child can perceive change and progress in her or his own work;
4. find motivating materials for children who usually avoid artwork;
5. nurture children's independent choice of art activities and projects;
6. exhibit all children's work samples, not just "good ones";
7. share art values and desirable processes with parents, for greater unity in approach;
8. plan experiences in and out of the classroom that tend to stimulate art projects;
9. help children to identify problems in art activities and to find ways to solve problems;

10. accept children's desire to describe their artwork or their refusal to do so;
11. avoid doing children's artwork for them;
12. help children perceive the need for skills, when appropriate, by suggesting discussions of intentions and procedures, or of problems encountered or resolved;
13. teach skills only when children are ready for them, such as fine motor control of crayon or brush, mixing of colors, or construction of desired shapes.

Artwork is therefore respected as uniquely the child's own in conception, process, and outcome for whatever purposes happen to be served. Teaching is concerned with frequency of art experiences, increasing complexity of art projects, and child independence and autonomy in initiating and in cleaning up art projects. These are the ways the art goals of self-knowing and self-valuing are developed.

Craft Projects

Craft activities are distinguished from art activities by the utilitarian nature of most craft projects, although no firm line can or should be drawn between them. Since craft projects involve children's purposefulness, they usually require planning, materials, problem solving, and sometimes tools. Discussions among children or between teacher and child often precede, accompany, or follow the project, so that language development is constant in all craft activities.

Craft projects are suggested to heighten children's enthusiasm for practicing key language and exploring related learnings. Craft products are expected to reflect the children's individual choices of materials; their skills; and cultural and community holidays, events, and artifacts. Table 14–4 lists specific craft projects, identifying materials needed and the key language involved. Craft projects listed include collages of various types; single-purpose books by color, number, or other characteristic; classification books; and mobiles. For example, a "shape" collage, or a mobile that can use many types of materials, can feature the following types of learning:

1. *Mathematics:*
   a. *Number:* more than or less than, matching sets, pairing, partitioning sets into subsets, creating equal and equivalent sets, counting, simple addition and subtraction, and serial order;
   b. *Geometry:* curved and straight lines, matching shapes, identical and similar shapes, joining shapes to make new shapes, open and closed curves, and spatial terms of location;
   c. *Measurement*: arbitrary and standard units for measure: comparing lengths as longer, shorter, or congruent (same length); comparing sizes as larger, smaller, or same size; and comparing weights as heavier or lighter.
2. *Science:* experimenting with properties of objects; transforming properties, balance, and motion.
3. *Geography:* positional terms, physical aspects of the environment, dimensionality, and directionality.

A mobile, as Table 14–4 suggests, may feature counting, names of numbers, and the names of objects used, such as wire hanger, string, buttons, feathers, springs, beads, or paper circles. Any vocabulary group can be practiced in some meaningful way through collage and mobile construction.

The holidays and cultural and ethnic celebrations of many kinds suggest another series of craft projects as listed in Table 14–5. As with Table 14–4, Thanksgiving cooking projects, of pies or cakes, for example, stress names of ingredients, tastes cooking actions, and cooking tools.

TABLE 14.4. Craft projects

	Craft project	Key language		Materials
1.	Make a single purpose collage:			
	a. Shape	circle triangle make a pattern copy a pattern color names round	square rectangle corners lines edges	construction paper, gummed shapes, toothpicks, washers, Mason jar rings, yarn, pipe cleaners, paper strips, paste, and stapler
	b. Texture: emphasize contrasting tactile and related properties	*hard, soft* *smooth, rough* *rigid, flexible* *flat, curved* *shiny, dull* *hollow, solid*		construction paper, glue, paste, stapler, or tape; assorted materials such as cotton, cork, aluminum foil, yarn, wire, wood, rubber, buttons, and straws
	c. Order by length: such as a flower garden	*tallest, shortest* *longest* color names *soft, smooth* stem petal flower leaf		construction paper with baseline marked, varying lengths of pipe cleaners, sticks, strips of paper for flower stems, gummed circles, crepe paper, cotton, ribbon, felt, buttons, and tissue paper for flowers
	d. Number: number page to indicate the number of objects.	number names object labels color labels same number		assorted collage materials, paper, paste, scissors, numeral stamps, and crayons
	e. Size: big or little, long or short	*big, little* *longer, shorter* name labels		two sizes of selected materials, such as buttons, cotton balls, or cardboard discs, two lengths of selected material, such as wooden sticks, pipe cleaners, or paper strips
	f. Position: feature objects above or below ground level or on land or water	*up above, down below* *over, under* *on top of, underneath* *circle, triangle, rectangle* *inside, outside* object labels classification categories such as *buildings* and *animals*		construction paper with horizontal lines, paste, crayons, boat or bird decals, cotton, stars, colored circles, pictures of trucks, planes, cars, subway, urban streets, people, buildings, felt, copper wire pictures of farm animals, trees, flowers, vegetables, rocks, worms, grass, and birds

TABLE 14.4. (continued)

	Craft project	Key language	Materials
2.	Make single purpose books:		paper, paste, tape, stapler, and assorted materials
	a. Color books	color names tactile properties	and objects of desired colors
	b. Shape books	*circle* *triangle* *rectangle* tactile properties	hole puncher, circles, triangles, squares of paper, fabric, cardboard, and stencils of shapes
	c. Number books	number names object labels *set, group, collection*	assorted objects of various sizes, such as macaroni, buttons, pipe cleaners, decals, cork, numeral stamps, and paste
	d. Pattern books	color names object labels patterning terms: *next* and *before*	objects suitable for "printing" with paint, such as plastic fork, cork, or wooden spool, plastic bottle cap; sponge cut for printing; sponge squares; paint; and paper
3.	Make classification books (may be combined with number books)	*farm animals* *pets* *growing things* *tools* *people* *vehicles* *toys*	assortment of decals, cutouts of a desired class mixed with other pictures, picture magazine, paper, and paste
4.	Make single purpose mobiles:	mobile language: *hang, swing, turn, spin, sway*	wire hanger, pieces of string, buttons, feathers, springs, beads, and paper circles
	a. Number	number names *a-three-mobile* object labels	
	b. Shape	*circle* *square* *triangle, rectangle* *spheres* or *balls* *rectangular solids* *cones*	wire hanger; pieces of string; tape; scissors; balls such as styrofoam, rubber, or ping pong; small boxes; precut shapes; and pipe cleaners
	c. Color	color names object names	wire hanger, pieces of string, tape, solid color objects, and pictures

TABLE 14.5. Holiday projects

Project	Key language	Materials
Columbus Day		
1. Box-like boats for floating and making exhibits	*rectangular solid* (hull) *triangle, rectangle* (sail) *float, sink* *outside, inside* *wet, dry*	scissors, paste, tape, stapler, milk cartons, styrofoam, cardboard paper, fabric, enamel paint, and water
Halloween		
2. masks for dramatic play and music: cut out, painted, crayoned, or pasted	*circle, square, triangle, rectangle* *soft, hard* *rough, smooth* *scary, funny*	scissors, paste, tape, stapler, construction paper or paper bags, string, yarn, and collage materials
3. Jack O'lantern: real or child-made pumpkins for dramatic play, music, or room decoration	*circle, square, triangle* *wet, dry* *soft, stringy, smooth, shiny* *scary, funny* *smells like . . .* *seeds, pulp, skin*	pumpkin, knife, construction paper, scissors, gummed shapes, cellophane paper, stapler, and tape
Thanksgiving		
4. Cookies and pies, cranberry sauce, and fresh vegetable sticks	object labels, cooking tools and ingredients measuring terms *recipe* cooking actions, such as *beating, whipping, kneading* or *blending* descriptive labels, such as *dry, crisp, doughy, hot, cool, cold, soft, smooth, powdery, wet, shape, sweet, spicy*	cooking ingredients: use either a cooking mix or flour, sugar, flavoring, and other desired ingredients pie ingredients cranberries and sugar fresh vegetables
5. Placemats for party decorations	color names *circle, square, triangle, rectangle* pattern names, such as *red, red, blue; circle, square*	construction paper, oaktag or fabric, gummed shapes or strips, other collage materials, sponge printing with waterpaint
Chanukah-Christmas		
6. Pencil holders	*cylinder, triangle, circle, square, rectangle* color names patterns object labels	cans for decorating with collage materials, paint, sequins, and shapes

TABLE 14.5. (continued)

	Project	Key language	Materials
7.	Wooden tie bars	*smooth, saw, screw*	wood, cup hooks, and enamel paint
8.	Picture frames	*circular, rectangular, square measure, length, longer, shorter*	cardboard, oaktag, collage materials, and printing materials
9.	Vanity boxes	*rectangular solids* object labels *wet, dry* size labels	wood, cardboard, collage, decorating materials, and paint
10.	Wooden pull-toy	*wheels, round, roll* rectangular solids	wheels, wood, string, and woodworking tools
11.	Gift-wrap paper	*patterns* *circle, square, triangle* other shape names color names names of objects used	shape prints with objects, sponges, shapes, collage materials, and tempera paint
12.	Tree decorations	*balls, spheres, cones* *sticky, pasty, wet, moist* *dry, hard, soft, powder*	papier-mâché, cut paper, paint and paper, cans, boxes, styrofoam, cotton, and paste
13.	Room decorations, such as mobiles and paper chains	color patterns object labels property labels	construction paper, paste, scissors, and stapler
President's birthday: Lincoln			
14.	Top hats	presidential name *cylinders, circle* measure, size	construction paper, paste, tape measure, and stapler
15.	Flag	*stripes, stars* *alternating pattern* *rectangle* color names	construction paper, colored paper strips, stars, sticks, paste, and scissors
President's birthday: George Washington			
16.	Three-cornered hat	presidential name *triangle, tricorn*	construction paper, paste, and stapler
Valentine's Day			
17.	Cards	color names, *hearts, friends* *mailbox, post office, stamps* *poems, rhymes*	paste, glue, stapler, construction paper, felt, scissors, doilies, cotton, pipe cleaners, metallic paper, crepe paper, wax paper, tissue paper, and yarn
18.	Mailbox	*rectangular solid* or *a box*	carton, decorations

TABLE 14.5. (continued)

Project	Key language	Materials
Easter		
19. Baskets	*fold, bend, overlap* shape labels	milk cartons, oaktag, pipe cleaners, decorative materials, paste, and stapler
20. Bonnets	*spheres, ties, textures* positional terms *bows, decorations* measurement terms for hat size	paper plates, construction paper, collage materials, doilies, styrofoam balls, crepe paper, lace, net, paste, and stapler
21. Dyeing eggs	*crayon resist* color names *stencils* smells	water, dye, vinegar, hard-boiled eggs, crayons, and tongs

Since craft projects usually have products of some practical usefulness, it is logical that they be used in some way. Mobiles are hung; books are used, read, and exhibited; boats are floated in water; kites are flown; and food, of course, must be eaten—alone or shared with guests. Craft projects may be individual, small group, or total group efforts. Other than individual projects, craft work requires a great deal of discussion, cooperation, and problem solving.

Art Goals

Since heightening self-awareness and increasing self-valuing and expressiveness are major goals in art, frequency of activity and satisfaction with the process and the products are necessary. Explorations of materials always precede planned uses. Good rules for safety and productivity in use of materials, along with effective and reliable clean up procedures, assure that art outcomes will please teachers as well as children. Children are quick to sense value judgments of their work. Teachers are reminded to value *process*, *persistence*, *exploratory efforts*, and *participation* in artwork. A further caution is to make objective rather than judgmental comments. "You used a lot of blue" is objective, while "that's a lovely dog" is judgmental. Children's art products serve to stimulate conversation and discussion. Teachers accomplish more by asking open-ended questions such as, "Do you want to tell me about your picture?" than they do by making comments or judgments.

SUMMARY

In both music and art, the prototype curriculum stresses children's pleasure and active participation to increase self-knowing and self-valuing. In music, developmental progress toward rhythm, tempo, pitch, timbre, dynamics, and melody are specific content goals that guide the teacher's selection of activities. In art, specific content goals involve developing representational methods, grouping, unity, variety, color, balance, movement, and aesthetic judgment. All content goals can be advanced through both planned and emerging (spontaneous) activities. Individual progress is valued, but grading and other judgmental forms of evaluation are not. Developmental progress, not instant mastery, is the desired outcome of music and art activities.

EXERCISES

1. Based on diagnostic checks in Appendix B, select and use one instructional model in music. Evaluate your consistency in implementing the design, the results, and your reaction to the model.
2. Select an art activity you have not previously tried and implement it with a small group of children. Analyze outcomes as in exercise one.

BIBLIOGRAPHY

Arnheim, Rudolf. *Art and Visual Perception: A Psychology of the Creative Eye*. Berkeley, Calif.: University of California Press, 1969.

———. *Visual Thinking*. Berkeley Calif.: University of California Press, 1969.

Cavanagh, Frances, and Pannell, Lucy, *Holiday Round Up*. Philadelphia: Macrae Smith, 1968.

Cherry, Clare. *Creative Movement for the Developing Child*. Rev. ed. Belmont, Calif.: Fearon Publishers, 1971.

Dobler, Lavinia. *Customs and Holidays around the World*. New York: Fleet Press, 1963.

Eisner, Elliott. *Educating Artistic Vision*. New York: Macmillan, 1972.

Feldman, Edmund. *Becoming Human through Art: Aesthetic Experience in the School*. Englewood Cliffs, N.J.: Prentice-Hall, 1970.

Hackett, Layne C. and Jensen, Robert G. *A Guide to Movement Exploration*. Palo Alto, Calif.: Peek Publications, 1961.

Haywood, Charles. *Folk Songs of the World*. New York: John Day, 1966.

Kellogg, Rhoda. *Analyzing Children's Art*. Palo Alto, Calif.: National Press Books, 1970.

Landeck, Beatrice, and Crook, Elizabeth. *Wake Up and Sing*. New York: Edward B. Marks, 1969.

Lark-Horovitz, B. *The Art of the Very Young: An Indicator of Individuality*. Columbus, Ohio: Charles E. Merrill, 1976.

Lowenfeld, Viktor, and Brittain, W. Lambert. *Creative and Mental Growth*, 5th ed. New York: Macmillan, 1970.

Robison, Helen F. *Exploring Teaching in Early Childhood Education*. Boston: Allyn and Bacon, 1977.

Seeger, Ruth Crawford. *American Folk Songs for Children*. Garden City, N.Y.: Doubleday, 1953.

Sheehy, Emma D. *Children Discover Music and Dance*. New York: Teachers College Press, Columbia University, 1977.

This Is Music. Boston; Allyn and Bacon, 1965.

15 Prototype Curriculum: Language Development and Beginning Reading

Though it is the codification of centuries of human experience, transformed by man's creative intelligence and preserved from generation to generation by the means it itself supplies, language still must be recreated in the individual.[1]

Communication is the major function of language.[2] The specific language humans learn depends on which one they grow up with. Successful communication, or sending and receiving messages, is an active process in which language carries information, ideas, and feelings. As children develop language, they are simultaneously expanding their ability to *decode*, or figure out what is being said, and to *encode*, or put their meanings into words. In our prototype curriculum, language goals permeate the whole program to provide a rich variety of activities that require communication with peers and adults.

All language is symbolic. Oral language stands for something in one's life experience. Written language is an abstraction of oral language, using graphic symbols to represent words and sounds. Written language has meaning only if the reader can relate it to oral language that is understood. Therefore, the reading program is built on a strong initial emphasis on oral language development. Graphic symbols, writing, and print are introduced only after oral language is sufficiently meaningful to take a more abstract form. Other elements of reading, such as perceptual motor skills and the cognitive skills of sorting, classifying, and generalizing, are integrated into the program as described in this chapter.

LANGUAGE DEVELOPMENT

Oral language skills include the ability to communicate by speaking to exchange information, test ideas, share experiences, and express feelings. Communication with another person succeeds if the participants have a common language with familiar vocabulary and syntax.

Over the past few decades, a large body of research has documented the complexity of the language learning process.[3] Two of the most popular myths have been exploded. The *first myth* is that *children learn language by imitation*. Imitation is necessary but not sufficient by itself. While it is known that children need to hear language to acquire it, the act of imitating what they hear does not account for the broad range of language forms they develop.

---

1. E. Brooks Smith, Kenneth S. Goodman, and Robert Meredith, *Language and Thinking in the Elementary School* (New York: Holt, Rinehart & Winston, 1970), p. 6.

2. Frank Smith, *Understanding Reading* (New York: Rinehart & Winston, 1971), chaps. 1–4, especially chap. 2, pp. 12–28.

3. A major impetus to the study of primary language learning occurred in the 1960s with the research at Harvard and Massachusetts Institute of Technology. Researchers of the period include Noam Chomsky, Jerome Bruner, Courtney Cazden, Ursula Belugi, and Robert Brown.

Children produce new forms of words they have heard and also create new words when needed. Everyone knows examples of children's sayings that startle and amuse adults because of their originality.[4] The *second myth* is that *children learn language by being corrected*. The research confirms that correction cannot occur with sufficient frequency to change verbal patterns. Therefore, something more than mere correction is involved.[5]

All theories of language development agree that experience, conceptualization, and communication continuously influence the way children develop language. Children demonstrate this continuing cycle as they explore their environment, sort perceptions, test generalizations, and ultimately extend perceptions through language and physical interactions. This theory indicates that children learn language not only by imitating what they hear, but also by making up rules about word usage and sentence structures. Without conscious awareness of adult grammar, children's own rules increasingly approximate those used in the immediate environment. As children hear more speech, they have more examples from which to make their rules, and they test their rules by using them more.

Kornei Chukovsky calls the language-learning power of young children awe-inspiring.

> It seems to me that beginning with age two every child becomes for a short period of time a linguistic genius. Later, beginning with the age of five to six, this talent begins to fade. There is no trace left in the eight-year-old of this creativity with words, since the need for it has passed; by this age the child already has fully mastered the basic principles of his native language.[6]

4. Kornei Chukovsky, *From Two to Five*. Berkeley, Calif.: University of California Press, 1963.

5. Courtney B. Cazden, "Suggestions from Studies of Early Language Acquisition," in Courtney Cazden, ed., *Language in Early Childhood Education* (Washington, D.C.: National Association for the Education of Young Children, 1972), pp. 6–7.

6. Chukovsky, *From Two to Five*, pp. 7–8.

It is the child's ability to organize perceptions about language, to construct rules of language usage, and to apply these rules in new situations that generates the design of this prototype language development program. Nourishment for the "linguistic genius" is provided through an activity-rich environment where there are many opportunities to communicate about common experiences.

Language and Thought

Contrasting views of the relationship between language and thought are presented by Piaget and Vygotsky. Piaget claims that thought precedes language, while Vygotsky emphasizes the influence of language on the shaping of ideas. Following the Piagetian view, construction of physical knowledge does not depend on language initially, but on manipulation and interaction. This view demotes language teaching to a minor role and favors children's active manipulation. The opposite view supports a major emphasis on language instruction to stimulate thinking and facilitate the organization of ideas. We prefer the middle position, which "embraces a concept of 'dialogue' in which language of children and the language of the adult teachers are brought into interplay at every stage of the development of language and thinking, including an initial 'discovery' period."[7]

While children are making discoveries about the physical world, they often lack the language to discuss it. Therefore, the teacher's language serves as an information resource that children need to talk about their findings. Vocabulary acquisition in this natural context gives children a way to handle ideas that are being developed. Language used to exchange ideas and feelings builds on experiences. Con-

7. Smith et al., *Language and Thinking in Elementary School*, p. 116.

sequently, language becomes a vehicle for thinking as children master symbolic form and accumulate experiences.

Dialects

All speakers learn the dialect of their families at first. Then, they add other dialects as they attend school, make friends, and communicate in broader language systems. *Dialectal flexibility*, or knowledge of more than one dialect, assures communication in a variety of settings.

Young children, who are barely mastering their primary dialect, have limited dialectal flexibility. But, as previously noted, the speed with which young children build vocabulary and general rules for oral language is remarkable. It would impede language development to interfere with this process. Children use the dialect they have. As they come in contact with other dialectal forms, in school or elsewhere, they expand their language repertoire.

Studies have demonstrated that each dialect has its own set of grammatical rules.[8] Learning a second dialect is both easier and more difficult than learning a first dialect. Learning the standard English dialect does not require nonstandard dialect speakers to learn everything new. Dialects, however, tend to interfere with each other because they have more rules in common than not. A second language offers sharp contrast, whereas a second dialect requires perceiving subtle changes.

William Labov found ten major differences in grammatical form between the dialect of inner-city black children and the dialect that is the basis for the school readers.[9] These differences identify some kinds of reading problems encountered in the early grades.

---

8. William Labov, *Language in the Inner City: Studies in Black English Vernacular* (Philadelphia: University of Pennsylvania Press, 1972).

9. Ibid., pp. 3–35.

A primary language goal in our prototype curriculum is to increase children's familiarity with standard English dialect without interfering with growing skills in their native dialects. This requires the development of activities that engage children in hearing and using unfamiliar language patterns. It also mandates a no-correction strategy for responding to spontaneous language. In essence, children learn a new dialect as they would a song or a poem—as an initial acquisition. They may learn the standard English dialect using the teacher as their model. However, to assure familiarity with standard English language forms, children are stimulated to produce the new forms. The language program in the prototype, therefore, stresses addition, expansion, and maximum opportunities for language use in active learning contexts.

GOALS AND TEACHING APPROACH

Language developent goals in this program aim for acquiring increasingly successful communication skills. *Communication* means speaking, listening, reading, and writing. For younger children the goal of developing oral language always precedes other language goals. Also, learning English as a second language or learning standard English usage always involves additive experiences—building on what children bring to school, valuing what they have, and expanding on it to include more communication skills. Goals for language development include not only skills in conversation and dialogue, but also the enjoyment of literature and poetry, which is discussed in the next section.

Specifically, the goals for language development, as listed in Tables 15–1 and 15–2 are to increase:

1. appropriate verbalization in the classroom;

2. verbal communication;
3. vocabulary;
4. production of standard syntactical form;
5. enjoyment of language playfulness and of rhyming, dramatization, and storytelling;
6. enjoyment of children's literature.

Language learning is included as part of all curriculum areas. Vocabulary development is nurtured through talking with children as they participate in many kinds of experiences. As noted in Chapter 12, children make their own choices of activity, so that their participation genuinely reflects interest. Voluntary involvement in program activities and necessary routines provides the substance of children's talk and of the development of oral language skills. Formal language drill is not included in this program.

As adults and children converse, the content of communication is valued over the language form. What a child says is more important than how the child says it. Native speech is accepted, whatever the level of mastery and regardless of dialect. New vocabulary and standard English usage, as noted in Table 15-1, is taught through games, chants, and playful activities that are separate and distinct from activities intended to provoke spontaneous use of language.

The teaching approach features talking and listening, initiating and responding. Teaching strategies include:

1. *providing a model* of talking, that is, using language for communication;
2. *supplying vocabulary words* in context and modeling standard syntactical form;
3. *inviting communication* by expressing interest in children's activities through observational comments, asking questions, and working with children in a participant role;
4. *extending communication* by:
   a. waiting a few seconds when a child finishes talking to allow for further comments or clarification;
   b. asking questions for elaboration and clarification;
   c. adding comments to test meaning or extend conversation;
   d. using synonyms in context to increase vocabulary acquisition;
5. *designing games and playful activities* for fun and laughter, activities which include new vocabulary and standard syntactical forms.

As noted in goals one and two of Table 15-1, which are developed in Instructional Models 15-1 and 15-2, vocabulary development is furthered through talking and listening. In activities where the teacher assumes the participant role, the teacher contributes vocabulary words and after listening asks questions to encourage clarification. New words are used in context so that vocabulary expansion continues naturally, without drills.

Games that involve verbal directions, together with various routine procedures, foster responding to instructions. Practice of standard syntax occurs in specifically designed games, chants, and playful activities. Teachers model standard speech forms but are cautioned to avoid interrupting children to correct immature or nonstandard forms.

Young children's *egocentric speech*—speech having many personal meanings—has been described by many writers. Young children use language literally and are slow to understand multiple meanings of words. However, teachers frequently forget this, often taking for granted that the meanings intended are the meanings that will be received.[10] For example, during a music period, a kindergarten teacher

---

10. Margaret Donaldson, *Children's Minds* (New York: W.W. Norton, 1978), pp. 10-12.

TABLE 15.1. Language development: goals and activities

Goals	Teacher-prepared activities	Naturally occurring program activities
*1. Expand vocabulary and meanings of language in context, using activities in *all* curriculum areas. Use language to share experiences, ideas, and feelings.	Making materials by mixing, such as play-dough and cooking. Physical-action activities and games: • follow-the-leader with accompanying language • follow-the-leader with command-action games. Building chants to accompany action, such as "jumping, jumping," "sawing, sawing," or "walking on sidewalk." "Finding" activities, such as Treasure Hunt, using verbal clues for position and name labels. Lotto games and labeling pictures Story reading and story telling: meaning in context. Finger plays. Discussion periods with small groups of three to six children to discuss experiences or selected topics, such as, "What happened yesterday on the trip that you liked very much?" Sessions to discuss or plan a class event. Discussions about immediate experiences, such as dressing for outdoors, snack, and lunch. For individual and small groups of two to four children. Problem-solving discussion with a small group about a social, construction, or materials-use problem.	Spontaneous communication between children and between children and adults: Listening to others to obtain meaning and talking with others to communicate meaning. Continual interaction with language in the natural setting initiated in context with spontaneous and planned activities. Multiple meanings of words exposed by chance can become the basis for later teacher planned activities. Informally responding to child-initiated conversations on feelings, ideas, and experiences, with one or two children at a time. Having problem-solving discussions with children who bring immediate problems to teacher.

TABLE 15.1. (continued)

Goals	Teacher-prepared activities	Naturally occurring program activities
*2. Play with language sounds, rhythms, accent, and tone. Match same and different sounds for word endings or beginnings. Match or contrast phrases.	Rhyming and alliteration. Chanting. "Playing" with inflection. Puppetry. See Chapter 14 for additional activities in music.	On the playground, on trips, during activity periods, noting especially water table or sand table, clay, swings, and bicycling activities: Children initiate playful use of language anywhere and anytime. Teachers have many opportunities to foster play with language, showing appreciation and humor and becoming a participant.
3. Practice standard syntactical form.	Lotto games: caller says, "Who has _____?" and player says, "I have _____." Follow the leader, language and action: Say what the leader says and do what the leader does. Responsive chants: two-part chants using questions and answers or adding on phrases. An add-on chant for verb *to have* might be: • "I have a duck _____." • "I have a duck and a _____." • "I have a duck and a mouse and a _____."	Children correcting each other and modeling for each other in spontaneous communication: Since communication of feelings, attitudes, ideas and perceptions takes precedence over syntactical form, teacher's correction of children's speech is not recommended. Instead, without breaking the flow of communication, teachers model correct forms whenever possible.

was observed to use the word *circle* as both a noun and a verb in successive sentences:

> Lets make a *circle* by joining hands. That's right, everybody *circle* up. Now, you begin to *circle* round with the music.

The children responded appropriately to the direction when circle was used as a noun, but were at a loss to understand the direction *circle round*, meaning "march along the circular path." As an important language resource, this teacher could have supported communication skills, diminished confusion, and guided children to more complex understanding had he been alert to the group's limited vocabulary and flexibility in word usage.

> **INSTRUCTIONAL MODEL 15.1**
> **Language Development:**
> **Using Language as Communication**
> (From Table 15.1, Goal One)
>
> *Goals:*
> 1. Children talk spontaneously to each other and to the teacher.
> 2. Children name materials and use descriptive words as they participate in play activities.
>
> *Group Size:* 2 to 4
>
> *Materials:*
> - *Play-dough ingredients:* salt, flour, water, and food coloring
> - *Tools:* mixing bowls, utensils such as spoons and knives, cookie cutters, rolling pins
>
> *Procedure:*
> 1. Place materials on the table and invite children to make play-dough.
> 2. Help children name the materials as they use them.
> 3. Guide children to put two cups of flour and one cup salt into a mixing bowl, encouraging them to feel the dry mixture.
> 4. Have children add water or colored water a little at a time, taking turns stirring the mixture as water is added.
> 5. Use words supplied by children and offer synonyms as needed.
> 6. As children increase their spontaneous speech, decrease verbal participation.
>
> *Key Language:*
>
> | | | | |
> |---|---|---|---|
> | flour | water | color names | smooth |
> | dry | powdery | mixture | moist |
> | salt | coloring | soft | wet |
> | white | sticky | cup | lumpy |
>
> *Variations:* Other examples of activities that stimulate children's spontaneous speech are clay modeling, block play, housekeeping play, water play, playing with puppets, eating, and cooking.

LITERATURE

The wealth of children's books available poses a challenge to teachers to select wisely. Realistic fiction, folktales, and fantasy abound in prose and poetry. A great range of serious and amusing themes and plots are offered. Simple labeling picture books, picture story books, classic nursery tales and rhymes, and the vast new children's literature and poetry of our time all compete for our selection. Besides books, Bernice Cullinan and Carolyn Carmichael cite literature as including the "great oral tradition of the story teller," with media materials such as films, recordings, slides, and television as important resources.[11]

11. Bernice E. Cullinan and Carolyn W. Carmichael, eds., *Literature and Young Children* (Urbana, Ill.: National Council of Teachers of English, 1977), p. vii.

INSTRUCTIONAL MODEL 15.2
Language Development:
Rhyming Words and Nonsense Syllables
(From Table 15.1, Goal Two)

Goals:
1. Children recognize rhymes.
2. Children produce simple and nonsense rhymes and practice rhyming.

Group Size: 5

Materials: Nursery or folk rhymes with which children are familiar. (*Folk rhymes* refer to such traditional ditties as those children chant to jump rope or bounce balls. See the examples and further references given at the end of this instructional model.)

A. LEARNING RHYMES AND PRODUCING RHYMES

Procedure:
1. Recite the rhyme clearly and rhythmically, inviting the children to recite it with you.
2. Suggest appropriate action or invite children to suggest action to accompany the rhyme. For example, if the rhyme is "One, Two, Buckle My Shoe," the action may be pretending to buckle one's shoe.
3. Select a series of rhymes for children to learn, so that they soon have a repertoire of learned rhymes.
4. After children have learned a series of rhymes, ask children to make up rhymes to add to the ones they have learned. For example, with the rhyme "One, Two Buckle My Shoe," say, "I can think of a different rhyme for 'One, Two, Buckle My Shoe.' I can say, 'One, Two, who are you?' What can you say?"
5. Offer examples freely until children begin to catch on to the rhyming quality.
6. Accept nonsense rhymes as well as word rhymes, since both reflect understanding of the concept of rhyme.

B. PRACTICING RHYMING

Materials: boxes of miniature objects

Procedure:
1. Select small objects with names that rhyme, such as *cat-bat* or *sock-rock*.
2. Ask children to take objects out of the box and help them name the objects.
3. Say, "Let's play a game. Derrick will pick out an object and tell me its name, and I will find an object with a rhyming name. Then someone else will pick out an object." Demonstrate rhyming by matching the object with one that has a rhyming name.

INSTRUCTIONAL MODEL 15.2 (continued)

4. Continue to demonstrate rhyming until each child has had several turns to select an object.
5. Gradually invite children to help you find an object with a rhyming name.
6. As the children learn the rhyming pairs, change your role and select the first object. Ask a child to match a rhyming name.
7. Then change the objects selected for rhyming practice to introduce new rhymes.
8. Then use pictures along with the objects.
9. Then use pictures without the objects.
10. Then encourage children to make up rhyming couplets.
11. Word cards can be used with children who are building a sight-word vocabulary in the primary grades. The cards can be made by the teacher, or children can write their own word cards.

C. INDEPENDENT ACTIVITIES:

1. Invite children to play the game without you.
2. Invite children to clip pictures from magazines and paste rhyming pairs in a booklet. Write the word names on the page in manuscript or invite the child to write or use letter stamps.
3. Invite children to dictate to you their own rhyming couplets or to write them themselves.

Examples of Folk Rhymes:

1. Rain, rain, go away. Come again another day. Little Johnny wants to play.
2. It's raining, it's pouring, The old man is snoring. He got into bed and bumped his head, and couldn't get up in the morning.
3. Snow, snow, faster. Ally, ally, blaster. The old woman's baking a pie. She'll let me eat some bye and bye.
4. A knife and a fork. A bottle and a cork. That's the way to spell New York.
5. I'm rubber and you're glue. What you say to me will bounce back and stick to you.

Further References:

1. Withers, Carl. *A Rocket in My Pocket: The Rhymes and Chants of Young Americans.* New York: Holt & Co., 1948.
2. Opie, Iona, and Opie, Peter. *The Oxford Dictionary of Nursery Rhymes.* Oxford, England: The Clarendon Press, 1951.
3. Evans, Patricia. *Rimbles.* New York: Doubleday, 1961.

The value of literary experiences in the lives and language of children has been well established. Familiarity with literature is regarded as the foundation for successful reading. The following quotations illustrate some of the ways in which literature contributes to children's well-being and growth:

Emotional growth	". . . delight of beauty, wonder and humor: or the despair of sorrow, injustice and ugliness" becomes available through literature.[12]
Cognitive growth	". . . The basic myths of art and literature provide the organizing principles by which knowledge of the human condition is rendered into a form that makes thinking possible. . . ."[13]
Cultural transmission	"The literature enbodies the culture, projects its ideals and values, and teaches individuals and subsequent generations how to belong to it."[14]
Emotional catharsis	"The imagery created when a folk tale is well told has the power to touch the deepest of human feelings and emotions. In a vicarious way, it serves to allay fears, fulfill ambitions and provide love. It strengthens, renews and leaves the listener ready to resume the struggles and stresses of everyday living."[15]
Language development	"Children are word collectors. They play with language. They are fascinated by its sounds. When we read to them, we expose them to the beauty of literary language and a wider variety of language forms than they hear in other situations."[16]
Self-concept development	"Imaginative thinking evoked by reading enables a child to develop a notion of credibility about himself and his immediate world. It allows him to view the real world in better perspective, to understand why and how things happen and to cope with life in a wholesome and positive manner."[17]
Total development	Literature provokes children to explore life and living.[18]

In addition, literature provides aesthetic experience, enhancing children's sensitivity to beauty in the natural world, to language, and to people while simultaneously whetting their appetites for reading.

Literary tastes vary, which accounts for the differing sets of published criteria for selecting children's books. Consequently, a program designed to contribute to children's growth in any of the areas indicated in the previous list of quotations is likely to include diverse types of literary experiences, depending on children's development and background. Smith, Goodman, and Meredith note that "the child must be able to meet the book at least halfway" in

12. Charlotte S. Huck and Doris Y. Kuhn, *Children's Literature in the Elementary School*, 3rd ed. (New York: Holt, Rinehart & Winston, 1979), p. 7.
13. Jerome Bruner, "Learning and Thinking," *Harvard Educational Review*, 29 (Summer 1959): 186.
14. Smith et al., *Language and Thinking*, p. 290.
15. Betty Coody, *Using Literature with Young Children* (Dubuque, Iowa: Wm. C. Brown, 1973), p. 22.

16. Cullinan and Carmichael, *Literature and Young Children*, p. 2.
17. Patricia J. Cianciolo, ed., and Picture Book Committee of the National Council of Teachers of English, *Picture Books for Children* (Chicago: American Library Association, 1973), p. 19.
18. Smith et al., *Language and Thinking*, pp. 291–292.

terms of life experiences, emotional development, and conceptual level.[19]

The distinction between fiction and nonfiction is relatively clear. Confusion arises in distinguishing realistic fiction from nonfiction. A great deal of realistic fiction is published for young children to add to their stock of knowledge. Fictional characters such as a fire fighter, farmer, nurse, and taxi driver are used to define job roles and functions. Often these realistic stories package nonfiction information in a more personal format. If the story line is barely discernible, it is likely that children will regard the book as nonfiction or a source of information.

In addition to story and poetry reading and to storytelling, literary experiences may take such forms as story dramatization, creative dramatization, puppetry, flannel-board story telling, and story creation.

Goals and Teaching Approach

The long-term goal in this area is that children use literature for aesthetic, cognitive, and informational purposes. *Aesthetic purposes* include enjoyment of reading; sensitivity to the rhythm, melody, and images of language; and increased understanding of the complexity of human experience and feelings. *Cognitive purposes* feature organizing perceptions, feelings, and ideas in linguistic forms. *Informational purposes* satisfy the needs for knowledge and survival.

While it is difficult to reduce these broad goals to more specific ones, it is useful to identify children's behaviors that may contribute to the long-term goals. Active involvement by choice in literary experiences is the strongest indicator that children are increasing their interest and are learning from these experiences.

---

19. Ibid., p. 301.

A list of such behaviors would include:

1. choosing books, whether for picture reading or actual reading;
2. requesting teachers to read or tell a story;
3. creating stories;
4. recreating stories spontaneously, by narrating or by using puppets, dramatic props, or make-believe props;
5. sharing stories, inviting others to participate in reading or listening;
6. requesting a book for informational purposes;
7. discussing a story spontaneously;
8. insisting on obtaining and using library cards;
9. bringing favorite storybooks from home to share in school;
10. making progress in reading skills and in independent reading.

A broad selection of fiction, nonfiction, poetry, and prose is recommended to meet the needs and interests of the members of the group. Teachers can rotate books from library storage to an open shelf that children maintain with little supervision. Local libraries usually enrich classroom offerings. Making regular visits to the library with the children assures that their selection of books will reflect their interests.

The following guidelines define the role of literature in children's language and reading experiences:

1. *Story reading is usually limited to small groups or individuals.* Successful story reading requires the listener to invest the content with personal meaning, to relate it to one's experiences, and to digest what is heard. Children vary in their ability to tolerate distractions while listening and to sustain involvement.

2. *Fiction is read without the teacher interrupting to ask questions or initiating discussion of pictures, story line, or other facets of the book.* A story is intended to create an experience for the listener-reader, and continuity is critical to its success. Therefore, literary experiences *are not* interrupted for testing comprehension, recalling facts, defining words, or other traditional academic goals. Of course, teachers who know how to dramatize a story will use various ways to heighten suspense and stress imminence of a climax or resolution of a conflict.
3. *Story telling occurs in small groups.* Stories are selected in which word pictures and gestures of the storyteller can carry the meaning. Communication is clearer in small groups.
4. *Story dramatization grows out of repetition of story reading and story telling, when children know the story "by heart."* Successful story dramatization occurs when children know a story so well they can put it in their own words, while also recalling juicy phrases.
5. *Creative dramatization or acting out stories children make up follows skills in dramatizing familiar stories.* The teacher encourages children to dramatize well-known stories before creating their own.
6. *Story reading procedures differ from reviews of information books.* Information books invite discussions at any point, and the completion of the book is a matter of choice. As noted in item two, story reading loses much when it is fragmented.

Table 15-2 summarizes the goals and activities for experiences with literature, noting ways to extend media resources and capitalize on children's expressed interest. For example, for goal one, "to enjoy stories as literature," tape-recorded stories by the teacher extend children's opportunities to hear a story when teachers are otherwise occupied.

Instructional Models 15-3 and 15-4, which follow Table 15-2, illustrate the teaching approach described in the previous list. They feature children's voluntary involvement and honor the distinction between fiction and nonfiction books.

TABLE 15.2. Literature: goals and activities

	Goals	Teacher-prepared activities	Naturally occurring program activities
*1.	Enjoy stories as literature.	Story listening as a literary experience; reading stories without seeking explanatory feedback from the listeners in process. Tape-recorded stories by teacher: Children listen to tapes, with or without head sets, and look at accompanying books. Repetitive listening is encouraged.	Story recordings with or without accompanying pictures or books, chosen by children.

TABLE 15.2. (continued)

Goals	Teacher-prepared activities	Naturally occurring program activities
2. Retell stories.	As a literary experience, children and teachers retelling stories, based on previous readings, without discussing detail, mood, plot, characters, or story line. All story recapitulations by the children are accepted without adult correction, but children may correct each other. When unresolved conflict occurs, reread the story.	Telling stories to "babies" in house play area. Showing pictures and retelling stories to classmates in library area while role playing a teacher, parent, or sibling. Solitary reading and story telling to oneself while looking at pictures or leafing through books.
*3. Dramatize a favorite story.	Dramatizing a well-known story: Teacher helps cast children in roles, offers simple costumes or props, and serves as narrator, unless a child can be given this task. Teacher helps structure dramatization by helping children: • Summarize the story. • Sequence the story for what comes first, next, last. • Decide how to develop action and to communicate. • Keep the activity orderly and not overly long. • Offer book selections at appropriate comfort levels of reading. • Feature book titles on a bulletin board with book jackets or pictures.	As children begin to dramatize characters and stories spontaneously, participating if needed, passing narration to children whenever possible. Children using dress-up clothes and costumes and props, puppets, or flannelboard figures. Spontaneous use of dress-up clothes, costumes, puppets, cutouts, or other materials to dramatize a familiar story or to create a dramatic episode. Conveying appreciation of children's choices for book reading in free-choice activities.
4. Create a story.	Encouraging children to create a new story after they begin to demonstrate interest and skill in dramatizing a familiar story.	

TABLE 15.2. (continued)

Goals	Teacher-prepared activities	Naturally occurring program activities
5. Use nonfiction as an informational resource.	Providing informational books at the children's level of reading, in response to their expressed interest in environmental phenomena, economic activity and job roles, mechanical operations, and physical laws. Introduce new material to extend or revive interest.	
6. Choose storybooks to read.	Offering book selections at appropriate comfort levels of reading. Featuring book titles on bulletin board with book jackets or pictures. Offering children the opportunity to keep a list of books read, including dates of starting and completing the book. Suggesting to children that they retell books read to others, recommending favorites. Encouraging artwork about books read. Suggesting book swaps or mutual lending of individually owned books.	Conveying appreciation of children's choices for book reading in free-choice activities. Helping children select purchases at a school book fair.

BEGINNING READING AND WRITING

Since reading is the process of understanding handwritten and printed messages, successful readers are those who receive the messages accurately and with reasonable speed. Unsuccessful readers face difficulty in decoding, speed, or comprehension.

Formal reading instruction tends to divert the energies of beginning readers toward figuring out the relationship between the sounds and symbols, thus diminishing the focus on meaning. Beginning readers spend most of their time on skills, the need for which they will rapidly outgrow.[20] "Fluent readers strive to grasp chunks of meaning when they encounter print," in contrast to early readers, who are learning how sounds relate to letters and how one word relates to another.[21]

Reading is distinguished from speaking by the reduction in cues and lack of feedback from the message source. That is, the book cannot say, "No, I really meant this...." Whereas, in direct communication, when misunderstand-

20. Smith, *Understanding Reading.*
21. Dorothy Strickland, "On Reading," *Childhood Education*, November–December, 1979, p. 69.

> **INSTRUCTIONAL MODEL 15-3**
> **Literature: Listening to Stories and Books**
> (From Table 15-2, Goal One)
>
> *Goal:*
> Children choose to listen to and enjoy stories and books read by teachers.
>
> *Group Size:* 1, 2, 5
>
> *Materials:*
> stories composed by children on the basis of common school experiences
> stories dictated or written by individual children
> trade books
> tape recorder and cassettes
>
> *Procedure:*
> 1. Keep story-reading groups small and arrange for occasional individual listening experiences.
> 2. Respect children's right to choose to listen or not listen to the story or book the teacher selects.
> 3. Rotate children's opportunities to select the story, regularly reviewing and changing the book selection on the shelves.
> 4. Avoid reading to children when classroom noises are at a high level. At such times, offer children tape recordings and headsets or remove the group to another, quieter room or corner.
> 5. Avoid stopping to discuss events in the story or to ask questions. Accept children's spontaneous comments while maintaining the reading flow. Review familiar stories selectively.
> 6. If the picture book is primarily informational, encourage discussion throughout and terminate the activity when children or teacher lose interest. Finishing the book is not an objective.
> 7. If a picture book is a series of one- or two-page episodes, discontinue reading when interest flags. If children indicate interest, foster discussion of an episode before continuing to the next one.
> 8. If the teacher reads a story written by a child, or if the child is willing to read her or his story, the teacher approves story writing without judging the story.

ings occur in either *decoding* (hearing a word) or *encoding* (phrasing the intended meaning), the speaker has the opportunity to try again to send the intended message. Speakers also use cues of stress, intonation, and often facial or body gestures to clarify meanings. Responders do the same. Consequently, to successfully recognize the ideas, experiences, information, and attitudes conveyed by the written communication, the reader must bring enough previous experience to the reading process.

Observing that reading "is not just learned in school," Kenneth Goodman notes that there are several purposes for reading.[22] Readers obtain the following kinds of information:

22. Kenneth S. Goodman, "Viewpoints: From a Researcher," *Language Arts*, 57, no. 8 (November–December 1980): 846–847.

PROTOTYPE CURRICULUM: LANGUAGE DEVELOPMENT AND BEGINNING READING

INSTRUCTIONAL MODEL 15-4
Literature: Creative Dramatization
(From Table 15-2, Goal Three)

Goals:
1. Children dramatize and narrate familiar stories.
2. Children dramatize events in sequence.

Group Size: 5 to all

Materials:
simple props for dramatization, such as (1) a scarf or (2) a teacher-made "animal face" that consists of paper headband and two long "ears"

Procedure:
1. Help children recall the sequence of the story.
2. Help children identify the characters and specify the action.
3. Cast roles either by assigning them or by asking for volunteers.
4. Direct a practice session by narrating or otherwise helping children to act the story. Encourage children to use their own words and to develop their own actions. Avoid memorization.
5. Refrain from correcting children's speech or actions. Gradually help children recall more details about the role or provide further sources of information, such as rereading the story.
6. Decrease your leadership role as children grow more skillful in dramatizations.
7. Multiply roles to include as many children as possible in the dramatization. For example, in *Caps for Sale,* there can be any number of monkeys; in *Ask Mr. Bear,* there can be any number of animals.

---

1. *Environmental information* includes messages communicated through street signs, traffic signals, house numbers, billboards, labels on public facilities, names of stores and other economic centers, and transportation routes. Young children begin reading environmental information very early.
2. *Functional or object-related information* accompanies manufactured products and includes directions for assembly and use of furniture, toys, games, and machinery. Many young children have also begun to "read" pictured instructions for use of toys and games before they are scheduled to read in formal programs. Later this may take the form of job-related reading, which involves the use of manuals and instruction booklets.
3. *Current events information* includes not only newspaper sources but also magazines and flyers, such as announcements of a political rally. Whether children come in contact with sources of current events depends on home patterns of acquisition and use of such sources.
4. *Familiar textbook information* sources range from simple, single-subject texts, on farm animals, for example, to textbooks with complex subject matter. Children's experience with such books is usually dependent on adult involvement.

In addition to these informational purposes, reading is also a leisure-time activity, one chosen for pleasure and fun.[23]

Hence, most children have already begun to read long before the school initiates a beginning reading program. Children's reading experiences for information and pleasure provide the basis for a beginning reading program. Although children's pleasure reading may vary from cartoons to picture books, children's contact with printed messages assures that teaching reading does not begin with a "blank slate."

APPROACHES TO BEGINNING READING

Generations of Americans have learned to read by a variety of methods; the "incredible fact seems to be that each of these methods worked."[24] Although not everyone was successful with the same method, Robert Aukerman's observation reminds us that all systems have worked for some pupils. This implies that there are some elements common to all beginning reading programs, or that successful readers must be combining key elements of the process in some way that is necessary to success.

Beginning reading programs basically reflect one of two major approaches—based on skill and based on experience.[25] Programs that feature skills place heavy emphasis on *phonics* —word and letter patterns—for strong decoding skills. The language-experience approach emphasizes content and meaning, using the child's natural language as the beginning reading content. Concern here is for comprehension and encoding competence.

The *phonetic or skills approach* to reading requires building skills through knowledge of the sounds associated with the symbols. Once learned, individual letter sounds are combined to lead to word reading and finally to sentence reading. In the phonetic approach, children practice visual discrimination of letters and words, auditory discrimination of sounds (separately and in combination), letter writing, and spelling patterns. Skills are developed independently and cumulatively in an order prescribed by the particular reading system.

Auditory and visual discrimination skills are critical to successful reading if the phonetic approach is used. Comparing and contrasting consonant sounds and letter patterns in words, as in rhyming, leads to recognition of "word families" (for example, *cat, bat, hat,* and *mat*, might form one such family). An outstanding advantage of the skills approach is the early reader's ability to decode new words and content not previously encountered. Decoding skills, say those who favor this approach, lead to earlier independence in reading, than with other approaches, and to generalizing the rules to cover vast areas of handwritten or printed language.

One major problem with using the phonetic approach to beginning reading stems from the irregularity of the alphabet sounds in the English language. The many exceptions to the phonetic rules can create extensive confusion for the beginning reader who is converging the sounds of a set of letters. Critics of the phonics approach point out that skill in decoding words by converging sounds does not assure meaningful reading. Nor does this approach feature comprehension at the beginning stages.[26]

The *language-experience approach* to beginning reading utilizes the children's own language and experiences to produce written material for reading. Important words in the children's vocabulary become the initial reading vocabulary. Written words are associated with experiences, ideas, and feelings, and pictorial material is used to support children's comprehension. Visual discrimination skills

---

23. Ibid.
24. Robert C. Aukerman, *Approaches to Beginning Reading* (New York: John Wiley, 1971), p. 1.
25. Mary A. Jensen and Bette A. Hanson, "Helping Young Children Learn to Read: What Research Says to Teachers," *Young Children*, November 1980, pp. 61–71.

26. Aukerman, *Approaches to Beginning Reading*, chapter 2, pp. 9–89.

are developed as children match words, phrases, and sentences and find similarities and differences in the shapes of words. Sound-symbol relationships, or the phonics skills, are usually fitted in when the teacher decides the children can benefit from them. Supporters of this approach praise the natural way children can "grow into reading" from seeing their own words written to learning a useful sight-word vocabulary. The approach seems unpressured and follows a clear sequence from the familiar (children's own language), to the unfamiliar (the language of books). It saves the child from unnecessary advance drill in phonics, which is offered when it is needed—at the time the child is motivated to learn skills.

Critics of the language-experience approach cite the haphazard pattern of acquiring reading vocabulary words. Since the reading materials grow out of children's language, it is not possible to sequence word lists in advance or to assure appropriate decoding skills. Sound-symbol relationships are not featured, and therefore, critics contend, children are not taught how to decode unfamiliar words.[27]

In both approaches, writing skills are included as part of the beginning reading process. The skill programs require children to copy sets of letters that are the basis for word families, to construct words using common spelling patterns, and to write word lists. The language-experience programs focus children's writing practice on words, phrases, and sentences dictated by the children and on word cards of personal "favorite words."

Analysis of reading programs reveals these common elements, although their importance and the ways they are promoted vary:

1. *Language development:* As discussed previously, oral language experience is a prerequisite for beginning reading.
2. *Visual discrimination:* Skills in distinguishing printed forms and the figure from the background are required.
3. *Auditory discrimination:* Reading includes identifying similarities and differences in language sounds and matching and contrasting words and parts of words.
4. *Directionality for reading:* Writing, as well as reading, requires the ability to track with the eye left to right and top to bottom in two-dimensional space.
5. *Eye-hand coordination:* Skills are required to perceive and reproduce letters and words and to track by hand along the reading path.
6. *Cognitive development:* Reading requires the skills of sorting, classification, and generalization, applied to language sounds, word shapes, and meanings. Readers also have to recognize part-whole relationships.
7. *Symbolic thinking:* To read pictures requires giving meaning to pictured objects and events, interpreting feelings, and mapping print to oral language.
8. *Sequencing:* Readers have to identify and understand the order of actions and events in sequences and time frames.

Not only do both major approaches address the same elements of reading, they also employ overlapping teaching strategies. A current analysis of teaching tactics identifies similarities in:[28]

1. matching activity, with the focus varying from skills to comprehension;
2. using letter, picture, and contextual cues for reading;
3. identifying similarities and differences in forms and ideas;
4. sequencing by constructing and reconstructing words and events;
5. making a word bank;
6. following left-to-right directions and marking words as read.

27. Ibid., chap. 6 and 7, pp. 229–325.

28. Jensen and Hanson, "Helping Young Children," p. 63.

The goal of instruction in all reading programs is to produce fluent readers who enjoy reading. Differences in reading programs lie not in overall, long-term goals but in the short-term goal of decoding versus comprehension and in the emphasis on when and how to teach the needed skills.

A COMPREHENSIVE APPROACH

Our prototype includes activities using aspects of both approaches to beginning reading. Encoding and decoding goals are included without preferring either one. While school systems usually make commitments to a reading program through the purchase of commercial materials, such materials rarely bind the whole instructional reading program. We take the position that an activity-rich program such as we suggest can include elements of both approaches simultaneously, but not necessarily within the same activity.

As noted earlier, young children come to school already reading—obtaining environmental information from signs, advertisements, and pictorial directions. They also demonstrate growing ability in such reading skills as matching language sounds, making visual discriminations of written forms, and obtaining meaning from written symbols. They tell and retell stories, narrating their experiences in sequence, clarifying their language meanings, and translating experience into language.

Visual Discrimination

The ability to make increasingly refined discriminations grows with experience and with concurrent growth in the cognitive skills of dealing with abstract and symbolic forms. (For a discussion of sequencing from the concrete to abstract, refer to Chapter 6). Among activities that feature visual discrimination in the curriculum areas are:

1. *Mathematics:* matching and sorting geometric forms; linear patterning; using lines, circles, and other geometric forms; copying sets to match a model set; matching and copying numerals; and linear measurement;
2. *Science:* comparing and contrasting objects by their attributes, matching identical and similar objects, and sorting and classifying;
3. *Music:* Responding to physical, pictorial, and sound cues in musical-action activities;
4. *Arts and crafts:* creating, matching, and constructing shapes and illustrating stories and personal experiences;
5. *Geography:* matching and comparing labels in the local environment that are related to movement and pathways and replicating signs in the classroom;
6. *Economics:* matching labels on food products in the classroom and in stores, comparing price labels, and using signs and labels in classroom dramatic-play activities.

Specifically, beginning reading activities, as outlined in Table 15–3, include reading signals and pictures, sequencing pictures, matching symbols (including numerals, alphabet letters and words), and reading words and sentences, (see Instructional Model 15–5).

Children use visual discrimination skills in all types of planned and spontaneous program activities. The teacher has many opportunities to extend discriminations without formalizing practice or interrupting children's involvement in activities. Additionally, specific playful activities and games focus children's practice on skills as needed.

TABLE 15.3. Beginning reading: pictures, signs, and symbols

Goals	Teacher-prepared activities	Naturally occurring program activities
1. Read signals and respond appropriately.	Playing signal-action response games: 1. Teachers use: • two action signals; • two picture signals; • two written symbols, such as hieroglyphics; • word signals, such as children's name cards. 2. Children respond with action: • stop-action, such as a stop-and-go game; • two-motion game, such as jumping and clapping.	Giving signals for changing program activities; for example, a five-minute warning before cleanup.
2. Respond to picture stimulators.	Presenting single pictures of high interest that stimulate children to look for detail and to generate meanings from the picture. Comparing and contrasting pictures of similar activities or sequences of action in a set of pictures.	Posted wall pictures that are timely and of high interest provoking examination and discussion by children as they move freely about; such discussion may be extended. Posting artwork of children, which also serves as discussion stimuli to children.
3. Sequence a set of pictures based on cues of action or events.	Sequencing in left-to-right direction with sequence cards: use sequences of photographs of a class activity or trip; sequences of a familiar activity using magazine pictures, commercial sets of pictures, cutouts from discarded books, or flannel board and flannel cutouts.	Leaving packets of sentence cards open for use. Children reading magazines with picture essays. Playing spontaneously with flannel board and a packet of flannel cutouts.

TABLE 15.3. (continued)

Goals	Teacher-prepared activities	Naturally occurring program activities
4. Match symbols and sets of symbols to action or a picture.	See patterning activities for sets of objects and symbols in linear array. See instructional models for mathematics, geometry, matching shape and number, and making identical sets.	From open shelves, using a kit of mixed sets of symbols, letters, numbers, and shapes to match pairs of identical symbols.
5. Match upper- and lower-case alphabet letters.	Lotto or other matching-game format. Stamping matched pairs of letter stamps. Providing sets of alphabet letters in oaktag, flannel, sandpaper, or wood. Using a typewriter to type upper and lower case forms of a letter.	Matching number and letter labels on classroom door, mailboxes and homes. Spontaneous use of letter stamps, sets of letters, or typewriter.
*6. Recognize and replicate names.	Using helper charts with name cards and picture cues of jobs. Playing small-group action games with name cards and cues. Playing card games with three to six sets of name cards for matching, for example: • draw-a-card, as in Old Maid; • concentration type games. Using name cards and sets of cutout letters or lettercards to match to the written name card. Using name cards with letter stamps to replicate one's own name. Using name cards with sets of precut lines and circles to construct letters of name.	Labeling cubbies, children's arts-and-crafts work, and posted attendance sheets in large print. Labeling take-home envelopes individually with each child's name. Posting charts of lower- and upper-case alphabet letters, for noting, identifying, and copying, by choice. Using letter stamps of cardboard, sandpaper, or felt letters.

TABLE 15.3. (continued)

Goals	Teacher-prepared activities	Naturally occurring program activities
	Using name cards with pre-cut letters or stencils for tracing letters. Providing children with lined paper and pencils for voluntary name writing, matching a teacher-made name card. Using a primer typewriter to type a name matched to teacher-made or child-made name card. *Note:* Work first with first names; add surnames later.	
7. Read and write words and sentences.	Creating a class-experience booklet with children, using one to two words or one short sentence per page and illustrating with photographs, drawings, or paste-ups: Duplicate the booklet so each child illustrates his or her copy. Creating a personal-experience booklet with an individual child. Limit script to one to two words or one sentence per page. Labeling artwork selectively with children (not labeling all the artwork automatically). Creating word signs with children to use in activities. For example, "open" or "closed" for store play, office hours for a doctor, or destination names for an airline trip. Recreating with children a simple recipe for finger paint or fruit salad. Duplicate and give each child a copy.	Reviewing a familiar picture storybook, restating the narrative and following written script with the finger. Reading posted signs and labels with one to two words. Using word signs and props in activities requested by children or suggested by teacher. Reading a class library book.

> **INSTRUCTIONAL MODEL 15-5**
> **Beginning Reading: Name Recognition and Replication without Writing**
> (From Table 15-3, Goal Six)
>
> *Goals:* Children recognize and replicate their names with writing.
>
> *Materials:* Provide for each child:
>   alphabet letters of first name made of flannel, precut cardboard, or plastic envelope
>   name card—first name only, written in standard manuscript
>   individual flannel board or other base.
>
> *Procedure:*
> 1. Invite one child at a time to find his or her name card, giving help as needed.
> 2. Give the letters of the first name in an envelope and ask the child to match these to his or her name card. If necessary, demonstrate with the first letter.
> 3. Help check the child's work by comparing letter to letter onward from left to right. Refrain from testing the child's knowledge of letter names by telling the child if he or she falters.
> 4. As children become skillful, add new challenges by including extra letters in the envelope or by adding the appropriate letters of the surname.
> 5. Note: make simple oaktag envelopes for each child, large enough to contain loose letters and the card with the name written in manuscript. At first, the name card may be taped to the outside of the envelope, first name only. The surname may be added later.

Auditory Discrimination

Some activities that feature auditory discrimination are:

1. *Music:* responding to rhythm and melody, pitch and timbre; comparing and contrasting the sounds of the instruments; creating different musical sounds with voice, instruments, and objects;
2. *Science:* discriminating environmental sounds.
3. *Geography:* environmental walks focusing on movement and pathways, using sound cues, directionality, street signs, and traffic symbols.

Rhyming and language play, cited in goals of language development and incorporated into games specifically designed to feature language sounds, are the primary ways for developing specific auditory discrimination skills. Other ways are featured in the curriculum areas of music, science, and geography.

Directionality for Reading and Writing

Curriculum activities featuring directionality include:

1. *Mathematics:* In the process of checking, use linear patterning, which focuses on beginning at the left and moving to the right.
2. *Music and geography:* Focus on orientation in space as a move toward mastery of directionality.

Activities for goal three, Table 15-3 incorporate practice in reading directionality.

Eye-hand Coordination

Improvement in eye-hand coordination permeates all activities in which children are active—in arts and crafts construction with manipulative materials, woodworking, dramatic play, and the routines of cleanup and donning clothing.

Cognitive Development

As noted earlier, cognitive development is another pervasive program feature. All curriculum content areas stress cognitive challenges, problem solving, and use of cognitive skills.

Symbolism and Sequencing

Literature and language development, as discussed earlier in this chapter, continuously emphasize these elements. The use of picture cues in music and movement activities is an example of the way in which the various aspects of the program are integrated to contribute to program goals.

Program Design

Beginning reading goals are approached through specifically designed activities (as noted in Table 15-3) and supported in pervasive teaching strategies (as outlined earlier in the chapter). Children participate in activities by choice, so the teacher is challenged to design projects that will attract and hold their interest. Lack of progress in beginning reading alerts the teacher to design more effective activities.

The design encourages work with individual children and small groups, relating instruction to the specific needs of each child. It requires a great deal of story reading by teachers and story recreating and creating by children. Experience, action, and communication are viewed as interrelated. Some skills, regarded as generally facilitative, are offered early, others when needed. Primers, workbooks, and readers from various programs can be used selectively. In lower elementary grades, where teachers are obligated to schedule formal instructional periods in reading, games may be added to further needed skills, along with fun and laughter. When children practice desired skills in a happy context, mastery is more likely to occur than when practice is restricted to mandated periods.

Writing

Writing practice can take many forms. A popular practice activity is to offer children models of lines and curves to copy on double-sized writing spaces. Other activities, based on the Montessori program, include providing oaktag or wooden models of letters to trace and sandpaper models of alphabet letters for finger tracing. Writing skill is often practiced after arranging wooden, felt, or oaktag letters into words and sentences; after typing letters, words, and sentences on a sturdy primer typewriter; or after using letter stamps with an inked stamp pad.

Writing skills are developed following the same pattern used in other areas of the prototype program. Children begin writing after extensive manipulative experiences with letters, which may be made of flannel, sandpaper, wood, or cardboard, and which may be movable or on fixed bases. They begin by putting together words to replicate their names and other words of interest. As they demonstrate interest and skill in writing through spontaneous efforts to make letter shapes, they are encouraged to copy their names. With growth in reading, writing interests expand and children begin to seek to write more than their names (see Instructional Model 15-5). The gradual process that progresses from copying a word to reproducing a word from memory parallels progress in other elements in reading. When children can reproduce written letters from memory, they are launched into writing. Further growth depends on interest generated through program activities.

SUMMARY

Language development, growth in literary experiences, and beginning reading are major goals in this program. The long-term goal is to produce fluent readers who enjoy reading. Acquisition of the native language occurs most rapidly in the early years, so that children have acquired the rudiments of communication before entering school. Language as a communication tool develops most rapidly when used to fulfill its purpose of exchanging messages. Our prototype program features respect for children's natural language and fosters communication in all areas of the program. Dialects are also respected, while the standard English dialect is added. Teachers communicate with children by listening and talking, initiating and responding in an action-based environment, as children engage in activities of choice and of interest.

Literary experiences to foster personal development and meet curriculum goals include the activities of story reading, and story telling, dramatization, and puppetry in the forms of fiction and nonfiction, prose and poetry. Literary experiences are provided for children, primarily in small groups or individually.

Beginning reading and writing include focus on common elements of the reading process evidenced in all programs, whether based on skills or language experience. Skills for reading are featured in many aspects of the program, as well as activities specifically designed to focus on one or more skills.

EXERCISES

1. Select two different books to read to children, one informational book and one literary, and tape record your reading.
   a. After listening to the tape, analyze your presentation for differences in continuity, discussions, children's questions and interest, and teacher's questions.
   b. Summarize any conclusions you make for needed changes in presentation.
   c. Repeat taping of reading the same two books to other children and analyze the tape again.
2. Observe or work with a small group on beginning reading.
   a. Identify problems and questions concerning reading materials, methods, grouping, duration of lesson, setting, or other features.
   b. Summarize briefly needs for change.

BIBLIOGRAPHY

Aukerman, Robert C. *Approaches to Beginning Reading.* New York: John Wiley, 1971.

Bruner, Jerome. "Learning and Thinking." *Harvard Educational Review,* 29 (Summer 1959): 184–192.

Cazden, Courtney B. "Suggestions from Studies of Early Language Acquisition." In Courtney Cazden, ed., *Language in Early Childhood Education.* Washington, D.C.: National Association for the Education of Young Children, 1972.

Chukovsky, Kornei. *From Two to Five.* Berkeley, Calif.: University of California Press, 1963.

Cianciolo, P. J., ed., and Picture Book Committee of the National Council of Teachers of English. *Picture Books for Children.* Chicago: American Library Association, 1973.

Coody, Betty. *Using Literature with Young Children.* Dubuque, Iowa: Wm. C. Brown, 1973.

Cullinan, Bernice E., and Carmichael, Carolyn W., eds. *Literature and Young Children.* Urbana, Ill.: National Council of Teachers of English, 1977.

Donaldson, Margaret. *Children's Minds.* New York: W. W. Norton, 1978.

Goodman, Kenneth S. "Viewpoints: From a Researcher." *Language Arts*, 57, no. 8 (November-December 1980): 846–847.

Huck, Charlotte S., and Kuhn, Doris Y. *Children's Literature in the Elementary School.* 3rd ed. New York: Holt, Rinehart & Winston, 1979.

Jensen, Mary A., and Hanson, Bette A. "Helping Young Children Learn to Read: What Research Says to Teachers." *Young Children*, November, 1980.

Labov, William. *Language in the Inner City: Studies in Black English Vernacular.* Philadelphia: University of Pennsylvania Press, 1972.

Smith, E. Brooks; Goodman, Kenneth S.; and Meredith, Robert. *Language and Thinking in the Elementary School.* New York: Holt, Rinehart & Winston, 1970.

Smith, Frank. *Understanding Reading.* New York: Holt, Rinehart & Winston, 1971.

Strickland, Dorothy. "On Reading." *Childhood Education*, November–December, 1979.

IV Curriculum Resources

A creative curriculum design, we have suggested, requires a framework that is coherent and that feels right. Such a design necessarily draws on the cultural and physical features of the surrounding community and on the many resources it offers for first-hand experiencing. To be contemporary and fill current needs, the design must also be in tune with the strong social and political forces of the times.

Teachers learn the resources of their own community personally, through colleagues and printed sources and through parents and community agencies. Keeping current with social and political forces results from wide reading and especially graduate study.

This section suggests the ways in which curriculum designs evolve from the resources in each community and from the ideas that are timely. Marrying vital resources to selected curriculum components leads to uniquely relevant learning experiences for children.

16 Resources for a Vital Curriculum

A curriculum must always draw strength, excitement, relevance, and dynamism from the human, cultural, and environmental resources available. Strength comes from the immediacy and availability of the resources. Even young children know when they are dealing with content that excites their families and friends. How else can one explain the interest young children demonstrated in the nuclear accident near Harrisburg, Pennsylvania, or in the traveling King Tut exhibit? Dynamism implies action and movement, which for young children means personal participation and experiences with new interest and ideas.

Resources that can support any curriculum design are reviewed in this chapter in the three broad categories of the natural environment, geographic resources, and people. It is our premise that programs flourish when they reflect the resources and interests that are unique to the local area. While other chapters in this book offer guidelines for identifying the ways in which activities foster cognitive, academic, social, physical, and emotional development and learning, this chapter describes the resources that serve as the substance of productive activity designs. These resources function appropriately as the "stuff," of curriculum, rather than as enrichment or added attractions.

Contemporary cultural resources that are rapidly spreading throughout the country include:

1. live music of all kinds;
2. square, folk, and disco dancing;
3. arts and crafts of every kind—photography, painting, glass blowing, pottery, quilt making, rug making, bookbinding, print making, batiking, woodworking, leather work, jewelry making, and many more;
4. traveling art exhibits, new local galleries, museums, and concert halls that provide more exposure to artists and more viewing to art-conscious people;
5. radio and television programs that bring rich museum collections and first-rate concerts and operas from far away into family living rooms.

An increasingly better-educated, leisure-oriented, and art-hungry populace seeks to create or experience creations of other people's art. These vast new audiences for art and music often include young children in the family party.

Environmental interests, even broader, are found everywhere in health-related activities such as jogging, roller skating, tennis, cross-country skiing, water sports, hiking, rock climbing, backpacking, and camping. Outdoor enthusiasts include gardeners, bird-watchers, and nature walkers. Campaigns to improve the physical environment are beamed at children as well as adults. Publicity of many types attempts to raise people's consciousness about their responsibilities for environmental improvement.

These cultural interests and activities are the life blood of relevant curriculum content in early childhood classrooms. The use of these resources depends on the conceptual framework of the program. How children's learning is selected, sequenced, and implemented reflects the teacher's commitment to a particular approach to early childhood education, as discussed in Section One. In this chapter, possible activities are suggested to illustrate how resources may serve curriculum development in almost any design.

This chapter will discuss curriculum resources in terms of:

1. the natural environment, including weather, plant, and animal life;
2. human geography, or patterns of land use;
3. human resources, or how people affect children's learning.

THE NATURAL ENVIRONMENT

Walks in the school neighborhood often focus on the natural environment with its weather variations and related growth cycles. Here children can study stability and change in the weather.

Weather

The weather phenomena of an area offer predictable, as well as occasional, unpredictable sets of events. The unpredictable event, such as a rainbow, is a novelty providing excitement. However, rainbows are too rare in most settings to become dependable curriculum resources. Consequently, it is the predictable events that offer the greatest curriculum possibilities.

Predictable weather phenomena, such as rain, wind, snow, fog, clouds, thunder, lightning, and seasonal plant cycles, may be:

1. predicted in advance,
2. observed in process,
3. observed for effects,
4. mediated.

For example, rain can be:

1. *predicted in advance* by observing signals of approach, such as dark clouds, wind, distant thunder, and lightning;
2. *observed in process*, noting such features as wetting of plant life, streets, automobiles, and people; puddling; and water run-off patterns;
3. *observed for effects*, such as raised water levels on streams or lakes, visible water paths, or inundated areas;
4. *studied* by creating rain effects, such as making dams or changes in water channels.

Selection of activities depends on children's interest, age, and prior experience. A more experienced group may deal with a major environmental concern, such as erosion. Noting erosion in a planted area, for example, children may consider how to alter the water path to be a realistic problem-solving activity. Concern for preserving natural resources adds immediacy to experimental problem solving and repeated testing of solutions. Such activities stir children to seek the meaning of observed changes. As children discuss their findings, vocabulary and language usage grow in active exchange.

Table 16–1 lists some ways to use rain as a curriculum resource in early childhood classrooms. Specific examples are given of observation in process, observation of effects, predicting procedures, and mediating procedures for soil-, sand-, and water-pouring tasks. The table illustrates a way to plan and review weather study, identifying activities and learning in concepts and skills. Activities that can be featured during the snow season are also listed.

RESOURCES FOR A VITAL CURRICULUM

TABLE 16.1. Resources in the natural environment

Resource and possible activities	Concept building	Skill development
Precipitation Rain: • *Predicting* based on such clues as cloud formations, temperature, sound, humidity, wind, barometric pressure, and the behavior of animals, especially birds; listening to weather forecasts on radio and television. • *Observing* rain-related changes in the environment. • *Recording* frequency: class graphs frequency weekly, monthly, and seasonally. • *Exploring effects*, finding "wetness" after rain; water accumulation; water run-off patterns; effects on plants, shrubs, and trees, such as falling leaves, branches, and bark; reading rain gauge. • *Mediating effects* based on observed changes: design and test some ways to alter water pathways, such as creating dams for water run-off, covering seedlings with protective covers, and diverting run-off to different channels. • *Collecting rain* in catch buckets, measuring the amount, and comparing the amounts in different-sized catch buckets. • *Charting monthly rainfall* in inches, using a rain gauge.	Rain occurs in cycles: visible cycle includes *signals* (such as clouds, wind, lightning, and thunder) and *effects* (such as wet surfaces or broken tree limbs). *Key Ideas:* forces interact; moving water is a force. The universe is constantly changing. Erosion changes various natural and man-made objects such as stream banks and pot holes. The force of moving water may affect people adversely or beneficially. Adverse effects: floods; fields too wet to plant; destruction of harvests, bridges, and roadways; flooded houses. Desirable effects: clean roads and streets; planted fields watered; reservoirs filled for drinking water; lakes and streams filled for navigation, fishing, and recreation (boats and swimming). Effects of erosion can be mediated. Water movement can be redirected, speed and force can be reduced, or both. People can control or minimize damage from natural occurrences or, if this is impossible, damage can often be repaired. Liquid measure, *more* and *less*. Rainfall can be measured using a standard measure. Records and symbols preserve information—use bar charts for monthly records.	Observation skills. Vocabulary development. Prediction skills. Math skills of graphing. Numerical comparison of sets. Ordering sets. Comparison and contrast. Measurement. Making inferences. Forming hypotheses. Testing hypotheses, seeking confirming data. Problem-solving skills, including identifying problems, making hypotheses, and testing them. Finding questions to ask and finding ways to answer them. Measurement skills for liquid volume. Using symbols to make charts and records of collected information.

TABLE 16.1. (continued)

Resource and possible activities	Concept building	Skill development
Snow: • *Predicting:* as for rain. • *Observing:* exploring coldness and melting. Feeling snow, collecting and storing it in the room, refrigerator, or freezer. Examining melted snow for dirt and debris. Watching snow melt outdoors and watching water run-off. • *Manipulating:* making snowballs, snow structures, and snow people. Shoveling snow; stamping down snow; making "people" or other forms in snow; and drawing in snow. • *Identifying effects* on people and objects in the environment. Movement: slipping, sliding, skidding. Clothing: boots, mittens, parkas Schedules: changes and delays in transportation, in work and recreation schedules, in planned activities	Weather data and weather cycles. Temperature changes and effects on snow. Change in temperature affects the state of some materials. Snow has a variety of characteristics. Uses of snow for fun. *Key Ideas:* Interrelationships exist between living things and the natural environment. Human beings, animals, and plants adapt to the natural environment. Effects of snow on transportation, work, recreation, schedules, and planned activities.	Exploring properties of objects. Language development. Gross and fine motor skills. Observation skills. Expressive art skills: drawing and construction. Sequencing events. Seeing relationships between events, cause-and-effect relationships, time-and-space relationships.
Wind: • *Observing and describing effects:* watching the movement of objects; feeling wind on the face and body; and viewing such effects on plants as seed dispersal. • *Classifying effects* as desirable, undesirable; under conditions of strong or mild wind, warm or cold weather, playing cards outdoors, or drawing on papers.	Cause-and-effect relationships in terms of force, speed, and distance. Wind scatters seeds, replanting fields and forests. Effects of wind may be desirable or undesirable to people based on circumstances. People adapt to nature. People use wind as energy. People measure wind direction and force. Protection from wind.	Observation and communication skills. Perceptual skills. Cause-and-effect relationships. Classifying: vocabulary development. Sequencing events. Evaluating effects. Problem-solving skills on how to shield animals and objects from the wind. Placement of shield and stability of shield.

TABLE 16.1. (continued)

Resource and possible activities	Concept building	Skill development
• *Mediating effects:* Building windshields for selected purposes. Experimenting with different sizes and shapes of windshields. Making instruments for wind power. Making pinwheels and testing them. Making and flying kites. Experimenting to find ways to make kites fly higher or faster. Making wind or weather vanes, noting wind changes and rates. Drying clothes in wind. Drying wet chalkboard by hand fanning or with wind from windows.	Tools can measure wind. Evaporation can be hastened by wind as force and energy.	Adaptation to natural events. Use of natural energy source. Making tools to measure wind.

As learning activities develop, teachers may want to refer to texts on meteorology to assure accuracy and breadth of content. Teachers will find not only new information, but also newer organizing ideas to pattern and categorize facts. Teachers may like the broad integrating key-concept approach, such as Gerald Craig's six large science patterns,[1] or the modern discovery-action programs,[2] or the more traditional content clusters found in standard science texts for the elementary school.

Teachers, secure in their own understanding, can plan for more than fact collection by building in process goals, such as solving problems, setting problems or seeking causal, temporal, or quantitative relationships. Time relationships at this early age begin as gross ideas of *now*, *before*, and *after* and gradually grow with experience and further development.

---

1. Initially introduced in Gerald S. Craig, *Science for the Elementary School Teacher* (Boston: Ginn, 1947). Elaborated on and expanded in *National Society for the Study of Education, Forty-Sixth Yearbook,* part 1: *Science Education in American Schools,* sec. 2 (Chicago: University of Chicago Press, 1947), pp. 60–105. A concise summary of these concepts especially intended for teachers of young children may be found in Mary Sheckles, *Building Children's Science Concepts* (New York: Teachers College Press, 1958). In this summary, Sheckles adds one additional concept to Craig's six, thus establishing seven basic, or overriding, concepts in science education.

2. For a clear and readable review of six discovery-action programs that were developed initially in the 1960s under federal grants, see Barbara Waters, *Science Can Be Elementary: Discovery Action Programs for K–3* (New York: Citation Press, 1973).

Replicating Natural Occurrences

Experiences that occur naturally can often be fashioned in the classroom. This increases possibilities for comparison and contrast of events, for changes, for transformations, and for problem resolutions.[3] As children repeat experiences in the classroom, they can begin to test their hunches and understanding. The major benefits of replicating experiences in the classroom are that:

1. children can inquire, discover, and think through experiences based on repeated trials over which they have some control;
2. the teacher feels no urgency to complete the instruction before nature changes the conditions;
3. there is time to plan for desired integration of this content with other processes and skills;
4. there is time to follow individual children's interests.

Since the weather cycle cannot be controlled, replication of some conditions in the classroom allows for some control. Ecological learning can be developed through such participant experiences.

In one kindergarten classroom, the water-table activities concentrated on exploring water trails in a multilevel system of containers with spigots, overflow tubes, catch basins, and water runs (see Figure 16–1). Over a period of several weeks, the children spent many hours experimenting with such concepts as gravity, speed, force, liquid quantity, and fluidity. Children can deal with these forces without naming them, although some insist on knowing the labels. Finding out what happens when water is poured quickly, slowly, and through sprinkling cans on different soils suggests further ecological study.

The Sun

As a pervasive natural resource, the sun offers children interesting ways to study shadows, heating effects, and color fading. Although direct observation of the sun is unsafe and usually unrewarding, the effects of the sun can be studied both in process and after the fact.

Initially, children discover shadows in relation to themselves or other people. Shadows challenge logic when elongated shapes and other distortions lead children to compare the object with its shadow. A further step is observing the shadow patterns cast by the same object at different times of the day. A simple sun dial can be made by implanting a vertical stick in soil. Children can observe the sun dial at regular intervals, marking the movement of the shadow by copying its length on the ground. On pavement, chalk marks can be made. In this way the children find themselves making a clock face simply by drawing a circle around a vertical marker.

The heat of the sun suggests other activities. Noticeable during the warmer seasons, sunlight shows effects on such heat-sensitive objects as one's own body, ice cubes, soft plastic, or flowers and leaves. One can also compare exposed and shaded surfaces of an object for their relative temperatures. When children talk spontaneously about their explorations, teachers see purpose in extending learning to how people adapt to the sun's heat and light. Children may wish to construct sun-protective objects, such as hats, parasols, and shelters.

---

3. In *Building Children's Science Concepts*, Sheckles suggests a wide variety of activities, that may be developed in the classroom, that relate to basic areas of knowledge in the sciences and coordinate with the seven large concepts that may be fostered by participation in these activities. Also, activity ideas usually are included in the teachers' texts to illustrate how science ideas apply to concrete situations. In addition, special science programs, such as the discovery action programs and the publishers' programs, include detailed activities that are clustered and goal-related.

RESOURCES FOR A VITAL CURRICULUM 271

FIGURE 16.1. Illustration of water table with water runs

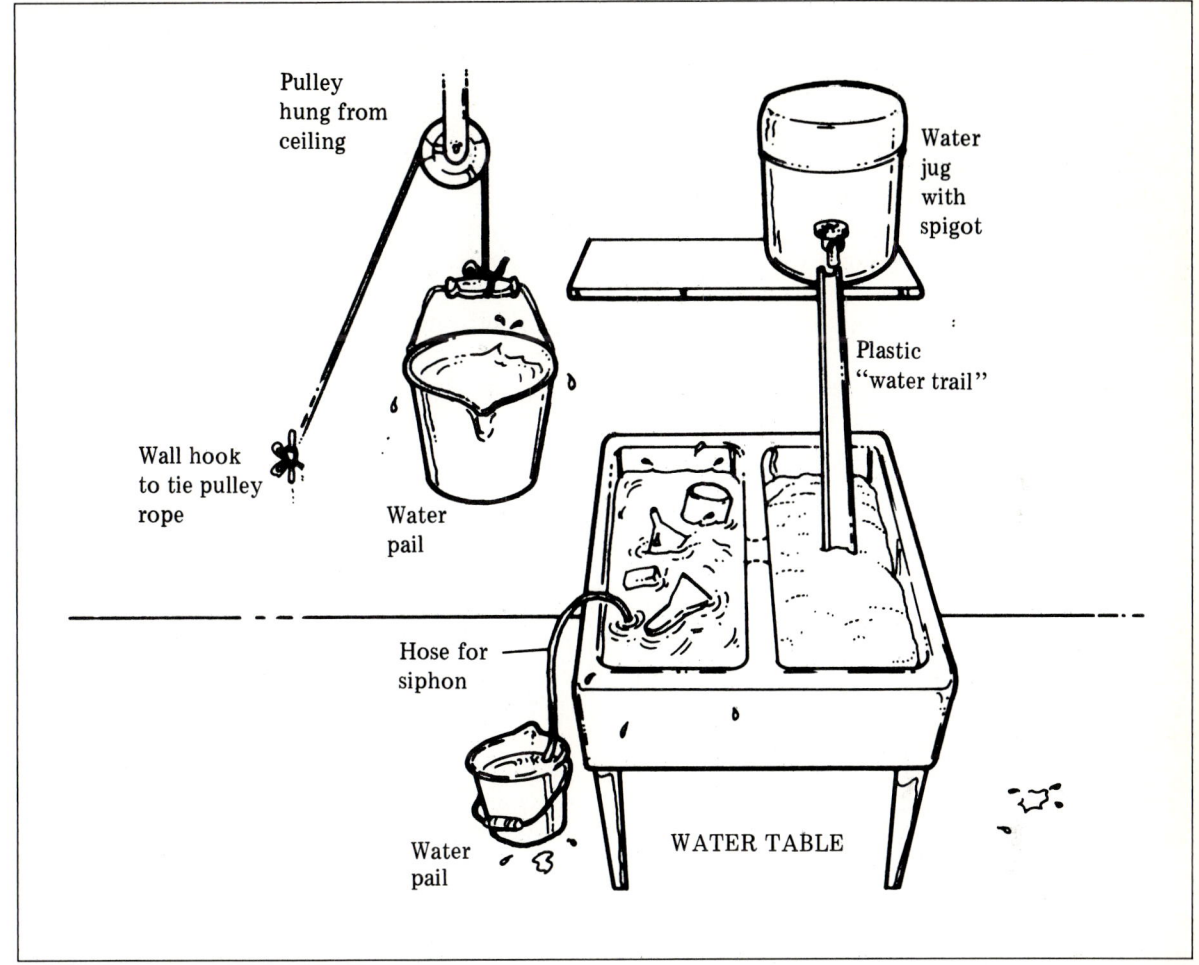

Heat, of course, produces energy. A simple use of the sun's heat as energy can be shown in making yogurt on a sunny, warm day. Teachers know how exciting it is to see large thermometers register temperature increases when the column of mercury lengthens. Evaporation also challenges children to wonder about cause-effect relationships, for example, when the chalk board dries.

The sun, therefore, offers many opportunities to play with, observe, wonder about, discuss, and experiment with such high-interest content as shadows and heating effects. The many ways in which the sun's heat is a source of energy for plant, animal, and human life can be explored in the old and new uses of solar energy. Greenhouses, cold frames, solar roof panels, and many other simple and complex ways of harnessing solar energy are to be found everywhere.

As children explore the natural environment, the many adjustments people make to weather phenomena can be organized to begin to shape concepts of adaptability in nature.

Ways of adaptation to weather include dressing appropriately, using special gadgets such as fans or umbrellas, changing one's rate of movement, using adapted vehicles to cope with special weather conditions, and enjoying recreation appropriate to the weather.

Children can observe the effects of snow on people, animals, and objects in the environment. They note changes in the speed of locomotion and changes in dressing and eating patterns that alter with the weather. Other repetitive weather occurrences may be analyzed for similar use, as illustrated in Table 16–1, which lists resources and learning activities for this purpose.

Plant Life

Luxuriant landscapes offer extensive materials to be collected, compared, sorted, discussed, named, and otherwise studied. In less abundant sites, indoor plantings and various media (such as slides, films, television, and pictures) can supplement intensive local study.

Plant study includes beginning to understand the cycle of growth and renewal, focusing on:

1. kinds of plants;
2. ways of plant renewal, such as seeds, runners, cuttings, and bulbs;
3. needs for survival and growth;
4. process goals, such as comparison and contrast, sorting, classification, and *seriation* (arranging in some order such as length).

In plant study, children can experiment and control outcomes. Cause-and-effect relationships become apparent as children gain some control over their immediate environment.

Process goals with plant study Process goals are easily achieved with studies of plants. Leaf and flower collections and rock and soil collections stimulate comparing and contrasting objects, sorting and classifying sets of materials, and experimenting to discover their properties.

Collecting experiences may highlight similarities in location as well as in the nature of the objects themselves, that is, one can organize one's findings in terms of where the objects were found. Samples of objects found on the ground or under the tree lead to the problem of finding out which objects were originally a part of the tree. Twigs, branches, bark, leaves, berries, pine cones, seed pods, and seeds represent parts of the plant system. Rocks and soil represent parts of other systems. Differentiating the plant system from the surrounding area is itself a major conceptual and classification problem. Still another system includes human trash, such as tin cans, bottles, boxes, paper, and other man-made objects. Thus, sorting tasks may include sorting (1) by location, (2) by properties of objects, (3) by natural versus man-made origin, and (4) within natural systems by plant versus nonplant origin. All of these sorting tasks require much activity, manipulation, and invention of sorting concepts.

Transferring plant study to the classroom requires replicating the external system where possible. Thus, children can repeat experiences in ways not possible outdoors, experimenting with conditions for growth and survival on a day-to-day basis. However, placing plants in the classroom may not necessarily involve children in meaningful study. It is necessary to relate classroom experiences to outdoor observations to assure that plants will be more than decorative.

Growing plants can be measured by comparing leaf size, stem length, and flower and seed size. Measurements can be charted by using samples of the plant parts, by using string or paper strips, by graphing, or by tallying. Drawings or photographs make charts clearer. Interesting recording and graphing ideas may be found in the Nuffield Project materials, to be used when appropriate to integrate math and science learning activities.[4]

4. *Nuffield Mathematics Project Booklets* (New York: John Wiley, 1969).

Play opportunities Children who play outdoors typically move into constructive and dramatic play, including tree climbing. Where a tree house or platform can be added without danger to the tree or the children, a parent-teacher-child construction project may be an appropriate school activity. A tire, rope swing, or rope ladder may be included. Some trees are better suited to ground-level platforms, with portable types of equipment, such as tents or movable shelters.

Population-dense inner city environments often permit access to trees and natural ground cover only in public parks, where these are suitable for young children. Adventure playgrounds, "vest-pocket" parks, and roof top play areas are alternate designs for inner-city children.[5]

Teaching suggestions Following the procedure recommended earlier for the weather-cycle content, it is suggested that the teacher list the kinds of plantings that grow or are cultivated in the neighborhood. Table 16–2 indicates activities and learning related to a variety of natural plant resources. Note that the activities range from more loosely structured arts-and-crafts experiences to planned collections and systematic studies. The use of natural materials in art has become very popular, and children can make wall hangings and other art forms making maximum use of their own ideas.

However, ecological concerns dictate that care be exercised in using natural materials so as not to endanger the balance of nature. Appropriate study of natural resources always includes ecological concerns, which we believe are best taught in the context of active learning experiences, when interest is high.

---

5. Adventure playgrounds is an idea developed recently in England. Instead of manufactured play equipment, such as slides and swings, only raw materials are provided, such as boards and bricks.

Geological Formations

Geological formations of the local area include hills, valleys, rock formations, waterways and water basins, forests, bogs, deserts, meadows, caves, and mines. Inclines and declines in land formations lend themselves to active physical exploration with considerable cognitive outcomes. Steeper hills challenge young learners to explore visually as well as physically. Objects and people lose some of their familiar characteristics when seen at a distance or from a height, stimulating reflection on the difference between near and far and on changing perspective.

Correlating movement to soil conditions flows from actively exploring land surfaces. Rocky hills are unsuitable for sliding and rolling. Wagons and tricycles sink into soft, sandy surfaces. Experiments can continue in the classroom at the sand or salt table, where children can roll miniature cars and trucks on level or inclined paths. Piaget emphasized, you will recall, that children construct physical knowledge out of activity and manipulation of objects that offer direct feedback without the need for explanations by the teacher.

Children's physical activity fosters knowledge of the factors that influence speed and distance over surfaces, especially force, friction, and energy. Ground cover; inclines; curves; angles on roadways, pathways, and open fields; and land surfaces are all part of children's active outdoor experiences.

Environments containing bodies of water offer opportunities for examining their uses for business and pleasure. Science activities, after a well-focused trip, may include observing floating and sinking objects in water, movement of people and vehicles on land, and the mechanics of loading and unloading merchandise. The provision of simple pulleys, ropes, and small berry baskets or other containers is likely to stimulate exciting activities in the mechanics of loading, especially in the block area of the classroom. Initial waterway exploration may stimulate activities in physical

TABLE 16.2. Resources in the natural environment: trees, plants and vegetation

Resources and possible activities	Concept building	Skill development
Uncultivated ground cover—grass, weeds, clover, and small bushy plants: • Collect samples of the variety of plant growth, such as ground cover, for comparison and contrast of leaf formations, tactile properties, size, and shape. • Sort collections. • Match leaves to pictures. • Use in craft projects as decoration or to replicate ground cover. • Make a resource book of samples of local ground cover. Store in clear plastic for future use.	Parts of plants have unique characteristics. Leaves of all plants have some common properties. Natural materials may be preserved. There is variety in uncultivated ground covering plants. Materials may be arranged so that like things are put together in some ways. Plants and vegetation have natural beauty in texture, color, shape, and arrangement.	Visual discrimination. Comparison and contrast. Sorting and classifying. Tallying or graphing quantities. Seriating: ordering by size or color. Matching object to picture or symbol. Completing a planned craft project.
Flowering plants, uncultivated and cultivated: • Adopt a plant: record growth pattern, flowering cycle, colors, numbers of flowers and flower petals, duration of flowering season, leaf growth, and height. • Observation walk: record evidence of different-colored flowers in the environment by making a color chart. • Begin plants in the classroom. • Record growth and change. • Compare plant growth. • Preserve flowers in water or pressed in wax paper.	Plants have a variety of systems by which they reproduce. Plants have growth patterns. Change in the environment is universal. Plants are part of an ecosystem and are affected by all parts of the system. We help to maintain ecological balance by refraining from destructive acts and by helping to replant where necessary. Plants vary in growth, speed, pattern, and in needs for water, light, and food. Forms of preservation include drying and placing in water, among other ways.	Recording skills. Vocabulary skills and language development. Comparison and contrast. Measurement skills. Communicating observations. Classifications and ecological learning and concerns. Contrasting moist and dry.

TABLE 16.2. (continued)

Resources and possible activities	Concept building	Skill development

Trees
 • *Measuring:* comparing measures of height, and thickness of trunk and of span of branches; leaf size.
 • *Estimating:* types of trees most numerous in locality.
 • *Comparing and contrasting* properties:
   Collect leaves and sort by shape and color or other attribute.
   Collect seed pods, pine cones, bark, and branches on ground under trees; compare and contrast.
   Make collages of tree wastes.
   Collect man-made objects found under trees. Examine budding trees, rate of bud growth, and differences between trees.
   Compare animal life in trees, crawling animals such as ants and spiders, rodents, squirrels, and birds.
   Identify foods different animals eat.
   Compare size and construction of animal homes in trees.
   Use photographs of animals to compare and match with observations.
 • *Tree-planting* ceremonies.
 • *Play:* use trees in dramatic play and as props for athletic activities.
	There are varieties of measuring devices, both arbitrary and standard.
	 Trees vary in terms of such physical properties as size, leaf shape, fruit and flowers, color, bark texture, and trunk thickness.
	 Trees change by cycles of growth and decay in seasons.
	 Tree rings give evidence of the tree's age.
	 Trees are invaluable resources for wood, food, shade, and climate maintenance.
	 There is ecological balance between trees and animals.
	 Variety exists in animal life.
	 Trees can be planted to renew tree resources.
	 Use natural environment for recreation while respecting ecological balance.
		Estimating and comparing sizes and lengths.
		 Gross and arbitrary measures and standard measures.
		 Problem solving, such as how to measure circumference.
		 Sorting.
		 Perceptual skills.
		 Observation skills.
		 Measuring skills: timetables.
		 Vocabulary development.
		 Descriptive terms and noun labels.
		 Classifying: natural objects and man-made.
		 Using magnifying glasses and field glasses.
		 Matching object to picture.
		 Planting skills.
		 Caring for the environment: use but do not destroy.

science, ecology, geography, and economics. For example, economic concepts may focus on how goods are shipped, how the labor force is involved in loading operations, and what the differences are in movement on water and land surfaces. The recreational uses of waterways are well known.

Animals

Depending on personal preferences, teachers may choose for study animals ranging in size from the small, nonthreatening ladybug to the full-grown rabbit. Those who enjoy caring for animals find many ways to include them in the curriculum. Some are animal-shy, preferring ant farms to animals that demand more intimate care.

The ground provides a home for many small animals that may be studied in their natural habitat or collected in see-through bottles or plastic boxes. There are texts now offering instruction on how to construct an ant farm for teachers who prefer to do so.[6]

Animal study need not be confined to direct handling of animals. In fact, animal-shy teachers may build a comfort level by starting with children's experiences in many aspects of animal life, including:

1. animal sounds;
2. animal tracks or other signals of their presence, such as food scraps, body wastes, footprints, holes in the ground, mounds, webs, fossils, or nests;
3. animal adaptation to the environment through nest building, hole digging, migrating, changing color, or hibernating;
4. animals making food nests, storing food, or using feeders.

---

6. Glenn O. Blough and Marjorie H. Campbell, *Making and Using Classroom Science Materials* (New York: Dryden Press, 1954), pp. 51–53.

The teacher who finds it difficult to care for animals in the classroom can encourage children to observe the ways of animals in their natural habitat. Observing birds, insects, squirrels, chipmunks, and other small mammals, as well as fish, tadpoles, and frogs, is possible in most areas. In the classroom, field glasses and good field guidebooks may produce rewarding learning experiences.

Table 16–3 summarizes activity designs for learning about the ways animals live in the natural habitat and about ways to explore animals' living patterns. Included are such activity suggestions as trips to zoos, parks, fields, forests, or untrafficked areas to find animal sounds, footprints, or ground holes or to locate birds, ants, or spiders. Concepts to pursue on trips or in school activities range from distinguishing types of animal shelters to understanding metamorphosis. Skills include perceptual, auditory, sorting, and classifying skills, as well as making inferences, relating cause and effect, and increasing language skills. Ecological concerns are listed for early learning. Teachers should not forget that there are many enchanting children's books about animals, how they are born, grow, and adapt to the environment.

HUMAN GEOGRAPHY

Many people who have studied geography learned chiefly the names of places on a map. People often learned about crops and sometimes noted shipping and railroad centers. Although there was some imaginative teaching, school geography tended to be a long string of isolated facts to be memorized.

As early as the mid-1930s pioneers in education such as Lucy Sprague Mitchell were transforming geography into a vital study of the process of change in which physical and human geography interact with each other. Mitchell's approach to geography emphasized the interdependence of human beings and the environ-

TABLE 16.3. Using natural resources: animals

Resource and possible activities	Concept building	Skill development
Animal signs outdoors: • *Sounds:* trips to local parks, meadows, or undeveloped or uncultivated areas, such as marsh, fields, or wooded plots. • *Tracks:* trips to untrafficked areas to find such evidence of animals as footprints, webs, food scraps, and ground holes.	There is variety in nature. Animals have identifiable characteristics. There is variety in nature, especially in eating and movement patterns. Animals adapt and create their own shelters. Life patterns of animals have an impact on the environment. There is interdependence in nature.	Auditory discrimination. Sorting by auditory and visual characteristics. Vocabulary. Cause-and-effect relationships: making inferences and testing them. Visual discrimination. Relating events.
Natural Habitat: • Find and observe animal homes, nests, burrows, and enclosed spaces such as holes in trees. • Find and observe birds, worms, ants, spiders, squirrels, and chipmunks. • Place emphasis on special observations: movement forms, speed, patterns of locomotion, comparative sizes and shapes of body parts, and group behavior of animals. • Use literature to enhance focus and organization of observation experiences. • Visit local zoo.	Animal species vary in living patterns, survival tracks and habits, and natural forms of protection against danger. All species have in common natural sources of food, protection, and patterns of defense against danger. There is variety and differentiation in nature. There is interdependence in nature. Animals use camouflage. There are seasonal changes in animal habits and habitats. People have an impact on animals. Some animals make dramatic changes in development known as metamorphosis.	All perceptual skills. Language skills in description and communication. Skills of inquiry. Making inferences and testing them. Cause-and-effect relationships. Sorting and classifying.
School Yard: • Make a bird feeder, squirrel feeder, or other feeder to serve the needs of a local animal.	People should value animal survival. Many species of animals are in danger of being wiped out forever.	Construction skills. Observation skills.

TABLE 16.3. (continued)

Resource and possible activities	Concept building	Skill development
Classroom: • Recreate basic survival conditions for small animals that are locally available, such as worms, ants, and spiders. Observe animal habits. Indoor pets may be a gerbil, turtle, parakeet, rabbit, hamster, fish, or other animal adaptable to enclosed life of a classroom. • Pair male and female for mating and reproducing. • Observe the newborn. • Adopt a class pet. (Note: having a classroom animal always presents some potential danger to the children, the animal, or both. Assessing such dangers is critical in deciding whether to have a pet and if so, what kind.) • Feed animals, clean cages or containers, and maintain an optimum environment for them.	Survival conditions include aspects of the environment, such as temperature, food, rest, safety, and exercise. Animal habits vary; animals of the same species have the same basic habits. Humans should have respect for animal survival. Animals and foods are related in ecological chains. Animals have life cycle patterns of birth, reproduction, and growth. People should show altruism in care of animals.	Construction skills to make classroom habitats. Problem-solving skills in construction. Information acquisition from books, specialists, or other appropriate sources. Observation skills. Question-asking skills. Kindness to animals. Cause-and-effect relationships: making inferences and testing them. Responsibility for chores.

ment,[7] a promising avenue for early childhood programs.

Young children are natural geographers. Roads, cars, buildings, hills, and landscapes are repeatedly constructed in block buildings, clay modeling, and artwork. These mostly spontaneous activities suggest organizing curriculum activities around existing interests. Adding to Mitchell's pioneering work, new geographic knowledge helps people understand how each element in their environment affects and influences all the other elements within the system.

Geography is currently a study of the processes by which physical and spatial aspects of the environment are transformed. Five interdependent dimensions of geographical space are:

1. the population and its attributes, such as levels of crowding, education, and income;

---

7. Lucy Sprague Mitchell, *Young Geographers* (New York: Bank Street College of Education, 1971).

2. the environmental attributes, such as weather and climate, proximity to other population centers, waterways, and land forms;
3. the organizational aspects, including economic, political, and other organizational institutions;
4. the social-psychological aspects, or the relationships of social groups to each other;
5. the technological aspect, or the level and extent of mechanization.[8]

The surface of the land, one major component within a geographic system, may be altered by people, environmental conditions, or both.

Analysis of surface attributes includes the *patterns of movement* and the *related pathways*, or channels. People move on foot and in vehicles. Vehicles move on fixed pathways or open pathways. Subways of some urban centers represent movement along fixed pathways, while buses, trucks, and cars have greater route flexibility.

Ideas and information move through the mails and telephones, through media such as television, and by other communication routes, such as the man-made satellite from which television programs are reflected to faraway places.

Where there are patterns of movement, there are *intersections*, or points where movement channels meet. *Intersections* dominate the physical landscape. A heavily trafficked intersection is usually associated with a high density of services for vehicles, meals, overnight facilities, and recreation. Where the pattern of human activity shifts, such as the change from urban to suburban shopping centers, a related change occurs in increased traffic density.

Systematic geographical study may be based on the components just discussed, that is:

---

8. Helen F. Robison and Sydney L. Schwartz, *Learning at an Early Age*, vol. 2 (Englewood Cliffs, N.J.: Prentice-Hall, 1972), p. 195.

1. *Surface use*, such as residential, commercial, recreational, religious, agricultural, or industrial;
2. a. *Movement* of people, things, or ideas from one place to another;
   b. *Channels*, the paths that movements take;
3. *Intersections*, where channels meet or cross.

Children can explore any community to develop geographic concepts. The local community can provide opportunities to observe and differentiate geographic observations. How people and objects move can be noted and classified. There are planned pathways for movement, such as sidewalks and roadways, that children can identify. While sidewalks are planned for people, there are intersections where people and vehicles move, mostly in alternating patterns.

One group of four-year-olds became involved in mapping experiences after a series of focused observation walks. In a walk around the school block, children identified different land uses. They found homes, a church, storage buildings, garages, driveways, a street and sidewalks. Subsequent walks built on this introductory experience, as children sought to answer such questions as "How many streets must we cross to get to the pet store?" and "What are the different routes we can follow?" Shortly after these focused walks, the children's geographic interests began to show up in block constructions. They used blocks to work through their geographic concepts of channels for movement, such as streets and sidewalks. Intersections posed the most challenge. The children wondered how intersections are controlled. What rules are indicated in the form of traffic lights and signs? If there are no such signs, how are collisions avoided?

Concern for safe crossing at intersections has long been reflected in schools, although the geographic understanding that supports safe practice is frequently ignored. Consequently, safety instruction in the form of memorized rules is not always successful. Knowledge about intersections may dramatize the collision potential between people and vehicles. Dependable adaptations in behavior are more likely to grow from understanding than from remembered cautions.

The ways in which the geographic environment is explored and analyzed by young children depends on the developmental stage of the children, the geographic situations that are accessible, and the experiential background of both children and teachers. When children experience an unusual perspective from a bridge or from the roof of a building, for example, intersections may fascinate one group while mapping may interest another.

Activities related to human geography, including sample learning outcomes, are suggested in Table 16-4. Since concept building and skill development are long-term processes, the concepts and skills listed are developmental and gradual, requiring construction of individual meanings by each child.

Geographic learning can be enhanced in the design of the outdoor play area. Figure 16-2 illustrates an unusual playground for a Japanese kindergarten. Note the waterways, which lace the playground and surround interest centers. This imaginative design uses water pathways in contrast to people pathways and provides endless opportunities to explore water movement, erosion, and channels. American preschools in the Sun Belt—areas with hot summers—may reconsider ways to design playgrounds for young children for more interesting and productive types of activities.

HUMAN RESOURCES

For the young child, still learning her or his own identity, contacts with people beyond the family feed self-awareness and expand understanding about others. These contacts can be maximized through careful planning. This section focuses on relationships with people and on their impact on learning.

The children and the teaching staff who congregate daily in a common set of experiences make up the core of the learning group. Beyond the primary unit of the class group are those persons who come to the classroom daily to transport the children or for regular program services, such as food delivery. Some people, such as a participating parent, may stay a while each day. Other regular visitors may be a senior citizen, a child from an upper elementary grade, or a student from a high school. Any of these persons may become important in the children's world for brief periods. Some classroom visitors may interact with the children as helpers, collaborators, or leaders, as older children often do. Almost every group of children has its "resident engineers," children who follow repair persons around, whether the job is replacing a light bulb or clearing a sink drain. These children savor every action, tool, and procedure, sometimes asking endless questions and often imitating the repair person's behavior.

The resource area surrounding the school presents a broad panorama of people. Looking out of the window or walking in the vicinity, children can observe:

1. public service employees monitoring traffic, picking up refuse, driving buses, and delivering mail;
2. community residents engaged in daily activities, such as joggers, family groups, and people on the way to work;
3. outdoor economic activities of construction workers, bus and truck drivers, telephone and electrical service workers, road repairers, and newspaper deliverers;
4. indoor economic activities of commercial and professional persons in stores and office buildings.

Commercial employees children can see include shopkeepers, clerks, food store workers, and cashiers. Members of the professional

TABLE 16.4. Human geography

Resource and possible activities	Concept building	Skill development
Pathways Streets and sidewalks: • Observe movement of people, animals, and objects on sidewalks and streets. • Categorize them, using variables children select. • Identify intersections. • Observe signals for control of movement to avoid collision at intersections. • Recreate a signal or control system in the classroom, in the block corner or elsewhere. Dramatize how the system works and what happens when it fails. • Plan and construct pathways, boundaries, and waterways on an outdoor playground. Use a hose or outdoor spigot if no natural water source is available, if weather permits. (See Figure 16–2.) • Reconstruct pathways with blocks and other classroom props, such as paper or cloth strips, or on playground. Shiny metal such as aluminum may symbolize water pathways, or children may prefer to paint or crayon paper in blues, greens, or other colors. • Formulate rules orally and in writing (child or teacher).	Movement on pathways differs in terms of form, speed, direction, density, and function. Pathways intersect. Collisions may occur at intersections. Procedures, such as signals, reduce the likelihood of collisions at intersections. Safety rules are designed to protect people, animals, and vehicles at intersections. Properties of water. Pathways and boundaries are needed for people and water. Desire lines are paths created spontaneously. Mapping concepts. There are multiple forms of land use. Directionality concepts: 1. Two-way streets have sidedness for travel in each direction. 2. Spatial relationships include meanings of *in front of*, *behind*, *across*, as in the placement of signs, people, and vehicles, and of directions of left and right.	Visual discrimination skills. Sorting skills. Vocabulary development: language labels and communication skills. Street crossing skills: reading signs, traffic control signal lights, and signals of traffic officers. Concepts of rules and commitments. Problem solving. Construction skills. Measurement. Task planning. Responsibility for task. Symbol learning: one thing standing for another, such as miniature car representing a full-sized car or a paper strip representing a sidewalk.

TABLE 16.4. (continued)

Resource and possible activities	Concept building	Skill development
Alternative perspectives on environmental attributes: • Walking or bus trips to achieve mapping perspective: go to upper floors, roof, overpasses, or bridges to identify geographic attributes, looking down on pathways, buildings, and open land. • Drive over a bridge or up a hill to gain perspective on a specified area. • Use field glasses for close-up views. • Use a camera to capture the view from different perspectives. Compare photographs. • Give children control of simple cameras and help them plan before they take pictures. • Assemble photographs in booklets, with group-dictated or prepared comments written by children or teacher. • Encourage other arts-and-crafts activities (such as tempera paint, clay, collages, scissors, paper and paste, or blocks) to express growing concepts.	Some things look different from different perspectives. Decentering size and distance concepts help to relate different views of the same object or place. Taking a bird's-eye view, makes it possible to conceptualize how things look from above. Children experience images or new ideas about size, distance, and changing perspectives. Symbols relate to objects by pictures, maps, words, signs, marks, and scales.	Mapping skills. Comparison of size and distance. Measurement skills: arbitrary measure. Sorting and classifying. Expressing concepts in arts and crafts, verbal forms, and constructional forms. Simple photographic skills. Language skills. Task formulation and completion. Participating in group projects. Social skills.
Forms of land use: • Walking trips around the school block and school neighborhood: 1. *Listing forms of land use*, such as house or apartment building; one story or	There are multiple forms of land use. Forms of land use can be categorized in many ways. Houses vary in size, shape, construction, and number of families in residence.	Language and communication skills. Knowledge of local community forms of land use. Observation. Sorting and classification. Construction skills.

TABLE 16.4. (continued)

Resource and possible activities	Concept building	Skill development
multistory buildings; stores; restaurants; offices for services; clinics for the community; real estate, legal, or other services; government offices; churches; hospitals; recreation (parks, movies, playgrounds, playing fields, theaters); gas stations, shopping plazas, or other. 2. *Photographing* types of buildings. 3. *Counting* buildings. 4. *Comparing* buildings for height, number of floors, size, and type of construction. • *In class follow-up:* replicating a street in terms of land use and size and number of buildings. Use blocks and block accessories, cereal boxes, or other construction materials. • *People-made artifacts*, such as mailboxes, fire alarm boxes, telephone poles and lines, electric poles and lines, posters and billboards, television cables: 1. *Identify* different ways messages are communicated. 2. *Identify* people who help in communication, such as delivery or maintenance personnel.	Offices house many different services. The community has a variety of stores and other buildings. There are many recreational uses of land. Objects stand for other objects. Math concepts of number, height, and size: environmental attributes can be represented in many ways. Spatial relationships. Directionality. Communication occurs in a variety of ways: written, spoken, by picture, and by code (telegraph). People and special equipment make communication possible in many ways. Communication concepts include personnel activities, equipment, procedures, and purposes. Communication content includes esthetic, practical, industrial, commercial, and scientific types of information. There are senders and receivers. Concepts of time: instant delivery by television or telephone can be compared with delayed delivery by mail or telegraph.	Size comparisons. Spatial relationships. Symbolization. Representation. Counting skills. Measuring and estimating. Observation. Language skills. Visual discrimination. Sorting and categorizing. Symbolization. Left-right discrimination. Communication forms using speech, symbols, writing, dramatization, and electronic equipment (radio, television, tape recorders, and others). Language skills. Social skills for group participation. Self-discipline on trips. Observation. Copying and imitating communication workers in play, in dramatic play, and in construction and language media. Purchase and use of stamps. Mailing letters.

TABLE 16.4. (continued)

Resource and possible activities	Concept building	Skill development
• *In class follow-up:* 1. For a Valentine's Day or a similar purpose, establish a classroom communication system requiring artwork, writing, addressing envelopes, mailing and mail delivery, including purchase, design, and use of stamps. 2. Arrange a mock television broadcast that requires laying cable wires, broadcast equipment, and TV sets, and planning and rehearsing for broadcasts. Radio broadcasts can also be suggested. 3. Arrange for trips to (a) a local post office to mail letters and to take a guided tour; or (b) to a radio or television studio, if possible, to observe personnel, equipment, and procedures. 4. Invite a mail carrier, a member of a local radio or television station, or someone from a telegraph office to visit the classroom to discuss professional activities, equipment, and procedures, demonstrating any that are possible.		

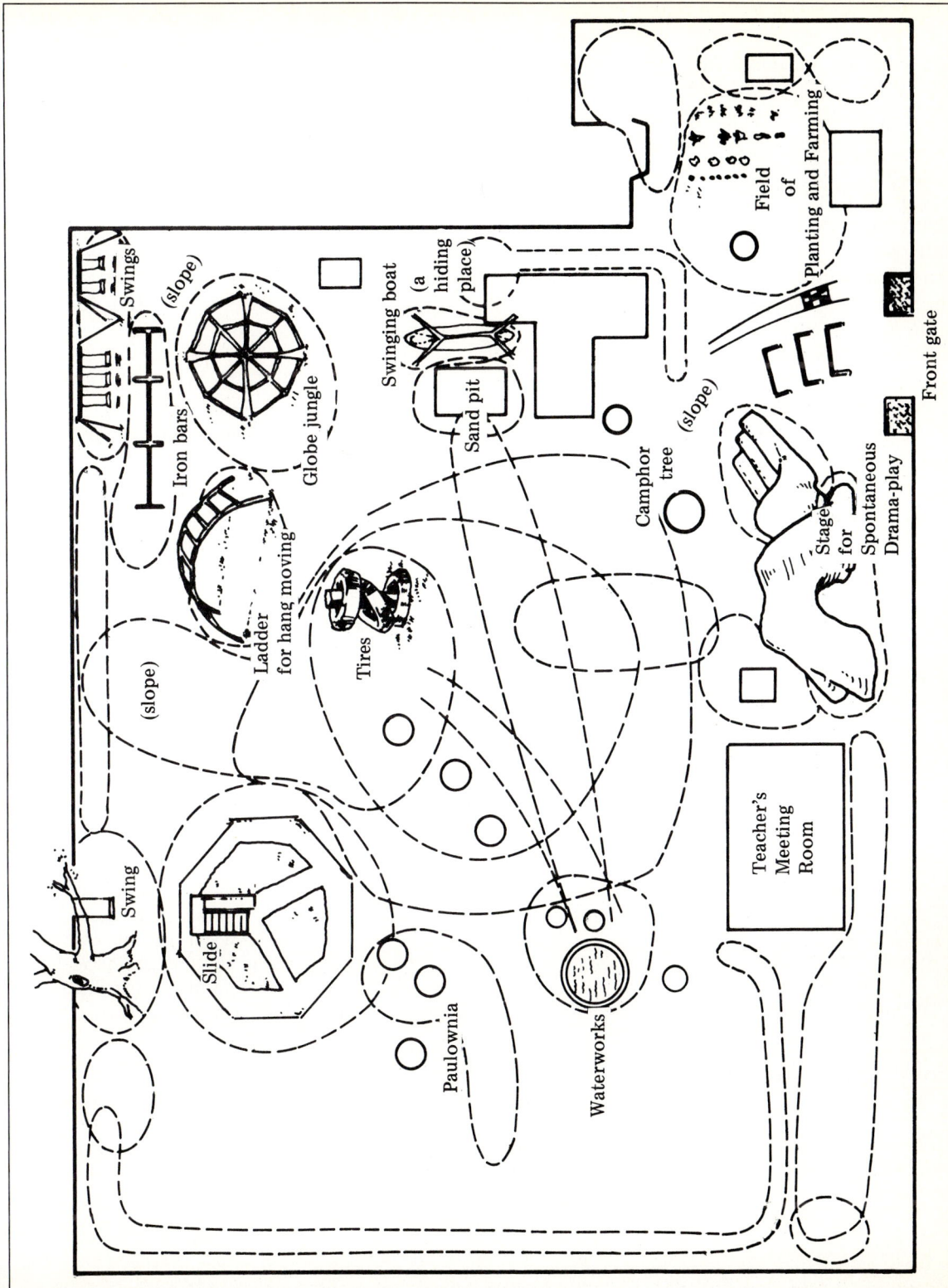

FIGURE 16.2. Visit to Uguisudani Sakura kindergarten—Map of play areas

groups and the skilled trades are often within walking distance of the school and can be visited in their own setting. Some of them may be able to accept an invitation to visit the classroom. Many people can be included in curriculum plans more than once and are glad to come. Others require careful planning for a single contact.

Each community has its unique set of economic and cultural activities, its own human resources. The diversity of activities invites the curriculum planner to dip selectively. Table 16-5 lists some of the ways in which these contacts in the classroom may contribute to curriculum development. The table begins with regular members of the class and then sketches persons who are at increasing distance from the primary classroom group. Note that the table reviews these resources in terms of increasing distance from the classroom and decreasing frequency of access. The more remote the resource, the greater the need for clarity of goal, since repeated visits are less likely.

All communities have occasional events, such as arts-and-crafts fairs, where, as a planned part of the curriculum, children can make contributions to the preparation or become active participants. For example, circus promoters often provide free or low-priced tickets for school groups. A trip to the circus includes such a wide array of possibilities for curriculum that teaching choices are imperative. The following possibilities are illustrative but not exhaustive:

1. developing language through vocabulary and word meanings;
2. developing oral language skills through narrating experiences;
3. sequencing events in advance and in review;
4. comparing and contrasting objects, animals, activities, and actions;
5. identifying job roles at the circus;
6. using and observing different forms of transportation, in transit and at the circus;

TABLE 16.5. Summary of human resources—frequency of contact and potential learnings

Frequency of contact	Nature of human resource (other than teaching staff)	Curriculum potential
Daily: all day	Class members. Older children. Helping adults.	Learning about role models and sources of knowledge, developing self-image and self-concept, gaining emotional and physical support, and increasing skill and cognitive development.
Daily: limited periods	Visitors. Persons appearing at arrival and dismissal, such as parents, siblings, family, and friends. Service personnel, such as food services, repair persons, and maintenance staff.	Expanding role models. Learning about occupations. Increasing self-concept. Developing social skills, such as acceptable modes of interaction.

TABLE 16.5. (continued)

Frequency of contact	Nature of human resource (other than teaching staff)	Curriculum potential
Occasional visitors	Classroom service personnel: • maintenance and repair persons; • delivery persons (for school supplies); • supervisory personnel. Classroom visitors: • parents interested in enrolling children; • licensing agents, such as fire inspectors, and health inspectors; • interested professionals from other schools and training institutions; journalists; and politicians.	Teacher's modeling of receiving visitors, helping strangers feel comfortable, finding out how others meet new situations, and acquiring social skills, social knowledge, and social practice. Job role model providing information on job-related activities.
Visible daily or weekly from inside the classroom	Municipal service workers: • refuse pickup; • mail delivery; • street maintenance; • traffic control. Community people: • on the way to work; • joggers; • shoppers; • family groups; • school children; • senior citizens; • commercial deliveries by car and truck; • large trucking, loading and unloading.	Identifying and observing activities in environment. Organizing knowledge of community activities and extending understanding of interrelatedness of the self, family, and community. Identifying personal preferences, interests, skills and sharing these with others. Observing many aspects of life in the community.
Occasional: planned visits or class visitations by persons from the community	Local commercial employees: all kinds of retail stores, salespersons, checkers, clerks, packers or wrappers, store managers, and owners. Community professionals and specialists: • medical and hospital personnel; • firefighters; • law enforcement personnel;	Learning economic concepts: forms of goods and services, job-related roles, interdependence and variety, role models, production and distribution staffs, and activities. Learning sociology concepts: community membership, community needs for services, cultural and ethnic needs, values, traditions, and role models.

TABLE 16.5. (continued)

Frequency of contact	Nature of human resource (other than teaching staff)	Curriculum potential
Single visits	• sanitation workers; • people in the craft trades: shoemakers, leather craft workers, and electronic and electrical specialists such as radio and television repair persons; • bus, subway, and other local transport personnel; • airline employees; • auto mechanics, auto, bicycle, parking lot staffs; • window washers; • restaurateurs and chefs; • athletes; • farmers; • musicians; • artists and art in museums, galleries, and studios; Commercial and manufacturing plant employees: people who work in any local manufacturing plant, such as a milk bottling or yarn and fabric center; printers of newspapers, books, journals, and other forms of information.	Learning geography concepts: pathways and movement, interactions, types of land-surface use, types of buildings, transportation, and commercial centers. Learning music and art concepts: rhythmic patterns in the environment, compositions in environments, colors, sounds, melodies, harmonies, and dissonance. Learning science concepts: ecology and the environment; interdependence in nature; animal life; changes in the environment; seasonal cycles; food chains; weather patterns; sun, moon, planets, and stars; sand, rock, and soil.

7. noticing music cues, announcements, and climaxes;
8. comparing and contrasting decorative forms;
9. looking at or reading written symbols;
10. observing humor, jokes, and farce;
11. observing animals in the circus.

The circus, which provides high excitement through maximum stimulation of all the senses, challenges teachers to find ways to reduce the scattering of attention and help focus on discrete parts of the total setting. While the circus represents one end of the spectrum of human resources, it illustrates the need for selective planning to avoid overstimulation or its opposite, dullness.

Using Human Resources

Once teachers identify the resources that are suitable and useful, they can decide whether safety or other factors militate against plans for on-site visits to, for example, a gasoline station. For curriculum purposes, people are suitable for:

1. personal interactions in spontaneous ways;
2. planned interactions, interviews, observations, and activities;
3. spontaneous and planned activities.

Interviews, observations, and activities may occur within the classroom or in the setting where people work or play. Plans to include specific people in the curriculum require consideration of outcomes, that is, will productive experiences take place?

The Class Group

In the classroom, children interact as a group that lives together, sharing personal joys and crises, interests and attitudes, wishes and dreams. While there are predictable expectations for the quality of relationships in this setting, the members of the peer group influence each other in many unpredictable ways. Children teach each other directly and indirectly; they also challenge, stimulate, and motivate each other. Teachers frequently capitalize on this peer teaching by encouraging one child to show another some procedure or skill. A recent study confirmed the acceptability and significance of peer learning, especially in its informativeness and precise communication.[9]

Some ideas for curriculum planning can be derived from the research on the effects of the peer group on learning. Merei found that, in a group of young children, there is the tendency to develop a "group tradition and a set of standards which give structure and content to group activities."[10] He also found that small groups within the larger preschool class established limits on the group in terms of functioning and use of materials. These groups resisted intrusion by older children or others who were in the class but not in the subgroup. Merei's research alerts teachers to the dynamics of group control within the classroom. Teachers who listen actively to the conversations children have with each other as they are exposed to new experiences can note whether and how the conforming phenomena tend to limit the children's intake. Teachers can identify not only group influences on learning, but also ways in which individuals teach each other in their intimate, one-to-one relationships. Sometimes teachers separate children who limit each other's activities unnecessarily.

We have discovered from a research project that as early as age four, children identify the members of the group who always have the "right" answer during instructional periods. In one situation, after the teacher agreed to remove the rapid responders from a review session, she discovered that only three of fifteen children had acquired the intended learning. The others echoed the answers they heard. The teacher, after repeating this experiment, became convinced that four-year-olds know whom to copy.

Many teachers find a major group interest developing out of the driving persistence of one child in some special topic or activity, such as machines, dinosaurs, music, acrobatic exercises, or rock hunting. Children not only infect the class with new interests, but they also set higher standards of achievement through their own accomplishments.

---

9. Catherine R. Cooper, Susan Ayers-Lopez, and Angela Marquis, "Children's Discourse During Peer Learning in Experimental and Naturalistic Situations" (paper presented at the annual meeting of the American Educational Research Association, Boston, Massachusetts, April 1980, pp. 16–17.

10. F. Merei, as reported by Joan Swift, "Effects of Early Group Experience: The Nursery School and Day Nursery," in Martin Hoffman and Lois Hoffman, eds., *Review of Child Development Research*, vol. 1 (New York: Russell Sage Foundation, 1964), pp. 274–275.

Thus, the children who comprise a classroom unit are themselves important resources for peer learning. The dynamics of interaction within the group give teachers needed information for curriculum development, grouping and teaching.

Older School Children

As noted on Table 16-5, older children provide a mixture of peer and adult qualities in their relationships with younger children, who adore them as playmates. However, older school children are often unable to deal with the strong emotions of anger, frustration, or fear. They also tend to be rigid and literal. The responsibilities of young helpers must be clearly limited. As models, older children can considerably enrich the school environment, provided teachers maintain the necessary watchfulness to prevent inappropriate modeling, bossiness, or overcontrol.

Occasional Visitors

Occasional visitors may bring into the classroom new information about job roles, hobbies, crafts, the arts, athletics, health and safety, different cultures, and ethnic traditions. While visitors are often asked to cook an ethnic dish, other suitable activities include making artifacts such as a piñata or *dredl*, teaching a song in a foreign language, or reading to one child.

Parents or community residents who are artists may be persuaded to bring their materials to the classroom and work quietly along with the children. Adult practitioners demonstrating their vocations give importance to art activities. Musicians, dancers, acrobats, weavers, carpenters, electricians, and chefs can all make interesting contributions to the curriculum.

Potential visitors who think they have nothing to offer can be reminded that they might share:

1. photographs, songs, or dances about other times and other places;
2. representative dishes of an ethnic group;
3. recordings of folk music;
4. myths, folktales, poetry, and stories;
5. personal biographies (children always want to know what other people's childhood was like);
6. skills in sewing, crocheting, knitting, embroidery, electrical work, leather work, or any other art or craft;
7. proficiency in a language other than English.

The excitement, novelty, and stimulation that occasional visitors impart are invaluable in adding needed variety, surprise, and new interests to any curriculum.

Trips to Meet People in the Community

Trips on foot or by vehicle to visit resource persons require careful planning with children. An advantage of visitation is the realistic view children perceive of working environments. However, this may be a distracting factor, preventing a clear focus on the purpose of the visit. The classroom may allow concentration on the visitor without distractions. When some children visited a supermarket and noted the manager, for example, the scene was too frenetic to offer much information. Afterward, when the manager agreed to visit the classroom, an unhurried discussion brought out many questions and answers.

Opportunities are abundant for expanding the set of curriculum activities based on community persons as occasional resources. For example, interest in a local ice cream vendor may lead to:

1. a series of cooking experiences—making ice cream, ices, frozen custard, and frozen yogurt;
2. trips to find other kinds of street vendors or other places where ice cream may be purchased;
3. a class fund-raising project selling some kind of food or drink to older children, parents, and visitors, replicating activities observed, practiced, or both.

Parents as Resources

The early development of nursery schools in this country involved parents in many roles. The parent-cooperative nursery school movement, which peaked in the 1940s and 1950s, provided a model for ways in which parents might contribute to curriculum and teaching in the program.[11] In addition to providing management, administrative, and teaching support, parents contributed to the curriculum, much as visitors and community persons still do.

Parents' interests, hobbies, skills, and special talents were offered to children in many ways. Both mothers and fathers became active in program development. Some led cooking activities with children. Musical parents gave concerts or started musical activities. Carpentry work with children was developed by parents. Some professional parents helped take the fear out of doctors' and dentists' visits; others initiated eye examinations. Parents are often the most accessible and responsive resource beyond the teaching team.

Early childhood programs seem to be decreasing the participation of parents. In a recent Florida State University study, in which teachers rank-ordered the value of selected teaching competencies, "use of parents and community resources" was reported as the least-valued and least-used competency.[12] Because mothers are increasingly becoming full-time workers or students, teachers must not assume they are unwilling or unable to arrange some forms of classroom participation.

Written Guides for Classroom Visitors

Wherever people visit classrooms, there are problems of consistency of expectations for children. In some cases, oral orientations seek to provide this. However, verbal suggestions can only be successful when visits are anticipated and planned for with the visitors. In many cases, this is impossible.

The obvious alternative to oral orientation is prepared written materials. Such materials include:

1. a list of classroom routines and responsibilities of adults and children;
2. classroom rules;
3. the regular daily schedule;
4. procedures for emergencies concerning health or safety;
5. guidelines followed in the classroom for dealing with social conflict or other emotional situations;
6. guides for ways to enter children's learning situations, usually consisting of "do's" and "don'ts."

Contemporary drop-in centers have the greatest turnover in staff and children and the greatest need for standardized guidelines for

---

11. Katherine W. Taylor, *Parent Cooperative Nursery Schools.* (New York: Teachers College Bureau of Publications, 1954).

12. *Development of General N-6 Teacher Competencies: Synopsis of Final Report* (Florida State University Right to Read project, DOE Contract #770-121, November 1978), pp. 26-32.

working with children.[13] But whenever visitors are sought or accepted as volunteers or participants, respect for their contributions includes some orientation for successful participation in an ongoing classroom. Plans for use of human resources, therefore, should include some consideration of important influences on learning by peer group, parents, older school children, and occasional visitors.

SUMMARY

In this chapter, detailed suggestions are made for using cultural and environmental resources for an exciting and relevant curriculum. Growing interest throughout the country in ecological balance; respect for plant and animal life; renewed emphasis on nature, health maintenance, and self-expression through physical activities and the arts—all are related to substantial curriculum possibilities. It is appropriate for young children in learning centers to enter the major interests and activities of their own time and at their own level.

Many resources for stimulating children's activities are found in the natural environment. Weather, plant and animal life, and natural earth formations are all fruitful sources for active learning efforts. Trips, repeated observations, in-class replications of outdoor forces and patterns, children's expressive activities verbally and through the arts, and endless possibilities for play are indicated here.

Geographic and economic activities are suggested, as part of the environmental studies children are likely to find absorbing and understandable. Specific concepts and activities flow from modern scholarly work in these areas.

Skill development of any specific type can be integrated with these activities.

Process goals are suggested in all cases, along with ways of building concepts, vocabulary, and skills. Since most of these goals can be included in most programs, teachers are free to use their own designs and adapt these resources in appropriate ways.

Teachers are alerted to possible needs for updating their own knowledge to guide children to conceptualizations that change with new discoveries and with different ways to pattern ideas and processes.

Finally, people as curriculum resources and their effects on children's learnings are reviewed. Trips and on-site visits to many places of work are discussed and contrasted with in-class visits. People who affect children's learning in the classroom are identified as peers, older children who act as aids or monitors, parents, school staff personnel, and visitors. The need to reverse the underutilization of parents as a curricular resource is stressed.

EXERCISES

1. Make a list of categories of community resources that would be helpful to use in teaching.
    a. Scout your community to check resources available in each category.
    b. Plan an instructional activity that utilizes some of the identified resources, based on children's interest and teaching goals.
2. Identify human resources available in the school, classroom, or both, using Table 16–5.
    a. Note frequency, closeness, and nature of contact.
    b. Observe children's interest.
    c. Note and specify curriculum potential.

---

13. One such written guide for participating college students and a campus child care center has been expanded into a text for participants. See Bruce Grossman and Carol Keyes, *Helping Children Grow: The Adult Role* (Wayne, N.J.: Avery, 1978).

BIBLIOGRAPHY

Blough, Glenn O., and Campbell, Marjorie H. *Making and Using Classroom Science Materials.* New York: Dryden Press, 1954.

Cooper, Catherine R.; Ayers-Lopez, Susan; and Marquis, Angela. "Children's Discourse during Peer Learning in Experimental and Naturalistic Situations." Paper presented at the annual meeting of the American Educational Research Association, Boston, Massachusetts, April, 1980.

Craig, Gerald S. *Science for the Elementary School Teacher.* Boston: Ginn, 1947.

Development of General N-6 Teacher Competencies: Synopsis of Final Report. Florida State University Right to Read project. DOE Contract #770-121, November 1978.

Grossman, Bruce, and Keyes, Carol. *Helping Children Grow: The Adult Role.* Wayne, N.J.: Avery, 1978.

Merei, F., as reported by Joan Swift. "Effects of Early Group Experience: The Nursery School and Day Nursery." In Martin Hoffman and Lois Hoffman, eds., *Review of Child Development Research.* Vol. 1. New York: Russell Sage Foundation, 1964.

Mitchell, Lucy Sprague. *Young Geographers.* New York: Bank Street College of Education, 1971.

National Society for the Study of Education, Forty-Sixth Yearbook. Part 1: *Science Education in American Schools.* Chicago: University of Chicago Press, 1947.

Nuffield Mathematics Project Booklets. New York: John Wiley, 1969.

Robison, Helen F. and Schwartz, Sydney L. *Learnng at an Early Age.* Vol. 2. Englewood Cliffs, N.J.: Prentice-Hall, 1972.

Sheckles, Mary. *Building Children's Science Concepts.* New York: Teachers College Press, 1958.

Taylor, Katherine W. *Parent Cooperative Nursery Schools.* New York: Teachers College Bureau of Publications, 1954.

Waters, Barbara. *Science Can Be Elementary: Discovery Action Programs for K-3.* New York: Citation Press, 1973.

17 Social and Political Forces and the Curriculum

Profound social change is taking place with unprecedented rapidity everywhere around the globe, especially in the United States. Long-held assumptions are being challenged, while new demands are taking on increasing urgency. Huge population shifts are occurring either in response to technological change here or abroad, or in response to political and economic conditions, and the rapid pace of change itself is bringing political problems to the boil. Mobility is a feature of American life that contributes to a great variety of tensions and problems on the educational scene. It is not just that people move; their ideas change and interact in unpredictable ways with their expectations and experiences.

Changing populations, or changing population characteristics, instantly challenge curriculum. Most big cities and many smaller ones in the United States are coping with problems in bilingual education because immigrants are no longer confining themselves primarily to the great port cities of entry but are settling everywhere they perceive opportunities for jobs, housing, and education. It gives some perspective to know that these are not solely the problems of the United States. England, France, Switzerland, Canada, Belgium, Australia, and Israel are among the many countries in the world today beset with schooling problems for new immigrant groups or with unresolved problems of which language shall predominate in schools.

Other changes also challenge Americans. Do you remember when every textbook reference to a child was unquestionably *he*? The rejection of sexual bias in general references to people has come about as the result of strong social and political forces driving into everyone's consciousness the need to avoid sex bias. The strength of these forces pushed a proposed equal-rights amendment close to national acceptance.

How does such a dynamic social force affect early childhood curriculum making? It is well known that preschool classes in the past generally demonstrated sex bias by arranging block play as a boys' area, with vehicles and other equipment in one corner, while making the housekeeping area a separate center for girls, with dolls, dress-up clothes, and other props for role-playing the traditional, at-home mother and housekeeper. When carpentry was available, observers noted how differently boys and girls were treated in this area. Boys were less protected, were encouraged to try harder, and also were urged to help girls who could not hammer or saw. Teachers gave lip-service to equality, but in many subtle ways, female teachers diverted boys from "too-female" activities, and vice versa.

Eliminating sex bias from the content of children's experiences is turning out to be a major challenge to teachers as curriculum shapers. Attitudes and expectations, reinforced by television programs, children's storybooks,

295

and children's own families, are difficult to change. Selecting children's books that foster nonsexist views, engaging in discussions that diminish male-female stereotypes, and encouraging children to participate in diverse types of activity irrespective of traditional sex-role expectations are a few of the ways in which teachers help children construct nonsexist attitudes.

In addition to sexism, contemporary social changes are affecting not only the content of early childhood curriculum directly, but also objectives, expectations, values, and methods of educating. Dramatic changes in education can be ascribed to such major trends as:

1. family changes: single-parent families, younger mothers, working mothers, and changing family composition;
2. heightened mobility: prejudice against newcomers or strangers and adjustment problems of the newly arrived;
3. racism and sexism;
4. poverty being combatted through schooling: bilingual and bicultural programs;
5. growing national dispersion of immigrants, especially from Hispanic countries;
6. value changes;
7. community involvement in curriculum decisions.

This chapter deals with some of these profound social and political changes and their impact on curriculum content, methodology, and objectives in early childhood education.

CHANGING FAMILY COMPOSITION

The nuclear family was the model of much analysis in sociological, psychological, and educational literature up until the sixties. A family consisting of two parents and at least two children—down from the post–World War II larger family of four to six children—seemed to be the most usual type. Grandparents had already begun living separately from the younger generation, except in unusual cases of illness or economic disaster, but clearly the pattern of bridging the generations in a single household was a thing of the past.

It was true that in various minority groups, different models of family had long been in existence to meet needs that could not be met in nuclear family units. Extended families developed—made up chiefly of related individuals but in many cases of persons unrelated by blood or marriage—in need of various forms of mutual assistance and nurturance. The intense period of dissent in the sixties accentuated this trend, and it spread to mainstream families, where it had not previously been common. These extended families, with related and unrelated persons, sometimes formed communes, in cities as well as in suburban and rural areas, redefining the family and its functions to suit their own needs.

Many families now include remarried couples who bring together children from previous marriages. Some children shuttle between divorced parents, who may have joint custody. Some children are being reared by fathers. The teacher's sensitivity must be well developed to accept the many kinds of families in which children live.

Working Mothers

The central place of the family in the child's educability has been stressed by Urie Bronfenbrenner, who said that "the family seems to be the most effective and economical system for fostering and sustaining the child's development."[1] "Without family involvement,"

---

1. Urie Bronfenbrenner, "Is Early Intervention Effective?," in Ashley Montagu, ed., *Race and I.Q.* (London: Oxford University Press, 1975), p. 316.

Bronfenbrenner says, "intervention is likely to be unsuccessful, and what few effects are achieved are likely to disappear once the intervention is discontinued." However, he added that "ecological intervention is needed for many poor families, to provide adequate medical care, nutrition, housing, jobs, as well as status for parenthood."[2] Valuing parenting but stressing the need for supporting parents adequately, Bronfenbrenner voices optimism for the family's capacity to rear effective and happy children once society provides more humane conditions of life for all families.

As of October 1977, there were about 9.2 million children in the United States in the three-to-five age group.[3] While only about 50 percent of this group were reported to be enrolled in schools, it has been estimated that over 88 percent, or 8.2 million of these children were in some kind of school or out-of-home arrangement.[4] At least 90 percent of the five-year-olds were in schools. What is new is the increasing proportion of younger children, including infants, who are now being cared for daily outside of their own homes. William Pierce points out that, out of necessity, working mothers have been finding all kinds of out-of-home arrangements, while political debates rage over whether mothers of small children should work. Further impressive changes Pierce cites include these:

1. A majority of mothers with children under eighteen now work.
2. About 40 percent of mothers with children under three now work.
3. By 1986, a majority of mothers with children under three are expected to be working.

2. Ibid., p. 317.
3. National Center for Educational Statistics, U.S. Department of Health, Education, and Welfare, *Digest of Education Statistics, 1978–1979.*
4. William L. Pierce, "Who's Watching the Children?" *American Educator*, 3, no. 1 (Spring 1979): p. 11.

He describes the agonizing controversies stimulated by the wholesale movement into the work force of mothers of young children:[5]

1. whether single mothers should be forced into the employment market, by retrenchment-minded legislators, when most of these women have few job skills and there is a dearth of jobs with adequate wages to support a family;
2. whether "cheap" daycare can be substituted for adequate daycare with acceptable social costs;
3. whether subsidies should be provided to mothers who prefer to raise their young children at home;
4. whether resources should be reallocated to working mothers, the needy aged, the young handicapped, or to other needy groups;
5. whether after-school supervision of school-aged children of working mothers should be greatly increased.

Single Parents

Since almost a third of all American families are now headed by single parents, mostly women, the schools' conception of the family is rapidly becoming more complex. School-home collaboration requires innovative thinking, and problems abound concerning sick children with no one at home to take charge. Problems include the larger proportion of nutritional needs that now occur during school hours, the dwindling supply of home instruction, and supervision of children's health, safety, physical, and recreational activities and their relationships with people. These changes contributed to the findings of the President's Commission on School Finance, which stated

5. Ibid., p. 12.

that the United States must rid itself of three assumptions:[6]

1. that the sole objective of education is the acquisition of information and the development of simple skills;
2. that present ways of teaching and learning and of organizing the schools for instruction are the only or preferred ways to conduct an adequate educational program.
3. that education can function adequately without considering the child's total environment, including its resources for learning and its handicaps.

An important aim of education, they added, is to teach students to learn and to develop interests in continued study.

These are examples of the new objectives that grow out of changing family patterns. With more younger children than ever before spending their waking hours outside of the home and having less interaction with parents and families, "making it" on one's own becomes a higher priority than ever before.

Younger Parents

The immaturity in terms of age, education, and experience of many new mothers poses another problem. It places a heavy responsibility on schools and social agencies to work closely with "child-mothers," who are too young and too unprepared for motherhood. An alarming feature of the decreasing age of new mothers is the high degree of birth defects associated with such early reproduction, swelling the rolls of the handicapped at a time when medical progress and better health care might otherwise be expected to show declining rates in handicaps.

---

6. President's Commission on School Finance, *Schools, People and Money: Final Report* (Washington, D.C.: U.S. Government Printing Office, 1972), p. 26.

Limited prenatal care and greater risks for very young mothers seem to be the contributing factors.

Teachers are challenged to find better ways to communicate and collaborate with very young mothers. Many of the latter are unmarried and without skills in either homemaking or child rearing and without marketable skills required for self-support. Various governmental programs are developing for prevention, assistance, or both, especially in the ten-to-fifteen-year-old age group where this alarming trend toward young motherhood has developed. Sympathetic teachers can help these young mothers seek solutions to overwhelming problems.

MOBILITY

The great mobility of Americans, with one family out of five moving annually, is especially hard on young children, who face discontinuities in their developing friendships. Children from mobile families lack familiarity with a particular neighborhood, a sense of security with known neighbors, and comprehension and assimilation of the changes they experience. Frequent moves to new neighborhoods usually mean family isolation among strangers when stresses are great and support needs are crucial. Feelings of belonging and acceptance may be difficult to reestablish once insecurity is felt. Teachers are especially important persons in helping to anchor children to a new institution and new friendships.

Discrimination

In some situations, the new child finds not only well-established relationships that exclude him or her but also ugly racist or ethnic prejudice. Self-hatred and extreme aggressiveness in the face of prejudice are two of the more antisocial forms of coping with rejection, contempt, or demeaning treatment.

Prejudice against such groups as migrant farm workers tends to be more openly expressed because of the transient character of their work and residence. However, prejudice is not confined to one kind of group or family. Often, communities and their schools have not developed patterns for absorbing new members and accommodating differences in traditions, culture, and values. Reactions to the unfamiliar frequently are expressed as an unwillingness to accept or respect differences; that is, prejudice.

Migrant workers and their families are not the only ones who move around a great deal. Families relocate because of better job opportunities or for reasons of health. Moves into rural or semirural areas are often made to escape the facelessness and anomie of the big city, where it is hard to know and trust one's neighbors. Some families are fleeing city pollution, sheer bigness, or overscheduled lives. Others want to return to the land, to recapture an earlier way of life, which many city folk think of as being less tense, more satisfying, more personally controlled. Jobs probably top the list of reasons for family moves.

The schools face a challenge to help avoid discrimination against children in this mobile society, by teaching the constitutional values of justice, equality, and human dignity, regardless of local prejudice.

Curriculum Continuity

How does family mobility affect local school control and curriculum decisions? It is inevitable that a homogenizing effect is developing. Such factors as federal aid to education with specific national priorities and the extensive use of national norms for achievement in reading and mathematics contribute to this trend. Our national system of textbook distribution, as well as the mass media, quickly publicize new ideas and educational procedures. Local groups still exercise control, but within a framework of the broader community of educational professionals and the political controls of money and resources.

Children moving into communities that have not offered any form of bilingual instruction often face painful transitional periods of adjustment. Value clashes occur between those who believe the school should offer instruction only in English and those who seek a more bicultural, bilingual accommodation.

SEXISM

Margaret Mead, in her introduction to an Italian book on sexism, says:

> The basic theme of the book is that home and school, book and toy manufacturers, and mass media are all contributing to stereotypes which interfere with a child's ability to grow up aspiring to diverse kinds of work and creativity.... The Italian version of sex stereotyping only serves to point up the French, the English and American versions of a common cultural lag.[7]

The renewed strength of the movement for sex equality in the sixties and seventies picked up where the movement died during the depression years of the thirties.

Those who work for equal rights for women emphasize that the intellectual differences between the sexes are affected by the differences in the ways in which they are reared and educated, treated socially, and trained. Psychologists point out that tests emphasizing intellectual differences that are culturally biased are being administered to children who have already been trained to the expected bias. Many contrasts have been noted in child-rearing practices that reward independence for boys and dependence for girls: athletics, adventure, and outdoor activities for boys and safe, stay-at-home, quiet activities for girls.

7. Margaret Mead, "Introduction to Elema Gianni Belotti," *What Are Little Girls Made Of?* (New York: Schocken Books, 1976), p. 11.

Achievement motivation is strongly regarded in boys, not in girls. In fact, girls are taught to fear success and its aftermath, especially its disadvantage in attracting male partners and husbands. Social expectations, established in the family, on jobs, in literature, television, and other mass media distinguish male from female traits, with far higher rewards for male traits.[8] Finally, it is said that women are not only taught to have female traits, but also to devalue themselves for having them, since they are perceived as inferior.

Efforts to eliminate sexism from American society are still far from widespread, nor is there yet a national consensus on this issue. Many women join organizations to fight the aims of women's liberation groups, fearing to lose a dependency status they regard as natural, familiar, and advantageous. Giving up this status is similar to growing up—it requires more independence and decision-making and less following of the dictates of others. It poses more risk and uncertainties, and it removes some of the protections that have come to seem essential and make some discrimination seem just. Since society acts to protect those who are weak and unable to fend for themselves, such as children, the aged, and the ill, it is difficult to give up protections for those who are dependent. Equality does not mean, of course, that women who are ill, aged, or destitute will lose any protections. It does emphasize that, by and large, women have the same potential as men to make decisions, to carry them out, and to choose their lifestyles, professions, and activities. It emphasizes individual decisions, not stereotyped expectations.

It seems likely that, as the ideal of sex equality becomes more generally accepted, more active efforts will be made to help women attain the equality accorded to them by law, which they are unaccustomed to exercising. Educational changes will be required to keep pace with legislation and social practices that seek to eliminate prejudice and discrimination. This is an issue on which there have been divisions among black and white women: black women claim often that racism is a far more vicious practice than sexism. It is likely that these two movements, with so much in common, will collaborate in many ways to counter both forms of discrimination.

Curricular content and methodology both need changes if children's uniqueness and strengths are to be emphasized and developed without irrelevant constraints of sex and race.

RACISM AND POVERTY

With its history of very rapid social change, the twentieth century is meeting head on many of the problems in eradicating racism in our society. Changes in racist laws, court decisions, administrative and other ways of moving toward a just society are regarded by conservatives as being too rapid or as undermining the traditional rights of whites. Radicals see very little accomplished when race still handicaps children educationally and adults vocationally and in other ways.

There will always be differences of opinion as to how American society can compensate for slavery and for perpetuating injustices that prevent true equality for all. Race is, of course, not the only determinant of social injustice victims. As previously noted, mobility, sexism, and poverty have been shown to be powerful causes of social inequality. Not all the poor are black. But far higher proportions of black families are poor, and therefore to be poor and black is to be among those who benefit least from the United States' affluent culture.

Governmental efforts in the sixties focused on education as the means for improving the prospects of the poor for greater participation in the benefits of American affluence. It was thought that better jobs and better lives would be open to children from poor minority

---

8. Barbara Grizzuti Harrison, *Unlearning the Lie: Sexism in School* (New York: Liveright, 1973), pp. 41-44.

families who received better education and graduated from high schools and colleges.[9] Many educational projects initiated in the sixties, especially Head Start and some programs in elementary and high schools, have had important positive effects across the country. Many outcomes have been hard to measure because all other things have not remained equal, and some longitudinal effects were neither studied nor detected. However, schools have initiated many different ways to improve instruction for children from poor minority families. There has surely been an increase in the motivation of children to stay in school, to graduate from college, and to enter the professions. The effects, however, are modest compared with expectations.

One recent study concluded that investment in early education has long term effects in three areas: in cognitive measures of IQ, in reduction of in-grade retention, and in reduction of numbers of children assigned to special education for the handicapped. According to this study, "the most important finding is that low-income children who received early education are better able to meet the minimal requirements of their schools."[10]

However, since 80 percent of children in private prekindergartens are white and about 70 percent in the publicly controlled sector are black, concern for a more integrated society adds weight to the movement for publicly controlled or funded preschool programs for all, with incentives for integrated classes.

It seems logical that a concerted effort that does not rely on education alone will improve the odds that children from poor and minority groups will have better prospects for "the good life." However, this argument does not relieve education of its responsibilities. The only just attitude schools can take is to do the very best that resources, human ingenuity, and compassion can make possible. While racism and ethnic prejudice have not been eradicated from American society, there is a high level of consciousness about its irrationality and cruelty, as well as its plain human injustice. The ideal is clear, although adherence may be variable.

POVERTY AND SCHOOLING

With the rapid increase of urbanism and civil rights activism, the rediscovering of poverty in the United States in the sixties led the large Democratic majorities in Congress to make history with new social legislation. The passage of the Elementary and Secondary Education Act in 1965 and the initiation of Head Start programs for preschool children opened a new role for the federal government in American education. The purpose of Head Start programs, generally, was to increase the chances that children from poor families would succeed in school. A powerful new stream of financial aid suddenly poured into schools and programs. Along with these new funds came new pressures for accountability, evaluation, and results.

The politicians managed to agree on programs and money policies. But there has been no agreement on the underlying theory of how to equalize educational opportunities for the disadvantaged, poor minority groups in the country. At least three different basic views of the causes of inadequate school performance of poor children, along with many possible paths to social reform, have been defined by sociologists, psychologists, anthropologists, educators, civil-rights leaders, and others.

---

9. J. McVicker Hunt, *Intelligence and Experience* (New York: Ronald Press, 1961); and J. McVicker Hunt, "The Psychological Bases for Using Preschool Enrichment as an Antidote for Cultural Deprivation," *Merrill-Palmer Quarterly*, 10 (1964): 220–240.

10. Irving Lazar, Virginia Ruth Hubbell, Harry Murray, Marilyn Rosche, and Jacqueline Royce, "The Persistence of Preschool Effects: A Long-Term Follow-Up of Fourteen Infant and Preschool Experiments" (New York State College of Human Ecology, Cornell University, Ithaca, September 1977), p. 2.

Three Models of Effects of Poverty on Children

The three basic views, or models, of poverty, held by various theorists and activists, can be called the *deficit, difference,* and *bicultural* models. Each has been defined in more than one way, but they can be differentiated as follows:

1. The deficit model was an early explanation of the poor functioning in schools of children from low-income families. At one extreme, the children were regarded as having lower intelligence than other children due to genetic inheritance of racially inferior potential. The environmentalists, however, attributed lower functioning not to biological causes but to the conditions of poverty, which were perceived to lack intellectual stimulation and opportunities for developing intellectual capacity more fully. Black children especially were viewed as nonverbal and linguistically incompetent because they used an "incorrect" version of English call *black dialect*, which lacks familiar structure and rules. This model, which conceives of the child as being incapable of succeeding in the contemporary school, generally led to plans for "remaking" the child to improve chances for school success. Racist views, of course, suggested that genetic inferiority could not be changed, only accepted. In some cases, the latter approach identified "associational" thinking, claiming that this, rather than more advanced conceptual modes, was an appropriate aim geared to the inferior capacity of poor children, even at mature levels. This view has lost most of its apparent credibility with the recent discovery that its major research base was spurious.

Currently, this deficit model requires adherents to choose between (1) taking children who have been forced to live largely outside of the mainstream of our society and fitting them into schools adapted to their special needs or (2) adapting the schools to the children who come to be educated. The question is whether to remake the child *or* remake the school.

2. *The difference model* contrasts two cultures as being equal but having great differences. Black dialects, for example, are described as being as structured as standard English, with logical rules.[11] Black children are observed to be highly verbal and creative in their ethnically unique forms of communication and expressiveness. Thus the different histories and experiences of the black and white cultures, including the different ways in which family and community have developed, are viewed as the basic problems of schooling within the white culture. This model generally leads to advocacy for school changes to accommodate the culture conflict for black children caught in the tensions created by the different value systems and lifestyles of the two cultures.

Sociolinguists such as William Labov have emphasized the similarity between black dialects and standard English, the need to respect both as being of equal value, and the need to teach children appropriate use of both dialects. Advocates of the difference model take a positive approach to planning curriculum, building on the strengths and current stage of development of the children without denigrating their language and culture. Standard English was to be added as a second dialect, not as a substitute for the child's black dialect. *Dialectal flexibility*, or the appropriate usage of each dialect, is viewed as an important school objective from this perspective.[12]

A major problem with this view is that schools see as one of their major objectives the teaching of standard English. As in most bilingual programs, teachers may not know the child's first language or dialect, but even when

11. William Labov, "The Logic of Nonstandard English," in Frederick Williams, ed., *Language and Poverty* (Chicago: Markham, 1970), pp. 153–189.

12. Joan Baratz and Stephen Baratz, "Early Childhood Intervention: The Social Scientific Basis of Institutionalized Racism," *Harvard Educational Review*, 39 (1970): 29–50.

they do, there is a tendency to give standard English more time, undervaluing the native tongue, if not outright, then in subtle, often unconscious ways. Many black educators and leaders are unimpressed with native tongues other than standard English, because only the latter has market value in jobs and in higher education. Others see great value in enhancing self-concepts and ethnic pride—attributes featured in maintaining one's first dialect.

Implementing the difference model would require great changes in the school curriculum almost everywhere, not only to maintain and develop the child's native tongue, but to teach children the role of different dialects in social, political, and vocational settings. Teaching the ways of different cultures would also be required.

3. *The bicultural model* emphasizes the multifaceted strengths and flexible adaptations of groups shaped by dual socialization. Charles Valentine, a spokesperson for this view, says that *biculturation* really explains how people learn and use both the mainstream culture and their own minority culture at the same time. While he does not claim that black children learn both cultures equally, he does point to television, schools, fashions, mass products, and the like as sources for learning the mainstream culture and practicing it to some extent.[13]

It is certainly evident that many Americans live in more than one culture, especially those who have maintained forms of religious or ethnic practices not found in mainstream society. Chinese and Jewish groups often maintain afterschool centers, to teach native languages and religion and instill pride in heritage and group identity. Other groups may have distinctively different cultures because of geographic isolation, occupational specialization, or other reasons. Separation of living areas from mainstream groups probably accounts for many differences in lifestyle among the children, but deliberate rejection by the mainstream is also a basic cause.

The major question in biculturation is the extent to which a culture maintains its separateness by choice—how much flexibility do families really have to move into or out of mainstream culture? If there is very little choice, the children will necessarily be much less familiar with the mainstream culture as day-to-day living and working members. Second-hand and vicarious experiences are very different in quality and usefulness from the everyday in-depth variety.

Two extremes flow from this model. The black Nationalist orientation is the radical alternative, requiring separation and avoidance of the mainstream culture. Separatists require their own schools, businesses, professions, institutions, and services to achieve adaptation to a minority culture on the American scene. The radicals also desire fundamental change in society, for greater justice and equality, but with their own values, attitudes, and interests.

The other extreme would be a bicultural school, very different from those now known, which would pursue the value of biculturalism in all aspects of curriculum, in school attitudes, and in methodologies employed. This interesting concept values cultural pluralism so highly that it seeks to embed it in schools in ways never before attempted. It would require either separate staffs capable of teaching the different cultures or people with an overriding commitment to their equality. It may be impossible to achieve largely because most American communities are not bicultural but multicultural. In big cities, many cultures vie for individuality and survival within the mainstream society. This model, however, emphasizes the pluralistic cultures in the United States and the contemporary longing for cultural identity.

---

13. Charles A. Valentine, "Models and Muddles concerning Inequality: A Reply to Critics," in *Challenging the Myths: The Schools, the Blacks, and the Poor* (Reprint series no. 5; Cambridge, Mass.: *Harvard Education Review*, 1975), pp. 191–197.

NATIONAL DISPERSION OF IMMIGRANTS

American teachers are well aware that in many classes children are enrolled who are not fluent in English or who do not speak English at all. Sensitivity in English-speaking classrooms to this plight varies.

A student teacher in a first-grade classroom noticed that one child was still sitting quietly in her seat after the class had gone to the school library. The student teacher, remembering this child understood no English, spoke to her briefly in Spanish, and the child immediately went to the library. On returning from the library, all the children except Rosa began copying sentences from the board, as instructed by the teacher. The teacher, pointing to the material on the board, told Rosa in Spanish, "Escribe," and Rosa promptly picked up her pencil to write. Did the teacher assume that Rosa would receive the same messages as the other children when no effort was made to make those messages understandable to the child? Why copy English sentences that could convey no meaning to this child at this time? In short, what expectations did the teacher have that this activity would constitute a meaningful form of learning for Rosa?

Before you conclude that Rosa's teacher was an insensitive, hard-hearted person, it should be noted that this is just an extreme example of the assimilationist philosophy about second-language learning. This teacher was, in fact, following her strongly held conviction that only in such a sink-or-swim approach would Rosa be sufficiently motivated to learn English rapidly and well. The teacher might cite the history of various immigrant groups to the United States, for which this assimilationist philosophy appeared to work. Unfortunately for this school of thought, recent research by educational historians does not support the efficacy of this approach, since the figures show very high failure rates.[14] In the past, language problems were cited as one of the major reasons for school failure.

A pluralist philosophy would argue for a bilingual, bicultural approach to teaching children whose first language is not English. Historically, this was one way in which Spanish, German, and other language groups were taught in various locations in the United States before World War I. However, in the psychological ambience of American participation in the war, it became unpatriotic to teach in any language other than English.

Currently, various forms of bridging the gap between the child's language and culture and the mainstream exist under the name of *bilingual education*, although most programs under this title are concerned only with bringing children to fluency in English as rapidly as possible. The most popular bilingual program constitutes a transitional program to teach children in the first (non-English) language only until second-language fluency (in English) is equal to the educational task. But maintenance of the child's first language is the goal of many groups, who maintain that, if children's first language is discouraged in school, there is cultural deprivation as well. Others argue that the United States is too monolingual, and that travel, trade, and international understanding all require more than one language.

Bilingual controversies are always more complex than they seem. Second-language learning seems to threaten the jobs of established groups in favor of those proficient in the child's first language.[15] Others are concerned that the result will be fluency in neither language and a decreased ability of the children to plan for higher education and better opportunities in life. Although Spanish is the second most frequently spoken language of the United States by far, it is interesting to note that in a multilingual city such as New York, there were 75,000 children in bilingual programs in 1979, in 37 different languages. This seems a staggering undertaking for all but the largest

---

14. Diane Ravitch, *The Great School Wars: New York City 1805-1973* (New York: Basic Books, 1974), pp. 167-178.

15. Ibid., p. 395.

educational systems. Television, language laboratories, and other forms of electronic equipment should offer many good resources from which skillful teachers might select the most promising to use with specific children.

So far, there is no way to judge the usefulness of any of the bilingual programs being developed across the country. It should be noted that offering bilingual education of some kind to children entering school without fluent English is a requirement that stems from court decisions, one originating in California from Chinese parents, the other in New York City from Hispanic groups. Agreement on the goals and effective methodologies for bilingual education is still lacking.

VALUE CHANGES

It is not difficult for the casual observer to detect evidence of sharp changes in values within one generation. Formerly, for example, as in many other cultures today, it was unthinkable to send elderly parents to old-age homes—children expected to care for their aging parents at home. Today, with the high mobility previously described, families can be separated by great distances. High rents keep apartments and homes too small to accommodate elderly relatives. Besides, there are now federal funds to cover the huge costs of medical and custodial care and to provide various forms of income maintenance. As a result, many educators fear that children are developing distorted concepts of old age. The "generation gap," surely stems as much from infrequent interactions between family members of all ages as it does from modern peer-group cultures.

While sociologists are far from agreement, most would probably be in accord with Clyde Kluckhohn's list of value changes in contemporary society:[16]

16. Clyde Kluckhohn, "Have There Been Discernible Shifts in American Values during the Past Generation?" In Elting Morison, ed., *The American Style* (New York: Harper & Row, 1958), p. 204.

1. Personal values are receding in favor of group values of an organization, community, social class, minority or interest group, or the like.
2. Psychological values, such as child-centeredness in rearing children and in mental health, are spreading.
3. Short-range security is prevailing over future success.
4. A rise in aesthetic values is notable, attributable in part to a better-educated population with more time for recreation and aesthetic pursuits.
5. Heterogeneity is valued over homogeneity. (This indicates far more acceptance of pluralistic values than most people think exists.)
6. The ideal of women as mothers and homemakers has changed to a complex view of their roles and choices.
7. Increased concern for standards and explicit values has been demonstrated.

Vietnam War dissenters and Watergate critics have helped to dramatize the search for stated values, religions, and philosophies. Other value changes could be added, such as increased values of spending over saving, of recreation over work, and of personal satisfactions over job security. While everyone would not subscribe to all these value changes, these are the kinds of preferences many people have been demonstrating in the marketplace, in job hunting, in mobility, in voting records, and in their public and private forms of organizational support. More concerted efforts are mounted, for example, to achieve school decentralization in big cities, or to oppose new sites for development of nuclear energy. Controversial issues in schools generate partisanship and divisions among groups. Issues include such procedures as heterogeneous versus homogeneous grouping, tracking, "transition" classes for kindergarten or first-grade children who are deemed "not ready" for promotion, prereading and reading systems, competency tests for children's promotion or graduation, as well as the values embedded in the curriculum.

Value changes, however, do not come about smoothly and cleanly. *Alienation* is the term used to describe an anxiety state resulting from rejection of traditional values without substituting a choice of new values from among the available options.[17] Many young people today are thought to be experiencing alienation because of the difficulty of making commitments and choices when so many choices are available. Where groups succeed in throwing off or avoiding alienation, they often work through community efforts to achieve and dramatize new value choices. The effort in the sixties by many black groups to establish a self-valuing goal with the slogan "black is beautiful" is one example of positive attempts to replace dysfunctional values with functional ones. Teachers of young children, therefore, cannot develop value orientation in the curriculum without collaboration from parents and community groups. Without clarity and consistency in value learning, little is accomplished.

Two substantial trends are evident in teaching children moral standards. One is the pattern of increasing the explicitness of the teacher's value systems. Some parents are no longer accepting implicit value systems taught in school. They want acceptance of more pluralistic systems of values with equality among various options, especially their own. The second trend is accommodating the teaching of values to children's reasoning levels, instead of indoctrinating children with mature standards. This means that teaching values is more explicit and preplanned than in the recent past.[18]

Children develop their own moral judgment through new curricula for classroom implementation. These use moral dilemmas for which various responses can be worked out, depending on the child's level of reasoning. The teacher encourages discussions among the children. This process requires children to participate very actively and the teacher to challenge and probe their thinking without didactic teaching. Teachers do not tell, they ask questions and argue with the children, pointing out some problems in the solutions children select. A dilemma may concern how to act when a child sees another child pocket someone's pencil or lunch snack. By working out fair and just solutions, children begin to make rules for their own ethical behavior. Verbalizing values and acting on them are very different forms of behavior. No one can say he or she knows how to teach moral *conduct*.

While some people still expect the schools to take the lead in remaking society, the prevailing view is that schools have neither the capability nor the responsibility for such roles. George Counts, in the thirties, was an articulate theorist who thought schools should lead the way to a more just society.[19] He viewed the schools as a powerful institution capable of functioning in a leadership role to realize the moral ideals of the culture. Contemporary writers rarely place the school in so central a position for bringing about social change.

Anthropologists and sociologists, among others, chiefly stress the interrelatedness of a society's institutions in mutually shaping the major values and ideas of a culture. Schools cannot operate independently of other acculturating institutions. Children's motivation, values, and aspirations cannot be solely school-based when other institutions play powerful roles in establishing norms, rewards, and opportunities.

17. Gerald E. MacDonald, *Values and the Valuing Process* (Morristown, N.J.: General Learning Press, 1976), p. 7.

18. Lawrence Kohlberg, "From 'Is' to 'Ought,' " in Theodore Mischel, ed., *Cognitive Development* (New York: Academic Press, 1971), pp. 222–226; and Lawrence Kohlberg, "Moral Development and the New Social Studies," *Social Education*, 37 (1973): 369–375.

19. George S. Counts, *Dare the Schools Build a New Social Order?* (New York: Arno Press, 1969; originally published in 1932).

In collaboration with other major social and political forces, schools are viewed as the major institution for socializing the young in accordance with educative needs and possibilities.

COMMUNITY INVOLVEMENT

All of the trends cited above have contributed to a resurgence of parent and community involvement in curriculum decisions. Formerly, teachers prevailed in claiming their professional rights and expertise to make decisions about curriculum, materials, and specific programs. Now, community groups, speaking for racial and ethnic concerns and for changing values about moral and sex education expect to participate in curricular decisions. Their participation often influences curriculum choices and staff selection.

A better-educated citizenry now considers mental and physical health, aesthetic interests, and good avenues to future vocational success to be very high priorities for their children. Much more is being asked of the schools than ever before.

In one school serving a middle- to upper-income group in a large urban center, the well-educated parents kept demanding "open classrooms" with inter-age grouping, while the teaching staff resisted strongly, unwilling to change to a new and untried system. The parents did ultimately prevail by winning several followers on the teaching staff, but not until a demoralizing controversy was finally resolved and several changes in staff were made. In another school, black and minority groups used political and social pressures to accomplish school changes. Objectives included a principal of their choice and an increase in the proportion of minority teachers appointed to the school. Observation of special festivities or celebrations, such as Martin Luther King Day or Puerto Rican Discovery Week have been achieved through minority group social activism.

In seeking the means to assure that the children will have equality of educational opportunity, equality of *access* is no longer viewed as an adequate goal by school critics. ". . . They have as their objective the reduction of the high correlations among socioeconomic status, local assessed valuation per pupil, expenditures per pupil, level of educational services, and student achievement."[20] What is now a socially acceptable goal for all children is equality of *achievement*, when such extraneous factors as social class, race, ethnicity, or the wealth of the community are removed.

Parent willingness to challenge teachers' decisions is also associated with the widespread unionization of teachers: parents now perceive that teachers are no less self-serving than members of other unions. Formerly, parents and teachers could agree that they were natural allies and on the same side on most major issues. Despite the liberal, public-spirited views on social issues that teachers' unions usually take, parents no longer automatically agree.

Now there is growing expectation that teachers will share with parents and the community the theory, the programs they expect to implement, the available options, the reasons for choices, and what is in store for the children. Parents require that they be treated as equals in discussing objective information and participating in decisions about their children's education. Teachers, therefore, must expect to be able to engage in such discussions within an educative framework, logically, objectively, and understandably.

---

20. Arthur E. Wise, "The Constitutional Challenge to Inequities in School Finance," in Emanuel Hurwitz, Jr., and Charles A. Tesconi, Jr., eds., *Challenge to Education* (New York: Dodd Mead, 1972), pp. 419–425. *See also* Martin Carnoy, ed., *Schooling in a Corporate Society* (New York: David McKay, 1972).

SUMMARY

In recasting their priorities, values, objectives, content, and methodologies, schools have much to accomplish to make adequate responses to the broad social movements that are attempting to create a more just society. Important social changes involved are changes in family composition and roles of family members, increased mobility and related prejudices toward strangers in a new community, racism and sexism, poverty, and the rise in community influence and control of school programs. There is heightened demand for improved quality of life for all. Great social and political issues challenge the schools to deal with their impact and to stay in touch with the real needs of society.

In the 1930s there was a movement, with George Counts as its articulate theorist, to put the schools in the lead in remaking society with more justice for all.[21] It was a very beguiling notion that schools, placed outside of the consuming-producing areas, could educate the young to institute a fairer society and a better life than that of the preceding generation. Few people advocate such leadership by schools today. Schools are an important institution in American culture; most people regard them as being among the basic acculturating forces, but not as primary change agents. The leadership that citizens see in the schools is the capability to focus clearly on contemporary needs and, in collaboration with other major institutions, to make appropriate educative responses to such needs.

EXERCISES

1. Attend a school board, or board-of-directors meeting.
    a. Identify value conflicts related to views of child development and learning and knowledge.
    b. Note political differences expressed.
    c. Write a brief statement you as an educator might have delivered to help resolve a conflict.
2. Review the enrollment in your class and note differences in:
    a. culture,
    b. race,
    c. economic background,
    d. religion,
    e. family composition,
    f. duration of residence in community.
3. Review your goals, values, and instructional plans and consider any need for revision to accommodate the differences noted in exercise 2.
4. If your review reveals great homogeneity in enrollment, consider ways for helping children to experience and understand diversity.

BIBLIOGRAPHY

Baratz, Joan, and Baratz, Stephen. "Early Childhood Intervention: The Social Scientific Basis of Institutionalized Racism." *Harvard Educational Review,* 39 (1970): 29-50.

Bronfenbrenner, Urie. "Is Early Intervention Effective?" In Ashley Montagu, ed., *Race and I.Q.* London: Oxford University Press, 1975.

Carnoy, Martin, ed. *Schooling in a Corporate Society.* New York: David McKay, 1972.

Counts, George S. *Dare the Schools Build a New Social Order?* New York: Arno Press, 1969. Originally published in 1932.

Harrison, Barbara Grizzuti. *Unlearning the Lie: Sexism in School.* New York: Liveright, 1973.

Hunt, J. McVicker. *Intelligence and Experience.* New York: Ronald Press, 1961.

———. "The Psychological Bases for Using Preschool Enrichment as an Antidote for Cultural Deprivation." *Merrill-Palmer Quarterly,* 10 (1964): 220-224.

Kluckhohn, Clyde. "Have There Been Discernible Shifts in American Values during the Past Generation?" In Elting Morison, ed. *The American Style.* New York: Harper & Row, 1958.

---

21. Counts, *Dare Schools Build a New Social Order?*

Kohlberg, Lawrence. "From 'Is' to 'Ought.'" In Theodore Mischel, ed., *Cognitive Development.* New York: Academic Press, 1971.

———. "Moral Development and the New Social Studies." *Social Education,* 37 (1973): 369–375.

Labov, William. "The Logic of Nonstandard English." In Frederick Williams, ed., *Language and Poverty.* Chicago: Markham, 1970.

Lazar, Irving; Hubbell, Virginia Ruth; Murray, Harry; Rosche, Marilyn; and Royce, Jacqueline. "The Persistence of Preschool Effects: A Long-Term Follow-Up of Fourteen Infant and Preschool Experiments." New York State College of Human Ecology, Cornell University, Ithaca, September 1977.

MacDonald, Gerald E. *Values and the Valuing Process.* Morristown, N.J.: General Learning Press, 1976.

Mead, Margaret. "Introduction to Elema Gianni Belotti." In *What Are Little Girls Made Of?* New York: Schocken Books, 1976.

National Center for Educational Statistics, U.S. Department of Health, Education and Welfare. *Digest of Educational Statistics, 1978–1979.*

Pierce, William L. "Who's Watching the Children?" *American Educator,* 3 no. 1 (Spring 1979): 10–13.

President's Commission on School Finance. *Schools, People and Money: Final Report.* Washington, D.C.: U.S. Government Printing Office, 1972.

Ravitch, Diane. *The Great School Wars: New York City 1805–1973.* New York: Basic Books, 1974.

Valentine, Charles A. "Models and Muddles Concerning Inequality: A Reply to Critics." In *Challenging the Myths: The Schools, the Blacks and the Poor.* Reprint series no. 5. Cambridge, Mass.: *Harvard Education Review,* 1975.

Wise, Arthur E. "The Constitutional Challenge to Inequities in School Finance." In Emanuel Hurwitz, Jr., and Charles A. Tesconi, Jr., eds., *Challenge to Education.* New York: Dodd Mead, 1972.

Appendix A   Tests

1. **The following are primarily *cognitive tests*, although it should be noted that they are also heavily language-based:**

American School Reading   cognitive
Readiness Test
Bobbs-Merrill Company

Description: Evaluates readiness to read. Eight subtests:
    Picture vocabulary
    Discrimination of forms
    Letter-form recognition
    Letter-combination recognition
    Word recognition
    Word matching
    Following directions
    Memory for designs

Administration: Group test
    Time: 1 hour, untimed
    Age: Beginning first grade

Scores: Eight subtest scores, plus total score, percentile rank, stanine, and predicted reading grade.

Basic Concept Inventory   cognitive
(BCI)
Follett Publishing Company

Description: Tests knowledge of basic concepts often used in verbal directions, for example, *not, more than, between, next to, tallest,* and *biggest.* Assesses concepts necessary for success in first grade. Identifies children deficient in these basic concepts and diagnoses the specific problems. Criterion-referenced test.

Administration: Individual test
    Time: 30–60 minutes, untimed
    Age: Preschool to grade 3

Scores: Four scores: basic concepts, statements and word combinations, pattern awareness, and total.

Basic School Skills   cognitive
Inventory
Follett Publishing Company

Description: Identifies areas important to academic success. Seven performance areas:
    Basic information
    Self-help
    Handwriting
    Oral communication
    Reading readiness
    Number readiness
    Classroom behavior

Administration: Individual test
    Time: 15–20 minutes plus class observation, untimed
    Age: 4–7 years

Detroit Tests of   cognitive
Learning Aptitude
Bobbs-Merrill Publishing Company

Description: Assesses capacity to learn. Nineteen subtests including:
- Reasoning and comprehension
- Practical judgment
- Time and space
- Verbal number and motor abilities
- Visual and auditory attention

Administration: Group test
    Time: Not given
    Age: 3–14 years

Scores: Not given.

Gates-MacGinitie   cognitive
Readiness Skills Test
Psychological Corporation

Description: General and reading readiness assessed. Eight skills tested:
- Listening comprehension—measures ability to understand story
- Auditory discrimination—ability to distinguish between two words of similar sound
- Visual discrimination—ability to distinguish between printed forms of two words
- Following directions
- Letter recognition
- Visual-motor coordination—completing letters printed
- Auditory blending—joining parts of words
- Word recognition—ability to recognize words in isolation

Administration: Group test
Time: Approximately 2 hours, untimed
Age: Grades K.8–1.2

Scores: Standard scores, percentiles for total score, stanines for subtests, and norms.

Boehm Test of Basic   cognitive
Concepts
Psychological Corporation

Description: Assesses preschool children's understanding of basic concepts that are used in preschool and elementary school curricula. These include concepts children need to know to understand teachers' instructions. Fifty basic concepts are assessed, dealing with understanding of space (location, orientation, and dimensions), time and quantity (number), and other miscellaneous items. Pinpoints deficits and suggests remediation. Does *not* assess intelligence.

Administration: Individual or group. Spanish translation available.
    Time: Approximately 30 minutes, untimed
    Age: K to grade 2

Scores: Percentiles, percent passing each item by grade and by socioeconomic status level, and total score.

Cooperative Preschool   cognitive
Inventory, Revised Edition
Cooperative Testing Service

Description: Previously titled the Caldwell Preschool Inventory. Measures areas of achievement necessary for school success:
- Numerical relations
- Sensory attributes
- Personal-social responsiveness
- Associative vocabulary

Administration: Individual test
    Time: 15 minutes, untimed
    Age: 3–6 years

Scores: Three subtest scores, plus total score, percentiles, and norms for middle- and lower-class children.

CTBS Readiness Test   cognitive
CTB/McGraw-Hill

Description: Assesses skills necessary for reading. Tests prereading skills:
- Letter names
- Letter forms
- Listening for information
- Letter sounds
- Visual discrimination
- Sound Matching

Administration: Group test
   Time: 2 hours, 39 minutes, timed
   Age: Grades K.0–1.3

Scores: Total normed score, expected normed reading score (estimate of reading score if given test at the end of first grade), and expected reading performance.

Metropolitan Readiness   cognitive
Test, 1976 Edition
Psychological Corporation

Description: Measures skills necessary for success in beginning reading and mathematics:
   Auditory discrimination
   Visual discrimination
   Language comprehension
   Quantitative concepts

A. *Level I* has six subtests:
   Auditory memory
   Rhyming
   Letter recognition
   Visual matching
   School language and listening
   Quantitative language
   Copying (optional)

Administration: Group test
Time: 80–90 minutes
Age: Grades K–1 (for low-level children)

Scores: Grade norms, stanines for two skill areas (visual and language), percentiles, and national norms for battery composite.

B. *Level II* has six prereading subtests plus three optional tests:
   Beginning consonants
   Sound-letter correspondence
   Visual matching
   Finding patterns
   School language
   Listening
   Quantitative concepts (optional)
   Quantitative operations (optional)
   Copying (optional)

Administration: Group test
   Time: Tests 1–6, approximately 80 minutes; tests 1–8, approximately 100 minutes

   Age: End of kindergarten or early grade 1

Scores: Norms, stanines for subtests, and percentile ranks.

Minnesota Preschool   cognitive
Scale
American Guidance Service

Description: Estimates verbal and nonverbal intelligence:
   Verbal: language comprehension, language facility, memory of objects, incomplete pictures, and digits.
   Nonverbal: drawing; blockbuilding; discrimination, recognition, and tracing forms; recognition of omitted parts in pictures; and imitating portions of clock hands.

Administration: Individual test
   Time: 30 minutes, untimed
   Age: 1.5–6 years

Scores: Three scores: verbal, nonverbal, and total. IQ equivalents given.

Peabody Picture   cognitive
Vocabulary Test
American Guidance Service

Description: Assesses verbal intelligence. One hundred fifty plates, each containing four pictures. Examiner presents stimulus word. Examinee is required to point to the picture that illustrates meaning.
   Time: Approximately 15 minutes, untimed
   Age: 2.5 years to adult

Scores: Percentile rank, mental age, standard score, age norms for mental age, and IQ.

Stanford Early School   cognitive
Achievement Test
Psychological Corporation

Description: Assesses cognitive abilities on entering kindergarten, leaving kindergarten, or entering first grade. Spanish adaptation available. Level I has four subtests:
   Environment: General knowledge about both social and natural environments

Mathematics: Quantitative skills—counting; numeration; measurement; and conservation of number, space, and volume

Letters and sounds: Recognition of letters (upper and lower case) and auditory perception of beginning sounds

Aural comprehension: Abilities to attend to, organize, interpret, draw inferences from, and retain what has been heard

Level II adds the following:

Word reading: Recognition of single printed words

Sentence reading: Understanding sentence structure

Administration: Group test
    Time: Level I—1 hour, 30 minutes; Level II—2 hours, 20 minutes
    Age: Level I—Grades K.1–1.1; Level II—1.1–1.8

Scores: Percentile ranks and stanines for subtests and total scores, scaled scores and grade equivalents, four subtest scores, and total score.

Test of Basic Experiences,   cognitive
Second Edition
CTB/McGraw-Hill

Description: Measures how well children are prepared for participation in classroom instruction. Two levels: K and L. Each level has four tests:
    Language
    Mathematics
    Science
    Social studies

Administration: Group test
    Time: Approximately 25 minutes for each test, untimed
    Age: Level K—preschool and kindergarten
        Level L—kindergarten and grade 1

Scores: Percentiles, stanines, and standard scores.

2. **Language tests** include these:

Assessment of Children's   language
Language Comprehension
Consulting Psychologists Press

Description: Evaluates receptive language and diagnoses difficulties. Fifty vocabulary words are combined into two-, three-, and four-element phrases. Children point to a picture in response to a phrase given by the examiner.

Administration: Group or individual test
    Time: 10–15 minutes
    Age: 2–6 years

Scores: Four scores: vocabulary, two-word phrases, three-word phrases, four-word phrases.

Inventory of Language   language
Abilities
Educational Performance Associates

Description: Assesses possible language learning disabilities in the following areas:
    Auditory reception
    Visual reception
    Auditory association
    Memory
    Visual memory
    Grammatical closure
    Visual closure
    Auditory closure
    Sound blending

Administration: Individual test
    Time: Not given
    Age: Grades K–2

Scores: Not given.

Spanish/English Language   language
Performance Screening
CTB/McGraw-Hill

Description: Provides an objective measure of children's dominant language for placement in bilingual programs.

Administration: Individual. Administered by bilingual adult.
Time: 10–15 minutes, untimed
Age: Grades K–2

Scores: Compares performance in one language with performance in the other. Children are not compared with other children.

Test of Basic Experiences: language
Language Subtest
CTB/McGraw-Hill

Description: Assesses basic language concepts: vocal, sentence structure, verbal tense, sound-symbol relationships, letter recognition, listening skills, and perceptions for use of symbols. Also includes items using nonsense words and requires derivation of meaning from context.

Administration: Group test
Time: Approximately 25 minutes
Age: Level I—prekindergarten and K
Level II—K–1

Scores: Not given.

3. The following are *motor development tests:*

Bruininks-Oseretsky Test of motor
Motor Proficiency
American Guidance Service

Description: Identifies children with motor dysfunctions and developmental handicaps. Measures eight areas of motor skills:
Running speed and agility
Balance
Bilateral coordination
Strength
Upper-limb coordination
Response speed
Visual-motor control
Upper-limb speed and dexterity

Administration: Individual test
Time: 45–60 minutes, untimed
Age: 4.5–14.5 years

Scores: Three scores: gross motor, fine motor, and battery composite. Age-based standard scores, percentile ranks, and age equivalents for subtests.

Short Form: Fourteen items from complete battery.
Time: 15–20 minutes
Score: Single score of general motor proficiency.

Developmental Test of motor
Visual-Motor Integration
Follett Publishing Company

Description: Evaluates degree to which visual-motor behavior is integrated in the child. Identifies children with problems. Test consists of twenty-four geometric forms arranged in order of increasing difficulty. Child is required to copy forms in test booklet.

Administration: Group or individual
Time: 15–20 minutes
Age: 2–15 years

Scores: Age norms.

Lincoln-Oseretsky Motor motor
Development Scale
Western Psychological Services

Description: Assesses motor development, unilateral and bilateral. Thirty-six items arranged in order of increasing difficulty, including:
Hand and arm movements measuring speed, dexterity, coordination, and rhythm
Gross motor involving balance and jumping
Scored for both left and right hands and for coordination and speed of movements.

Administration: Individual test
Time: Not given
Age: 6–14 years

Scores: Percentiles and norms.

Southern California Kinesthesia and Tactile Perception Test — motor
Western Psychological Services

Description: Measures dysfunction in somesthetic perception. Evaluates use of tactile and kinesthetic information. Six subtests:
- Kinesthesia (arm movements)
- Manual form perception (form recognition)
- Finger identification
- Graphesthesia
- Localization of tactile stimuli
- Double tactile stimuli perception

Administration: Individual test
  Time: Not given
  Age: 4–8 years

Scores: Six scores, one for each subtest.

4. **Social-emotional development tests, including tests of self-concept, are as follows:**

Animal Crackers: A Test of Motivation to Achieve — social-emotional
CTB/McGraw-Hill

Description: Measures motivation to achieve in learning. Five subtests:
- School enjoyment
- Self-confidence
- Purposiveness
- Instrumental activity
- Self-evaluation

Sixty items: two animals per item with two statements about each. Children are asked to choose the one of the pair that is like them or likes what they like.

Administration: Individual or group
  Time: Individual—30–40 minutes;
    group —45–60 minutes
  Age: Preschool–grade 1

Scores: Five subscores, plus total score and percentile rank.

California Preschool Social Competency Scale — social-emotional
Consulting Psychologists Press

Description: Evaluates adequacy of interpersonal behavior and degree of assumption of social responsibility. Thirty items: each contains four descriptive statements posed in behavioral terms representing varying degrees of competence that are rated by teacher.

Administration: Teacher ratings
  Time: untimed
  Age: 2.5–5.5 years

Scores: Age percentiles, norms by occupational level, and total sample.

Primary Self-Concept Inventory — social-emotional
Learning Concepts, Inc.

Description: Identifies children who have low self-concept. Measures self-concept in three domains, each of which contains two factors:
- Personal self (physical size, emotional state)
- Social self (peer acceptance, helpfulness)
- Intellectual self (success, student self)

Stories with picture presented; children are required to match item most like them.

Administration: Individual or group
  Time: 10–15 minutes
  Age: Grades K–6

Scores: Six factor scores, three domain scores, total self-concept score. Standardized on black, Mexican-American, American Indian, and Anglo populations.

Responsive Self-Concept Test — social-emotional
Far West Laboratory for Educational Research and Development

Description: Assesses self-concept. Teacher rating scale and picture projective test. Factors measured:

Appropriate emotional affect
Good relationship with family
Good peer relationships
Efficient verbal participation
Positive approach to learning
Realistic reactions to success and failure
Self-satisfaction
Realistic level of aspiration

Administration: Individual test
   Time: Untimed
   Age: Grades 1–2

Scores: Not given.

Self-Concept and   social-emotional
Motivation Inventory
(What Face Would You Wear?)
Person-O-Metrics

Description: Measures self-concept with regard to school:
   Role expectation
   Achievement needs
   Failure avoidance
   Self-adequacy

Child responds by marking on faces (happy, sad, etc.) with crayon.

Administration: Group test
   Time: 25–30 minutes, untimed
   Age: Preschool to kindergarten

Scores: Three scores: motivation (goal and achievement needs, achievement investment), self-concept (role expectation, self-adequacy), and total score. Grade level norms given.

Vineland Social   social-emotional
Maturity Scale
American Guidance Service

Description: Checklist that measures stage of social competence. Six categories:
   Self-help (general, eating, dressing)
   Locomotion
   Occupation
   Communication
   Self-direction
   Socialization

Administration: Observation and interview with parent. Individual test.
   Time: 20–30 minutes, untimed
   Age: Birth to maturity

Scores: Total score converted to age score and social quotient (SQ).

5. ***Identification of learning disabilities tests*[1] include:**

Jordan Left Right   Identifying possible
Reversal Test   learning disability
Academic Therapy
Publications

Description: Measures number and letter reversals, diagnoses minimal neurological impairment, and screens for neurological reading problems.

Administration: Individual or group test
   Time: Approximately 20 minutes
   Age: 5–12 years

Scores: Norms, subtest, and total scores.

Psychoeducational   Identifying possible
Evaluation of the   learning disability
Preschool Child
Grune & Stratton

Description: Evaluates level of functioning and possible specific deficits. Tests:
   Physical functioning and sensory status
   Perceptual functioning
   Competence in learning for short-term retention
   Language competence
   Cognitive functioning

Administration: Individual test
   Time: Untimed
   Age: Preschool to grade 1

Scores: Purpose is not to record a numerical score, but rather an analytic in-depth description of child's needs.

1. Vallett's test, although widely used, is omitted here because of the special training required for administration and scoring.

McCarthy Screening Test
Psychological Corporation
Identifying possible learning disability

Description: Tests ability to perform schoolwork. (Identifies children for special-education placement.) Seven component scales:
- Puzzle-solving
- Verbal memory
- Right-left orientation
- Leg coordination
- Draw-a-design
- Numerical memory
- Conceptual grouping

Administration: Individual test
  Time: 20–25 minutes
  Ages: 4–6.5 years

Scores: Not given.

Preschool Attainment Record, Research Edition
American Guidance Service
Identifying possible learning disability

Description: Global assessment of physical, social, and intellectual functions of children. Useful for children with sensory impairment, speech and language difficulty, emotional disturbance, neuro-muscular impairment, resistance to other testing, cultural difference. Structured interview with adult who knows child and observation. Assesses:
- Ambulation
- Manipulation
- Rapport
- Communication
- Responsibility
- Information
- Ideation
- Creativity

Administration: Individual test
  Time: 20–30 minutes
  Age: 6 months to 7 years

Scores: Total score converted to age score and attainment quotient (AQ). Norms being prepared.

6. **Visual functioning** is tested by:

Motor-Free Visual Perception Test
Academic Therapy Publications
Visual

Description: Assesses visual perceptual ability without involving a motor component. Items fall into five categories:
- Spatial relationships
- Visual discrimination
- Figure-ground relationships
- Visual closure
- Visual memory

Children are required to point to the correct alternative for each item.

Administration: Individual test
  Time: 10 minutes or less
  Age: 4.0–8.11 years

Scores: Five subtests and total score. Standardized for learning-disabled, motorically impaired, and physically handicapped children.

Appendix B   Teacher-made Diagnostic Recording Forms

DIAGNOSTIC CHECK RECORDING FORM
Terms of Spatial Relationships

Instructions:
1. Check one child at a time.
2. Hands child a miniature truck and two blocks and labels them.
3. Makes the following requests:
   a. *"Place blocks* on top of *the truck."*
   b. *"Place the blocks* in back of *the truck."*
   c. *"Place the blocks* underneath *the truck."*
   d. *"Place the blocks* in front of *the truck."*
   e. *"Place the truck* between *the blocks."*

Scoring: + means correct, − means incorrect, 0 means no response

Child's name	On top of	In back of	Underneath	In front of	Between	Comments

DIAGNOSTIC CHECK RECORDING FORM
Same and Different Musical Sounds

Instructions:
1. Work with one child at a time.
2. Use a xylophone and a drum.
3. Strike instruments as indicated below.

Scoring: + correct, − incorrect, 0 no response

Child's name	Instruments in view				Instruments not in view			
	Drum 1 beat— 1 beat	Drum and xylo 1 beat, 1 tone	Xylo, same tone twice	Xylo, 2 different tones, C and G	Drum 1 beat— 1 beat	Drum and xylo, 1 beat, 1 tone	Xylo, same tone twice	Xylo, different tones C and G

DIAGNOSTIC CHECK
Identifying and Naming Alphabet Letters

Materials:
Magnaboard and set of upper- and lower-case alphabet letters.

Instructions:
1. Check one child at a time.

2. Place all upper-case letters on magnetic board out of sequence.

3. Ask child to give you the letters he or she knows: *"Take off a letter that you know and give it to me. Tell me the name of the letter."*

4. After child has selected all the familiar letters, ask the child to select, from those remaining, each letter you name.

5. Repeat the procedure for lower-case letters.

Scoring:
+ + Selected and produced name of letter correctly
+   Responded correctly to teacher request
−   incorrect
0   no response

DIAGNOSTIC CHECK RECORDING FORM
Upper-Case Letters

Child's name	A	B	C	D	E	F	G	H	I	J	K	L	M	N	O	P	Q	R	S	T	U	V	W	X	Y	Z

DIAGNOSTIC CHECK RECORDING FORM
Lower-Case Letters

Child's name	a	b	c	d	e	f	g	h	i	j	k	l	m	n	o	p	q	r	s	t	u	v	w	x	y	z

DIAGNOSTIC CHECK
Numeral Replication

Materials:
Pencil or crayon, three sheets of 8½-by-11-inch unlined paper, and number cards one to nine.

Instructions:
1. Check one child at a time.

2. Give the child crayon, pencil, and sheets of drawing paper.

Note: If necessary, the following three tasks may be offered at different times.

3. *Task I:* Show the child one numeral at a time, out of sequence, such as 3, 5, 2, 7, 8, 4, stating the number name. Ask child to write the number on the paper.

4. *Task II:* Remove the cards and give the child new paper. State the number names out of sequence, asking the child to write the stated number.

5. *Task III:* Give child another sheet of paper and ask him to write down all the numbers he can remember.

6. Mark each sheet with the child's name, task number, and date; then file for future reference and record of progress.

DIAGNOSTIC CHECK
Liquid Measurement

Materials:
Transparent quart container, two eight-ounce transparent cups, water. Work at sink or use large pitchers.

Instructions:
1. Check one child at a time.
2. For each task:
    a. Pour water in the two containers, as described in item three below.
    b. Give the child one container and keep the other, saying, *"This one is yours, and this one is mine."* Asks the child: *"Do we have the same amount of water, or does one of us have more?"* If the child says one has more, then ask, *"Who has more, you or I?"*
    c. After each task, the child empties both containers.
3. Tasks:
    a. Two eight-ounce cups full of water.
    b. Two eight-ounce cups, one full, one half full.
    c. A quart container full of water and one eight-ounce cup full of water.
    d. A quart container one-eighth full and one eight-ounce cup full.

Scoring:
+ for correct, − for incorrect, 0 for no response.

Date _____

Child's name	2 eight-ounce cups — full	2 eight-ounce cups — 1 full, 1 one half full	1 qt. — full; 1 eight-ounce cup — full	1 qt. — 1/8 full 1 eight-ounce cup — full

DIAGNOSTIC CHECK RECORDING FORM
Functional Sorting

Materials:
- Eating utensils, such as miniature fork, spoon, cup, saucer;
- Miniature doll and doll clothes;
- Red crayon, yellow pencil, and blue ball-point pen.

Instructions:
1. Check one child at a time.
2. Place collection of objects on the table and ask the child to put the objects into groups that go together.
3. After sorting, point to a pile and ask, "Why do these objects go together?"
4. Record the list of objects in each pile. Record the child's exact response.

Child's name	Group 1	Child's statement*	Group 2	Child's statement*	Group 3	Child's statement*

*Child's verbatim statement of criteria for sorting.

DIAGNOSTIC CHECK RECORDING FORM
Grouping Objects That Go Together

Instructions:
1. Check one child at a time.
2. Color and material—use one of the options listed below:
    a. four crayons, two colors (for example, two red and two green);
    b. four blocks, two colors—same as for crayons;
    c. four pegs, two colors—same as for crayons.
3. Present one set of materials to the child and ask the child to put together the *objects that go together,* in two piles. Ask child why the objects in each group go together and record response exactly. Scramble objects together and ask child to make three piles of *objects that go together.* Again, ask why objects in each pile go together.

Name of Child _____ Date _____

Circle the items selected by child					*Why they go together (record exact response)*

Two-Pile Sort
First Pile
    Crayons   R   R   G   G
    Blocks   R   R   G   G
    Pegs   R   R   G   G
Second Pile
    Crayons   R   R   G   G
    Blocks   R   R   G   G
    Pegs   R   R   G   G

Three-Pile Sort
First Pile
    Crayons   R   R   G   G
    Blocks   R   R   G   G
    Pegs   R   R   G   G
Second Pile
    Crayons   R   R   G   G
    Blocks   R   R   G   G
    Pegs   R   R   G   G
Third Pile
    Crayons   R   R   G   G
    Blocks   R   R   G   G
    Pegs   R   R   G   G

DIAGNOSTIC CHECK RECORDING FORM
Gross Differences in Size of Sets

Instructions:
A. Task I—*Identifies*
1. Make four model sets of beans, one set each of 20, 10, 10 and 2. Each set is placed on a separate sheet of white 8½" × 11" construction paper.
2. Select one set of ten beans, saying: *"This is my set of beans. You show me which group of beans has less than my group."*
3. Repeat step two and ask the child to find the set which *has more than my set*.

B. Task II—*Creates*
1. Place a set of five beans on a piece of white 8½" × 11" construction paper.
2. Ask child to make a set of beans on his or her paper that has *more than* her set.
3. Collect all beans, again place a set of five beans on the child's paper and ask the child to make a set that has *less than* her or his set of five beans.

Scoring: + correct, − incorrect, 0 no response.

Child's name	Task I—identifies		Task II—creates	
	More than	Less than	More than	Less than

DIAGNOSTIC CHECK
Comparing Sets by One to One Matching

Materials:
- Poker chips — six red, six blue, and one white.

- Colored cubes — two yellow, one purple and two green.

Instructions:
1. Check one child at a time.

2. Create each pair of sets in turn as specified below.

3. After setting up the first pair of sets, say, *"Find out which set has more objects."* If child gives the answer without using a matching procedure, say: *"Show me how you find out which set has more objects."*

4. Repeat step three for each pair of sets specified.

5. Tasks:
    a. Set 1: a line of six red poker chips.
       Set 2: a line of five blue poker chips.

    b. Set 1: a bunch of five blue poker chips.
       Set 2: a bunch of four red poker chips.

    c. Set 1: a bunch of poker chips consisting of two red, three blue, and 1 white.
       Set 2: a bunch of poker chips consisting of two yellow, one purple, and two green.

Scoring:
- + +   matching procedure used with prompting
- +   matching procedure used without prompting
- −   matching done incorrectly
- 0   no response

TEACHER-MADE DIAGNOSTIC RECORDING FORMS

DIAGNOSTIC CHECK RECORDING FORM
Comparing Sets by One to One Matching

Child's name	Task A	Task B	Task C	Comments*

Teacher _____ Date _____

*Note briefly any unusual variations in approach to the task.

DIAGNOSTIC CHECK RECORDING FORM
Patterning

Instructions:
1. Check one child at a time.
2. Teacher and child each have four red cubes and four blue cubes or checkers.
3. Sitting next to the child, make an alternating pattern of red and blue in a row, using eight cubes: R B R B R B R B
4. Ask child to make a pattern *"just like my pattern."*
5. Make a pattern of two red and two blue, using all eight cubes. Again ask child to copy it: R R B B R R B B
6. Mark + for correct. If incorrect, mark the child's pattern as made, such as R R R B B R.

Child's name	*Alternating R — B:* single alternation	*Alternating RR — BB:* double alternation

DIAGNOSTIC CHECK
Application of Number to Size of Sets

Materials:
Use sets of objects *different* from those used in the math learning sequences. For example, crayons in two colors, such as red and green, and a container or box.

Procedure:
1. Check one child at a time.
2. Construct each set as described in item three below. After each task, ask the child to put objects back in the box.
3. Check the child on the following tasks, in sequence, saying each time: *"How many crayons are here?"*
   a. Set of five green crayons.
   b. Set of three red crayons.
   c. Set of four green crayons.
   d. Set of two red crayons.
   e. Set of one green crayon.
   f. Set of three red and two green crayons.
   g. Set of two red and one green crayons.

Scoring: + correct, − incorrect, 0 no response

	All one color					Two colors	
Child's name	Five green	Three red	Four green	Two red	One green	Three red, two green	Two red, one green

Teacher _____ Date _____

Index

AUTHORS

Abt Associates, 175
Adams, Raymond S., 133, 143
Arnheim, Rudolf, 223, 225, 234
Aronoff, Frances W., 94
Aukerman, Robert C., 252, 260
Axline, Virginia, 112, 113, 119
Ayers-Lopez, Susan, 289, 293

Bandura, Albert, 58, 59, 61, 62
Baratz, Joan, 302, 308
Baratz, Stephen, 302, 308
Belotti, Elena Gianni, 299, 309
Belugi, Ursula, 236
Berman, Louise, 108, 119
Bersoff, Donald, 148, 157
Berson, Minnie P., 121, 130
Bevlin, Marjorie Elliott, 3, 8
Biber, Barbara, 22, 26, 56, 62
Biddle, Bruce J., 133, 137, 143
Bjorklund, Gail, 10, 11, 16
Blough, Glenn O., 276, 293
Bonmarito, James N., 157
Boyer, E. Gil, 156
Brittain, W. Lambert, 222, 234
Bronfenbrenner, Urie, 296, 297, 308
Brown, Robert, 236
Bruner, Jerome, 36, 37, 40, 42, 83, 94, 236, 245, 260
Butts, R. Freeman, 25, 26

Campbell, Marjorie H., 276, 293
Carmichael, Carolyn W., 242, 245, 260
Carnoy, Martin, 308
Cartwright, Carol A., 156
Cartwright, George P., 156
Cavanagh, Frances, 234
Cazden, Courtney, 236, 237, 260
Chase, William W., 121, 130

Cherry, Clare, 130, 234
Chomsky, Noam, 236
Chukovsky, Kornei, 237, 260
Cianciolo, Patricia J., 245, 260
Combs, Arthur, 108, 110, 119
Coody, Betty, 245, 260
Cooper, Catherine R., 289, 293
Cooper, James M., 157
Coopersmith, Stanley, 108, 114, 119
Copeland, Richard, 152, 157, 177, 210
Counts, George S., 306, 308
Craig, Gerald, 36, 37, 42, 269, 293
Cremin, Lawrence, A., 25, 26
Crook, Elizabeth, 234
Cullinan, Bernice E., 242, 245, 260

Dalcroze, Emile Jacques, 217
Dales, Ruth, 32, 42
Davis, C. M., 15, 16
Day, Mary Carol, 22, 49, 56, 62
Dearden, R. F., 14, 16
DeVries, Rheta, 22, 27, 55, 60, 62, 142, 143, 152, 153, 157, 211
Dinkmeyer, Donald, 108, 110, 119
Dobler, Lavinia, 234
Dolly, John, 148, 157
Donaldson, Margaret, 211, 239, 261
Duckworth, Eleanor, 64, 94
Dunkin, Michael, 133, 143

Eisner, Elliott, 233, 234
Elkind, David, 51, 52, 62
Engel, B. S., 157
Erikson, Erik, 58, 61, 62
Evans, Ellis, 23, 27, 29, 42, 48, 62
Evans, Patricia, 244

Feldman, Edmund B., 213, 234
Forman, George E., 22, 27, 55, 62, 91, 94, 153, 157

Fowler, William, 121, 130
Fraiberg, Selma, 109, 112, 119
Freud, Sigmund, 58
Frost, Joe L., 121, 130

Gagné, Robert M., 88, 94
Gendlin, Eugene, 110, 119
Gesell, Arnold, 45, 61, 62
Ginott, Haim, 113, 119
Good, Harry, 24, 27
Good, Ronald, 92, 95, 152, 157, 177, 211
Goodman, Kenneth S., 236, 250, 261
Gordon, Ira, 157
Grossman, Bruce, 292, 293

Haas, Glen, 36, 40, 42
Hackett, Layne C., 217, 234
Hanson, Bette A., 252, 253, 261
Hardeman, Mildred, 102, 104
Harlan, Jean Curgin, 211
Harms, Thelma, 122, 130, 211
Harrison, Barbara Grizzuti, 300, 308
Havighurst, Robert, 60, 61, 62
Haywood, Charles, 234
Hirst, Paul H., 37, 38, 42
Hoepfner, Ralph, 157
Hoffman, Lois W., 114, 119, 289, 293
Hoffman, Martin L., 114, 119, 289, 293
Holt, Bess-Gene, 211
Hom, Harry L., Jr., 59, 62
Hubbell, Virginia Ruth, 301, 309
Huck, Charlotte S., 245, 261
Hunt, J. McVicker, 301, 308
Hurwitz, Emanuel, 307, 309
Hymes, James L., 111, 113, 119

Ilg, Frances, 45, 62
Isaacs, Nathan, 102, 104

INDEX 335

Jensen, Mary A., 252, 253, 261
Jensen, Robert G., 217, 234
Johnson, Mauritz N., 12, 16
Johnson, Orval G., 157

Kamii, Constance, 22, 27, 55, 60, 62, 142, 143, 152, 153, 157, 211
Karafin, Gail, 156
Karnes, Merle, 21, 22, 27
Katz, Lillian, 133, 138, 143
Kellogg, Rhoda, 223, 225, 234
Keyes, Carol, 292, 293
Kluckhohn, Clyde, 305, 308
Kofsky, Ellin, 95
Kohlberg, Lawrence, 44, 51, 62, 306, 308
Kuhn, Doris Y., 245, 261
Kuschner, David S., 22, 27, 55, 62, 91, 94, 153, 157

Labov, William, 238, 261, 302, 309
Landeck, Beatrice, 234
Landreth, Catherine, 4, 8
Lark-Horovitz, B., 226, 234
Laurendeau, Monique, 211
Lawton, Denis, 38, 42
Lazar, Irving, 301, 309
Leeper, Sarah, 32, 42
Lovell, Kenneth, 211
Lowenfeld, Viktor, 223, 234

Maccoby, Eleanor M., 19, 27
MacDonald, Gerald E., 306, 309
McKee, Judy Spitler, 122
McNeil, John D., 99, 104
Mager, Robert, 157
Marconnit, George D., 12
Marquis, Angela, 289, 293
Mead, Margaret, 299, 309
Meredith, Robert, 236
Merei, F., 289, 293
Mitchell, Lucy Sprague, 34, 42, 276, 278, 293
Monroe, Marion, 81, 95
Montagu, Ashley, 296, 308

Montessori, Maria, 31, 42
Murray, Harry, 301, 309

Nickelsburg, Janet, 211
Nummedal, S. G., 157

Opie, Iona, 244
Opie, Peter, 244

Pannell, Lucy, 234
Parker, Ronald, 22, 49, 56, 62
Patterson, Cecil H., 108, 119
Phenix, Phillip H., 37, 38, 42
Piaget, Jean, 25, 50, 51, 52, 57, 62, 70, 142, 153, 225
Pierce, William L., 297, 309
Pinard, Adrien, 211
Pring, Richard, 38, 42

Ravitch, Diane, 304, 309
Reisman, Fredericka, 152, 157
Renner, John, 211
Resnick, Lauren B., 49, 57, 62
Robinson, Paul A., 59, 62
Robison, Helen F., 122, 130, 133, 143, 211, 234, 279, 293
Roderick, Jessie, 108, 119
Rogers, Carl, 110, 119
Rosche, Marilyn, 301, 309
Rosner, Jerome, 49, 57, 62
Royce, Jacqueline, 301, 309
Rowe, Mary Budd, 89, 95, 140, 143

Sanders, Norris, 141, 143
Saunders, Ruth, 138, 142, 143
Schwartz, Sydney L., 122, 130, 133, 143, 279, 293
Seeger, Ruth Crawford, 234
Sheckles, Mary, 269, 270, 293
Sheehy, Emma D., 234
Shepard, Lorne, 110, 119
Shlien, John, 110, 119
Short, Edmund, 12

Sigel, Irving, 138, 142, 143
Simon, Anita, 156
Skipper, Doris, 32, 42
Smith, E. Brooks, 236, 237, 245, 249, 261
Smith, Frank, 236, 261
Snygg, Donald, 110, 119
Spache, George, 81, 95
Stafford, Don, 211
Steenburgen, Frances, 157
Stern, C., 157
Stevens, Barry, 110, 119
Strickland, Dorothy, 249, 261
Swift, Joan, 114, 119, 289, 293

Taba, Hilda, 12, 16, 21, 27
Taylor, Katherine W., 291, 293
Teller, James, 24, 27
Tesconi, Charles A., Jr., 307, 309
Teska, James, 21, 22, 27
Thomas, Edwin J., 133, 143
Tillman, Murray, 148, 157
Tuckman, Bruce W., 145, 157

Valentine, Charles A., 303, 309
Van Dusen, Wilson, 110, 119

Walker, Deborah Klein, 157
Wang, Margaret C., 49, 57, 62
Waters, Barbara, 269, 293
Weber, Evelyn, 24, 27
Weinstein, Carol, 123, 130
Williams, Frederick, 309
Wise, Arthur E., 307, 309
Withers, Carl, 244
Witherspoon, Ralph, 32, 42

Yamamoto, Kaoru, 108, 119
Yardley, Alice, 211

Zais, Robert S., 12, 16
Zehrbach, R. Reid, 21, 22, 27
Zeller, Marian, 19, 27
Zimmerman, Barry J., 59, 62

SUBJECTS

Academically oriented program, 15
 (see also Curriculum content)
 instructional activities for, 129
 room arangement for, 121
 skill goals in, 18
Academic goals (see Goals, categories of; Objectives)
Accommodation, 51 (see also Piaget, summary)
Accountability, 6-7, 32, 104, 301
 movements in, 25
Achievement, motivation related to sexism, 300

Activities, 13, 31-33, 34, 41, 71, 82
 (see also Instructional models)
 arts and crafts, 132, 213, 223-234
 cognitive activities, 71: patterning, 71-73
 construction, 132
 dance, 132, 211-221
 drama, 133
 dramatic play, 13: in prototype, 167, 169, 172, 178-210, 214-234, 238-259
 formal practice, 79, 214, 223
 independence in, 126-129
 for key concepts in music, 84
 for key concepts in physics, 83-84
 physical motor activities, 71, 91, 273

for planting, 87
playful, exploratory, 72, 168, 170, 214, 223
for preserving leaves in wax paper, 86-87
in prototype, 167, 169, 172, 178-210, 214-234, 238-259
self-imposed tasks, 79, 214
singing, 132, 222
for studying animals, 276-278
for studying geography, 278-280
for studying geological formations, 273-276
for studying plant life, 272-273
for studying rain, 266-269
for studying the sun, 270-272

Affective goals (see Goals, affective; Goals of prototype; Objectives, content of)
Aggression, 110
Aims (see Curriculum aims; Goals; Objectives; Values)
Alienation, 306
Ambience, 12
Anecdotal recording, 150
Art in prototype, 213, 223-234
  activities and projects, 227-234
  Arnheim's theory of, 225
  art concepts, 225-227
  art values, 225-226
  cognitive theory of, 224-225
  concepts in, 225-226
  craft projects for, 228-233
  developmental stages in, 223
  Gestalt view of, 225
  goals in, 224-234
  grouping of forms in, 225
  instructional approach to, 226-229
  psychodynamic view of, 225
  relation to mathematics, 228
  universal shapes in, 223
Assessment, 14 (see also Evaluation)
Assimilation, 51 (see also Piaget, summary)
Assimilationist philosophy, second-language learning in, 304
Auditory discrimination, 81-82 (see also Beginning reading)
Auditory sequential memory, 252 (see also Language processing skills)
Autonomy, 52, 58

Back-to-basics movement, goals in, 25
Bank Street College model, 56
Behavior analysis, 48
Behaviorism (see also Neobehaviorist theories; Social learning theory)
  teaching procedures to accord with, 134-139
Behaviorist, 68, 70
  control of stimuli for specified outcomes, 108
  reinforcement for behavior modification, 47, 111, 113
  relationship to views of child development, 134-135
  shaping desired behavior, 111
  teacher roles of, 134-139
  training to meet social-emotional needs, 111
  view of punishment, 112, 114
  view of self-concept, 108, 111
Behaviorist programs, 19
  relationship to curriculum, 48-49
Behaviorist view (see Cultural training view)
Beginning reading, 252-254 (see also Curriculum prototype; Curriculum tables; Instructional models; Reading)
  auditory discrimination, 252, 258
  common elements in programs, 253-254
  common teaching strategies for, 253-254
  directionality for, 258
  eye-hand coordination for, 259
  language experience approach to, 252-253
  phonetic approach to, 252
  problems in, 252-253
  teaching approach for, 259
  visual discrimination in, 252-254
Bicultural model, 302-303
Biculturation, relation to cultural pluralism, 303
Bilingualism
  instruction in, 299
  statistics of, 302, 304
Black dialect, related to standard English, 302
Black nationalist orientation, 303
Branching (see Cues)

Changing family patterns, 296-298
  single parents, 297-298
  working mothers, 296-297
  younger parents, 298
Chants, 239 (see also Language development; Music)
Checklists for observation, 150-151
Child development, 40, 66, 75, 85, 162
  in art, 223-225
  psychological patterns, 33
  relationship to teacher roles for, 134-135
  views of, in prototype, 168-169, 174
Children with handicaps
  contributing to self-concepts of, 114-117
  contributing to self-esteem of, 114
  learning from, 114-117
  mainstreaming, 114
Classification (see Piaget)
Classifying (see also Piaget)
  class inclusion, 92
  grouping, 76
  hierarchical classification, 92
  multiple classification, 93
  in plant study, 272
  in prototype, 168
  sorting, 76, 92-94: exhaustive sorting, 92; perceptual bases for, 93; personal-functional, 93; relational, 93; resemblance, 92
Classroom management, 11 (see also Rules; Routines; Use of space)
  affect, 12
  ambience, 12
  group dynamics, 12
  learning context, 12
  in prototype, 167, 170, 173
Cognitive development, 19, 65, 66, 90
  comparing, contrasting, 141
  concrete operations stage, 90
  decentering, 90
  distancing, 142
  predicting, 141
  preoperational stage, 90: egocentrism, 90; impulsivity, 90; precausal reasoning, 90
  problem solving, 141
  processes activated by questions, 141-143
  reason logically, 90
  use of "why" questions, 142
Cognitive developmental view, 44, 51-56 (see also Curriculum tables; Goals; Objectives)
  curriculum implications of, 55-57
  Piagetian theory, 52-55
  teaching roles in, 55
Communication skills (see Language development, goals of)
Community involvement, 307
  goals for, 307
Compensatory program, 15
Competencies, 15
Concepts
  acquisition of, 85
  of adaptability, 271
  of directionality, 79, 229
  of a discipline, 81
  of evaporation, 271
  of geography, 278-280
  of geometry, 89
  of heat as energy, 270
  key concepts, 167: in economics, 167-168; in geography, 167; in mathematics, 89, 167, 169; in music and art, 84, 167, 214, 225-226; in reading, 167; in science, 83, 167
  of measurement, 89
  of music, 84
  of number, 89
  of ordered relationships, 79
  in physics, 83-84: balance, 84; distance, 83; force, 83; motion, 83; speed, 83; weight, 84
  positional, 80-81, 229
  of preservation of objects, 86
  of shadows, 270
  of time, 89-90, 269
  of weather, 266-269
Conditioned response (see Behaviorism; Behaviorist; Reinforcement)
Constructivism (see Cognitive developmental view; Interactionist; Piaget)
Context of learning, 170-171, 173-174
  informality of, 170
Controversial issues, 305
Creative dramatization, 247 (see also Literature, teaching procedures for)
Criterion-referenced test data, 155 (see also Tests)
Cues, 49
Cultural pluralism, 34, 303
  philosophy of, 304
Cultural traditions, 34
Cultural training view, 44, 47-51 (see also Behaviorist)
  arguments for and against, 49-50
  behavior analysis, 48
  curriculum implications of, 48-49, 56-57
  goals of, 50

INDEX

reinforcement, 47
  teaching implications of, 51
Cumulative learning theory, 57 (see also Cultural training view)
Curriculum aims, 18–27 (see also Goals)
Curriculum components, 8, 161 (see also Curriculum variables)
Curriculum content, 13, 75
  from academic disciplines, 29, 32, 36, 40, 42, 66: key concepts, 36–40, 91; strengths and limitations, 38–40; structured disciplines, 36–37, 81
  basics, 42
  behavior-based, 40
  citizenship education, 32
  classes of, 29–42
  content focus, 13
  fact accumulation, 29–31, 42, 66, 85: strengths and limitations, 31
  holistic view, 29, 40–41, 42: humanistic, 40; self-perception, 40; social relationships, 40; strengths and limitations, 40; undifferentiated, 40
  logic of subject mater, 33, 66
  nonsexist, 40
  prereading, 81
  process-based, 66
  projects, 33
  reading, 81
  skill accumulation, 29, 31–32, 42: strengths and limitations, 31–32
  subject areas, 29, 32–33, 42: health and safety, 32; language arts, 32; social studies, 32; strengths and limitations, 33
  subject-centered, 33, 81
  themes, 29, 33–36, 42: strengths and limitations, 36, 40
  three Rs, 42
  units, 33, 34
Curriculum continuity, 299
Curriculum definitions, 12–13, 15
  comparison of, 15–16
  process-oriented, 15
  product-oriented, 15
Curriculum design problems, 4–7, 100–104
  articulation, 100–101
  balance, 103
  curriculum roots, 102–103
  establishing objectives, 103
  knowledge of content, 102
  process-product arguments, 103–104
  universal or individualized, 102
Curriculum form, 10–16
  child's experiences, 10, 12, 16
  formal, 40, 107
  happening, 10, 11, 16, 40, 68
  informal, 40, 79, 80, 89
  plans for teaching, 10, 12–16, 40: short- and long-range, 13
  program, 10, 16, 68
  of prototype, 161, 162, 172–173
  syllabus, 10, 14–16, 40
Curriculum framework, 7–8, 14, 90

Curriculum, hidden (see Hidden curriculum)
Curriculum plans (see also Curriculum tables; Instructional models; Sequencing Curriculum)
  activities, 13
  content, 13
  long-range, 13
  processes, 13
  short-range, 13
  writing, 14–15
  using, 14–15
Curriculum prototype, 160–261 (see also Geography)
  language and reading content of, 236–261
  mathematics and science content of, 177–211
  music and art content of, 213–234
  summary of features, 173–175
Curriculum tables
  for art, 229–233
  for beginning reading, 255–257
  for language development, 240–241
  for literature and dramatization, 247–249, 251
  for mathematics: geometry, 203; materials resources, 178–180, 182; measurement, 204–205; number, 194–197
  for music, 215–216, 222, 224
  for science: animals, 207; common beginnings with mathematics, 183–185; physical laws, 208; plants, 206
Curriculum variables
  content sequence, 64–94
  criteria for selection, 97–102
  form of, 11–15
  purpose and values of, 19–26
  views of knowledge for, 29–42
  views of child development and learning for, 44–62

Decentering (see Piaget, and Observing children, systematic recording)
Decoding (see Beginning Reading; Reading)
Deficit model, 302–303
Designing curriculum, 3, 97–104 (see also Curriculum design problems; Curriculum prototype)
Design of space, 121–124 (see also Use of space)
Development (see also Child development)
  definition of, 44
  normative approach to, 45
  theories of, 44
Diagnostic assessment
  formal procedures, 30, 153–156
  informal procedures, 30, 145–152
  types of, 145
Diagnostic procedures, informal, 68, 145–152
  anecdotal recordings, 150
  checklists and records, 150–151

observation of children, 147–150
  unobtrusive measures, 151–152
  work samples, 146–147
Diagnostic procedures, formal, 153–156
  administering, 154
  standardized tests, 153–154
  teacher-made tests, 155–156
  use of results, 154
Diagnostic teaching
  Piagetian-based programs, 152–153
  sequential levels in learning, 152–153
  teaching principles, 152–153
Dialectal flexibility, 302 (see also Dialects)
Dialects, 238–239 (see also Language development)
Difference model, 302–303
Disadvantaged, economically, 19
Disciplines of knowledge, 29, 32
  anthropology, 32
  economics, 32
  geography, 32
  history, 32
  political science, 32
  sequencing, 83
  sociology, 32
Discovery learning, 4–5, 40
DISTAR, 56

Early childhood programs, 14
Early education
  effects of, 301
Ecological concerns, 273, 276 (see also Environmentalists)
Egocentricity (see Piaget, summary; Tests)
Egocentric speech, 239
Empathy and sympathy (see Social learning theory)
Encoding (see Beginning reading; Reading)
Environmentalists, 302
Equilibration, 51 (see also Piaget, summary)
Erikson's view of psychosocial development, 168 (see also Psychosocial developmental view)
Errorless learning, 48, 50 (see also Behavior analysis; Behaviorist; Reinforcement)
Ethnic needs of children, 12
  curriculum roots for, 102–103
Extended family, 296
Evaluation, 14–15, 21–23, 301
  of use of space, 122–124
Event sampling (see Observing children)

Family
  intervention in, 296–297
Feedback, 107, 110 (see also Behaviorism; Behaviorist)
Follow-Through program, 15, 19
  goals and values of, 23
Freudian theory, 24

Generation gap, 305
Geographic resources, 265-276
Geography, 276-280
　　concern for safe crossing of streets, 279
　　goals of, 205
　　intersections, 279
　　Mitchell's approach to, 276
　　pathways or channels, 279
　　patterns of movement, 279
Goals, 13, 15, 18-27 (*see also* Curriculum tables; Objectives)
　　affective, 19-21
　　categories of, 18-22
　　function of, 18, 23
　　long-term and short-term, 18, 21-23
　　primary, secondary, 21
　　skill, 19-20
　　social movements' influence on, 25-26
　　sources of influence, 24-25
　　tradition of, 24-25
Goals of prototype, 162, 166-167, 172-174
　　of activity, 171, 217
　　affective goals, 162-163, 170
　　cognitive, 162-163
　　for language, 162, 166-167
　　in language, literature, and reading, 238-258
　　long-term, 162, 165-167
　　in mathematics and science, 178-210
　　in music and art, 213-224, 225-233
　　in reading, 254-260
　　short-term, 163, 165-166
Grammatical closure (*see* Language processing skills)
Group dynamics, 12
Grouping children (*see* Heterogeneous grouping; Homogeneous grouping)
Group membership, goals for, 165-166

Harvard studies
　　of retarded infants, 45
Heterogeneous grouping, 305
Hidden curriculum, 12, 163
Homogeneous grouping
　　maturationist view, 46, 305
Humanism (*see* Humanist-field theory)
Humanist-field theory
　　accepting feelings in, 111-113
　　central role of self in, 110
　　goals of, 25, 27
　　holistic view of, 110
　　nondirective approach in, 112
　　phenomenological views in, 110
　　of self-concept, 108, 110-111
　　teaching procedures to accord with, 113-114
　　view of punishment in, 112-114
Human resources for learning, 280-292
　　the class group as, 289-290
　　community residents, 290-291
　　community workers, 280, 286-290
　　curriculum potential of, 286-288
　　frequency of contact with, 286-288
　　older school children, 290
　　parents as, 291-292
　　peer relationships, 289
　　trips to meet community members, 290-291
　　use of, 288-289
　　visitors to classroom, 280, 290
　　written guides for classroom visitors, 291-292

Individual differences, 88
Individual development goals (*see* Goals; Objectives)
Indoor space (*see* Use of space)
Illinois test for psycholinguistic abilities, 154
Imitation learning (*see* Social learning theory)
Immigrants, dispersion of, 296, 304-305
Instructional models (*see also* Activities)
　　for beginning reading, 258
　　for language development, 242-244
　　for literature, 250
　　for mathematics: number, 191-193, 198-202
　　for music, 218-221
　　for science and mathematics: sorting and classifying, 186-190
　　for science: animals, 209-210
Instructional sequences, 162 (*see also* Sequencing curriculum
Interaction, 107
　　as contributing to self-concept, 108
Interactionist, 68, 70, 91 (*see also* Cognitive developmental view; Piaget)
　　approach in prototype, 169
　　characteristic teaching roles of, 134-137
　　relationship to views of child development of, 134-135
Interest centers, 121 (*see also* Use of space)

Key concepts (*see* Concepts)
Key language (*see* Curriculum tables; Instructional models)
Kindergarten
　　Froebel's curriculum, 24
　　history of, 24-25
Knowledge, views of, 29, 161
　　selection of, for prototype, 167-169, 174
Knowledge goals (*see* Curriculum tables; Objectives)

Language development
　　content of communication, 239
　　dialectal flexibility, 238
　　by generating rules, 237
　　goals of, 238-239 (*see also* Curriculum tables)
　　by imitation, 236-237
　　in language and reading, 236-260
　　language form, 239
　　in mathematics and science, 177-210
　　meanings, 81
　　in music and art, 215-234
　　oral language, 236-239
　　picture reading, 81
　　process of, 236
　　teaching approach for, 238-239
　　theories, 237-238
　　and thought, 237-238
　　in use of community resources, 286
　　use of games for, 239
　　vocabulary acquisition in, 237, 239
Language processing skills, 21
　　auditory-sequential memory, 21
　　grammatical closure, 21
Learning
　　approaches to, 44
　　behaviorist view of, 47-48
　　definition of, 44
　　outcomes, 162-166, 173-175, 280
　　theory, 86, 91, 92, 168
Learning disabilities, 79
　　lack of orientation in space, 79
　　lack of psychomotor control, 79
　　perceptual distortion, 79
Learning outcomes (*see* Learning)
Literature
　　fiction and nonfiction, 246
　　goals of, 246-249
　　kinds of activities, 246
　　purposes of, 246
　　tastes in, 245
　　teaching procedures for, 247-249
　　values of, 245

Mainstream culture, 296, 303-304
Mainstreaming, 102
Materials for learning, 213 (*see also* Use of space)
　　accessibility of, 121
　　in art, 227-233
　　in mathematics and science, 178-180, 182
　　in music, 215-223
　　placement of, 121
　　resources for learning, 265-292
Mathematics: geometry, 177-178, 197, 199, 203-205 (*see also* Art, activities and projects)
　　language shape labels, 199
　　sequence of goals, 199
Mathematics: measurement, 177-178, 202
　　activity sequences, 205
　　arbitrary measure, 202
　　conservation, 202
　　in plant study, 272
　　standard measure, 202
　　tasks, 202
Mathematics: number, 177-178, 190-199
　　activity sequences, 191
　　drill, 190, 193
　　equivalent sets, 191-193
　　goals, 181, 183-185, 186

number meanings, 177–178, 190–191
sets, 177–178, 190–191, 197
symbols, 193
Mathematics materials (*see also* Materials for learning)
  criteria for selection, 181
  identical, 181–182
  measuring, 182
  props for, 182
  related, 181–182
  similar, 181–182
Maturationist view, 44–46, 68, 70
  characteristic teaching roles for, 134–137
  curriculum implications of, 46, 56–57
  Gesell's contribution to, 45
  Piaget's contribution to, 52
  relationship to child development views of, 134–135
Methodology, 161–163, 171–174 (*see also* Instructional models; Social-emotional development; Teaching roles; Teaching strategies)
Metropolitan readiness test, 154 (*see also* Diagnostic procedures, formal)
Migrant workers, 299
Mobility, family, 295–296, 298–300, 305
  causes of, 295, 299
  discrimination, 298–299
  prejudice, 298–299
Modeling (*see* Social learning theory)
Montessori (*see also* Maturationist view)
  schools, 15
  teaching procedures of, 127
  theory of, 15
Moral development, 38, 90
Moral education, 38, 306–307
Movement education, goals of, 25
Music, in prototype, 213–223
  activities, 214–223
  concepts in, 214
  Dalcroze method, 217
  goals for, 213
  instructional approach to, 214
  instruments, 222–223
  movement, 214–222
  singing, 222–223
  use of directional terms in, 222
  use of positional terms in, 222

Native speech, 239 (*see also* Dialects)
Naturally occurring program activities (*see* Curriculum tables)
Naturalistic approach, 79–80, 89, 278
Natural resources for learning, 265–276
  rain as a resource, 266–269
  use of weather data for, 266–272
Neobehaviorist theories, 47 (*see also* Cultural training view)
Nuclear family, 296

Objectives, 15, 18–27, 161 (*see also* Goals)
  broad vs. specific, 21
  categorizing, 19–23
  content of, 19–21
  function of, 18, 23
  general vs. specific, 18–19, 21–23
  long-term, 18–19, 161, 174, 213–217, 223–225
  short-term, 21–23, 161, 174, 213
Observation by children, 107, 168, 273, 276
Observing children, 14
  anecdotal recording, 150
  checklists and records, 150–151
  child-maintained system, 151
  formal vs. informal, 147
  purposes of, 147–148
  sample checklist, 150
  systematic recording, 148–149
  unobtrusive measures, 151–152
Organization of materials, 11 (*see also* Use of space)
Outcomes, 18–23 (*see also* Goals; Values)
Outdoor space (*see* Use of space)

Patterning, 178, 193, 197–199
Perception bound (*see* Piaget, summary)
Perceptual-motor development, 90
Phonics, 252–253 (*see also* Beginning reading)
Physical development, 90
Piaget, 29, 40, 70, 90–92, 112, 114, 142, 164, 174, 273
  concrete operations, 54–55
  curriculum implications, 55
  intuitive/preoperational stage, 53–54
  sensorimotor stage, 52–53
  summary, 52–55
Piagetian (*see* Piaget)
Play, 168, 170, 174, 214, 273
  balance in, 103
  different views of, 56
Poetry reading, 242–244
Population changes, 295
Poverty
  need for financial aid, 301
  racism, 300–301
  school failure, 301–303
  schooling effects, 301–304
Prepared environment (*see also* Montessori)
  maturationist view, 46
President's commission of school finance, 297–298
Primary education project, 49
Principles of practice, 69, 107
  variety of, 69, 71
Process goals, 11, 13, 15, 55, 272 (*see also*, Curriculum tables; Instructional models; Piaget; Science)
Process-product arguments, 103–104
Professional autonomy, 5–7

Programs
  British infant school, 29
  developmental, 15
  Follow-Through, 15, 163
  Head Start, 15, 19, 23, 301
  Montessori, 15, 16, 29
  as in prototype, 162
Prompts (*see* Cues)
Prototype curriculum (*see* Curriculum prototype; Curriculum tables; Instructional Models)
Psychoanalytic theory
  adjusting to external realities in, 111, 113
  concept of mental health in, 109
  exploring causes of behavior in, 112
  psychodynamic approach to, 109–110
  redirection of unsocial impulses in, 109
  role of ego in, 109
  of self-concept, 108, 111
  teaching procedures to accord with, 111–114
  view of punishment in, 112, 114
Psychosocial developmental view
  curriculum implications of, 58
  of Erikson, 58
Public school kindergartens (*see* Kindergarten)
Punishment, 112 (*see also* Reinforcement)
Purposes, 18–27 (*see also* Curriculum aims; Goals)

Racism, 300–302
  and law, 300
  and poverty, 300–301
Readiness, 32, 68 (*see also* Diagnostic procedures, formal)
  maturationist view, 46
  for reading, 81
  tests, 154–157
  for use of hot iron, 85
Reading, 81
  approaches to, 252–254
  cognitive skills in, 236
  a comprehensive approach to, 254
  in curriculum areas, 254
  decoding/encoding, 250, 252
  definition of, 249
  perceptual-motor skills, 236
  purposes of, 250–252, 254
Reading in prototype (*see* Curriculum in prototype; Curriculum tables; Instructional models)
Reinforcement, 47–51, 69, 172
  behavior analysis, 48
  punishment, 47
  reinforcers, 47
Reliability (*see* Observing children, systematic recording)
Representation, 68, 71, 213
Resources for learning, 265–292
  cultural resources, 265
  environmental resources, 265:
    natural environment, 265–276
  human resources, 265

Room arrangement, 121 (see also Use of space)
Routines, 5-6, 75, 94
 approaches to, 125-126
 component parts of, 126
 related to goal, 126
 skill practice in, 126
Rules, 124-125
 approaches to, 124-125
 necessity of, 124
 purpose of, 124-125

School decentralization, 305
School enrollment, 297, 301
School failures, causes of, 301-303
Science, in prototype
 activities, 177-180, 183: naturally occurring, 177-180; planned, 177-180; sequencing of, 181-183, 185; teacher role in, 181, 185
 animals, 205, 207, 209-210
 changes, 177
 comparison and contrast, 177, 183
 goals in, 183-190, 205-211
 key concepts in, 205
 key language in, 178-180
 learning processes, 177, 180, 181, 183
 life sciences, 177
 materials resources for, 178-180
 physical laws, 205, 208
 physical sciences, 177
 plants, 205-206
 prediction, 185, 190
 properties of objects, 177-180
 skills of inquiry, 177, 180, 181, 183
 sorting and classifying, 177-178
Science and mathematics
 common beginnings of, 177, 183-185
 language goals in, 183, 186, 188, 189
Scope and sequence, 15 (see also Sequencing curriculum)
Second language learning, 238 (see also Dialects)
Self-actualization programs, 19
Self-concept, 107-119
 of children with handicaps, 114-117
 as developed in prototype, 213, 223, 233
 effect of teaching team on, 118
 self as abstraction, 108
Self-esteem, 107-119
 of children with handicaps, 114-117
 as developed in prototype, 164, 165, 170, 213, 223, 233
 teacher modeling as a strategy for, 117
 team approach for children with handicaps, 117-118
Sensorimotor stage (see Piaget, summary)
Sequencing curriculum, 64-95
 in academic disciplines, 81
 by child development, 66, 68, 78, 79, 83, 84, 86, 88, 90, 91, 94: by stage development, 90, 91

by concrete to abstract, 66, 68, 70-72, 74, 81-82, 88, 94, 169
from exploration to problem solving, 66, 69, 94
by fact accumulation, 75: teaching implications of, 75: based on logic of content, 76; based on process, 76
from facts to concepts, 66, 69, 75, 94, 169
by key concepts, 83: in music, 84; in physics, 83, 92; in planting, 188
from known to unknown, 66, 69, 88, 94, 169
from logic of content, 66-68, 75, 79, 86, 91
by number of variables, 71-75
by numerical order, 68
through review of prior knowledge, 85-86
from self-concentration to social skills, 66, 69, 79, 94
by simple to complex, 66, 69, 71-74, 76-77, 81-82, 88, 90-91, 94, 169, 223
by skill accumulation, 76-81: automatic performance, 77
in subjects, 81, 88
by task analysis, 88
by themes, 84, 86-88
Sexism, 34, 295-296, 299-300
 equal rights related to, 299-300
Skills, 29, 31
 academic, 31, 76-77, 79, 167-169
 cleaning skills, 31
 cognitive, 77-78, 84, 164, 167-169, 217
 development of, 85
 eye-hand coordination, 79
 name-writing, 79-80
 perceptual-motor, 81
 personal management skills, 31
 physical motor, 31, 76-78, 80-81, 169
 pouring, 31
 reading, 81
 scissors, 77
 social, 76, 77
 specified in prototype, 161, 169, 181-210, 213-217, 223-225, 238-257
 in study of weather, 266-269
 tool control, 79
Social change, 295
 impact on curriculum, 12
Social developmental view
 curriculum implications, 60
 Havighurst, 60-61
Social-emotional development, 65, 90, 107-119
 adapting social skills in, 111
 coping with strong feelings in, 111, 114
 dealing with inner feelings for, 111
 facilitating learning for, 111
 guidelines for dealing with behavior, 114-117
 helping children to cope with, 111, 114

learning new social skills for, 111, 114
 peer group acceptance for, 114
 as in prototype, 170, 173
 relearning behavior for, 114
 teaching strategies for, 111-119, 113-114
Social forces, 12, 24-25
Social goals (see Curriculum tables; Objectives, content of)
Socialization, acculturation, 306-307
Social learning theory, 47, 108-109
 Bandura, 58-60
 curriculum implications, 59-60
 as implemented in prototype, 168-169, 174
 role of interactions in, 109
 role of modeling in, 109
Social transmission, 51 (see also Piaget, summary)
Social utility goals (see Goals, categories of)
Sorting and classification in prototype, 178-181, 183-188, 197 (see also Classifying; Piaget, summary)
 changes in, 184-185, 189-190
 instructional models for, 186-190
Sound-symbol relationships (see Phonics; Reading)
Spontaneous (see Naturalistic approach; Play)
Stage-development theory
 of Erikson, 58-61
 of Havighurst, 60-61
 of Piaget, 52-55
Stage-related characteristics (see Stage-development theory)
Standard syntax, 239 (see also Language development)
Stimulus and response (see Behaviorist; Reinforcement)
Story dramatization, 247 (see also Literature, teaching procedures for)
Story reading, 246-247 (see also Literature, teaching procedures for)
Storytelling procedures, 247
Symbol learning, 168, 173 (see also Curriculum prototype)

Task analysis, 89-90
 in clock-reading, 89
Teacher-made tests, 155-156 (see also Diagnostic procedures, formal; Diagnostic procedures, informal)
Teaching roles
 as affected by personal attributes, 132, 133
 caretaker, 134-135
 challenger, 133, 135, 171
 definition of, 133-134, 143
 evaluator, 134-135, 171-172
 information giver, 13, 171
 manager, 134-135, 171
 nurturer, 133, 171
 observer, 134-135, 171

participant, 134–135, 171
planning, 11
in prototype, 169, 171
reinforcer, 133, 171–172
role possibilities, 133–135
for social-emotional development, 111–114
to stimulate play, 168
suggested for natural study, 273
tutor, 133, 171
as viewed by classroom style, 132
Teaching strategies, 132, 135–143
behavior control, 137
cognitive processes, 141–143
definition of, 135–137, 143
direct teaching, 135
eliciting verbalization, 136
giving directions, 136
giving feedback, 136
improving questioning strategies, 142–143
information-giving, 136
inviting to a task, 136
manipulating materials, 136
modeling, 136
observing, 137
probing, 136
in prototype, 171–172, 174
questioning, 136–143, 172: complex types, 139; diagnostic types, 137–138; embedded types, 139; functions of, 137; instructional types, 137–138; linguistic structure of, 138–140; open- and close-ended types, 139–140; psychological function of, 140–142; simple types, 138–139; use of Bloom's taxonomy for, 141–142; wait time for, 140–144
recording, 137
running machines, 136
testing, 137, 172
Teaching style, 21 (*see also* Teaching roles; Teaching strategies)
modeling, 58–60
Teaching team, 117–118
attributes of effective teamwork for, 117–118
differentiated staffing for, 117
effects of on children's self-concepts, 118
optimal involvement of members of, 118
Teaching values (*see* Moral Education)
Tests (*see also* Diagnostic procedures; Readiness, tests; Teacher-made tests)
problems, 154–155
testing conditions, 156
Textbooks
national distribution of, 299
sexism in, 295–296
Time-sampling (*see* Observing children, anecdotal recording, systematic recording)
Traffic patterns, 121–124
Transitional class, 46

Use of space
boundaries for, 122–124
clarity of, 122
guidelines for, 122
pathways in, 122
placement of centers, 122
problems in, 122–124
visible order in, 122

Validity (*see* Observing Children, anecdotal recording, systematic recording)
Values, 18–27 (*see also* Curriculum prototype; Goals; Use of space)
changing of, 305–307
of prototype, 162
Variables (*see* Curriculum variables)
Visual discrimination, 81 (*see also* Beginning reading)
Vocabulary development, 81, 167, 168, 217, 286 (*see also* Beginning reading; Language development)

Women's liberation, 300 (*see also* Sexism)
Working mothers, 296–297
Writing (*see* Beginning reading)
Written guide, 14

Younger parents, 298
birth defects with, 298

ABOUT THE AUTHORS

Sydney Schwartz, associate professor at Queens College for over ten years as a member of the Early Childhood faculty, teaches graduate and undergraduate courses. She first worked with Professor Robison in curriculum research in 1965, which culminated in their first set of books jointly authored, in 1972.

Dr. Schwartz has led an extensive number of inservice projects across the country, from Anchorage, Alaska, to her home in New York City. Her local activities in New York City have included school evaluation studies, as well as mini-courses and workshops.

Dr. Schwartz's most recent activities have been to serve as director of a Title XX daycare training project and as a contributor to an administration and supervision program.

Helen F. Robison received both her master's degree and doctorate in education from Teacher's College, Columbia University. She is Professor of Education, Director of Early Childhood and Elementary Education, and Director of Student Teaching at Bernard M. Baruch College, City University of New York. Her teaching experience also includes nursery school, first grade, and administrative positions in parent cooperative nursery schools.

Professor Robison has also served as consultant on early childhood programs throughout the United States, Mexico, and Japan, including a federally funded public school bilingual-curriculum program in New York City.

She is author or coauthor of several books, including *Exploring Teaching in Early Childhood Education*, second edition, also published by Allyn and Bacon.

THE EVANS LIBRARY
FULTON-MONTGOMERY COMMUNITY COLLEGE
2805 STATE HIGHWAY 67
JOHNSTOWN, NEW YORK 12095-3790